Department of National Defence

Directorate of History

Occasional Paper Number Two

———————

Ministère de la Défense nationale

Service historique

Document occasionnel numéro 2

Series Editor/Rédacteur de la collection
Brereton Greenhous

THE
CANADIAN MILITARY EXPERIENCE
1867-1967: A BIBLIOGRAPHY

BIBLIOGRAPHIE DE
LA VIE MILITAIRE AU CANADA
1867-1967

O.A. COOKE
Directorate of History / Service historique

Published by Authority of the Minister of National Defence
Publication autorisée par le ministre de la Défense nationale

FOREWORD — AVANT-PROPOS

Occasional papers are published by the Directorate of History at National Defence Headquarters in Ottawa. They contain information that, although it is of great interest, is too detailed for inclusion in the official histories of the Canadian armed forces. The first such book was T.W. Melnyk's *Canadian Flying Operations in South East Asia, 1941-1945,* published in 1976.

Occasional Paper No. 2, O.A. Cooke's *The Canadian Military Experience, 1867-1967: a Bibliography* represents years of patient investigation to fill a serious gap in our knowledge about published sources of Canadian military history. The extraordinary number of books and pamphlets in this field tends to belie the popular impression that Canadians are an unmilitary people. To be sure, careful examination will show that there are relatively few works of great substance, but that is not the point. What is important is that for the first hundred years after Confederation there was sufficient public interest to warrant the efforts required to write and publish over 2000 books and pamphlets purely on military affairs. They all need to be consulted by historians of Canada's military past, and we can say with some assurance from this evidence that the subject has enjoyed a continuing and dynamic interest in the nation.

The editor would have had to expand this bibliography significantly had he included titles dealing with political and social affairs that also touched on military topics. Such titles have therefore been omitted. They are readily found in standard Canadian bibliographies such as those mentioned in Part A of the text. The purpose of this book is to guide readers to purely military titles that are often left out of all the listings now in print.

The Canadian military experience is of course bound up in geography. The 3000-mile border with the United States, the transatlantic economic and political ties with European nations, the coastline that includes our polar regions as well as two very long seaboards, on the Atlantic and Pacific Oceans, have on the one hand placed Canada in a position of some strategic importance and on the other have always rendered it vulnerable to military threats from powerful neighbours. The entries that deal adequately with such questions should be fairly self-evident, even though no attempt has been made to provide annotations for the list. But the military experience is also bound up in personalities and outlooks formed by the various backgrounds of the authors here represented. Whether they had military experience themselves or not, on land, sea or air, they were all formed by the circumstances of their lives, by such things as education, religion, political leanings and climate. Understanding the Canadian military means understanding these people, and in that respect the present bibliography is unique, containing information that in some cases has never been tapped. We hope therefore that this Occasional Paper will be of use to the scholar, the military buff and the general reader alike. And we hope it will lay the basis for a continuing and complete record of writings in this field.

———————

La Direction du Service historique du Quartier général de la Défense nationale, à Ottawa, publie parfois des ouvrages qui, même s'ils sont d'un grand intérêt, sont trop détaillés pour paraître dans les histoires officielles des Forces armées du Canada. Le premier de ces ouvrages, *Les opérations aériennes du Canada dans le Sud-Est asiatique, 1941-1945,* de T.W. Melnyk, a été publié en 1976.

Le deuxième ouvrage, *Bibliographie de la vie militaire au Canada, 1867-1967,* édité par O.A. Cooke, représente plusieurs années de travail acharné pour combler une profonde lacune de nos connaissances des documents publiés sur l'histoire militaire du Canada. Le nombre incroyable de volumes et de brochures publiés dans ce domaine tend à démentir l'impression générale voulant que les Canadiens ne soient pas un peuple militaire dans l'âme. Bien sûr, un examen attentif montrera qu'il y a relativement peu d'ouvrages de grande valeur, mais là n'est pas la question. Ce qui importe c'est qu'au cours des cent années qui ont suivi la Confédération le public a montré suffisamment d'intérêt pour qu'on fasse l'effort d'écrire et de publier plus de 2000 livres et brochures sur des sujets purement militaires. Les historiens s'intéressant au passé militaire du Canada se doivent de les consulter et nous pouvons dire avec quelque assurance à partir de ces chiffres que le sujet a connu et continue de connaître une grande vogue au pays.

Le rédacteur aurait dû augmenter considérablement cette bibliographie s'il y avait inclus les titres des ouvrages portant sur des questions politiques et sociales qui touchent également à des sujets militaires. Il les a donc laissés de côté. On peut néanmoins facilement trouver ces titres dans les bibliographies régulières du Canada comme celles mentionnées dans la partie A du texte. Le présent ouvrage vise plutôt à orienter les lecteurs vers les volumes purement militaires, qu'on ne retrouve pas dans les listes imprimées actuelles.

L'expérience militaire du Canada est évidemment reliée à la géographie du pays. Sa frontière de 3000 milles avec les Etats-Unis, ses liens politiques et économiques avec les pays d'Europe, son littoral qui comprend les régions polaires et les rives des océans Atlantique et Pacifique ont, d'une part, placé le Canada dans une position importante sur le plan stratégique et l'ont, d'autre part, toujours rendu vulnérable à la menace militaire de ses puissants voisins. Il suffit de lire les titres des ouvrages pour savoir lesquels sont consacrés à ces questions, même si l'on n'a pas jugé bon d'ajouter des notes explicatives à la liste. Mais la vie militaire est aussi liée à certaines personnalités et à la perspective que nous donnent les origines des divers auteurs ici représentés. Qu'ils aient ou non servi dans l'infanterie, la marine ou l'aviation, ils ont tous été formés par les expériences qu'ils ont vécues, par l'éducation qu'ils ont reçue, par leur religion, leurs tendances politiques et le climat politique. Comprendre la vie militaire au Canada, c'est comprendre ces auteurs; à cet égard, la présente bibliographie est unique, car elle contient des sources de renseignements qui parfois n'ont jamais encore été utilisées. Nous souhaitons que le présent ouvrage soit de quelque utilité à l'érudit, au mordu de la chose militaire et au public en général. Nous espérons en outre qu'il constitue le point de départ d'un dossier complet et sans cesse renouvelé des ouvrages parus dans ce domaine.

W.A.B. Douglas
Director / Directeur
Directorate of History / Service historique

November / novembre 1979

TABLE OF CONTENTS
TABLE DES MATIÈRES

INTRODUCTION

Canadian military history and military matters have not been well represented in the past in retrospective bibliographies of Canadiana or in international military bibliographies. Although a small number of very useful listings of some aspects of Canadian military history, such as those on unit histories or of the writings of such prolific military authors as C.P. Stacey or G.F.G. Stanley, have been produced, no comprehensive list of references to guide the researcher interested in Canada's military past has been published.

What has been attempted here is a bibliography of published primary sources and secondary works on Canadian military topics, excluding poetry and fiction (with one exception), covering the period from Confederation to service unification — the first century of Canada's armed forces.

Entries in the bibliography represent printed monographs, books and pamphlets (to a minimum of ten pages), and serial titles. The prime criteria for inclusion were that the work be chiefly or uniquely both Canadian and military in its contents dealing with the 1867-1967 period.

Many in-house publications, of the training pamphlet or regulations type, have been included, but only insofar as they tell us something of the armed forces themselves, rather than details of tactical doctrine or of pieces of equipment. Works by or about Canadians serving with the armed forces of other countries have been included, as well as materials relating to the military history of Newfoundland since 1867.

In order to restrict the bibliography to a reasonable size, periodical articles are not listed individually. Instead, serial titles of mainly Canadian and military content have been included, interfiled with monograph titles in the appropriate sections of the bibliography. Newspapers and newsletters have been excluded, but unit magazines and yearbooks regularly containing material of historical interest about the unit are found here.

Materials on soldiers' rehabilitation have not been considered. Veterans' publications and works about veterans have been included only if they deal directly with the wartime activities of individuals or units.

It is obvious from these criteria that a certain amount of subjective judgement has had to be exercised on the inclusion of individual items. This is most obvious in Part B, "Defence Policy and General Works," in which the criteria of mainly or uniquely Canadian and military content have been most difficult to apply.

In general, first editions of books have been listed. Later editions have been included only if they have been greatly enlarged or are much different in their bibliographic description. An effort was made to inspect each work to verify its bibliographic description and subject relevance. Some works were unobtainable, but have been included on the basis of entries in reliable bibliographies.

In compiling this bibliography, I have relied heavily on the holdings of the major military and academic libraries of the Ottawa, Kingston and Toronto areas. No critical evaluation or selection has been made, for what may seem a weak book to the compiler might well provide vital information to a researcher working from a different viewpoint.

Materials have been arranged so that individual entries are sometimes repeated in several different sections of the bibliography. For example, a regimental history of an infantry regiment raised in 1885 and existing to the present day appears in all four time-periods of the land forces section. A work on some aspect of the Royal Canadian Air Force and the Canadian Army in the Second World War would appear in the 1939-1945 parts of both the land and air forces sections. In all, the bibliography contains approximately 2200 different entries.

I wish to express thanks to the historians and other staff of the Directorate of History for their individual expertise in collecting many entries for the bibliography and for their time in tracking down and verifying copies of works. I am grateful to the staffs of the military, academic and public libraries of Ottawa, Kingston and Toronto for their assistance, and particularly to the Royal Canadian Military Institute, Toronto, for making its private library freely available. Thanks must also go to Mr. T. LaRue, Saskatoon, for details of works in his collection, and especially to Elizabeth Chenier for assistance in editing and typing the text.

No bibliography is ever complete and this is certainly no exception. Further entries for a revised edition are welcome. Anyone submitting new titles should send them to:

> Canadian Military History Bibliography Project,
> Directorate of History,
> National Defence Headquarters,
> Ottawa, Ontario.
> K1A 0K2

The location of the copy seen for each new entry would be much appreciated.

O.A. Cooke

*An asterisk opposite an item indicates that it is also listed in the bibliography in the other official language.

Par le passé fort peu d'ouvrages sur l'histoire et la vie militaire au Canada figuraient dans les recueils rétrospectifs de publications sur le Canada ou dans les bibliographies militaires internationales. Même si l'on a constitué quelques listes très utiles d'oeuvres consacrées à certains aspects de l'histoire militaire canadienne, notamment l'histoire des unités, ou des écrits d'auteurs militaires aussi prolifiques que C.P. Stacey ou G.F.G. Stanley, il n'existe aucune liste complète sur laquelle peut se fonder le chercheur qui s'intéresse au passé militaire du Canada.

Nous avons donc tenté de dresser ici la liste des sources premières publiées et des oeuvres secondaires, hormis la poésie et la fiction (sauf une seule exception), consacrées à la vie militaire canadienne depuis la Confédération jusqu'à l'unification des Forces — ce qui représente les cent premières années des Forces armées canadiennes.

La bibliographie regroupe des monographies, des livres et des brochures d'au moins dix pages, ainsi que des titres de périodiques. Notre choix des oeuvres s'est fondé sur le critère primordial suivant: le sujet devait être uniquement ou principalement canadien et militaire à la fois, et traiter de la période 1867-1967.

Plusieurs publications internes du ministère, telles les manuels d'instruction ou de règlements, ont été retenues, mais seulement dans la mesure où elles nous renseignent sur les forces armées en plus de donner des détails de pièces d'équipement ou d'ordre tactique. Les ouvrages de Canadiens servant au sein de forces armées d'autres pays ou consacrés à ceux-ci, ainsi que ceux touchant l'histoire militaire de Terre-Neuve depuis 1867, ont également été catalogués.

Afin d'éviter de surcharger la bibliographie, les articles de périodiques ne sont pas répertoriés séparément. Nous avons plutôt retenu les titres des périodiques à fonds principalement militaire et canadien, que nous avons insérés avec les monographies dans les sections appropriées de la bibliographie. Les journaux et les lettres au rédacteur ont été laissés de côté, mais les revues et les livrets annuels des unités contenant régulièrement des articles d'intérêt historique ont été catalogués.

Les ouvrages portant sur la réadaptation des soldats ont été rejetés. Les publications des anciens combattants et les ouvrages qui leur sont consacrés n'ont été retenus que s'ils portaient directement sur les activités de temps de guerre des soldats ou des unités.

Comme vous le voyez, une bonne part de subjectivité a régi le choix des ouvrages. La chose est encore plus évidente dans la partie B intitulée «Les politiques sur la défense et généralités» où le caractère principalement ou uniquement canadien et militaire des ouvrages a été très difficile à cerner.

En général, nous avons retenu les premières éditions des livres. Les éditions ultérieures n'ont été répertoriées que si leur contenu a été considérablement augmenté ou si leur description bibliographique a été largement modifiée. Nous nous sommes efforcés de vérifier la description bibliographique et la pertinence de chaque ouvrage. Il a été impossible de se procurer certains d'entre eux, mais nous les avons quand même catalogués parce qu'ils figuraient dans des bibliographies fiables.

Pour dresser cette bibliographie, nous nous sommes considérablement basés sur les ouvrages détenus par les principales bibliothèques universitaires et militaires des régions d'Ottawa, de Kingston et de Toronto. Il n'y a pas eu d'évaluation ou de choix critiques, car l'ouvrage qui peut nous avoir semblé de peu d'importance pourrait fournir des renseignements inestimables au chercheur qui a un autre point de vue.

Les ouvrages ont été classés de façon que le même titre figure parfois dans plusieurs sections de la bibliographie. Par exemple, l'histoire d'un régiment d'infanterie formé en 1885 et existant encore aujourd'hui paraît dans chacune des quatre grandes époques de la section consacrée aux forces terrestres. Un ouvrage portant sur certains aspects de l'Aviation royale du Canada et de l'Armée canadienne pendant la Seconde Guerre mondiale figurerait dans la partie 1939-1945 de la section des forces terrestres et de la section des forces aériennes. En tout, la bibliographie renferme environ 2200 titres différents.

Nous tenons à exprimer notre reconnaissance aux historiens et au personnel du Service historique, dont le précieux concours nous a permis de relever beaucoup de titres et qui ont consacré de leur temps à la recherche et à la vérification des ouvrages. Nous remercions également le personnel des bibliothèques militaires, universitaires et publiques d'Ottawa, de Kingston et de Toronto pour l'aide qu'il nous a apporté et notamment le Royal Canadian Military Institute de Toronto qui nous a permis de consulter sa bibliothèque privée. Nous remercions en outre Monsieur T. LaRue de Saskatoon pour les renseignements qu'il nous a communiqués sur les oeuvres de sa collection et notamment Elizabeth Chenier pour l'aide qu'elle nous a fournie pour rédiger et dactylographier ce texte.

Aucune bibliographie n'est jamais complète et celle-ci ne fait pas exception à la règle. C'est avec plaisir que nous ajouterons d'autres titres à notre édition revue et corrigée.

Toute personne désirant nous présenter d'autres titres doit le faire en s'adressant au:

> Projet de bibliographie sur l'histoire militaire du Canada,
> Service historique,
> Quartier général de la Défense nationale,
> Ottawa (Ontario).
> K1A 0K2

Veuillez également nous indiquer où trouver chaque nouvel ouvrage.

O.A. Cooke

*Un astérisque en regard d'un ouvrage indique qu'il figure également dans la bibliographie dans l'autre langue officielle.

A. BIBLIOGRAPHY — BIBLIOGRAPHIE

In addition to the works listed below, other bibliographies, not primarily both Canadian and military, are relevant. General Canadian historical bibliographies, such as J.L. Granatstein and Paul Stevens, eds., *Canada since 1867; a Bibliographical Guide* (Toronto: Hakkert, 1974), 170 pp., or Claude Thibault, *Bibliographia Canadiana* (Don Mills, Ont.: Longman Canada, 1973), 795 pp., list many works on the Canadian military experience among references to other facets of our history. More specialized references will be found in regional bibliographies, such as Bruce Peel, *A Bibliography of the Prairie Provinces to 1953* (Toronto: Univ. of Toronto Press, 1956), 680 pp. (also later editions).

Similarly, international military bibliographies also contain Canadian materials. General works, like Gwyn M. Bayliss, *Bibliographic Guide to the Two World Wars; an Annotated Survey of English-Language Reference Materials* (London: Bowker, 1977), 578 pp., or Commission internationale d'histoire militaire, Comité de bibliographie, *Bulletin de bibliographie,* No. 1- (Lausanne, Suisse: Centre d'histoire, 1978-), or such specific topical bibliographies as Myron J. Smith, *World War II at Sea; a Bibliography of Sources in English* (Metuchen, N.J.: Scarecrow Press, 1976), 3 vols., are useful.

En plus des oeuvres citées on devra consulter d'autres bibliographies dont l'intérêt primordial est ni canadien, ni militaire. Certaines bibliographies générales en histoire du Canada citent des ouvrages à caractère militaire parmi les nombreuses études sur divers aspects de notre histoire, telles celle de J.L. Granatstein et Paul Stevens, eds., *Canada since 1867; a Bibliographical Guide* (Toronto: Hakkert, 1974), 170 pp., ou celle de Claude Thibault, *Bibliographia Canadiana* (Don Mills, Ont.: Longman Canada, 1973), 795 pp. On trouvera aussi des études plus spécialisées à même les bibliographies régionales, telles celle de Bruce Peel, *A Bibliography of the Prairie Provinces to 1953* (Toronto: Univ. of Toronto Press, 1956), 680 pp. (et éditions suivantes).

Quelques travaux canadiens sont aussi publiés dans des bibliographies militaires à caractère international. Des études générales sont utiles, telles celle de Gwyn M. Bayliss, *Bibliographic Guide to the Two World Wars; an Annotated Survey of English-Language Reference Materials* (London: Bowker, 1977), 578 pp., celle de Commission internationale d'histoire militaire, Comité de bibliographie, *Bulletin de bibliographie,* No. 1- (Lausanne, Suisse: Centre d'histoire, 1978-), ou encore celle de Myron J. Smith, *World War II at Sea; a Bibliography of Sources in English* (Metuchen, N.J.: Scarecrow Press, 1976), 3 vols., qui traite évidemment d'un aspect bibliographique particulier.

Canada. Committee on the Defences of Canada. *The Defences of Canada, 1st January, 1886.* Ottawa: Queen's Printer, 1886. 171 pp.
Caption title: Report, by the Secretary, upon the Correspondence Submitted to the Committee.

Canada. Dept. of National Defence. Directorate of Strategic and Air Defence Operational Research. *A Selected Bibliography of Peacekeeping (Revised) (U).* Gordon S. Smith, comp. (ORD Report no. 66/R14.) Ottawa: Queen's Printer, 1966. 35 pp.

Canada. Director of Public Information. *Selected List of Wartime Pamphlets.* No. 1-2? Ottawa: King's Printer, 1941-?

Canada. Public Archives. Manuscript Division. *Preliminary Inventory; Record Group 9; Department of Militia and Defence, 1776-1922.* Ottawa: Queen's Printer, 1957. 36 pp.

Canadian Institute of International Affairs. Toronto Men's Branch. Defence Study Group. *Problems of National Defence; a Study Guide and Bibliography,* by Brian A. Crane, Sydney Peck, and Tom Wickett. Toronto: Canadian Institute of International Affairs, 1962. 14 pp.

Cross, Michael, and Robert Bothwell, eds. *Policy by Other Means; Essays in Honour of C.P. Stacey.* Toronto: Clarke, Irwin, 1972. 258 pp.

Dhand, H., L. Hunt and L. Goshawk. *Louis Riel; an Annotated Bibliography.* Saskatoon, Sask.: Univ. of Saskatchewan, 1972. 41 pp.

Dornbusch, C.E., comp. *The Canadian Army, 1855-1958; Regimental Histories and a Guide to the Regiments.* Cornwallville, N.Y.: Hope Farm Press, 1959. 216 pp.

_____. *The Canadian Army, 1855-1955; Regimental Histories and a Guide to the Regiments.* Cornwallville, N.Y.: n.p., 1957. 162 1.

_____. *The Canadian Army, 1855-1965; Lineages; Regimental Histories.* Cornwallville, N.Y.: Hope Farm Press, 1966. 179 pp.

Dornbusch, C.E., comp. *Preliminary List of Canadian Regimental Histories.* Cornwallville, N.Y.: n.p., 1955. 49 pp.

Fancy, Margaret, comp. *A Bibliography of the Works of George Francis Gillman Stanley.* (Bibliography Series, no. 1.) Sackville, N.B.: Ralph Richard Bell Library, Mount Allison Univ., 1976. 52 pp.

Kerr, W.K. *Bibliography of Canadian Reports in Aviation Medicine, 1939-1945.* n.p.: Defence Research Board, 1962. v.p.

_____. *Canada's Part in the Great War; Reprints of Bibliographies.* Toronto: Canadian Historical Review, n.d. v.p.

O'Brien, Jerome W., and Glenn T. Wright. *Sources for the Study of the Second World War./Documents sur la deuxième guerre mondiale.* (Public Archives of Canada Public Records Division Special Publications Series./Archives publiques du Canada Division des archives fédérales collection de publications spéciales.) Ottawa: Supply and Services Canada/Approvisionnements et Services Canada, 1979. 22/24 pp.
Bilingual text./Texte bilingue.

Saskatchewan. Provincial Library. Bibliographic Services. *Louis Riel; a Bibliography.* Ved Parkash Arora, comp. Regina: Queen's Printer, 1972. 66 pp.

Stewart, Charles H. *The Service of British Regiments in Canada and North America; a Resume, with a Chronological List of Uniforms Portrayed in Sources Consulted; Based on Regimental Histories Held in Department of National Defence Library.* (Department of National Defence Library Publication no. 1.) Ottawa: Queen's Printer, 1962. v.p.

B. DEFENCE POLICY AND GENERAL WORKS
— LES POLITIQUES SUR LA DÉFENSE ET GÉNÉRALITÉS

Adams, E.G. *Disarmament and Prosperity for Canada.* Toronto: Canadian Peace Congress, [1962?]. 34 pp.

Agreement Amending and Extending the British Commonwealth Air Training Plan Agreement of December 17, 1939, Relating to Training of Pilots and Aircraft Crews in Canada and their Subsequent Service, between the United Kingdom, Canada, Australia and New Zealand, dated at Ottawa, June 5, 1942. Ottawa: King's Printer, 1942. 28 pp.

Air Force College Journal. Toronto: privately printed, 1956-64. 9 vols.
Title varies.

Aitchison, J.H. *Canada at War; Report of Two Round Tables of the Annual Conference of the Canadian Institute of International Affairs, London, Ontario, May, 1940.* Toronto: Canadian Institute of International Affairs, 1940. 19 pp.

Amery, L.S. *Canadian Citizenship and Imperial Defence.* Toronto: privately printed, [1910]. 11 pp.

Andrew, G.C. *Canada at War; a Report of a Round Table Held by the Canadian Institute of International Affairs at its Eighth Annual Conference, Kingston, Ontario, May 1941.* Toronto: Canadian Institute of International Affairs, 1941. 11 pp.

Angers, François-Albert. *Le bilan canadien d'un conflit.* (Actualités, no. 12.) Montréal: Editions de l'Action nationale, [1946?]. 46 pp.

_____. *Est-ce ainsi qu'on fait la guerre sainte? Conscription des femmes, moralité dans l'armée; "C'est non encore une fois!"* (Actualités, no. 9.) Montréal: Editions de l'Action nationale, [1943?]. 21 pp.

_____. *Pourquoi nous n'accepterons "jamais" la conscription pour service outre-mer.* (Actualités, no. 8.) Montréal: Editions de l'Action nationale, [1942]. 22 pp.

Anglin, Douglas G. *The St. Pierre and Miquelon Affaire of 1941; a Study in Diplomacy in the North Atlantic Quadrangle.* [Toronto]: Univ. of Toronto Press, 1966. 219 pp.

Armstrong, Elizabeth H. *The Crisis of Quebec, 1914-18.* New York: Columbia Univ. Press, 1937. 270 pp.

_____. *French Canadian Opinion on the War, January, 1940 — June, 1941.* (Contemporary Affairs, no. 12.) Toronto: Ryerson Press, 1942. 44 pp.

Asselin, Olivar. *Pourquoi je m'enrôle.* Montréal: s.i., 1916. 50 pp.

_____. *Trois textes sur la liberté.* (Collection Reconnaissances HMH.) Montréal: Editions HMH, 1970. 195 pp.

Atherton, W.H. *A Report of the First National Unity and Win the War Convention, Held in Montreal, May 21-25, 1917./Rapport de la première Convention de l'unité nationale et pour gagner la guerre, tenue à Montréal, du 21 au 25 mai 1917.* Montreal: Canadian Unity and Win the War League, n.d./s.d. 49 pp. *Bilingual text./Texte bilingue.*

Bishop, William A. *Winged Peace.* New York: Viking Press, 1944. 175 pp.

Borden, (Sir) Robert L. *Canada at War; Speeches delivered by Rt. Hon. Sir Robert Laird Borden, K.C., P.C., G.C.M.G., before Canadian Clubs, Toronto, Montreal, Halifax, Winnipeg, December 1914.* n.p.: n.d. 31 pp.

_____. *Canada at War; Speeches delivered by Rt. Hon. Sir Robert Laird Borden, K.C., P.C., G.C.M.G. in Canada and the United Kingdom, June-September, 1918.* n.p.: n.d. 31 pp.

_____. *Canada at War; Speeches Delivered by Rt. Hon. Sir Robert Laird Borden, K.C., P.C., G.C.M.G., in Canada and the United Kingdom, December, 1916 — May, 1917.* n.p.: n.d. 28 pp.

_____. *Canada at War; Speeches Delivered by Rt. Hon. Sir Robert Laird Borden, K.C., P.C., G.C.M.G., in England, Canada, and the United States, July-December, 1915.* n.p.: n.d. 58 pp.

_____. *Manifestos, 1916-17.* Ottawa: King's Printer, 1918. 16 pp.

_____. *The Naval Aid Bill; Speech Delivered by Right Honourable R.L. Borden.* Ottawa: King's Printer, 1912. 31 pp.

_____. *Robert Laird Borden; his Memoirs.* Henry Borden, ed. Toronto: Macmillan, 1938. 2 vols.

_____. *The War and the Future.* Percy Hurd, comp. London: Hodder and Stoughton, 1917. 162 pp.

Bourassa, Henri. *Canadian Nationalism and the War.* Montreal: n.p., 1916. 31 pp.

*Bourassa, Henri. *La conscription.* Montréal: Editions du Devoir, 1917. 46 pp.

*_____. *Conscription.* Montreal: Le Devoir, 1917. 46 pp.

_____. *Le Devoir et la guerre; le conflit des races; discours prononcé au banquet des amis du DEVOIR, le 12 janvier 1916.* Montréal: Imprimerie du Devoir, [1916]. 45 pp.

_____. *The Duty of Canada at the Present Hour; an Address Meant to be Delivered at Ottawa, in November and December, 1914, but Twice Suppressed in the Name of "Loyalty and Patriotism".* Montreal: Le Devoir, [1915?]. 43 pp.

_____. *La mission Jellicoe; nouvelle poussée d'impérialisme.* [Montréal]: Editions du Devoir, 1920. 37 pp.

_____. *Le projet de loi navale; sa nature, ses conséquences; discours prononcé au monument national le 20 janvier 1910.* Montréal: Le Devoir, [1910]. 37 pp.

_____. *Que devons-nous à l'Angleterre? La défense nationale; la révolution impérialiste; le tribut à l'empire.* Montréal: [Le Devoir], 1915. 420 pp.

_____. *Why the Navy Act Should be Repealed; Imperial Problems.* Montreal: Le Devoir, 1912. 62 pp.

_____. *"Win the War" and Lose Canada.* (The Case Against Conscription, 1.) Montreal: Le Devoir, 1917. 14 pp.

Boyd, John. *The Naval Question; in the Light of Canada's National Interests.* Montreal: n.p., 1912. 24 pp.

Brewin, Andrew. *Stand on Guard; the Search for a Canadian Defence Policy.* Toronto: McClelland & Stewart, 1965. 140 pp.

Brewin, Andrew, and Kenneth McNaught. *Debate on Defence; Two Viewpoints on Canadian Foreign Policy.* Toronto: Ontario Woodsworth Memorial Foundation, 1960. 27 pp.

*Brouillette, Benoît. *Canada's Strategic Position.* (Current Affairs for the Canadian Forces, vol. II, no. 2.) Ottawa: King's Printer, 1952. 22 pp.

*_____. *La position stratégique du Canada.* (Actualités; revue destinée aux Forces canadiennes, vol. II, no. 2.) Ottawa: Imprimeur du Roi, 1952. 22 pp.

Buchan, John, *see* Tweedsmuir, John Buchan, baron.

Buchan, Susan Charlotte (Grosvenor), *see* Tweedsmuir, Susan Charlotte (Grosvenor) Buchan, baroness.

Buchner, W.R. *Canada, Ours to Defend.* London, Ont.: privately printed, [1961]. 99 pp.

Buck, Tim. *Canada in the Coming Offensive.* Toronto: privately printed, 1943. 40 pp.

_____. *For Victory in the War and Prosperity in the Peace; Speech Delivered at Spadina Riding Labor Nominating Convention, Feb. 5, 1943.* Toronto: privately printed, [1943?]. 15 pp.

_____. *A National Front for Victory.* n.p.:[1941?]. 22 pp.

_____. *Organize Canada for Total War! The Decisive Year of the War, 1942.* n.p.: [1942?]. 64 pp.

_____. *The Way Forward to Total War; Lessons of the Plebiscite; Smash the Fascists in Quebec.* Toronto: privately printed, [1942]. 20 pp.

Burns, E.L.M. *Between Arab and Israeli.* Toronto: Clarke, Irwin, 1962. 336 pp.

_____. *Megamurder.* Toronto: Clarke, Irwin, 1966. 288 pp.

_____. *A Seat at the Table; the Struggle for Disarmament.* Toronto: Clarke, Irwin, 1972. 268 pp.

Canada. Army Headquarters. *A Brief History of the Canada — United States Permanent Joint Board on Defence, 1940-1960.* Ottawa: Queen's Printer, 1960. 16 pp.

*Canada. Canadian Forces Headquarters. Directorate of History. *The Armed Forces of Canada, 1867-1967; a Century of Achievement.* D.J. Goodspeed, ed. Ottawa: Queen's Printer, 1967. 289 pp.

Canada. Defence Construction (1951) Limited. *Annual Report.* n.p.: 1951-   .

Canada. Dept. of Defence Production. *Canada — United States Defence Development Sharing.* Ottawa: Queen's Printer, 1962. 68 pp.

_____. *Canada — United States Defence Production Sharing.* Ottawa: Queen's Printer, 1960. 122 pp.

_____. *Canadian Defence Products.* Ottawa: Queen's Printer, 1964. 345 pp.

*_____. *Report.* Ottawa: King's Printer, 1952-69.

*Canada. Dept. of External Affairs. *Canada and NATO.* (Current Affairs for the Canadian Forces, vol. III, no. 1.) Ottawa: Queen's Printer, 1952. 22 pp.

*_____. *Canada and the Korean Crisis.* Ottawa: King's Printer, 1950. 36 pp.

*Canada. Dept. of Militia and Defence. *Annual Report.* Ottawa: Queen's Printer, 1867-1922.
Title varies. Until 1883 was State of the Militia of the Dominion of Canada, with further variation in some years.

_____. *Minutes of the Militia Council.* Ottawa: King's Printer, 1905-21. 23 vols.

Canada. Dept. of National Defence. *The Battle of Brains; Canadian Citizenship and the Issues of the War.* Ottawa: King's Printer, 1943. 182 pp.

*_____. *Report.* Ottawa: King's Printer, 1923-59.
Title varies. Annual most years.

_____. *Where Do We Go From Here? Facts for the Guidance of Canadian Army Personnel.* n.p.: [1945]. 28 pp.

*_____. *White Paper on Defence.* Ottawa: Queen's Printer, 1964. 30 pp.

Canada. Dept. of National Defence. Operational Research Division. *Some Problems Met in the Allocation of Defence Resources in Canada,* by G.R. Lindsey. (ORD Informal Paper, no. 67/P4.) Ottawa: n.p., 1967. 41 pp.

Canada. Dept. of National War Services. *Annual Report.* Ottawa: King's Printer, 1945. 3 vols.

Canada. Dept. of the Secretary of State. *Copies of Proclamations, Orders in Council and Documents Relating to the European War.* Ottawa: King's Printer, 1915. 5 vols.

_____. *Correspondence Relating to the Fenian Invasion, and the Rebellion of the Southern States.* Ottawa: Queen's Printer, 1869. 176 pp.

*Canada. Director of Public Information. *Canada at War.* No. 1-45. Ottawa: King's Printer, 1941-45.

_____. *Canada's Part in the Great War.* Ottawa: n.p., 1919. 64 pp.
Also issued by Information Branch, Dept. of External Affairs.

_____. *Canada's War Effort, 1914-1918.* Ottawa: King's Printer, 1918. 31 pp.

*Canada. Forces armées. Quartier général des Forces canadiennes. Direction des services historiques. *Les Forces armées du Canada; un siècle de grandes réalisations.* D.J. Goodspeed, rédacteur. Ottawa: Imprimeur de la Reine, 1967. 289 pp.

*Canada. Ministère de la Défense nationale. *Livre blanc sur la défense.* Ottawa: Imprimeur de la Reine, 1964. 34 pp.

*Canada. Ministère de la Défense nationale. *Rapport.* Ottawa: Imprimeur du Roi, 1923-59.
Divergence du titre. Annuel, la plupart des années.

*Canada. Ministère de la Milice et de la Défense. *Rapport annuel.* Ottawa: Imprimeur de la Reine, 1867-1922.
Divergence du titre. Jusqu'à 1883 le titre était <u>Rapport annuel sur l'état de la Milice de la Puissance du Canada</u>; divers titres suivirent pendant quelques années.

*Canada. Ministère de la production de défense. *Rapport.* Ottawa: Imprimeur de la Reine, 1952-69.

*Canada. Ministère des Affaires extérieures. *Le Canada et la crise coréenne.* Ottawa: Imprimeur du Roi, 1950. 40 pp.

*_____. *Le Canada et l'OTAN.* (Actualités; revue destinée aux Forces canadiennes, vol. III, no. 1.) Ottawa: Imprimeur de la Reine, 1952. 22 pp.

Canada. Munition Resources Commission. *Final Report of the Work of the Commission, November, 1915, to March, 1919, Inclusive.* Toronto: Industrial and Technical Press, 1920. 260 pp.

*Canada. Parlement. *Conférence de la limitation des armements tenue à Washington du 12 novembre 1922, au 6 février 1922, rapport du délégué du Canada comprenant les traités et résolutions.* (Document parlementaire, no. 47.) Ottawa: Imprimeur du Roi, 1923. 236 pp.

*_____. *Copies des décrets du conseil, correspondance, etc., échangés entre le gouvernement impérial et le gouvernement canadien touchant l'organisation d'un état-major général impérial.* (Document parlementaire, no. 99.) Ottawa: Imprimeur du Roi, 1909. 23 pp.

*_____. *Copies du décret en conseil nommant le major général comte de Dundonald commandant de la milice canadienne, 20 mai 1902, et du décret en conseil relevant le comte de Dundonald du commandement de la milice canadienne, 14 juin 1904, ainsi que de la correspondance et des autres documents s'y rattachant.* (Document de la session, no. 113, 113a.) Ottawa: Imprimeur du Roi, 1904. 42 pp.

*_____. *Correspondance concernant la discontinuation de l'usage de la carabine Ross dans l'armée canadienne.* (Document parlementaire, no. 44.) Ottawa: Imprimeur du Roi, 1917. 12 pp.

*_____. *Correspondance relative à l'envoi de contingents militaires coloniaux dans le sud africain.* (Document de la session, no. 20, 20a.) Ottawa: Imprimeur de la Reine, 1900. 54 pp.

*Canada. Parlement. *Mémoire des membres militaires du Conseil de la Milice au Ministre de la Milice et de la Défense; et aussi mémoire du Membre financier du dit Conseil concernant le budget de milice pour l'exercise 1905-1906.* (Document de la session, no. 130.) Ottawa: Imprimeur du Roi, 1905. 25 pp.

*_____. *Réponse à une adresse de la Chambre des Communes en date du 29 novembre 1911, demandant copie de toute la correspondance échangée à la suite de la Conférence impériale entre le gouvernement du Canada et le gouvernement de Sa Majesté au sujet du Service naval du Canada ou d'une manière quelconque y afférant.* (Document parlementaire, no. 40d.) Ottawa: Imprimeur du Roi, 1912. 19 pp.

*Canada. Parlement. Chambre des Communes. Comité permanent de la défense nationale. *Procès-verbaux et témoignages.* Ottawa: Imprimeur de la Reine, 1966-68.

*Canada. Parlement. Chambre des Communes. Comité spécial chargé d'étudier le bill no. 133. *Procès-verbaux et témoignages.* No. 1-8. Ottawa: Imprimeur du Roi, 1950.

*Canada. Parlement. Chambre des Communes. Comité spécial de la défense. *Etudes spéciales à l'intention du Comité spécial de la Chambre des Communes concernant les questions relatives à la défense.* Ottawa: Imprimeur de la Reine, 1965. 196 pp.

*_____. *Procès-verbaux et témoignages.* Ottawa: Imprimeur de la Reine, 1963-65.

*Canada. Parlement. Chambre des Communes. Comité spécial de la défense nationale. *Procès-verbaux et témoignages.* Ottawa: Imprimeur du Roi, 1950.

*Canada. Parlement. Chambre des Communes. Comité spécial de la loi sur les mesures de guerre. *Procès-verbaux et témoignages.* Ottawa: Imprimeur de la Reine, 1960-61. 53 pp.

*Canada. Parlement. Chambre des Communes. Comité spécial d'enquête sur les dépenses de guerre. *Procès-verbaux et témoignages.* Ottawa: Imprimeur du Roi, 1940-45.

*Canada. Parlement. Chambre des Communes. Comité spécial d'enquête sur les règlements concernant la défense du Canada. *Procès-verbaux et témoignages.* No. 1-2. Ottawa: Imprimeur du Roi, 1944.

*Canada. Parlement. Chambre des Communes. Comité spécial des dépenses aux fins de la défense. *Procès-verbaux et témoignages.* Ottawa: Imprimeur du Roi, 1951-60.

*Canada. Parlement. Chambre des Communes. Comité spécial des dépenses et économies de guerre. *Procès-verbaux et témoignages.* Ottawa: Imprimeur du Roi, 1945-46.

*Canada. Parliament. *Conference on the Limitation of Armament Held at Washington, November 12, 1921, to February 6, 1922; Report of the Canadian Delegate including Treaties and Resolutions.* (Sessional Paper, no. 47.) Ottawa: King's Printer, 1922. 222 pp.

*_____. *Copies of Orders in Council, Correspondence, &c., between the Imperial and Canadian Governments, Relating to the Organization of an Imperial General Staff.* (Sessional Paper, no. 99.) Ottawa: King's Printer, 1909. 22 pp.

*_____. *Copies of the Order in Council Appointing Major General, the Earl of Dundonald, to the Command of the Canadian Militia, 20th May, 1902, and the Order in Council Relieving from the Command of the Canadian Militia, 14th June, 1904, and also, Correspondence and Other Papers Connected Therewith.* (Sessional Paper, no. 113, 113a.) Ottawa: King's Printer, 1904. 41 pp.

*_____. *Correspondence Relating to the Despatch of Colonial Military Contingents to South Africa.* (Sessional Paper, no. 20, 20a.) Ottawa: Queen's Printer, 1900. 51 pp.

*_____. *Correspondence Relating to the Withdrawal of the Ross Rifle from the Canadian Army Corps.* (Sessional Paper, no. 44.) Ottawa: King's Printer, 1917. 12 pp.

*_____. *Memorandum from the Military Members of the Militia Council to the Minister of Militia and Defence; and also Memorandum of the Finance Member of the Militia Council relating to the Militia Estimates for 1905-1906.* (Sessional Paper, no. 130.) Ottawa: King's Printer, 1905. 24 pp.

_____. *Report of the Delegates to England of their Correspondence with Her Majesty's Government on the Subject of Fortifications, Defence, Arms, etc.* Ottawa: Queen's Printer, 1869. 15 pp.

*_____. *Return to an Address of the House of Commons, dated November 29, 1911, for a Copy of all Correspondence between the Government of Canada and His Majesty's Government Subsequent to the Last Imperial Conference, Concerning the Naval Service of Canada and in Any Way Connected with it.* (Sessional Paper, no. 40d.) Ottawa: King's Printer, 1912. 18 pp.

*Canada. Parliament. House of Commons. Special Committee on Bill No. 133. *Minutes of Proceedings and Evidence.* No. 1-8. Ottawa: Queen's Printer, 1950.

Canada. Parliament. House of Commons. Special Committee on Boot Inquiry. *Proceedings and Evidence.* Ottawa: King's Printer, 1915.

Canada. Parliament. House of Commons. Special Committee on Defence. *Interim Report./Rapport intérimaire.* Ottawa: Queen's Printer/Imprimeur de la Reine, 1963. 24 pp.
Bilingual text./Texte bilingue.

*_____. *Minutes of Proceedings and Evidence.* Ottawa: Queen's Printer, 1963-65.

*_____. *Special Studies prepared for the Special Committee on Matters Relating to Defence.* Ottawa: Queen's Printer, 1965. 179 pp.

*Canada. Parliament. House of Commons. Special Committee on Defence Expenditure. *Minutes of Proceedings and Evidence.* Ottawa: King's Printer, 1951-60.

*Canada. Parliament. House of Commons. Special Committee on Defence of Canada Regulations. *Minutes of Proceedings and Evidence.* No. 1-2. Ottawa: King's Printer, 1944.

*Canada. Parliament. House of Commons. Special Committee on National Defence. *Minutes of Proceedings and Evidence.* Ottawa: King's Printer, 1950.

*Canada. Parliament. House of Commons. Special Committee on the War Measures Act. *Minutes of Proceedings and Evidence.* Ottawa: Queen's Printer, 1960-61. 48 pp.

*Canada. Parliament. House of Commons. Special Committee on War Expenditure. *Minutes of Proceedings and Evidence.* Ottawa: King's Printer, 1940-45.

*Canada. Parliament. House of Commons. Special Committee on War Expenditures and Economics. *Minutes of Proceedings and Evidence.* Ottawa: King's Printer, 1945-46.

*Canada. Parliament. House of Commons. Standing Committee on National Defence. *Minutes of Proceedings and Evidence.* Ottawa: Queen's Printer, 1966-68.

Canada. Privy Council. *Proclamations and Orders in Council Passed under the Authority of the War Measures Act; R.S.C. (1927) Chap. 206.* Ottawa: King's Printer, 1940-42. 8 vols.
Vols. IV-VIII titled: Proclamations and Orders in Council Relating to the War.

Canada. Royal Commission Concerning Purchase of War Supplies and Sale of Small Arms Ammunition. *Evidence.* The Honourable Sir Charles Davidson, Commissioner. Ottawa: King's Printer, 1917. 3 vols.

Canada. Royal Commission on Purchase of Surgical Field Dressings and Other Surgical Supplies. *Report of the Commissioner.* The Honourable Sir Charles Davidson, Commissioner. Ottawa: King's Printer, 1917. 28 pp.

Canada. Royal Commission on Shell Contracts. *Minutes of Evidence.* Ottawa: King's Printer, 1916. 2 vols.

Canada. Royal Comission on the Bren Machine Gun Contract. *Report.* Henry Hague Davis, Commissioner. Ottawa: King's Printer, 1939. 52 pp.

[Canada. Royal Commission to Inquire into the Purchase by and on Behalf of the Government of the Dominion of Canada, of Arms, Munitions, Implements, Materials, Horses, Supplies, and Other Things for the Purpose of the Present War.] *Report of the Commissioner Concerning Sale of Small Arms Ammunition.* Sir Charles Davidson, Commissioner. Ottawa: King's Printer, 1917. 56 pp.

*Canada. Service de l'Information. *Le Canada en guerre.* No. 1-45. Ottawa: Imprimeur du Roi, 1941-45.

Canada. War Purchasing Commission. [*Report.*] A.E. Kemp, Chairman. Ottawa: King's Printer, 1916-19. 6 vols.

Le Canada arme ses troupes. (Actualités; revue destinée aux Forces canadiennes, vol. VII, no. 11.) Ottawa: Imprimeur de la Reine, 1954. 27 pp.

Canada Arms Her Forces. (Current Affairs for the Canadian Forces, vol. VII, no. 11.) Ottawa: Queen's Printer, 1954. 31 pp.

Canada; Neighbor at War; a University of Chicago Round Table Broadcast. (Univ. of Chicago Round Table, no. 195.) Chicago: Univ. of Chicago, 1941. 29 pp.

Canada's Effort in the Great War to March, 1917. Moose Jaw, Sask.: privately printed, [1917]. 79 pp.

Canadian Broadcasting Corporation. Publications Branch. *We have been There; Authoritative Reports by Qualified Observers who have Returned from the War Zones, as Presented over the CBC National Network.* Toronto: Canadian Broadcasting Corporation, 1941-42. 2 vols.

Canadian Defence League. *The Canadian Defence League, Organized May 5th, 1909.* Toronto: n.p., 1913. 48 pp.

Canadian Defence Quarterly. Vol. I-XVI. Ottawa: privately printed, 1923-39.

Canadian Defence Quarterly./Revue canadienne de défense. Vol. I- . Toronto: Baxter Pub., 1971- .

Canadian Institute of International Affairs. Toronto Men's Branch. Defence Study Group. *Problems of National Defence; a Study Guide and Bibliography,* by Brian A. Crane, Sydney Peck, and Tom Wickett. Toronto: Canadian Institute of International Affairs, 1962. 14 pp.

Canadian Liberal Party. Central Information Office. *Canada and the Navy; Australia and New Zealand; Methods of Naval Defence; the Policies of other Self-Governing British Dominions and their Bearing upon the Naval Controversy in Canada.* (Publication no. 9.) Ottawa: privately printed, 1913. 23 pp.

_____. *Canada and the Navy; Canada's Position in Military and Naval Defence; an Outline of Important Events.* (Publication no. 7.) Ottawa: privately printed, 1913. 16 pp.

_____. *Canada and the Navy; Is There an Emergency? Conflicting Opinions Examined in the Light of Facts.* (Publication no. 6.) Ottawa: privately printed, 1913. 24 pp.

_____. *Canada and the Navy; the Memorandum Prepared by the Board of Admiralty on the General Naval Situation.* (Publication no. 5.) Ottawa: privately printed, 1913. 16 pp.

_____. *Canada and the Navy; the Real Emergency; the Nationalist-Conservative Alliance and some of its Consequences; how British Interests have been Sacrificed to Serve Party Ends.* (Publication no. 8.) Ottawa: privately printed, 1913. 20 pp.

_____. *Canada and the Navy; the Two Policies; 100 Reasons Why the Laurier is Better than the Borden Policy!* (Publication no. 12.) Ottawa: privately printed, 1913. 15 pp.

_____. *Canadian Defence and the Navy Question.* Ottawa: privately printed, 1915. 80 pp.

_____. *Correspondence of General Sir Sam Hughes, ex-Minister of Militia, and the Right Hon. Sir Robert Borden, G.C.M.G., at the Time Sir Sam Resigned; Sir Sam Accused of Insubordination but Dismissed for Writing the Premier an Insulting Letter; Read the "Charges and Accusations".* (Publication no. 52.) Ottawa: privately printed, [1917]. 16 pp.

_____. *A Series of Pamphlets and Leaflets on Canada and the Navy Issued by the Liberal Information Office during the 1912-13 Session of Parliament.* Ottawa: privately printed, n.d. v.p.

_____. *Shell and Fuse Contracts; a Million Dollar Rake-off; Taken from Government Records.* (Publication no. 49.) Ottawa: privately printed, [1917]. 12 pp.

_____. *War Contract Scandals, as Investigated by the Public Accounts Committee of the House of Commons, 1915; also the Purchase of Boots, as Investigated by the Special "Boot Committee" Appointed by the House of Commons, Ottawa, 1915.* Ottawa: privately printed, 1915. 47 pp.

The Canadian Military Gazette. Vol. I-LXIII. Ottawa: privately printed, 1885-1948.

The Canadian Military Journal. Vol. I- . Beauceville, P.Q., Montreal: privately printed, 1934- .
  Title 1934-1943: Salute.

Canadian Military Medals and Insignia Journal. Vol. I- . Guelph, Ont.: privately printed, 1965- .
  Title varies.

Canadian Military Review./Revue militaire canadienne. Vol. I-II. Québec, P.Q.: privately printed/imprimé privé, 1880-81?

Canadian National Railways. *Canada's National Railways; their Part in the War.* Toronto: privately printed, n.d. 167 pp.

Canadian Nationalism and the War. Montreal: n.p., 1916. 31 pp.

The Canadian War. No. 1-12. Toronto: n.p., 1914-15.

Canadian War Museum./Musée de guerre. Ottawa: Queen's Printer/Imprimeur de la Reine, 1969. 1 vol., unpaged./1 tome, non-paginé.
  Bilingual text./Texte bilingue.

Capon, Alan R. *His Faults Lie Gently; the Incredible Sam Hughes.* Lindsay, Ont.: F.W. Hall, 1969. 159 pp.

Carnegie, David. *The History of Munitions Supply in Canada, 1914-1918.* London: Longmans, Green, 1925. 336 pp.

Carter, G. *The British Commonwealth and International Security; the Role of the Dominions, 1919-1939.* Toronto: Ryerson Press, 1947. 326 pp.

Chase-Casgrain, T. *Address by Hon. T. Chase-Casgrain, K.C., M.P., Postmaster General, Delivered at a Luncheon Given in His Honour by the Canadian Club, Vancouver, B.C., on the 16th of August, 1915.* n.p.: [1915]. 23 pp.

Chassé, Noël. *Avant la poussée finale.* Québec, P.Q.: Imprimerie "L'évènement", 1918. 98 pp.

Churchill, (Sir) Winston Leonard Spencer. *Churchill in Ottawa.* [Ottawa: King's Printer, n.d.] 1 vol., unpaged.

[Coffin, W.F.] *Thoughts on Defence; from a Canadian Point of View,* by a Canadian. Montreal: J. Lovell, 1870. 55 pp.

Comments on the Senate's Rejection of the Naval Aid Bill. Ottawa: Ottawa Print. Co., [1913]. 27 pp.

Conant, Melvin. *The Long Polar Watch; Canada and the Defence of North America.* New York: Harper, 1962. 204 pp.

Conn, Stetson, and Byron Fairchild. *The Western Hemisphere; the Framework of Hemisphere Defense.* (United States Army in World War II.) Washington: U.S. Govt. Print. Off., 1960. 470 pp.

Conscription 1917. Essays by A.M. Wilhms and others. (Canadian Historical Readings, 8.) Toronto: Univ. of Toronto Press, n.d. 77 pp.

*Le Conseil du service militaire. *Pour la défense du Canada.* Ottawa: imprimé privé, 1917. 29 pp.

[Conservative Party (Canada).] *Imperial Defence; the Record of the Liberal Party; Persistent Opposition to any Proposals which would Bind Canada Closer to the Motherland; Refused to Share the Burden.* Ottawa: Federal Press Agency, 1915. 16 pp.

_____. *Imperial Naval Defence; the Record of the Liberal Party.* Ottawa: Federal Press Agency, 1915. 32 pp.

_____. *The Collapse of the "Boot Scandal"; Liberal Campaign of Falsehood a Total Failure; but it has Robbed the Canadian Workingman of Millions of Dollars.* Ottawa: Federal Press Agency, n.d. 11 pp.

Co-operative Commonwealth Federation. National Office. *A New Order shall Arise; Statements on the Policy of the Co-operative Commonwealth Federation (C.C.F.) in the Present Struggle Against the Nazis and Fascists, Consisting of an Address by M.J. Coldwell, M.P., C.C.F. National Chairman, Policy Resolutions Adopted by the 1940 National Convention of the C.C.F., Cables of Greetings Exchanged by the C.C.F. with the British Labour Party.* Ottawa: privately printed, n.d. 24 pp.

Cowan, John Scott. *See No Evil; a Study of the Chaos in Canadian Defence Policy.* Toronto: Annex Pub., 1963. 35 pp.

Cox, David. *Canadian Defence Policy; the Dilemmas of a Middle Power.* (Behind the Headlines, vol. XXVII, no. 5.) Toronto: Canadian Institute of International Affairs, 1968. 43 pp.

Crane, Brian. *An Introduction to Canadian Defence Policy.* Toronto: Canadian Institute of International Affairs, 1964. 75 pp.

Cross, Michael, and Robert Bothwell, eds. *Policy by Other Means; Essays in Honour of C.P. Stacey,* Toronto: Clarke, Irwin, 1972. 258 pp.

Cuff, R.D., and J.L. Granatstein. *Canadian-American Relations in Wartime; from the Great War to the Cold War.* Toronto: Hakkert, 1975. 205 pp.

Cuthbertson, Brian. *Canadian Military Independence in the Age of the Superpowers.* Toronto: Fitzhenry & Whiteside, 1977. 282 pp.

Dafoe, John W. *The Voice of Dafoe; a Selection of Editorials on Collective Security, 1931-1944.* W.L. Morton, ed. Toronto: Macmillan, 1945. 293 pp.

Dafoe, John W., ed. *Canada Fights; an American Democracy at War.* New York: Farrar & Rinehart, 1941. 280 pp.

Davidson, (Sir) Charles, *see* Canada. Royal Commission . . .

Davies, Raymond Arthur. *This is our Land; Ukranian Canadians against Hitler.* Toronto: Progress Books, 1943. 158 pp.

Davis, Henry Hague, *see* Canada. Royal Commission on the Bren Gun Contract.

Dawson, R. MacGregor. *The Conscription Crisis of 1944.* Toronto: Univ. of Toronto Press, 1961. 136 pp.

*Defence of Canada Regulations. Ottawa: King's Printer, 1939. 57 pp. *Reprinted and expanded 1940, 1941, 1942.*

De Malijay, Paul. *Le Colonel d'Orsonnens; considerations sur l'organisation militaire de la Confédération canadienne; observations critiques.* Montréal: Les presses à vapeur du Franc-Parleur, 1874. 58 pp.

Denison, George T. *Naval Defence; St. Andrew's Society Banquet; Colonel George T. Denison's Reply to the Toast of Army and Navy, 30th November, 1909.* n.p.: [1909]. 14 pp.

*Desjardins, L.G. *L'Angleterre, le Canada et la grande guerre.* Québec, P.Q.: s.i., 1917. 460 pp.

*_____. *England, Canada and the Great War.* Quebec, P.Q.: Chronicle Print., 1918. 422 pp.

De Wolfe, J.H., comp. *Our Heroes in the Great World War; Giving Facts and Details on Canada's Part in the Greatest War in History.* Ottawa: Patriotic Pub. Co., 1919. 415 pp.

Dillon, G.M. *Canadian Naval Forces since World War II; a Decision-making Analysis,* with comments by Dr. G.R. Lindsey and Professor Jonathan Wouk, with a reply from the author. (Dalhousie Univ. Center for Foreign Policy Studies Occasional Paper.) Halifax: Dalhousie Univ., 1972. 79 pp.

Diubaldo, R.J., and S.J. Scheinberg. *A Study of Canadian-American Defence Policy (1945-1975); Northern Issues and Strategic Resources.* (Dept. of National Defence Operational Research and Analysis Establishment ORAE Extra-Mural Paper no. 6.) Ottawa: n.p., 1978. 115 pp.

Douglas, W.A.B., and Brereton Greenhous. *Out of the Shadows; Canada in the Second World War.* Toronto: Oxford Univ. Press, 1977. 288 pp.

"Du Guesclin" [*pseud.*] *voir Notre marine de guerre.*

Dundonald, Douglas Mackinnon Baillie Hamilton Cochrane, 12th earl. *My Army Life.* London: E. Arnold, 1926. 342 pp.

Dziuban, Stanley W. *Military Relations between the United States and Canada, 1939-1945.* (United States Army in World War II; Special Studies.) Washington: U.S. Govt. Print. Off., 1959. 432 pp.

Eayrs, James. *Future Roles for the Armed Forces of Canada.* (Behind the Headlines, vol. XXVIII.) Toronto: Canadian Institute of International Affairs, 1969. 16 pp.

_____. *In Defence of Canada.* (Studies in the Structure of Power; Decision Making in Canada.) Toronto: Univ. of Toronto Press, 1964-72. 3 vols.

_____. *Northern Approaches; Canada and the Search for Peace.* Toronto: Macmillan, 1961. 195 pp.

Eggleston, Wilfrid. *Canada's Nuclear Story.* Toronto: Clarke, Irwin, 1965. 368 pp.

_____. *Scientists at War.* London: Oxford Univ. Press, 1950. 291 pp.

Evans, W. Sanford. *The Canadian Contingents and Canadian Imperialism; a Story and a Study.* Toronto: Publishers' Syndicate, 1901. 352 pp.

Ewart, John S. *Canada and British Wars.* n.p.: n.d. 88 pp.

A Few Words on Canada, by a Canadian. Ottawa: Hunter-Rose, 1871. 72 pp.

Finnie, Richard. *Canol; the Sub-Arctic Pipeline and Refinery Project Constructed by Bechtel-Price-Callahan for the Corps of Engineers, United States Army, 1942-1944.* San Francisco, Calif.: privately printed, 1945. 210 pp.

Fletcher, [Henry Charles]. *A Lecture Delivered at the Literary and Scientific Institute, Ottawa, by Col. Fletcher, Scots Fusilier Guards, Military Secretary, February, 1875.* Ottawa: n.p., n.d. 19 pp.

_____. *Memorandum on the Militia System of Canada.* Ottawa: Citizen Print. Co., 1873. 20 pp.

Foulkes, Charles. *Canadian Defence Policy in a Nuclear Age.* (Behind the Headlines, vol. XXI, no. 1.) Toronto: Canadian Institute of International Affairs, 1961. 20 pp.

_____. *Canadian Response to United States Strategy.* [(Carleton Univ. School of International Affairs Occasional Papers, 2.) Ottawa: Carleton Univ., 1968?] 20 pp.

French, John Denton Pinkstone French, 1st earl of Ypres. *Report by General Sir John French, G.C.B., G.C.V.O., K.C.M.G., Inspector General of the Imperial Forces, upon his Inspection of the Canadian Military Forces.* (Sessional Paper, no. 35a.) Ottawa: King's Printer, 1910. 38 pp.

Gellner, John. *Canada in NATO.* Toronto: Ryerson Press, 1970. 117 pp.

_____. *Problems of Canadian Defence.* (Behind the Headlines, vol. XVIII, no. 5.) Toronto: Canadian Institute of International Affairs, 1958. 16 pp.

Gibson, Colin. *"Air Power in Canada"; an Address by Col. the Hon. Colin Gibson, M.C., M.A., Minister of National Defence for Air, to the Empire Club of Toronto, February 28, 1946.* n.p.: n.d. 11 pp.

[Gillis, Clarence.] *Letter from Home.* Toronto: Canadian Forum, 1943. 32 pp.

Glazebrook, G. de T., and Winslow Benson. *Canada's Defence Policy; Report of Round Tables of the Fourth Annual Conference of the Canadian Institute of International Affairs.* Toronto: [Canadian Institute of International Affairs], 1937. 16 pp.

Godsell, Philip H. *The Romance of the Alaska Highway.* Toronto: Ryerson Press, 1944. 235 pp.

[Golden, L.L.L.] *Conscription,* by "Politicus" [*pseud.*] (Macmillan War Pamphlets, Canadian Series.) Toronto: Macmillan, 1941. 32 pp.

Good, Mabel Tinkiss. *Men of Valour.* Toronto: Macmillan, 1948. 137 pp.

Granatstein, J.L. *Canada's War; the Politics of the Mackenzie King Government, 1939-1945.* Toronto: Oxford Univ. Press, 1975. 436 pp.

_____. *Conscription in the Second World War, 1939-1945; a Study in Political Management.* (The Frontenac Library, Number 1.) Toronto: Ryerson Press, 1969. 85 pp.

Granatstein, J.L., and J.M. Hitsman. *Broken Promises; a History of Conscription in Canada.* Toronto: Oxford Univ. Press, 1977. 281 pp.

Granatstein, J.L., and R.D. Cuff, eds. *War and Society in North America.* Toronto: T. Nelson, 1971. 199 pp.

Gravel, Jean-Yves. *L'armée au Québec; un portrait social, 1868-1900.* Montréal: Les Editions du Boréal Express, 1974. 157 pp.

Gravel, Jean-Yves, éd. *Le Québec et la guerre, 1867-1960.* Montréal: Les Editions du Boréal Express, 1974. 173 pp.

The Great War and Canadian Society; an Oral History. Daphne Read, ed. Toronto: New Hogtown Press, 1978. 223 pp.

Haddow, Robert. *More Planes to Smash Fascism.* [Montreal?]: n.p., n.d. 18 pp.

Hall, H. Duncan. *North American Supply.* (History of the Second World War; United Kingdom Civil Series.) London: H.M. Stationery Office and Longmans, Green, 1955. 559 pp.

The Halship Saga; the War Effort of Halifax Shipyards, Limited; "An Illustrious War Achievement". [Halifax: n.p., n.d.] 1 vol., unpaged.

Hannon, Leslie F. *Canada at War.* (The Canadian Illustrated Library.) Toronto: McClelland and Stewart, 1968. 127 pp.

Harrison, W.E.C., and others. *Canada, the War and After.* (Live and Learn Books.) Toronto: Ryerson Press, 1942. 78 pp.

Harvey, Jean-Charles. *French Canada at War.* (Macmillan War Pamphlets, Canadian Series.) Toronto: Macmillan, 1941. 26 pp.

Haydon, Walter. *Canada and the War.* Bristol, Eng.: J.W. Arrowsmith, 1915. 90 pp.

Hertzman, Lewis, John W. Warnock and Thomas A. Hockin. *Alliances and Illusions; Canada and the NATO-NORAD Question.* Edmonton: Hurtig, 1969. 154 pp.

Hitchins, F.H. *Air Board, Canadian Air Force and Royal Canadian Air Force.* (National Museum of Man Mercury Series; Canadian War Museum Paper no. 2.) Ottawa: Queen's Printer, 1972. 475 pp.

Hitsman, J. Mackay. *Canadian Naval Policy.* Kingston, Ont.: Queen's Univ., 1940. 208 pp.

_____. *Military Inspection Services in Canada, 1855-1950.* Ottawa: [Queen's Printer, 1962.] 122 pp.

_____. *Safeguarding Canada, 1763-1871.* Toronto: Univ. of Toronto Press, 1968. 240 pp.

Hodgins, J. Herbert, and others, comps. *Women at War.* Montreal: MacLean Pub., 1943. 190 pp.

Hopkins, J. Castell. *The Province of Ontario in the War; a Record of Government and People.* Toronto: Warwick Bros. & Rutter, 1919. 123 pp.

Hunt, M.S., comp. *Nova Scotia's Part in the Great War.* Halifax: Veteran Pub., 1920. 466 pp.

Hurst, Alan M. *The Canadian Y.M.C.A. in World War II.* n.p.: n.d. 398 pp.

Hyde, H. Montgomery. *The Quiet Canadian; the Secret Service Story of Sir William Stephenson.* London: H. Hamilton, 1962. 255 pp.

Irwin, Ross W., and Edward E. Denby. *Orders, Decorations and Medals to Canadians.* n.p.: 1976. 63 pp.

Irwin, Ross W., comp. *A Guide to the War Medals and Decorations of Canada.* [Guelph, Ont.: privately printed], 1969. 114 pp.

Jackson, H.M. *Canadian Prime Ministers and the Canadian Militia.* n.p.: 1958. 11 pp.

James, F. Cyril. *The Impact and Aftermath of War; an Address Delivered before a Meeting of the Canadian Club at Toronto, Canada, on Monday, December 14, 1942.* Toronto: privately printed, [1942?]. 19 pp.

Jellicoe, John Rushworth Jellicoe, 1st earl. *Report of Admiral of the Fleet, Viscount Jellicoe of Scapa, G.C.B., O.M., G.C.V.O. on Mission to the Dominion of Canada, November-December, 1919.* Ottawa: n.p., n.d. 3 vols.
Vol. I also printed as Sessional Paper no. 61, 1920. Vol. II-III originally Secret.

*Jellicoe, John Rushworth Jellicoe, 1re earl. *Rapport de l'Amiral de la Flotte le Vicomte Jellicoe de Scapa, G.C.B., O.M., G.C.V.O., sur la mission navale au Canada en novembre et décembre 1919.* (Document de la session, no. 61.) Ottawa: Imprimeur du Roi, 1920. 59 pp.

Kardash, William. *Hitler's Agents in Canada; a Revealing Story of Potentially Dangerous Fifth Column Activities in Canada among Ukrainian Canadians.* Toronto: privately printed, 1942. 32 pp.

_____. *1942; Year of Victory; Defeat the Enemy on a Second Land Front in Western Europe.* Toronto: privately printed, [1942?]. 29 pp.

Kelsey Club, Winnipeg, Man. *Canadian Defence; What We have to Defend; Various Defence Policies.* Toronto: T. Nelson, 1937. 98 pp.

Kemp, A.E., *see* Canada. War Purchasing Commission.

Kennedy, J. de N. *History of the Department of Munitions and Supply; Canada in the Second World War.* [Ottawa]: King's Printer, 1950. 2 vols.

Kimble, George H.T. *Canadian Military Geography.* Ottawa: Queen's Printer, 1949. 196 pp.

King, W.L. Mackenzie. *Aggression in Hitler's Mind has no Limits; My Duty, as I see It, is to Seek above all to Preserve National Unity.* Winnipeg: privately printed, n.d. 23 pp.

_____. *Canada and the Fight for Freedom.* Toronto: Macmillan, 1944. 326 pp.

_____. *Canada and the War; Canada's Contribution to Freedom, Speech by Right Hon. W.L. Mackenzie King, M.P., Prime Minister of Canada, at a Dinner Tendered in his Honour by the Associated Canadian Organizations of New York City, New York, June 17, 1941.* Ottawa: King's Printer, 1941. 18 pp.

*_____. *Canada and the War; Canada's Fighting Men; an Address on the Opening of the Fourth Victory Loan Campaign, by Right Hon. W.L. Mackenzie King, M.P., Prime Minister of Canada, Toronto, April 19, 1943.* Ottawa: King's Printer, 1943. 15 pp.

*_____. *Canada and the War; Canada's Support of the Army Overseas; Broadcast by Right Hon. W.L. Mackenzie King, M.P., Prime Minister of Canada, Ottawa, November 8, 1944.* Ottawa: King's Printer, 1944. 11 pp.

_____. *Canada and the War; Mackenzie King to the People of Canada, 1940; a Series of Radio Broadcasts by Prime Minister Mackenzie King from Ottawa, February-March 1940.* Ottawa: National Liberal Federation, n.d., 104 pp.

*_____. *Canada and the War; Manpower and a Total War Effort; National Selective Service, Broadcast by Right Hon. W.L. Mackenzie King, M.P., Prime Minister of Canada, August 19, 1942.* Ottawa: King's Printer, 1942. 12 pp.

*_____. *Canada and the War; New Situations and Responsibilities. I. Canada's War Effort Viewed in Relation to the War Effort of the Allied Powers. II. Italy's Entry into the War, Broadcasts by Right Hon. W.L. Mackenzie King, M.P., Prime Minister of Canada, Friday, June 7, and Monday, June 10, 1940.* Ottawa: King's Printer, 1940. 18 pp.

*_____. *Canada and the War; the Defence of Common Liberties; an Address to the Pilgrims of the United States by Right Hon. W.L. Mackenzie King, M.P., Prime Minister of Canada, New York, December 2, 1942.* Ottawa: King's Printer, 1942. 11 pp.

_____. *Canada and the War; the Training of British Pilots and the Joint Air Training Plan; Mackenzie King Replies to Dr. Manion; a Radio Address by Right Honourable W.L. Mackenzie King, Ottawa, 8th March, 1940.* Ottawa: National Liberal Federation, n.d. 13 pp.

King, W.L. Mackenzie. *Canada and the War; the Unconditional Surrender of Italy (September 3, 1943); Four Years of War, 1939-1943, Broadcasts by Right Honourable W.L. Mackenzie King, M.P., Prime Minister of Canada, Ottawa, September 8 and 10, 1943.* Ottawa: King's Printer, 1943. 10 pp.

_____. *Canada and the War; Three Years of War; the Real Issue in the Struggle; Broadcast by Right Hon. W.L. Mackenzie King, M.P., Prime Minister of Canada, September 10, 1942.* Ottawa: King's Printer, 1942. 12 pp.

_____. *Canada and the War; Victory, Reconstruction and Peace.* n.p.: 1945. 142 pp.

_____. *Canada and the War; War Record of the Mackenzie King Administration; a Radio Address by Right Honourable W.L. Mackenzie King, Ottawa, 21st February, 1940.* Ottawa: National Liberal Federation, n.d. 20 pp.

*_____. *Canada at Britain's Side.* Toronto: Macmillan, 1941. 332 pp.

*_____. *Le Canada et la guerre.* Montréal: Editions B. Valiquette, n.d. 341 pp.

*_____. *Le Canada et la guerre; appui du Canada à son armée d'outre-mer, causerie radiophonique du très honorable W.L. Mackenzie King, M.P., premier ministre du Canada, Ottawa, 8 novembre 1944.* Ottawa: Imprimeur du Roi, 1944. 12 pp.

_____. *Le Canada et la guerre; effort total contre guerre total; un appel en faveur de l'épargne de guerre, radiodiffusé par le très hon. Mackenzie King, M.P., premier ministre du Canada, dimanche, le 2 février 1941.* Ottawa: Imprimeur du Roi, 1941. 12 pp.

*_____. *Le Canada et la guerre; la défense de nos communes libertés, discours prononcé lors du dîner des "Pilgrims of the United States" par le très hon. W.L. Mackenzie King, M.P., premier ministre du Canada, New-York, le 2 décembre 1942.* Ottawa: Imprimeur du Roi, 1942. 12 pp.

*_____. *Le Canada et la guerre; les forces combattantes du Canada, discours prononcé à l'ouverture de la campagne du quatrième emprunt de la victoire, par le très honorable W.L. Mackenzie King, premier ministre du Canada, Toronto, le 19 avril 1943.* Ottawa: Imprimeur du Roi, 1943. 15 pp.

*King, W.L. Mackenzie. *Le Canada et la guerre; nouvelles situations et nouvelles responsabilités.* I. *L'effort de guerre du Canada en regard de l'effort de guerre des puissances alliées.* II. *L'entrée de l'Italie dans la guerre, discours à la radio du très hon. W.L. Mackenzie King, M.P., premier ministre du Canada, le vendredi 7 juin et le lundi 10 juin 1940.* Ottawa: Imprimeur du Roi, 1940. 20 pp.

*_____. *Le Canada et la guerre; ressources humaines et effort de guerre total; service sélectif national, discours prononcé à la T.S.F. par le très honorable W.L. Mackenzie King, M.P., premier ministre du Canada, le 19 août, 1942.* Ottawa: Imprimeur du Roi, 1942. 13 pp.

_____. *National Security — the Issue in the Plebiscite; an Appeal to the Canadian Electorate for an Affirmative Vote on April 27th; an Address Broadcast by the Right Honourable W.L. Mackenzie King, M.P., Prime Minister of Canada, over the Canadian Broadcasting Network, April 7th, 1942.* Ottawa: King's Printer, 1942. 11 pp.

_____. *National Unity and National Survival; Responsibility to our Own and Future Generations; a Second Appeal to the Canadian Electorate for an Affirmative Vote on April 27th; an Address Broadcast by the Right Hon. W.L. Mackenzie King, M.P., Prime Minister of Canada, over the Canadian Broadcasting Corporation Network, April 24th, 1942.* Ottawa: King's Printer, 1942. 11 pp.

*_____. *L'organisation de l'effort de guerre du Canada; le Parlement et le Gouvernement; discours à la radio par le très honorable W.L. Mackenzie King, M.P., premier ministre du Canada, mardi, le 31 octobre 1939.* Ottawa: Imprimeur du Roi, 1939. 16 pp.

*_____. *The Organization of Canada's War Effort; Parliament and the Government; Broadcast by Right Hon. W.L. Mackenzie King, M.P., Prime Minister of Canada, Tuesday, October 31, 1939.* Ottawa: King's Printer, 1939. 16 pp.

_____. *Plan d'entraînement des aviateurs du Commonwealth britannique; discours à la radio par le très honorable W.L. Mackenzie King, M.P., premier ministre du Canada, le dimanche, 17 décembre 1939.* Ottawa: Imprimeur du Roi, 1939. 15 pp.

Kirkconnell, Watson. *Canada, Europe and Hitler.* Toronto: Oxford Univ. Press, 1939. 213 pp.

_____. *Our Ukranian Loyalists.* Winnipeg: privately printed, 1943. 28 pp.

_____. *Twilight of Liberty.* London: Oxford Univ. Press, 1941. 193 pp.

Kirkconnell, Watson. *The Ukranian Canadians and the War.* (Oxford Pamphlets on World Affairs, no. C.3.) Toronto: Oxford Univ. Press, 1940. 30 pp.

*Knight, Eric. *C'est votre terre qu'ils veulent.* Ottawa: [Imprimeur du Roi, 1942]. 11 pp.

*_____. *They Don't Want Swamps and Jungles.* Ottawa: [King's Printer, 1942]. 11 pp.

Kronenberg, Vernon J. *All Together Now; the Organization of the Department of National Defence in Canada, 1964-1972.* (Wellesley Paper, 3/1973.) Toronto: Canadian Institute of International Affairs, 1973. 124 pp.

Laflamme, Jean. *Les camps de détention au Québec durant la première guerre mondiale.* Montréal: s.i., 1973. 49 pp.

Lake, (Sir) P.H.N. *Report upon the Best Method of Giving Effect to the Recommendations of General Sir John French, Regarding the Canadian Militia.* (Sessional Paper, no. 35b.) Ottawa: King's Printer, 1910. 16 pp.

Lanctot, Gustave. *Trois ans de guerre, 1939-1942.* Montréal: G. Ducharme, 1943. 32 pp.

Lanks, Herbert R. *Highway to Alaska.* New York: D. Appleton, 1944. 200 pp.

Lash, Z.A. *Defence and Foreign Affairs; a Suggestion for the Empire.* Toronto: Macmillan, 1917. 86 pp.

Laurendeau, André. *La crise de la conscription, 1942.* Montréal: Editions du Jour, 1962. 157 pp.

Lauterpacht, E., ed. *The United Nations Emergency Force; Basic Documents.* London: Stevens, 1960. 49 pp.

Lawrence, W.H.C. *The Storm of '92; a Grandfather's Tale Told in 1932.* Toronto: Sheppard Pub. Co., 1889. 71 pp.
Mythical war in Canada.

Leacock, Stephen. *National Organization for War.* Ottawa: King's Printer, 1917. 11 pp.

Lee, William M. *Background to the White Paper on Defence.* Ottawa: n.p., 1964. 27 pp.

Leshchenko, L.O. *SRSR i Kanada v antyhitlerivis' kiĭ koalitsiĭ.* n.p.: 1973. 210 pp.

Letter from Home see Gillis, Clarence.

Lord Dundonald; les motifs de sa révocation. s.l.: s.i., [1904?]. 16 pp.

Lord Dundonald; Orders in Council and Correspondence Showing Why he was Removed from Office; Attacked Canada's Government in Defiance of Military Regulations. (Political Pointers, no. 5.) n.p.: [1904]. 72 pp.

Lower, A.R.M., and F.J. Parkinson, eds. *War and Reconstruction, Some Canadian Issues; Addresses Given at the Canadian Institute of Public Affairs, August 15 to 23, 1942.* Toronto: Ryerson Press, 1942. 106 pp.

MacCormac, John. *Canada; America's Problem.* New York: Viking Press, 1940. 287 pp.

Macdonald, Angus L. *Speeches of Angus L. Macdonald.* Toronto: Longmans, Green, 1960. 227 pp.

*McInnis, Edgar. *La menace contre le Canada.* (Actualités; revue destinée aux Forces canadiennes, vol. I, no. 1.) Ottawa: Imprimeur du Roi, 1951. 23 pp.

*_____. *The Threat to Canada.* (Current Affairs for the Canadian Forces, vol. I, no. 1.) Ottawa: King's Printer, 1951. 23 pp.

McLin, Jon B. *Canada's Changing Defence Policy, 1957-1963; the Problem of a Middle Power in Alliance.* Baltimore: Johns Hopkins, 1967. 251 pp.

Machum, George C., comp. *Canada's V.C.'s; the Story of Canadians who have been Awarded the Victoria Cross.* Toronto: McClelland & Stewart, 1956. 208 pp.

Martin, Paul. *Canada and the Quest for Peace.* New York: Columbia Univ. Press, 1967. 93 pp.

Massey, Hector J., ed. *The Canadian Military; a Profile.* n.p.: Copp Clarke, 1972. 290 pp.

Massey, Vincent. *The Sword of Lionheart and other Wartime Speeches.* Toronto: Ryerson Press, 1942. 117 pp.

Menzies, J.H. *Canada and the War; the Promise of the West.* Toronto: Copp, Clark, 1916. 117 pp.

Merritt, Wm. Hamilton. *Canada and National Service.* Toronto: Macmillan, 1917. 247 pp.

Michel, Jacques, [*pseud.*] *voir* Poisson, Camille.

*The Military Service Council. *For the Defence of Canada.* n.p.: 1917. 31 pp.

Miller, Carman. *Canada and the Boer War./Le Canada et la guerre des Boers.* Ottawa: National Film Board of Canada/Office national du film du Canada, [1970]. 18 pp. *Bilingual text./Texte bilingue.*

La Minerve, Montréal, P.Q. *Sir Adolphe Caron, G.C.M.G., Ministre de la Milice et ses détracteurs; ou huit années d'administration militaire.* Montréal: Cie. d'imprimerie et lithographie Gelhardt-Berthiaume, 1888. 34 p.

Minifie, James M. *Peacemaker or Powder-Monkey; Canada's Role in a Revolutionary World.* Toronto: McClelland and Stewart, 1960. 180 pp.

The Moccasin Prints. No. 1-6. Montreal: privately printed, 1912-13.

Monk, F.D. *Address by F.D. Monk, Esq., M.P., Lachine, August 18th, 1911.* n.p.: [1911]. 13 pp.

Montreal Daily Herald. *The Story of French Canada's War Effort; Full Industrial Strength and all Economic Resources Support Democracy.* Montreal: Daily Herald, 1941. 62 pp.

Morenus, Richard. *DEW Line; Distant Early Warning; the Miracle of America's First Line of Defence.* New York: Rand McNally, 1957. 184 pp.

Morris, Leslie. *Whose War? A Reply to the Liberal Party's Winnipeg Free Press.* Winnipeg: privately printed, [1943?]. 45 pp.

Morton, Desmond. *Ministers and Generals; Politics and the Canadian Militia, 1868-1904.* Toronto: Univ. of Toronto Press, 1970. 257 pp.

Murray, Howard. *The Munitionment of the Canadian Forces for Purposes of Defence; an Aide-Memoire; being a Study of Canada's Effort in the Supply of Propellants and Explosives during the War and Conclusions to be Drawn as Applying to Future Munitionment of the Military Forces of Canada.* [Ottawa: n.p., 1921.] 222 pp.
Projected in four volumes, but only the first may have been published.

Myers, C.V. *Oil to Alaska; Canol Unveiled.* Edmonton: Doublas Print. Co., [1944?]. 40 pp.

Nasmith, George Gallie. *On the Fringe of the Great Fight.* New York: Doran, n.d. 263 pp.

National Liberal Federation of Canada. *The Wartime Effort of a United Canada.* (National Liberal Federation of Canada Leaflets, [2nd Series] no. 10.) Ottawa: n.p., [1940]. 20 pp.

Notre marine de guerre; que fera-t-on de la marine Laurier-Brodeur? Est-il vrai qu'elle ne servira qu'à la défense du Canada? [par] "Du Guesclin" [*pseud.*] Montréal: Imprimerie Le Devoir, 1911. 130 pp.

O'Gorman, John J. *Canadians to Arms!* Toronto: Extension Print, 1916. 14 pp.

On our Naval Policy see Ross, Hendrie Drury.

Ontario Liberal Association. *Our Militia and Navy.* n.p.: [1911]. 36 pp.

Organization of Military Museums of Canada. *Bulletin.* Vol. I- . Ottawa: Queen's Printer, 1972- .

Ottawa Air Training Conference, 1942. *Report of the Conference.* Ottawa: King's Printer, 1942. 25 pp.

Papineau, [Talbot Mercer]. *Captain Papineau's letter to M. Henri Bourassa (Editor of "Le Devoir").* n.p.: n.d. 11 pp.

Peat, Louisa W. *Canada; New World Power.* Toronto: G.J. McLeod, 1945. 293 pp.

Peden, Murray. *Fall of an Arrow.* Stittsville, Ont.: Canada's Wings, 1978. 182 pp.

Penlington, Norman. *Canada and Imperialism, 1896-1899.* Toronto: Univ. of Toronto Press, 1965. 288 pp.

The Permanent Joint Board on Defence; Canada — United States, 1940-1975./La Commission permanente mixte de Défense; Canada — Etats-Unis, 1940-1975. n.p.: n.d./s.l.: s.i., s.d. 1 vol., unpaged./1 tome, non-paginé.
Bilingual text./Texte bilingue.

The Permanent Joint Board on Defence; Canada — United States, 1940-1965. Ottawa: Queen's Printer, 1965. 1 vol., unpaged.

Phillips-Wolley, Clive. *An Address Delivered by Clive Phillips-Wolley on Behalf of the Victoria-Esquimalt Branch, British Columbia, of the Navy League to an Audience in the City Hall, Victoria, B.C., Tuesday, May 14, 1907.* Victoria, B.C.: privately printed, n.d. 10 pp.

_____. *The Canadian Naval Question; Addresses Delivered by Clive Phillips-Wolley, F.R.C.S., Vice-President, Navy League.* Toronto: W. Briggs, 1910. 70 pp.

Plumptre, A.F.W. *Mobilizing Canada's Resources for War.* Toronto: Macmillan, 1941. 306 pp.

[Poisson, Camille.] *La participation des Canadiens français à la grande guerre; réponse à un livre récent de M. André Siegfried: "Le Canada, puissance internationale",* par Jacques Michel [*pseud.*] Montréal: Editions de l'A.C.-F., [1938]. 188 pp.

"Politicus" [*pseud.*] *see* Golden, L.L.L.

Pope, Maurice A. *Soldiers and Politicians; the Memoirs of Lt.-Gen. Maurice A. Pope, C.B., M.C.* Toronto: Univ. of Toronto Press, 1962. 462 pp.

Pope, R.H. *An Address Delivered by Mr. R.H. Pope at Sherbrooke, Que., on Feb 28th, 1910.* Cookshire, P.Q.: Chronicle Print, 1910. [14] pp.

[Power, Charles Gavan.] *A Party Politician; the Memoirs of Chubby Power.* Norman Ward, ed. Toronto: Macmillan, 1966. 419 pp.

Preston, Richard A. *Canada and "Imperial Defense"; a Study of the Origins of the British Commonwealth's Defense Organization, 1867-1919.* (Duke University Commonwealth-Studies Center; Publication Number 29.) Durham, N.C.: Duke Univ. Press, 1967. 576 pp.

_____. *Canadian Defence Policy and the Development of the Canadian Nation, 1867-1917.* (Canadian Historical Association Booklets, no. 25.) Ottawa: Canadian Historical Association, 1970. 22 pp.

_____. *The Defence of the Undefended Border; Planning for War in North America, 1867-1939.* Montreal: McGill-Queen's Univ. Press, 1977. 300 pp.

Provencher, Jean. *Québec sous la loi des mesures de guerre, 1918.* Montréal: Les Editions du Boreal Express, 1971. 147 pp.

Ranger, Robin. *The Canadian Contribution to the Control of Chemical and Biological Warfare.* (Wellesley Paper 5/1976.) Toronto: Canadian Institute of International Affairs, 1976. 66 pp.

Reader's Digest. *The Canadians at War, 1939/45.* Montreal: Reader's Digest, 1969. 2 vols.

Reford, Robert. *Making Defence Policy in Canada.* (Behind the Headlines, vol. XXII, no. 2.) Toronto: Canadian Institute of International Affairs, 1963. 23 pp.

_____. *Merchant of Death?* (Behind the Headlines, vol. XXVII, no. 4.) Toronto: Canadian Institute of International Affairs, 1968. 28 pp.

Regehr, Ernie. *Making a Killing; Canada's Arms Industry.* Toronto: McClelland and Stewart, 1975. 135 pp.

Règlements concernant la défense du Canada. Ottawa: Imprimeur du Roi, 1939. 58 pp.
    Réimprimé et développé 1940, 1941, 1942.

Renison, Robert John. *Impressions, September 16 to October 28, 1941; to Britain and Return.* [Toronto: privately printed, 1941?] 31 pp.

Robinson, C.W. *Canada and Canadian Defence; the Defensive Policy of the Dominion in Relation to the Character of her Frontier, the Events of the War of 1812-14, and her Position To-day.* Toronto: Musson Book Co., 1910. 186 pp.

Rosner, Gabriella. *The U.N. Emergency Force.* New York: Columbia Univ. Press, 1963. 294 pp.

[Ross, Hendrie Drury.] *On our Naval Policy.* Ottawa: n.p., [1908]. 14 pp.

*Roy, Ferdinand. *L'appel aux armes et la réponse canadienne-française; étude sur le conflit de races.* Québec, P.Q.: J.P. Garneau, 1917. 44 pp.

*_____. *The Call to Arms and the French Canadian Reply; a Study of the Conflict of Races.* J. Squair and J.S. Will, tr. Quebec, P.Q.: J.P. Garneau, 1918. 40 pp.

Roy, R.H. *For Most Conspicuous Bravery; a Biography of Major-General George R. Pearkes, V.C., through Two World Wars.* Vancouver: Univ. of British Columbia Press, 1977. 388 pp.

Royal Canadian Military Institute, Toronto, Ont. *Transactions.* Vol. 1- . Toronto: privately printed, 1890- .
Title varies. Selected Papers no. 1 was published in 1889. Superseded by Yearbook in 1947.

Sandwell, B.K. *Canada and the United States Neutrality.* (Oxford Pamphlets on World Affairs, no. C.2.) Toronto: Oxford Univ. Press, 1939. 34 pp.

Santor, Donald M. *Canadians at War, 1914-1918.* (Canadiana Scrapbook.) Scarborough, Ont.: Prentice-Hall, 1978. 48 pp.

Scoble, T.C. *The Utilization of Colonial Forces in Imperial Defence (Read before the Toronto (Canada) Militia Institute, on Saturday 25th October, 1879).* London: H.M. Stationery Office, n.d. 11 pp.

Shields, Thomas Todhunter. *Premier King's Plebiscite Speech in Commons Analyzed; an Address, Delivered in Jarvis Street Baptist Church, Toronto, Monday Evening, February 2nd, 1942.* n.p.: n.d. 32 pp.

Sherman, Michael E. *A Single Service for Canada?* (Adelphi Papers, no. 39.) London: Institute for Strategic Studies, 1967. 14 pp.

Sir Georges [sic] Cartier sur la défense du Canada. s.l.: s.i., [1909]. 13 pp.

*Smith, Goldwin. *Devant le tribunal de l'histoire; un plaidoyer en faveur des Canadiens qui ont condamné la guerre sud-africaine.* Henri Bourassa, tr. Montréal: Librairie Beauchemin 1903. 61 pp.

*Smith, Goldwin. *In the Court of History; an Apology for Canadians who were Opposed to the South African War.* Toronto: W. Tyrrell, 1902, 71 pp.

Smith, Sidney E. *Report on Disarmament Discussions, 1957.* Ottawa: Queen's Printer, 1958. 40 pp.

Snowy Owl; Journal of the Canadian Land Forces Command and Staff College. Kingston, Ont.: privately printed, 1952-73. 18 vols.
Title varies.

*Stacey, C.P. *Armes, hommes et gouvernements; les politiques de guerre du Canada, 1939-1945.* Ottawa: Imprimeur de la Reine, 1970. 747 pp.

*_____. *Arms, Men and Governments; the War Policies of Canada, 1939-1945.* Ottawa: Queen's Printer, 1970. 681 pp.

_____. *Canada and the British Army, 1846-1871; a Study in the Practice of Responsible Government.* (Royal Empire Society Imperial Studies Series, no. 11.) London: Longmans, Green, 1936. 287 pp.

_____. *Canada and the Second World War.* (Oxford Pamphlets on World Affairs, no. C.5.) Toronto: Oxford Univ. Press, 1940. 32 pp.

_____. *The Military Problems of Canada; a Survey of Defence Policies and Strategic Conditions Past and Present.* Toronto: Ryerson Press, 1940. 184 pp.

_____. *The Undefended Border; the Myth and the Reality.* (Canadian Historical Association Booklets, no. 1.) Ottawa: Canadian Historical Association, 1953. 19 pp.

Stacey, C.P., ed. *The Arts of War and Peace, 1914-1945.* (Historical Documents of Canada, Volume V.) Toronto: Macmillan, 1972. 656 pp.

Stairs, Denis. *The Diplomacy of Constraint; Canada, the Korean War, and the United States.* Toronto: Univ. of Toronto Press, 1974. 373 pp.

Stevens, G.R. *The Sun Is Setting on the Paleface Brave or Down the Drain a Billion a Year Goes.* Montreal: privately printed, [1968]. 16 pp.

Stevenson, William. *A Man Called Intrepid; the Secret War.* New York: Harcourt Brace Jovanovich, 1976. 468 pp.

Strange, Thomas Bland. *The Military Aspect of Canada; a Lecture Delivered at the Royal United Service Institution.* London: Harrison, [1879]. 66 pp.

Strange, William. *Canada, the Pacific and the War.* Toronto: T. Nelson, 1937. 220 pp.

Summary of Memorandum of Agreement between the Governments of the United Kingdom, Canada, Australia and New Zealand Relating to Training of Pilots and Aircraft Crews in Canada and their Subsequent Service. n.p.: [1942]. 12 pp.

Swettenham, John. *Allied Intervention in Russia, 1918-1919; and the Part Played by Canada.* Toronto: Ryerson Press, 1967. 315 pp.

_____. *Canada and the First World War.* Toronto: Ryerson Press, 1969. 160 pp.

_____. *McNaughton.* Toronto: Ryerson Press, 1968-69. 3 vols.

Swettenham, John, ed. *Valiant Men; Canada's Victoria Cross and George Cross Winners.* (Canadian War Museum Historical Publication Number 7.) Toronto: Hakkert, 1973. 234 pp.

Tackaberry, R.B. *Keeping the Peace; a Canadian Military Viewpoint on Peace-Keeping Operations.* (Behind the Headlines, vol. XXVI.) Toronto: Canadian Institute of International Affairs, 1966. 26 pp.

Talmadge, Marion, and Iris Gilmore. *NORAD; the North American Air Defense Command.* New York: Dodd, Mead, 1967. 29 pp.

Taylor, Alastair. *For Canada — both Swords and Ploughshares; a Plea for an Integrated Defence and Foreign Policy for Canada.* (Contemporary Affairs, no. 30.) Toronto: Canadian Institute of International Affairs, 1963. 67 pp.

Taylor, Alastair, David Cox and J.L. Granatstein. *Peacekeeping; International Challenge and Canadian Response.* (Contemporary Affairs, no. 39.) [Toronto]: Canadian Institute of International Affairs, 1968. 211 pp.

Thistle, Mel, ed. *The Mackenzie-McNaughton Wartime Letters,* with Introduction and Epilogue by C.J. Mackenzie. Toronto: Univ. of Toronto Press, 1975. 178 pp.

Thompson, John Herd. *The Harvests of War; the Prairie West, 1914-1918.* Toronto: McClelland and Stewart, 1978. 207 pp.

Thoughts on Defence see Coffin, W.F.

"Till the Hour of Victory"; Addresses by Right Honourable W.L. Mackenzie King, Prime Minister of Canada, Right Honourable Winston Churchill, Prime Minister of Great Britain, Right Honourable Ernest Lapointe, Minister of Justice, Delivered over the National Network of the Canadian Broadcasting Corporation, 1st June, 1941. Ottawa: King's Printer, 1941. 11 pp.

Toews, J.A. *Alternative Service in Canada during World War II.* Winnipeg: privately printed, [1959]. 127 pp.

Trotter, Reginald G. *North America and the War; a Canadian View.* (Oxford Pamphlets on World Affairs, no. C.7.) Toronto: Oxford Univ. Press, 1940. 40 pp.

Tucker, A.B. *Canada and the War.* (Oxford Pamphlets, 1914-1915.) London: Oxford Univ. Press, [1915]. 18 pp.

Turner, Arthur C. *Bulwark of the West; Implications and Problems of NATO.* (Contemporary Affairs, no. 24.) Toronto: Ryerson Press, 1953. 106 pp.

Tweedsmuir, John Buchan, baron. *Lord Minto; a Memoir,* by John Buchan. London: T. Nelson, 1924. 352 pp.

Tweedsmuir, Susan Charlotte (Grosvenor) Buchan, baroness. *Canada and the War,* by Lady Tweedsmuir. (March of Time Series, 7.) London: Pilot Press, 1942. 48 pp.

Univ. of California. Committee on International Relations. *Problems of Hemispheric Defense.* Berkeley, Calif.: Univ. of California Press, 1942. 139 pp.

Vachon, Stanislas. *Le Canada et la deuxième grande guerre; la puissance occulte, tome premier.* [Montréal: le Devoir, 1949.] 324 pp.
Des autres tomes n'étaient jamais publiés.

Vaillancourt, Emile. *Le Canada et les Nations unies.* Montréal: Beauchemin, 1942. 143 pp.

Vaughan, H.H. *The Manufacture of Munitions in Canada; Presidential Address, Annual Meeting, Ottawa, Feb. 10th, 1919.* n.p.: n.d. 91 pp.
Address to the Engineering Institute of Canada.

La verité sur la question de la défense navale. s.l.: s.i., s.d. 38 pp.

Warnock, John W. *Partner to Behemoth; the Military Policy of a Satellite Canada.* Toronto: New Press, 1970. 340 pp.

Warren, Falkland. *The Defence of Our Empire, with Special Reference to Canada.* n.p.: [1902]. 19 pp.

West, Christopher. *Canada and Seapower.* Toronto: McClelland & Goodchild, 1913. 172 pp.

_____. *The Defence of Canada; in the Light of Canadian History.* London: Dent, 1914. 16 pp.

Why Three Dreadnoughts? Ottawa: Modern Press, 1914. 54 pp.

Wickham, H.J. *Naval Defence of Canada.* Toronto: Murray, 1896. 11 pp.

Wilkinson, J.W. *Canada's Attitude both before and since the War with Regard to Naval Defence.* Toronto: n.p., 1918. 35 pp.

*Wilkinson, (Sir) George Henry, W.L. Mackenzie King and Winston S. Churchill. *Canada and the War; the Lord Mayor's Luncheon in Honour of the Prime Minister of Canada, Addresses by Right Hon. Sir George Henry Wilkinson, Lord Mayor of London, Right Hon. W.L. Mackenzie King, M.P., Prime Minister of Canada and Right Hon. Winston S. Churchill, C.H., M.P., Prime Minister of Great Britain, the Mansion House, London, England, September 4, 1941.* Ottawa: King's Printer, 1941. 16 pp.

*Wilkinson, (Sir) George-Henry, W.-L. Mackenzie King et Winston Churchill. *Le Canada et la guerre; dîner offert par le Lord-maire en l'honneur du premier ministre du Canada, discours des très honorable Sir George-Henry Wilkinson, Lord-maire de Londres, très honorable W.-L. Mackenzie King, M.P., premier ministre du Canada, et du très honorable Winston Churchill, C.H., M.P., premier ministre de Grande-Bretagne, à Mansion House, Londres, Angleterre, le 4 septembre 1941.* Ottawa: Imprimeur du Roi, 1941. 16 pp.

Williams-Taylor, (Sir) Frederick. *Sea Power in Relation to Canada . . . Address at Annual Banquet of the Navy League of Canada,* n.p.: [1929]. 11 pp.

Willson, (Sir) John. *Canada's Relation to the Great War; an Address by Sir John Willson before the University Club of Rochester, New York, February 19, 1916.* Toronto: News Pub. Co., 1916. 1 vol., unpaged.

Wilson, Barbara M., ed. *Ontario and the First World War, 1914-1918; a Collection of Documents.* (The Publications of the Champlain Society; Ontario Series, X.) Toronto: Champlain Society, 1977. 201 pp.

*Wood, Herbert Fairlie. *Singulier champ de bataille; les opérations en Corée et leurs effets sur la politique de défense du Canada.* (Histoire officielle de l'armée canadienne.) Ottawa: Imprimeur de la Reine, 1966. 354 pp.

*_____. *Strange Battleground; the Operations in Korea and their Effects on the Defence Policy of Canada.* (Official History of the Canadian Army.) Ottawa: Queen's Printer, 1966. 317 pp.

*Wood, Herbert Fairlie, and John Swettenham. *Silent Witnesses.* (Canadian War Museum Historical Publication Number 10; Department of Veterans Affairs Publication Number 6.) Toronto: Hakkert, 1974. 243 pp.

*Wood, Herbert Fairlie, et John Swettenham. *Témoins silencieux.* Jacques Gouin, tr. (Musée de guerre du Canada publication historique no. 10; Ministère des Affaires des anciens combattants publication no. 6.) Toronto: Hakkert, 1974. 249 pp.

Wood, William. *The British Command of the Sea and What it Means to Canada.* Toronto: Hunter, Rose, [1900]. 48 pp.

_____. *The Fight for Canada; a Naval and Military Sketch from the History of the Great Imperial War.* Toronto: Musson Book Co., 1905. 370 pp.

*Worthington, F.F. *Civil Defence and Armed Defence.* (Current Affairs for the Canadian Forces, vol. VII, no. 8.) Ottawa: Queen's Printer, 1954. 31 pp.

*_____. *La défense civile et la défense militaire.* (Actualités; revue destinée aux forces canadiennes, vol. VII, no. 8.) Ottawa: Imprimeur de la Reine, 1954. 31 pp.

Ypres, John Pinkstone French, 1st earl *see* French, John Pinkstone French, 1st earl of Ypres.

Zink, Lubor J. *Under the Mushroom Cloud.* Brandon, Man.: The Brandon Sun, 1962. 252 pp.

C. NAVAL FORCES — FORCES DE MARINE

1867-1914

Appleton, Thomas E. *Usque ad Mare; a History of the Canadian Coast Guard and Marine Services.* Ottawa: Queen's Printer, 1968. 318 pp.

Bourassa, Henri. *Le projet de loi navale; sa nature, ses conséquences; discours prononcé au monument national le 20 janvier 1910.* Montréal: le Devoir, [1910]. 37 pp.

Canada. Dept. of the Naval Service. *Instructions Relative to Recruiting for the Naval Service of Canada, 1910.* Ottawa: King's Printer, 1910. 35 pp.

_____. *Monthly Orders.* Ottawa: n.p., 1912-18.
Title varies. Naval Orders *(1918). Continued in mimeograph form until 1936.*

_____. *Naval Orders.* Ottawa: King's Printer, 1918-21. 6 vols. *Consolidation of* Monthly Orders, *1912-20. Title varies.*

_____. *Preliminary Training of Naval Cadets and Midshipmen, 1911.* n.p.: n.d. 29 pp.

*_____. *Report.* (Sessional Papers, no. 38 (1911-18), no. 39 (1919-21), no. 17a (1922).) Ottawa: King's Printer, 1911-22.

*Canada. Ministère du Service naval. *Rapport.* (Documents parlementaires, no. 38 (1911-18), no. 39 (1919-21), no. 17a (1922).) Ottawa: Imprimeur du Roi, 1911-22.

[Canada. Navy.] *Canadian Naval Force and Royal Canadian Navy, 1910-1914.* Ottawa: Queen's Printer, 1955. 38 pp.

*Canada. Parlement. *Réponse à une adresse de la Chambre des Communes en date du 29 novembre 1911, demandant copie de toute la correspondance échangée à la suite de la Conférence impériale entre le gouvernement du Canada et le gouvernement de Sa Majesté au sujet du Service naval du Canada ou d'une manière quelconque y afférant.* (Document parlementaire, no. 40d.) Ottawa: Imprimeur du Roi, 1912. 19 pp.

*Canada. Parliament. *Return to an Address of the House of Commons, dated November 29, 1911, for a Copy of all Correspondence between the Government of Canada and His Majesty's Government Subsequent to the Last Imperial Conference, Concerning the Naval Service of Canada, and in Any Way Connected with It.* (Sessional Paper, no. 40d.) Ottawa: King's Printer, 1912. 18 pp.

"Du Guesclin" [*pseud.*] *voir Notre marine de guerre.*

Gough, Barry M. *The Royal Navy and the North-West Coast of North America, 1810-1914; a Study of British Maritime Ascendency.* Vancouver: Univ. of British Columbia Press, 1971. 294 pp.

Gt. Brit. Admiralty. *Regulations for the Royal Naval Reserve Newfoundland.* London: H.M. Stationery Office, 1910. 41 pp.

[Gt. Brit. Colonial Defence Committee Canada.] *Halifax Defence Scheme.* London: H.M. Stationery Office, 1904?-12? *Amended annually.*

Longstaff, F.V. *Esquimalt Naval Base; a History of its Work and its Defences.* Vancouver: Clarke & Stuart, 1941. 189 pp.

McKee, Fraser M. *Volunteers for Sea Service; a Brief History of the Royal Canadian Naval Volunteer Reserve, its Predecessors and Successors, on its 50th Anniversary, 1973.* Toronto: privately printed, 1973. 69 pp.

Macpherson, K.R. *Canada's Fighting Ships.* (Canadian War Museum Historical Publication Number 12.) Toronto: Hakkert, 1975. 116 pp.

[Maritime Museum of Canda.] *Souvenir of the Maritime Museum of Canada, Halifax, Nova Scotia.* [Halifax: n.p., 195-?] 44 pp.

Notre marine de guerre; que fera-t-on de la marine Laurier-Brodeur? Est-il vrai qu'elle ne servira qu'à la défense du Canada? [par] "Du Guesclin" [*pseud.*] Montréal: Imprimerie Le Devoir, 1911. 130 pp.

Preston, Richard A. *Canada and "Imperial Defense"; a Study of the Origins of the British Commonwealth's Defense Organization, 1867-1919.* (Duke University Commonwealth-Studies Center; Publication Number 29.) Durham, N.C.: Duke Univ. Press, 1967. 576 pp.

Royal Canadian Navy, 1910-1960; the First Fifty Years. n.p.: 1960. v.p.

Smith, Waldo E.L. *The Navy Chaplain and his Parish.* Ottawa: Queen's Printer, 1967. 264 pp.

Stanley, George F.G., and Richard A. Preston. *A Short History of Kingston as a Military and Naval Centre.* Kingston, Ont.: Queen's Printer, [195-?]. 33 pp.

Swain, Hector. *History of the Naval Reserves in Newfoundland.* [St. John's, Nfld.: Provincial Archives, 1975.] 56 pp.

Tucker, Gilbert Norman. *A History of the Royal Canadian Navy.* Ottawa: King's Printer, 1951. 16 pp.

_____. *The Naval Service of Canada; its Official History.* Ottawa: King's Printer, 1952. 2 vols.

La verité sur la question de la défense navale. s.l.: s.i., s.d. 38 pp.

Wickham, H.J. *Naval Defence of Canada.* Toronto: Murray, 1896. 11 pp.

1914-1918

Appleton, Thomas E. *Usque ad Mare; a History of the Canadian Coast Guard and Marine Services.* Ottawa: Queen's Printer, 1968. 318 pp.

Art Gallery of Toronto. *Catalogue of an Exhibition of the Canadian War Memorials, October 1926.* Toronto: privately printed, [1926]. 21 pp.

Bank of Montreal. *Memorial of the Great War, 1914-1918; a Record of Service.* Montreal: privately printed, 1921. 261 pp.

Bidwell, R.E.S. *Random Memories.* Ottawa: privately printed, [1962. 21 pp.]

Bindon, Kathryn M. *More than Patriotism.* (A Personal Library Publication.) Don Mills, Ont.: Nelson, 1979. 192 pp.

Bird, Michael J. *The Town that Died; the True Story of the Greatest Man-made Explosion before Hiroshima.* New York: Putnam, 1962. 192 pp.

Canada. Dept. of the Naval Service. *The Canadian Navy List.* Ottawa: King's Printer, 1914-65.
Issued by the Dept. of National Defence from 1923.

_____. *Confidential Weekly Orders.* Ottawa: n.p., 1916-22.
Title varies: Confidential Naval Orders (December 1917 — June 1921), Naval Staff Orders from June 1921.

_____. *Correspondence Relating to the Purchase of Two Submarines by the Canadian Government.* (Sessional Paper, no. 158.) Ottawa: King's Printer, 1915. 35 pp.

Canada. Dept. of the Naval Service. *Monthly Orders.* Ottawa: n.p., 1912-18.
Title varies: Naval Orders (1918). Continued in mimeograph form until 1936.

_____. *Naval Orders.* Ottawa: King's Printer, 1918-21. 6 vols.
Consolidation of Monthly Orders, 1912-20. Title varies.

_____. *Pay and Allowances for Officers and Men of the Royal Canadian Navy.* Ottawa: King's Printer, 1918. 17 pp.

_____. *Regulations for Supply and Accounting of Provisions, Clothing and Mens Traps Issued to Vessels of HMC Patrol Service; Instructions to Stewards.* Ottawa: King's Printers, 1917. v.p.

*_____. *Report.* (Sessional Papers, no. 38 (1911-18), no. 39 (1919-21), no. 17a (1922).) Ottawa: King's Printer, 1911-22.

_____. *Uniform and Clothing Regulations for Petty Officers, Men and Boys, H.M. Canadian Naval Service.* Ottawa: King's Printer, 1918. 111 pp.

Canada. Dept. of the Naval Service. Intelligence Branch. *Naval Intelligence Reports.* No. I-C. Ottawa: n.p., 1917-18.

Canada. Director of Public Information. *Canada's Part in the Great War.* Ottawa: n.p., 1919. 64 pp.
Also issued by Information Branch, Dept. of External Affairs.

_____. *Canada's War Effort, 1914-1918.* Ottawa: King's Printer, 1918. 31 pp.

*Canada. Ministère du Service naval. *Rapport.* (Documents parlementaires, no. 38 (1911-18), no. 39 (1919-21), no. 17a (1922).) Ottawa: Imprimeur du Roi, 1911-22.

[Canada. Navy.] *Canadian Naval Force and Royal Canadian Navy, 1910-1914.* Ottawa: Queen's Printer, 1955. 38 pp.

Canadian Bank of Commerce. *Letters from the Front; being a Record of the Part Played by Officers of the Bank in the Great War, 1914-1919.* Toronto: privately printed, n.d. 2 vols.

Canadian War Records Office. *Art and war; Canadian War Memorials; a Selection of the Works Executed for the Canadian War Memorials Fund to Form a Record of Canada's Part in the Great War and a Memorial to those Canadians who have Made the Great Sacrifice.* London: n.p., 1919. 1 vol., unpaged.

_____. *Canadian War Memorials Exhibition, [New York] 1919.* n.p.: n.d. 48 pp.

_____. *Thirty Canadian V.C.'s; 23rd April 1915 to 20th March 1918.* London: Skeffington, n.d. 96 pp.

Carr, William Guy. *Out of the Mists.* London: Hutchinson, n.d. 176 pp.

Corporation of British Columbia Land Surveyors. *Roll of Honour; British Columbia Land Surveyors; 1914 the Great War 1918.* n.p.: privately printed, n.d. 1 vol., unpaged.

Creed, Catherine. *'Whose Debtors We Are.''* (Niagara Historical Society, 34.) Niagara, Ont.: Niagara Historical Society, 1922. 116 pp.

Dominion of Canada Roll of Honor; a Directory of Casualties (Deaths Only) of the World's Greatest War, 1914-1918, of the City of Toronto; Dedicated to Perpetuate Those who Made the Supreme Sacrifice, "They Shall Not be Forgotten". n.p.: C. McAlpine, 1919. 28 1.

Duguid, Archer Fortescue. *The Canadian Forces in the Great War, 1914-1919; the Record of Five Years of Active Service.* Ottawa: King's Printer, 1947. 14 pp.

Duguid, Archer Fortescue, *see also The Memorial Chamber in the Peace Tower . . .*

Duncan-Clark, S.J., and W.R. Plewman. *Pictorial History of the Great War; [including] Canada in the Great War,* by W.S. Wallace. Toronto: J.L. Nichols, 1919. 2 vols. in 1.

Fetherstonhaugh, R.C. *McGill University at War, 1914-1918; 1939-1945.* Montreal: McGill Univ., 1947. 437 pp.

Fighters for Freedom; Honor Roll of Halifax; the Great War, 1914-1919. Halifax: Service Pub. Co., [1919]. 191 pp.

[Garvin, Amelia Beers (Warnock).] *Canada's Peace Tower and Memorial Chamber, Designed by John A. Pearson, D. Arch., F.R.A.I.C., F.R.I.B.A., A.R.C.A., G.D.I.A., a Record and Interpretation by Katherine Hale [pseud.] Dedicated by the Architect to the Veterans of the Great War.* Toronto: Mundy-Goodfellow Print. Co., 1935. 29 pp.

Godenrath, Percy F. *Lest We Forget; a Record in Art of the Dominion's Part in the War (1914-1918) and a Memorial to those Canadians who Made the Great Sacrifice, being the Gift of the Over-Seas Military Forces to the Nation; a Brief History of the Collection of War Paintings, Etchings and Sculpture, Made Possible by the Work of the Canadian War Memorials Fund and the Canadian War Record Office.* Ottawa: n.p., 1934. 46 pp.

Gt. Brit. Imperial War Graves Commission. *Beaumont-Hamel (Newfoundland) Memorial; bearing the Names of those Sailors, Soldiers and Merchant Seamen from Newfoundland who Fell in the Great War and have no Known Graves.* London: H.M. Stationery Office, 1929. 45 pp.

Gt. Brit. Imperial War Graves Commission. *Memorials Erected at Halifax, Nova Scotia, and Victoria, British Columbia, Canada, Bearing the Names of those Sailors, Soldiers and Merchant Seamen of Canada who Fell in the Great War and have no Known Graves.* London: H.M. Stationery Office, 1930. 24 pp.

_____. *The War Graves of the British Empire; the Register of the Names of Those who Fell in the Great War and are Buried in Cemeteries and Churchyards in Nova Scotia, Prince Edward Island and New Brunswick, Canada.* London: H.M. Stationery Office, 1931. 92 pp.

_____. *The War Graves of the British Empire: the Register of the Names of Those who Fell in the Great War and are Buried in Cemeteries in Newfoundland.* London: H.M. Stationery Office, 1930. 19 pp.

_____. *The War Graves of the British Empire; the Register of the Names of Those who Fell in the Great War and are Buried in Cemeteries in the Province of British Columbia, Canada.* London: H.M. Stationery Office, 1931. 48 pp.

_____. *The War Graves of the British Empire; the Register of the Names of Those who Fell in the Great War and are Buried in Cemeteries in the Province of Manitoba, Canada.* London: H.M. Stationery Office, 1931. 48 pp.

_____. *The War Graves of the British Empire; the Register of the Names of Those who Fell in the Great War and are Buried in Cemeteries in the Province of Ontario, Canada.* London: H.M. Stationery Office, 1931. 2 vols.

_____. *The War Graves of the British Empire; the Register of the Names of Those who Fell in the Great War and are Buried in Cemeteries in the Province of Quebec, Canada.* London: H.M. Stationery Office, 1931. 64 pp.

_____. *The War Graves of the British Empire; the Register of the Names of Those who Fell in the Great War and are Buried in Cemeteries in the Provinces of Saskatchewan and Alberta, Canada.* London: H.M. Stationery Office, 1931. 63 pp.

Hale, Katherine, [*pseud.*] *see* Garvin, Amelia Beers (Warnock).

[Hallam, T. Douglas.] *The Spider Web; the Romance of a Flying-Boat Flight,* by P.I.X. [*pseud.*] Edinburgh: W. Blackwood, 1919. 278 pp.

Herrington, Walter S., and A.J. Wilson. *The War Work of the County of Lennox and Addington.* Napanee, Ont.: Beaver Press, 1922. 278 pp.

Hezzelwood, Oliver, *see* Trinity Methodist Church, Toronto, Ont.

*Kealy, J.D.F., and E.C. Russell. *A History of Canadian Naval Aviation, 1918-1962.* Ottawa: Queen's Printer, 1965. 164 pp.

*Kealy, J.D.F., et E.C. Russell. *Histoire de l'aéronavale canadienne, 1918-1962.* Ottawa: Imprimeur de la Reine, 1965. 185 pp.

Longstaff, F.V. *Esquimalt Naval Base; a History of its Work and its Defences.* Vancouver: Clarke & Stuart, 1941. 189 pp.

McGill Univ., Montreal, P.Q. *A Memorial Service for the McGill Men and Women who Gave Their Lives during the First and Second World Wars.* n.p.: [1946]. 1 vol., unpaged.

McKee, Fraser M. *Volunteers for Sea Service; a Brief History of the Royal Canadian Naval Volunteer Reserve, its Predecessors and Successors, on its 50th Anniversary, 1973.* Toronto: privately printed, 1973. 69 pp.

Macpherson, K.R. *Canada's Fighting Ships.* (Canadian War Museum Historical Publication Number 12.) Toronto: Hakkert, 1975. 116 pp.

[Maritime Museum of Canada.] *Souvenir of the Maritime Museum of Canada, Halifax, Nova Scotia.* [Halifax: n.p., 195-?] 44 pp.

The Memorial Chamber in the Peace Tower, Houses of Parliament, Ottawa, Canada, [by A.F. Duguid]. Ottawa: Photogelatine Engraving Co., n.d. [34] pp.

Metson, Graham, comp. *The Halifax Explosion, December 6, 1917.* Toronto: McGraw-Hill Ryerson, n.d. 173 pp.

Miller, James Martin, and H.S. Canfield. *The People's War Book; History, Encyclopedia and Chronology of the Great World War; and Canada's Part in the War,* by W.R. Plewman. Toronto: Imperial Pub. Co., 1919. 520 pp.

Ontario. Dept. of Education. *The Roll of Honour of the Ontario Teachers who Served in the Great War, 1914-1918.* Toronto: Ryerson Press, 1922. 72 pp.

Ontario Agricultural College, Guelph, Ont. *Ontario Agricultural College Honor and Service Rolls.* n.p.: n.d. 1 vol., unpaged.

P.I.X. [*pseud.*] *see* Hallam, T. Douglas.

Parkdale Collegiate Institute, Toronto, Ont. *Roll of Service in the Great War, 1914-1919.* n.p.: n.d. 22 pp.

_____. *Their Name Liveth; a Memoir of the Boys of Parkdale Collegiate Institute who Gave their Lives in the Great War.* Toronto: privately printed, n.d. 177 pp.

Peace Souvenir; Activities of Waterloo County in the Great War, 1914-1918. Kitchener, Ont.: Kitchener Daily Telegraph, 1919. 70 pp.

Plewman, W.R., *see* Miller, James Martin.

Preston, Richard A. *Canada and "Imperial Defense"; a Study of the Origins of the British Commonwealth's Defense Organization, 1867-1919.* (Duke University Commonwealth-Studies Center; Publication Number 29.) Durham, N.C.: Duke Univ. Press, 1967. 576 pp.

Queen's Univ., Kingston, Ont. *Overseas Record; Record of Graduates, Alumni, Members of Staff, and Students of Queen's University on Active Military (Overseas) Service (to June 1st, 1917) 1914-1917.* n.p.: [1917?]. 44 pp.

Royal Canadian Navy, 1910-1960; the First Fifty Years. n.p.: 1960. v.p.

Santor, Donald M. *Canadians at War, 1914-1918.* (Canadiana Scrapbook.) Scarborough, Ont.: Prentice-Hall, 1978. 48 pp.

Sea Breezes. Vol. I-III. Halifax: privately printed, 1914-22.
Journal of the Royal Naval College of Canada.

Smith, G. Oswald, *see University of Toronto . . . .*

Smith, Gaddis, *Britain's Clandestine Submarines, 1914-1915.* New Haven, Conn.: Yale Univ. Press, 1964. 155 pp.

Smith, Waldo E.L. *The Navy Chaplain and his Parish.* Ottawa: Queen's Printer, 1967. 264 pp.

Stanley, George F.G., and Richard A. Preston. *A Short History of Kingston as a Military and Naval Centre.* Kingston, Ont.: Queen's Printer, [195-?]. 33 pp.

Swain, Hector. *History of the Naval Reserves in Newfoundland.* [St. John's, Nfld.: Provincial Archives, 1975.] 56 pp.

Swettenham, John. *Canada and the First World War.* Toronto: Ryerson Press, 1969. 160 pp.

_____. *Canada and the First World War./La participation du Canada à la première guerre mondiale.* Ottawa: Canadian War Museum/Musée de guerre, n.d./s.d. 56/63 pp.
Bilingual text./Texte bilingue.

Thompson, Roy J.C. *Wings of the Canadian Armed Forces, 1913-1972.* [Dartmouth], N.S.: n.p., 1973. 106 pp.

Thorburn, Ella M., and Charlotte Whitton. *Canada's Chapel of Remembrance.* Toronto: British Book Service (Canada), 1961. 68 pp.

Trinity Methodist Church, Toronto, Ont. *Trinity War Book; a Recital of Service and Sacrifice in the Great War.* Oliver Hezzelwood, comp. Toronto: privately printed, 1921. 368 pp.

Tucker, Gilbert Norman. *A History of the Royal Canadian Navy.* Ottawa: King's Printer, 1951. 16 pp.

_____. *The Naval Service of Canada; its Official History.* Ottawa: King's Printer, 1952. 2 vols.

Univ. of British Columbia. *Record of Service, 1914-1918; University of British Columbia, McGill British Columbia, Vancouver College.* Vancouver: privately printed, 1924. 142 pp.

Univ. of Manitoba. *Roll of Honour, 1914-1918.* Winnipeg: privately printed, 1923. 150 pp.

Univ. of Toronto. Victoria College. *Acta Victoriana; War Supplement.* [Toronto]: n.p., 1919. 128 pp.

University of Toronto; Roll of Service, 1914-1918. G. Oswald Smith, ed. Toronto: Univ. of Toronto Press, 1921. 603 pp.

X., P.I., [*pseud.*] *see* Hallam, T. Douglas.

War Record of McGill Chapter of Delta Upsilon. Montreal: n.p., 1919. 47 pp.

Wodehouse, R.F. *A Check List of the War Collections of World War I, 1914-1918, and World War II, 1939-1945.* Ottawa: Queen's Printer, 1968. 239 pp.

Young, A.H., and W.A. Kirkwood, eds. *The War Memorial Volume of Trinity College, Toronto.* [Toronto]: Printers Guild, 1922. 165 pp.

1919-1945

Active Service Canteen, Toronto, 1939-1945. Toronto: n.p., 1945. 1 vol., unpaged.

Appleton, Thomas E. *Usque ad Mare; a History of the Canadian Coast Guard and Marine Services.* Ottawa: Queen's Printer, 1968. 318 pp.

Bank of Montreal. *Field of Honour; the Second World War, 1939-1945.* Montreal: n.p., 1950. 1 vol., unpaged.

Bartlett, E.H. *The Royal Canadian Navy.* (Macmillan War Pamphlets, Canadian Series.) Toronto: Macmillan, 1942. 30 pp.

Beckles, Gordon, [*pseud.*] *see* Willson, Gordon Beckles.

Bidwell, R.E.S. *Random Memories.* Ottawa: privately printed,
[1962. 21 pp.]

Birney, Earle, ed. *Record of Service in the Second World War; the
University of British Columbia; a Supplement to the University
of British Columbia War Memorial Manuscript Record.* Vancouver: privately printed. 1955. 46 pp.

Bourassa, Henri. *La mission Jellicoe; nouvelle poussée d'impérialisme.* [Montréal]: Editions du Devoir, 1920. 37 pp.

Bowering, Clifford H. *Service; the Story of the Canadian Legion,
1925-1960.* Ottawa: privately printed, 1960. 240 pp.

Broadfoot, Barry. *Six War Years, 1939-1945; Memories of Canadians
at Home and Abroad.* Toronto: Doubleday Canada, 1974.
417 pp.

Brock, Thomas Leith. *Fight the Good Fight; Looking in on the Recruit Class at the Royal Military College of Canada during a
Week in February, 1931.* Montreal: privately printed, 1964.
30 pp.

Brockington, Leonard W. *"D" Day on a Canadian Destroyer; a Talk
Broadcast on the CBC Trans-Canada Network, Sunday, June
18th, 1944.* n.p.: n.d. 14 pp.

Burton, E.F. *Canadian Naval Radar Officers; the Story of University
Graduates for whom Preliminary Training was Given in the De-
partment of Physics, University of Toronto.* Toronto: Univ. of
Toronto Press, 1946. 63 pp.

Canada. Armed Forces. H.M.C.S. Unicorn. *History of Unicorn,
1923-1973.* n.p.: n.d. v.p.

Canada. Dept. of National Defence. *Canadian Prisoners of War and
Missing Personnel in the Far East.* Ottawa: King's Printer, 1945.
59 1.

_____. *Defence Forces List, Canada (Naval, Military and Air
Forces).* Ottawa: King's Printer, 1930-39.
Title varies somewhat. Superseded The Militia List. *Superseded
by* The Canadian Navy List, The Canadian Army List *and* The
Royal Canadian Air Force List.

_____. *Digest of Opinions and Rulings; Ottawa; March 31,
1944; Compiled from the Records of the Office of the Judge
Advocate-General, at National Defence Headquarters.* n.p.:
[1944]. 353 pp., looseleaf.

_____. *Instructions for Engineer Services, Canada, 1936.*
Ottawa: King's Printer, 1936. 152 pp.

Canada. Dept. of National Defence. *The King's Regulations for the Government of His Majesty's Canadian Naval Service, 1945.* (B.R.C.N. 101-103.) Ottawa:. King's Printer, 1945. 3 vols., looseleaf.

*_____. *Report.* Ottawa: King's Printer, 1923-59.
Title varies. Annual most years.

_____. *Royal Canadian Naval Reserve Regulations.* Ottawa: n.p., [1926]. v.p.

Canada. Dept. of National Defence (Naval Service). *Naval Orders.* Ottawa: n.p., 1938-45.
Title varies: Naval Monthly Orders until September 1939. Continues mimeographed orders.

_____. *Regulations and Instructions for the Royal Canadian Fleet Reserve, 1939.* Ottawa: King's Printer, 1939. 32 pp.

_____. *Regulations and Instructions for the Royal Canadian Naval Reserve, 1940.* Ottawa: King's Printer, 1940. 103 pp.

_____. *Regulations and Instructions for the Royal Canadian Naval Reserve, 1932.* Ottawa: King's Printer, 1932. 102 pp.

_____. *Regulations and Instructions for the Royal Canadian Navy, 1937.* Ottawa: King's Printer, 1937. 269 pp.
Addendum published 1940.

_____. *Regulations for Royal Canadian Naval Volunteer Reserve, 1938.* Ottawa: King's Printer, 1938. 124 pp.

_____. *The Regulations for the Organization and Administration of the Women's Royal Canadian Naval Service.* Ottawa: King's Printer, 1942. 33 pp.

_____. *Royal Canadian Naval Reserve Regulations.* Vol. II: *Fishermen's Reserve (West Coast).* Ottawa: King's Printer, 1939. 24 pp.

_____. *Royal Canadian Naval Volunteer Reserve Regulations, 1930, and Regulations for Entry and Service of Instructional Staff for the Royal Canadian Naval Volunteer Reserve.* Ottawa: King's Printer, 1930. v.p.
Addendum issued 1933.

Canada. Dept. of National War Services. *Annual Report.* Ottawa: King's Printer, 1945. 3 vols.

Canada. Dept. of the Naval Service. *The Canadian Navy List.* Ottawa: King's Printer, 1914-65.
Issued by the Dept. of National Defence from 1923.

_____. *Confidential Weekly Orders.* Ottawa: n.p., 1916-22.
Title varies: Confidential Naval Orders (December 1917 — June 1921), Naval Staff Orders from June 1921.

Canada. Dept. of the Naval Service. *Naval Orders.* Ottawa: King's Printer, 1918-21. 6 vols.
Consolidation of Monthly Orders, 1912-20. Title varies.

_____. *Pay and Allowances, 1920, for Officers and Men of the Royal Canadian Navy.* Ottawa: King's Printer, 1920. 28 pp.

*_____. *Report.* (Sessional Papers, no. 38 (1911-18), no. 39 (1919-21), no. 17a (1922).) Ottawa: King's Printer, 1911-22.

Canada. Dept. of Veterans Affairs. *30th Anniversary of the D-Day Landings in Normandy, 1944 — June 6 — 1974./30e anniversaire des débarquements en Normandie au jour J, 1944 — le 6 juin — 1974.* n.p./s.l.: s.i., 1974. 22 pp.
Bilingual text./Texte bilingue.

*Canada. Director of Public Information. *Canada at War.* No. 1-45. Ottawa: King's Printer, 1941-45.

*Canada. Ministère de la défense nationale. *Rapport.* Ottawa: Imprimeur du Roi, 1923-59.
Divergence du titre. Annuel, la plupart des années.

*Canada. Ministère du Service naval. *Rapport.* (Documents parlementaires, no. 38 (1911-18), no. 39 (1919-21), no. 17a (1922).) Ottawa: Imprimeur du Roi, 1911-22.

Canada. National Gallery. *Exhibition of Canadian War Art.* Ottawa: King's Printer, 1945. 22 pp.

Canada. National Research Council. *History of the Associate Committee on Naval Medical Research.* Ottawa: n.p., 1948. 121 pp.

Canada. Naval Service Headquarters. *Particulars of Canadian War Vessels; Half-Yearly Return.* Ottawa: King's Printer, 1940-45. 8 vols.
No issue for July 1944. Title varies somewhat.

Canada. Naval Service Headquarters. Naval Historian. *The University Naval Training Divisions,* [by Philip Chaplin]. Ottawa: Queen's Printer, 1963. 24 pp.

Canada. Navy. *Entry of Officers in the Royal Canadian Navy, Conditions of Service, etc.* Ottawa: King's Printer, 1937. 24? pp.

_____. *Regulations and Instructions for the Royal Canadian Navy.* Ottawa: King's Printer, 1927. 407 pp.
Short title: Canadian Naval Regulations or CNR's. Originally issued under title: Consolidated Naval Orders, 1927. Title amended by Naval Order 62 of 1928.

*Canada. Parlement. Chambre des Communes. Comité spécial d'enquête sur les distinctions honorifiques et les décorations. *Procès-verbaux et témoignages.* No. 1-6. Ottawa: Imprimeur du Roi, 1942.

Canada. Parliament. House of Commons. Special Committee on Canteen Funds. *Minutes of Proceedings and Evidence.* No. 1-11. Ottawa: King's Printer, 1942.

*Canada. Parliament. House of Commons. Special Committee on Honours and Decorations. *Minutes of Proceedings and Evidence.* No. 1-6. Ottawa: King's Printer, 1942.

Canada. Royal Commission to Conduct an Inquiry into Certain Disorders Occurring May 7-8, 1945, in the City of Halifax. *Report on the Halifax Disorders, May 7th-8th, 1945.* Hon. Mr. Justice R.L. Kellock, Royal Commissioner. Ottawa: King's Printer, 1945. 61 pp.

*Canada. Service de l'Information. *Le Canada en guerre.* No. 1-45. Ottawa: Imprimeur du Roi, 1941-45.

*Le Canada dans la bataille de l'Atlantique. [Ottawa: Imprimeur du Roi, 1942.] 1 tome, non-paginé.

*Canada's Battle of the Atlantic. [Ottawa: King's Printer, 1942.] 1 vol., unpaged.

Canadian Bank of Commerce. *War Service Records, 1939-1945; an Account of the War Service of Members of the Staff during the Second World War.* D.P. Wagner and C.G. Siddall, eds. Toronto: Rous & Mann, 1947. 331 pp.

Canadian Broadcasting Corporation. Publications Branch. *We have been There; Authoritative Reports by Qualified Observers who have Returned from the War Zones, as Presented over the CBC National Network.* Toronto: Canadian Broadcasting Corporation, 1941-42. 2 vols.

Canadian Jewish Congress. *Canadian Jews in World War II.* Montreal: privately printed, 1947-48. 2 vols.

Canadian Legion War Services, Inc. *A Year of Service; a Summary of Activities on Behalf of His Majesty's Canadian Forces Rendered during Nineteen-Forty.* n.p.: n.d. 1 vol., unpaged.

Carr, William Guy. *Checkmate in the North; the Axis Planned to Invade America.* Toronto: Macmillan, 1944. 304 pp.

Catley, Harry. *Gate and Gaiters; a Book of Naval Humour and Anecdotes; Including a Glossary of Naval Language for the Uninformed.* Toronto: Thorn Press, 1949. 322 pp.

Chambers, Robert W. *Halifax in Wartime; a Collection of Drawings.* Halifax: The Halifax Herald and the Halifax Mail, 1943. 1 vol., unpaged.

Coale, Griffith. *North Atlantic Patrol, the Log of a Seagoing Artist.* New York: Farrar & Rinehart, 1942. 51 pp.

Commonwealth War Graves Commission. *The War Dead of the Commonwealth; the Register of the Names of Those who Fell in the 1939-1945 War and are Buried; Cemeteries in Canada; Cemeteries in Ontario.* London: H.M. Stationery Office, 1961. 2 vols.

_____. *The War Dead of the Commonwealth; the Register of the Names of Those who Fell in the 1939-1945 War and are Buried in Cemeteries in Canada; Cemeteries in British Columbia, Yukon Territory and Alberta.* Maidenhead, Eng.: [H.M. Stationery Office], 1972. 82 pp.

_____. *The War Dead of the Commonwealth; the Register of the Names of Those who Fell in the 1939-1945 War and are Buried in Cemeteries in Canada; Cemeteries in New Brunswick, Nova Scotia, Newfoundland and Prince Edward Island.* London: H.M. Stationery Office, 1962. 81 pp.

_____. *The War Dead of the Commonwealth; the Register of the Names of Those who Fell in the 1939-1945 War and are Buried in Cemeteries in Canada; Cemeteries in Quebec.* London: H.M. Stationery Office, 1962. 63 pp.

_____. *The War Dead of the Commonwealth; the Register of the Names of Those who Fell in the 1939-1945 War and are Buried in Cemeteries in Canada; Cemeteries in Saskatchewan and Manitoba.* London: [H.M. Stationery Office], 1963. 79 pp.

_____. *The War Dead of the Commonwealth; the Register of the Names of Those who Fell in the 1939-1945 War and have no known Grave; the Halifax Memorial.* London: [H.M. Stationery Office], 1968. 2 vols.

Creighton, (Sir) Kenelm. *Convoy Commodore.* London: W. Kimber, 1956. 205 pp.

Davison, Stan. *Canada's Greatest Navy! A Cartoon Seaman's Eye-View of our Sailors in World War Two.* Victoria, B.C.: privately printed, 1967. 132 pp.

Douglas, W.A.B., and Brereton Greenhous. *Out of the Shadows; Canada in the Second World War.* Toronto: Oxford Univ. Press, 1977. 288 pp.

Easton, Allan. *50 North; an Atlantic Battleground.* Toronto: Ryerson Press, 1963. 287 pp.

Ettenger, G.H. *History of the Associate Committee on Medical Research, Ottawa, 1938-1946.* Ottawa: n.p., n.d. 46 pp.

Fetherstonhaugh, R.C. *McGill University at War, 1914-1918; 1939-1945.* Montreal: McGill Univ., 1947. 437 pp.

[General Motors of Canada, Limited.] *Achievement.* n.p.: [1943]. 74 pp.

Gt. Brit. Imperial War Graves Commission. *The War Dead of the British Commonwealth and Empire; the Register of the Names of Those who Fell in the 1939-1945 War and are Buried in Cemeteries and Churchyards in Surrey; Brookwood Military Cemetery, Woking.* London: [H.M. Stationery Office], 1958. 3 vols.

Gregory, Walter, and Michael Ticehurst. *Memories of H.M.C.S. Trentonian; Alias K368; Trenton's Own Ship.* n.p.: [1979]. 72 pp.

Gutta Percha and Rubber, Limited. *A Selection of Badge Designs of the Canadian Forces.* Toronto: n.p., n.d. 16 pp., chiefly illus.

HMCS Cornwallis. Cornwallis, N.S.: n.p., n.d. 1 vol., unpaged.

Hermann, J. Douglas. *Report to the Minister of Veterans Affairs of a Study on Canadians who were Prisoners of War in Europe during World War II./Rapport présenté au Ministre des Affaires des anciens combattants au sujet d'une enquête portant sur les Canadiens prisonniers de guerre en Europe au cours de la seconde guerre mondiale.* Ottawa: Queen's Printer/Imprimeur de la Reine, 1973. 56/60 pp.
Bilingual text./Texte bilingue.

Hill, J. Kirkbride, comp. *The Price of Freedom.* Toronto: Ryerson Press, 1942-44. 2 vols.

Hitsman, M. Mackay. *Canadian Naval Policy.* Kingston, Ont.: Queen's Univ., 1940. 208 pp.

Hoare, John. *Tumult in the Clouds; a Story of the Fleet Air Arm.* London: Joseph, 1976. 208 pp.

Hodgins, J. Herbert, and others, comps. *Women at War.* Montreal: MacLean Pub., 1943. 190 pp.

Hopkins, Anthony. *Songs from the Front & Rear; Canadian Servicemen's Songs of the Second World War.* Edmonton: Hurtig Publishers, 1979. 192 pp.

Houghton, F.L., comp. *H.M.C.S. Skeena, 1931-1932; Commemorating her First Year in Commission.* Victoria, B.C.: privately printed, n.d. 80 pp.

Jellicoe, John Rushworth Jellicoe, 1st earl. *Report of Admiral of the Fleet, Viscount Jellicoe of Scapa, G.C.B., O.M., G.C.V.O., on Mission to the Dominion of Canada, November-December, 1919.* Ottawa: n.p., n.d. 3 vols.
Vol. I also printed as Sessional Paper no. 61, 1920. Vol. II-III originally Secret.

*Jellicoe, John Rushworth Jellicoe, 1re earl. *Rapport de l'Amiral de la Flotte le Vicomte Jellicoe de Scapa, G.C.B., O.M., G.C.V.O., sur la mission navale au Canada en novembre et décembre 1919.* (Document de la session, no. 61.) Ottawa: Imprimeur du Roi, 1920. 59 pp.

Journal of the Edmonton Military Institute. Vol. I-IV? Edmonton: Edmonton Military Institute, 1937-46?

*Kealy, J.D.F., and E.C. Russell. *A History of Canadian Naval Aviation, 1918-1962.* Ottawa: Queen's Printer, 1965. 164 pp.

*Kealy, J.D.F., et E.C. Russell. *Histoire de l'aéronavale canadienne, 1918-1962.* Ottawa: Imprimeur de la Reine, 1965. 185 pp.

Kellock, R.L., *see* Canada. Royal Commission to Conduct an Inquiry into Certain Disorders Occurring May 7-8, 1945, in the City of Halifax.

Kelsey Club, Winnipeg, Man. *Canadian Defence; What We have to Defend; Various Defence Policies.* Toronto: T. Nelson, 1937. 98 pp.

Laing, Gertrude. *A Community Organized for War; the Story of the Greater Winnipeg Co-ordinating Board for War Services and Affiliated Organizations, 1939-1946.* Winnipeg: n.p., 1948. 103 pp.

Lamb, James B. *The Corvette Navy; True Stories from Canada's Atlantic War.* Toronto: Macmillan, 1977. 179 pp.

Lawrence, Hal. *A Bloody War; One Man's Memories of the Canadian Navy, 1939-1945.* Toronto: Macmillan, 1979. 193 pp.

Leacock, Stephen, and Leslie Roberts. *Canada's War at Sea.* Montreal: A.M. Beatty, 1944. 2 vols. in 1.

The Log; Royal Roads Military College. Vol. V- . Victoria, B.C.: privately printed, 1942-   .

Longstaff, F.V. *Esquimalt Naval Base; a History of its Work and its Defences.* Vancouver: Clarke & Stuart, 1941. 189 pp.

Macdonald, Angus L. *Speeches of Angus L. Macdonald.* Toronto: Longmans, Green, 1960. 227 pp.

Macdonald, Grant. *Our Canadian Armed Services,* sketches by Grant Macdonald. Montreal: Gazette, 1943. 1 vol., chiefly illus.

_____. *Sailors.* Toronto: Macmillan, 1945. 153 pp.

McGill Univ., Montreal, P.Q. *A Memorial Service for the McGill Men and Women who Gave Their Lives during the First and Second World Wars.* n.p.: [1946]. 1 vol., unpaged.

McGrane, J.E. *The Exeter and the North Saskatchewan.* Lac La Biche, Alta.: privately printed, 1950. 107 pp.

McKee, Fraser M. *Volunteers for Sea Service; a Brief History of the Royal Canadian Naval Volunteer Reserve, its Predecessors and Successors, on its 50th Anniversary, 1973.* Toronto: privately printed, 1973. 69 pp.

Macpherson, K.R. *Canada's Fighting Ships.* (Canadian War Museum Historical Publication Number 12.) Toronto: Hakkert, 1975. 116 pp.

[Maritime Museum of Canada.] *Souvenir of the Maritime Museum of Canada, Halifax, Nova Scotia.* [Halifax: n.p., 195-?] 44 pp.

Milne, Gilbert A. *H.M.C.S.; one Photographer's Impressions of the Royal Canadian Navy in World War II.* Toronto: T. Allen, 1960. 141 pp.

Mowat, Farley. *The Grey Seas Under.* Toronto: McClelland and Stewart, 1958. 341 pp.

Nicholson, G.W.L. *More Fighting Newfoundlanders; a History of Newfoundland's Fighting Forces in the Second World War.* [St. John's, Nfld.]: Govt. of Nfld., 1969. 621 pp.

Nova Scotia. *Nova Scotia Helps the Fighting Man.* n.p.: [1942]. 32 pp.

Outerbridge, L.M., ed. *H.M.S. Puncher, D-Day — 1944 to V.E. and V.J. — 1945.* Vancouver: privately printed, n.d. 128 pp.

Preston, Richard A. *Canada's RMC; a History of the Royal Military College.* Toronto: Univ. of Toronto Press, 1969. 415 pp.

Proulx, Benjamin A. *Underground from Hongkong.* New York: Dutton, 1943. 214 pp.

Puddester, J., ed. *The Crow's Nest (Officers Club); 30th Anniversary Souvenir, 1942-1972.* St. John's, Nfld.: privately printed, 1972. 51 pp.

Pugsley, William H. *Sailor Remember.* Toronto: Collins, 1948. 185 pp.

_____. *Saints, Devils and Ordinary Seamen; Life on the Royal Canadian Navy's Lower Deck.* Toronto: Collins, 1945. 241 pp.

The Rally Magazine. Vol. 1-? Wrecclesham, Eng.: n.p., 1939?-? *A monthly magazine for Canadian Active Service Forces.*

Reader's Digest. *The Canadians at War, 1939/45.* Montreal: Reader's Digest, 1969. 2 vols.

_____. *The Tools of War, 1939/45, and a Chronology of Important Events.* Montreal: Reader's Digest, 1969. 96 pp.

Robertson, Heather, [comp.] *A Terrible Beauty; the Art of Canada at War*. Toronto: J. Lorimer, 1977. 239 pp.

Robertson, Peter. *Irréductible vérité/Relentless Verity/les photographes militaires canadiens depuis 1885/Canadian Military Photographers since 1885*. (Les Archives publiques du Canada/ Public Archives of Canada Series.) Québec, P.Q.: Les Presses de l'Université Laval, 1973. 233 pp.
Texte bilingue./Bilingual text.

Royal Canadian Navy Monthly Review (R.C.N.M.R.). Ottawa: King's Printer, 1942-45, 1947-48.

Royal Canadian Navy, 1910-1960; the First Fifty Years. n.p.: 1960. v.p.

Royal Military College of Canada, Kingston, Ont. *Regulations and Calendar of the Royal Military College of Canada, 1922.* Ottawa: King's Printer, 1923. 68 pp.

_____. *Standing Orders, Amended to January, 1924.* Ottawa: King's Printer, 1924. 120 pp.

_____. *Standing Orders, Amended to January, 1926.* Ottawa: King's Printer, 1926. 105 pp.

_____. *Standing Orders; the Royal Military College of Canada, 1938.* Ottawa: King's Printer, 1938. 67 pp.

The Royal Military College of Canada Review. Vol. I- . Kingston, Ont.: privately printed, 1920- .

Russell, E.C. *H.M.C.S. Haida; a Brief History*. n.p.: n.d. 56 pp.

Sallans, G.H. *With Canada's Fighting Men*. Ottawa: King's Printer, 1941. 46 pp.

*Savard, Adjutor. *The Defence of Our Land*. n.p.: 1943. 12 pp.

*_____. *La défense du territoire*. s.l.: s.i., 1943. 11 pp.

*Schull, Joseph. *The Far Distant Ships; an Official Account of Canadian Naval Operations in the Second World War*. Ottawa: Queen's Printer, 1952. 527 pp.

*_____. *Lointains navires; compte rendu officiel des opérations de la Marine canadienne au cours de la seconde grande guerre*. Ottawa: Imprimeur de la Reine, 1953. 605 pp.

_____. *Ships of the Great Days; Canada's Navy in World War II*. (Great Stories of Canada.) Toronto: Macmillan, 1962. 156 pp.

Sclater, William. *Haida*. Toronto: Oxford Univ. Press, 1947. 221 pp.

Sea Breezes. Vol. I-III. Halifax: privately printed, 1914-22.
Journal of the Royal Naval College of Canada.

Shea, A.A., and E. Estoriak. *Canada and the Short-Wave War.* (Behind the Headlines, vol. III.) Toronto: Canadian Institute of International Affairs, 1942. 36 pp.

Sheffield, E.F. *Portraits of the Officers in Charge of the 21st Officers' Disciplinary Course in H.M.C.S. "Cornwallis" and of the Twenty-three Members of the Class.* Grant Macdonald, illus. [n.p.: privately printed, 1943. 32 pp.]

Smith, Waldo E.L. *The Navy Chaplain and his Parish.* Ottawa: Queen's Printer, 1967. 264 pp.

*Stacey, C.P. *Armes, hommes et gouvernements; les politiques de guerre du Canada, 1939-1945.* Ottawa: Imprimeur de la Reine, 1970. 747 pp.

*_____. *Arms, Men and Governments; the War Policies of Canada, 1939-1945.* Ottawa: Queen's Printer, 1970. 681 pp.

Stanley, George F.G., and Richard A. Preston. *A Short History of Kingston as a Military and Naval Centre.* Kingston, Ont.: Queen's Printer, [195-?]. 33 pp.

Strange, William. *Into the Blitz; a British Journey.* Toronto: Macmillan, 1941. 318 pp.

_____. *Ships Mean Freedom.* Ottawa: King's Printer, [1942]. 63 pp.

_____. *Ships Mean Life.* [Toronto: privately printed, 1944.] 64 pp.

_____. *Ships Mean Security.* Ottawa: King's Printer, [1946]. 54 pp.

_____. *Ships Mean Victory.* [Toronto: privately printed, 1942.] 63 pp.

Swain, Hector. *History of the Naval Reserves in Newfoundland.* [St. John's, Nfld.: Provincial Archives, 1975.] 56 pp.

Swettenham, John. *D-Day./Jour-J.* Jacques Gouin, tr. Ottawa: National Museum of Man/Le Musée national de l'homme, [1970]. 27/30 pp.
Bilingual text./Texte bilingue.

Swettenham, John, and Fred Gaffen. *Canada's Atlantic War.* Toronto: Samuel-Stevens, 1979. 154 pp.

Thompson, Roy J.C. *Wings of the Canadian Armed Forces, 1913-1972.* [Dartmouth], N.S.: n.p., 1973. 106 pp.

Thornton, J.M. *H.M.C.S. Discovery and Deadman's Island; a Brief History . . . .* n.p.: [197-?]. 52 pp.

The Tiddley Times; the W.R.C.N.S. Magazine. Ottawa: King's Printer, ?-1945.

Trinity College School Old Boys at War, 1899-1902, 1914-1918, 1939-1945. Port Hope, Ont.: privately printed, 1948. 245 pp.

Tucker, Gilbert Norman. *A History of the Royal Canadian Navy.* Ottawa: King's Printer, 1951. 16 pp.

_____. *The Naval Service of Canada; its Official History.* Ottawa: King's Printer, 1952. 2 vols.

The University of Alberta in the War of 1939-45. Edmonton: n.p., 1948. 70 pp.

Waters, John M. *Bloody Winter.* Princeton, N.J.: Van Nostrand, 1967. 279 pp.

Whitehead, William. *Dieppe, 1942; Echoes of Disaster.* Terence Macartney-Filgate, ed. (A Personal Library Publication.) Don Mills, Ont.: Nelson, 1979. 187 pp., chiefly illus.

Whitton, Charlotte. *Canadian Women in the War Effort.* Toronto: Macmillan, 1942. 56 pp.

[Willson, Gordon Beckles.] *Canada Comes To England,* by Gordon Beckles [*pseud.*] London: Hodder and Stoughton, 1941. 166 pp.

Wodehouse, R.F. *A Check List of the War Collections of World War I, 1914-1918, and World War II, 1939-1945.* Ottawa: Queen's Printer, 1968. 239 pp.

Wright J., comp. *Music Ashore and Afloat; Famous Bands of the R.C.N.* Wallaceburg, Ont.: Standard Press, 1945. 1 vol., unpaged.

Young, George. *The Short Triangle; a Story of the Sea and Men who go Down to It in Ships; the Place, the Coasts of New England and Nova Scotia; the Time, Summer — 1942.* Lunenburg, N.S.: privately printed, 1975. 79 pp.

Young Men's Christian Associations, Canada. *The 1st Year; a War Service Record of the Canadian Y.M.C.A. from the Outbreak of the War.* n.p.: [1940]. 23 pp.

Young Men's Christian Associations, Canada. National Council. War Services Executive. *With Arthur Jones through 5 Years of War; a Report of Canadian Y.M.C.A. War Services.* n.p.: n.d. 1 vol., unpaged.

Young, Scott. *Red Shield in Action; a Record of Canadian Salvation Army War Services in the Second Great War.* Toronto: F.F. Clarke, 1949. 149 pp.

Air Force College Journal. Toronto: privately printed, 1956-64. 9 vols.
Title varies.

Appleton, Thomas E. *Usque ad Mare; a History of the Canadian Coast Guard and Marine Services.* Ottawa: Queen's Printer, 1968. 318 pp.

*Barton, William H. *Science and the Armed Services.* (Current Affairs for the Canadian Forces, vol. II, no. 1.) Ottawa: King's Printer, 1952. 22 pp.

*_____. *La science et les Services armés.* (Actualités; revue destinée aux Forces canadiennes, vol. II, no. 1.) Ottawa: Imprimeur du Roi, 1952. 22 pp.

Bidwell, R.E.S. *Random Memories.* Ottawa: privately printed, [1962. 21 pp.]

Bowering, Clifford H. *Service; the Story of the Canadian Legion, 1925-1960.* Ottawa: privately printed, 1960. 240 pp.

CNAV Endeavour AGOR 171 Oceanographic Research Vessel. Ottawa: Queen's Printer, 1965. 1 vol., unpaged.

Canada. Armed Forces. H.M.C.S. Unicorn. *History of Unicorn, 1923-1973.* n.p.: n.d. v.p.

Canada. Canadian Forces Headquarters. *Canadian Forces Administrative Orders.* Ottawa: n.p., 1965-71.
Issued as a non-chronological sequence in which orders were discarded when obsolete. Superseded by a bilingual format in 1972.

Canada. Court Martial Appeal Board. *Court Martial Appeal Reports.* Ottawa: Queen's Printer, 1957-73. 3 vols.

*Canada. Dept. of National Defence. *The Defence Research Board, Canada.* n.p.: n.d. 1 vol., unpaged.

_____. *Defence Research Board; the First Twenty-five Years./ Conseil de recherches pour la défense; les 25 premières années.* Ottawa: Queen's Printer/Imprimeur de la Reine, 1972. 46 pp.
Bilingual text./Texte bilingue.

_____. *The King's Regulations and Orders for the Royal Canadian Navy.* (BRCN 101-103.) Ottawa: King's Printer, 1951. 3 vols., looseleaf.

_____. *Manual of the Canadian Forces Medical Service in the Field, 1959.* Ottawa: Queen's Printer, 1959. 324 pp., looseleaf.

_____. *The Naval Officer.* Ottawa: Queen's Printer, 1956. 14 pp.

*Canada. Dept. of National Defence. *The Queen's Regulations and Orders for the Canadian Forces.* Ottawa: Queen's Printer, 1965. 3 vols., looseleaf.

_____. *The Queen's Regulations and Orders for the Royal Canadian Navy.* (BRCN 101-103.) Ottawa: Queen's Printer, 1952. 3 vols., looseleaf.

*_____. *Queens Regulations for the Canadian Services Colleges.* Ottawa: Queens Printer, 1958. 1 vol., unpaged.

*_____. *Report.* Ottawa: King's Printer, 1923-59.
Title varies. Annual most years.

*_____. *White Paper on Defence.* Ottawa: Queen's Printer, 1964. 30 pp.

Canada. Dept. of National Defence. Defence Research Board. *Annual Review./Revue annuelle.* n.p./s.l.: s.i., 1966- .
Bilingual text./Texte bilingue.

*Canada. Dept. of National Defence (Naval Service). *Report on Certain "Incidents" which Occurred on Board H.M.C. Ships Athabaskan, Crescent and Magnificent, and on Other Matters Concerning the Royal Canadian Navy Made to the Minister of National Defence by a Commission Duly Appointed for the above Purposes . . . . Ottawa, October, 1949.* Ottawa: King's Printer, 1949. 57 pp.

Canada. Dept. of Veterans Affairs. *Commemoration; Canadians in Korea, 1978./Souvenir; Canadiens en Corée, 1978.* n.p./s.l.: s.i., [1978. 14 pp.]
Bilingual text./Texte bilingue.

Canada. Dept. of the Naval Service. *The Canadian Navy List.* Ottawa: King's Printer, 1914-65.
Issued by the Dept. of National Defence from 1923.

*Canada. Marine. *Carrières de la Marine pour les diplômés et les étudiants d'université.* Ottawa: Imprimeur de la Reine, 1962. 28 pp.

_____. *Carrières et formation.* Ottawa: Imprimeur de la Reine, 1964. 32 pp.

*_____. *Formation et carrières dans la Marine à l'intention des élèves des écoles secondaires.* Ottawa: Imprimeur de la Reine, 1960. 64 pp.

*Canada. Marine. Commandement maritime de l'Atlantique. *Visite du comité spécial de la défence* [sic] *au Commandement maritime canadienne de l'Atlantique, juillet 1964; programme et renseignements.* s.l.: s.i., 1964. 1 tome, non-paginé.

*Canada. Ministère de la Défense nationale. *Le conseil de recherches pour la défense, Canada.* s.l.: s.i., s.d. 1 tome, non-paginé.

*_____. *Livre blanc sur la défense.* Ottawa: Imprimeur de la Reine, 1964. 34 pp.

*_____. *Ordonnances et règlements royaux applicables aux Forces canadiennes.* Ottawa: Imprimeur de la Reine, 1965. 3 tomes, feuilles mobiles.

*_____. *Rapport.* Ottawa: Imprimeur du Roi, 1923-59. *Divergence du titre. Annuel, la plupart des années.*

*_____. *Règlements royaux applicables aux Collèges des services armés du Canada.* Ottawa: Imprimeur de la Reine, 1958. 1 tome, non-paginé.

*Canada. Ministère de la Défense nationale (Service naval). *Rapport sur certains incidents survenus à bord de l'Athabaskan, du Crescent et du Magnificent et sur d'autres questions relatives à la Marine royale canadienne, rapport présenté au Ministre de la défense nationale par une Commission régulièrement nommée à ces fins.* Ottawa: Imprimeur du Roi, 1949. 62 pp.

Canada. National Defence Headquarters. *Supplement to Naval General Orders.* Ottawa: n.p., 1965. 1 vol., looseleaf.

Canada. Naval Service Headquarters. *General Orders.* [new series.] Ottawa: n.p., 1951-65. 3 vols., looseleaf.

_____. *General Orders.* [old series.] Ottawa: n.p., 1946-57.

_____. *Royal Canadian Navy Badges, Battle Honours, Mottoes.* Ottawa: Queen's Printer, 1964. 4 vols., looseleaf.

_____. *Uniform Instructions for the Royal Canadian Navy.* (BRCN 108.) Ottawa: Queen's Printer, 1951. 1 vol., looseleaf.

Canada. Naval Service Headquarters. Ad Hoc Committee on RCN Personnel Structure. *Report.* Ottawa: n.p., [1958]. v.p.

Canada. Naval Service Headquarters. Directorate of Naval Information. *The Sea, Ships and Men.* Toronto: Navy League of Canada, n.d. 48 pp.

Canada. Naval Service Headquarters. Naval Historian. *The University Naval Training Divisions,* [by Philip Chaplin]. Ottawa: Queen's Printer, 1963. 24 pp.

*Canada. Navy. *Education and Careers in the Navy for Canadian High School Students.* Ottawa: Queen's Printer, 1960. 64 pp.

_____. *General Information about the Pacific Command of the RCN.* Ottawa: Queen's Printer, 1961. 24 pp.

Canada. Navy. *Listing of Officers on the General and Special Lists; Containing a Listing of RCN and RCN(R) Officers on Continuous Naval Duty Serving on 1 December, 1959.* Ottawa: Queen's Printer, 1960. v.p.

*_____. *R.C.N. Careers for University Graduates and Undergraduates.* Ottawa: Queen's Printer, 1962. 28 pp.

_____. *Regulations and Orders for the Royal Canadian Sea Cadets.* (BRCN 105(64).) n.p.: 1964. 1 vol., looseleaf.

_____. *The Regulations for the Government of Royal Canadian Sea Cadet Corps, 1949.* n.p.: [1949]. 51 pp.

_____. *Royal Canadian Navy Divisional Officer's Handbook.* (BRCN 3059.) Ottawa: Queen's Printer, 1963. 241 pp.

_____. *Royal Canadian Navy Financial Manual.* (BRCN 625.) Ottawa: Queen's Printer, 1963. 2 vols.

_____. *Seaman's Handbook.* (BRCN 3029.) n.p.: [1960]. 366 pp.

_____. *Technical Apprenticeship Training, Royal Canadian Navy.* Ottawa: Queen's Printer, 1958. 14 pp.

_____. *Venture Plan.* Ottawa: Queen's Printer, 1958. 23 pp.

*Canada. Navy. Maritime Command, Atlantic. *Visit of the Special Committee on Defence to the Canadian Maritime Command Atlantic, July 1964; Programme and Information.* n.p.: 1964. 1 vol., unpaged.

Canada. Parliament. House of Commons. Special Committee on Canteen Funds. *Minutes of Proceedings and Evidence.* No. 1-10. Ottawa: King's Printer, 1947.

Canadian Defence Quarterly./Revue canadienne de défense. Vol. I- . Toronto: Baxter Pub., 1971- .

Casey, Douglas E., ed. *R.C.S.C.C. Rainbow.* n.p.: n.d. 64 pp.

Collège militaire royal de Saint-Jean. *Ouverture officielle./Official Opening.* s.l.: s.i., s.d./n.p.: n.d. 27 pp. *Texte bilingue./Bilingual text.*

The Commissioning Book of H.M.C.S. Warrior, January 24th 1946. Belfast: n.p., 1946. 32 pp.

The Commissioning of HMCS Algonquin, 3 November 1973, at Davie Shipbuilding Ltd., Lauzon, Quebec./Mise en service de l'Algonquin, le 3 novembre 1973, aux chantiers de la Davie Shipbuilding Ltd., Lauzon, Québec. n.p.: n.d./s.l.: s.i., s.d. 1 vol., unpaged./ 1 tome, non-paginé. *Bilingual text./Texte bilingue.*

The Commissioning of HMCS Annapolis, 19 December 1964, at Halifax Shipyards Limited, Halifax, N.S./Mise en service de l'Annapolis, 19 décembre 1964, à Halifax Shipyards Limited, Halifax (N.-E.). n.p.: n.d./s.l.: s.i., s.d. 1 vol., unpaged./ 1 tome, non-paginé.
Bilingual text./Texte bilingue.

The Commissioning of HMCS Assiniboine at Marine Industries Ltd., Sorel, P.Q., August 16, 1956. n.p.: n.d. 1 vol., unpaged.

The Commissioning of HMCS Athabaskan, 30 September 1972, at Davie Shipbuilding Ltd. Lauzon, Quebec./Mise en service de l'Athabaskan, le 30 septembre 1972, aux chantiers de la Davie Shipbuilding Ltd. Lauzon, Québec. n.p.: n.d./s.l.: s.i., s.d. 1 vol., unpaged./1 tome, non-paginé.
Bilingual text./Texte bilingue.

The Commissioning of HMCS Chaudière at Halifax Shipyards, Halifax, N.S., November 14, 1959. Ottawa: Queen's Printer, 1959. 1 vol., unpaged.

The Commissioning of HMCS Columbia at Burrard Dry Dock Co., Ltd., North Vancouver, B.C., November 7, 1959. Ottawa: Queen's Printer, 1959. 1 vol., unpaged.

The Commissioning of HMCS Fraser at Yarrows Limited, Esquimalt B.C., June 28, 1957. n.p.: n.d. 1 vol., unpaged.

The Commissioning of HMCS Gatineau at HMC Dockyard, Halifax, N.S., February 17, 1959. Ottawa: Queen's Printer, 1959. 1 vol., unpaged.

The Commissioning of HMCS Grilse at the United States Naval Submarine Base, New London, Groton, Connecticut, 11th May, 1961. Ottawa: Queen's Printer, 1961. 1 vol., unpaged.

The Commissioning of HMCS Kootenay at Burrard Dry Dock Co., Ltd., North Vancouver B.C., March 7, 1959. Ottawa: Queen's Printer, 1959. 1 vol., unpaged.

The Commissioning of HMCS Mackenzie at Canadian Vickers Ltd., Montreal, P.Q., October 6, 1962. Ottawa: Queen's Printer, 1962. 1 vol., unpaged.

The Commissioning of HMCS Margaree at Halifax Shipyards, Halifax, N.S., October 5, 1957. Ottawa: Queen's Printer, 1957. 1 vol., unpaged.

The Commissioning of HMCS Ojibwa, 23 September 1965, in Her Majesty's Dockyard, Chatham, Kent, England. Ottawa: Queen's Printer, 1965. 1 vol., unpaged.

The Commissioning of HMCS Ottawa, at Canadian Vickers Ltd., Montreal, P.Q., November 10, 1956. Ottawa: Queen's Printer, 1956. 1 vol., unpaged.

The Commissioning of HMCS Preserver at Saint John Shipbuilding and Dry Dock Co., Ltd., Saint John, N.B./Mise en service du Preserver à la Saint John Shipbuilding and Dry Dock Co., Ltd., Saint John, N.B. n.p.: n.d./s.l.: s.i., s.d. 1 vol., unpaged./ 1 tome, non-paginé.
Bilingual text./Texte bilingue.

The Commissioning of HMCS Protecteur, 30 August, 1969, at Saint John Shipbuilding and Dry Dock Co., Ltd., Saint John, N.B./Mise en service du Protecteur, 30 août 1969, à la Saint John Shipbuilding and Dry Dock Co., Ltd., Saint John, N.-B. n.p.: n.d./s.l.: s.i., s.d. 1 vol., unpaged./1 tome, non-paginé.
Bilingual text./Texte bilingue.

The Commissioning of HMCS Provider, 28 September, 1963, at Davie Shipbuilding Limited, Lauzon, Quebec./Mise en service du Provider, 28 septembre, 1963, à l'Arsenal de la Davie Shipbuilding Limited, Lauzon, Québec. n.p.: n.d./s.l.: s.i., s.d. 1 vol., unpaged./1 tome, non-paginé.
Bilingual text./Texte bilingue.

The Commissioning of HMCS Qu'Appelle, 14 September 1963, at Davie Shipbuilding Limited, Lauzon, Quebec./Mise en service du Qu'Appelle, 14 septembre 1963, à l'Arsenal de la Davie Shipbuilding Limited, Lauzon, Québec. n.p.: n.d./s.l.: s.i., s.d. 1 vol., unpaged./1 tome, non-paginé.
Bilingual text./Texte bilingue.

The Commissioning of HMCS Restigouche at Canadian Vickers Ltd., Montreal, P.Q., June 7, 1958. Ottawa: Queen's Printer, 1957. 1 vol., unpaged.
Some copies exist giving November 30, 1957, as commissioning date.

The Commissioning of HMCS Saguenay at Halifax Shipyards Ltd., Halifax, N.S., December 15, 1956. n.p.: n.d. 1 vol., unpaged.

The Commissioning of HMCS St. Croix at Marine Industries Ltd., Sorel, P.Q., October 4, 1958. Ottawa: Queen's Printer, 1958. 1 vol., unpaged.

The Commissioning of HMCS St. Laurent at Canadian Vickers Limited, Montreal, Quebec, Saturday, October 29, 1955. n.p.: n.d. 1 vol., unpaged.

The Commissioning of HMCS Saskatchewan, February 16, 1963, at Yarrows Limited, Esquimalt, B.C. Ottawa: Queen's Printer, 1963. 1 vol., unpaged.

The Commissioning of HMCS Skeena at Burrard Dry Dock Co., Ltd., North Vancouver, B.C., March 30, 1957. n.p.: n.d. 1 vol., unpaged.

The Commissioning of HMCS Terra Nova at Victoria Machinery Depot Co. Ltd., Victoria, B.C., June 6, 1959. Ottawa: Queen's Printer, 1959. 1 vol., unpaged.

The Commissioning of HMCS Yukon, May 25, 1963, at Burrard Dry Dock Co. Ltd., North Vancouver. Ottawa: Queen's Printer, 1963. 1 vol., unpaged.

Coup d'oeil sur le Collège militaire royal de Saint-Jean. Ottawa: Imprimeur de la Reine, 1959. 20 pp.

Crichton, Robert. *The Great Imposter.* New York: Random House, 1959. 218 pp.

The Crowsnest; the Royal Canadian Navy's Magazine. Vol. I-XVII. Ottawa: Queen's Printer, 1948-65.

Le Défilé; la revue du Collège militaire royal de Saint-Jean. St-Jean, P.Q.: imprimé privé, 1952-   .
Divergence du titre.

Dillon, G.M. *Canadian Naval Forces since World War II; a Decision-making Analysis,* with comments by Dr. G.R. Lindsey and Professor Jonathan Wouk, with a reply from the author. (Dalhousie Univ. Center for Foreign Policy Studies Occasional Paper.) Halifax: Dalhousie Univ., 1972. 79 pp.

Goodspeed, D.J. *A History of the Defence Research Board of Canada.* Ottawa: Queen's Printer, 1958. 259 pp.

*HMCS Labrador. (Current Affairs for the Canadian Forces, vol. IX, no. 2.) Ottawa: Queen's Printer, 1955. 31 pp.

Irvine, T.A. *The Ice was All Between.* Toronto: Longmans, Green, 1959. 216 pp.

*Kealy, J.D.F., and E.C. Russell. *A History of Canadian Naval Aviation, 1918-1962.* Ottawa: Queen's Printer, 1965. 164 pp.

*Kealy, J.D.F., et E.C. Russell. *Histoire de l'aéronavale canadienne, 1918-1962.* Ottawa: Imprimeur de la Reine, 1965. 185 pp.

Kilgour, Robert W. *A History of the Canadian Naval Auxiliary Vessels,* [1945-1967. Halifax: privately printed, 1967.] 44 pp.

Le "Labrador". (Actualités; revue destinée aux Forces canadiennes, vol. IX, no. 2.) Ottawa: Imprimeur de la Reine, 1955. 35 pp.

The Log; Royal Roads Military College. Vol. V- . Victoria, B.C.: privately printed, 1942-   .

*McCracken, George W. *Votre Marine.* (Actualités; revue destinée aux Forces canadiennes, vol. IV, no. 8.) Ottawa: Imprimeur de la Reine, 1953. 31 pp.

_____. *Your Navy.* (Current Affairs for the Canadian Forces, vol. IV, no. 8.) Ottawa: Queen's Printer, 1953. 31 pp.

McGrane, J.E. *The Exeter and the North Saskatchewan.* Lac La Biche, Alta.: privately printed, 1950. 107 pp.

McKee, Fraser M. *Volunteers for Sea Service; a Brief History of the Royal Canadian Naval Volunteer Reserve, its Predecessors and Successors, on its 50th Anniversary, 1973.* Toronto: privately printed, 1973. 69 pp.

Macpherson, K.R. *Canada's Fighting Ships.* (Canadian War Museum Historical Publication Number 12.) Toronto: Hakkert, 1975. 116 pp.

Marcoux, Jules, éd. *CMR, 1952-1977; album du 25e anniversaire./ 25th anniversary album.* St-Jean, P.Q.: s.i./n.p., 1977. 62 pp. *Texte bilingue./Bilingual text.*

[Maritime Museum of Canada.] *Souvenir of the Maritime Museum of Canada, Halifax, Nova Scotia.* [Halifax: n.p, 195-?] 44 pp.

The Medical and Dental Services of the Canadian Forces. (Current Affairs for the Canadian Forces, vol. VI, no. 1.) Ottawa: Queen's Printer, 1954. 31 pp.

The Naming and Commissioning of HMCS Huron, 16 December 1972, at Marine Industries Ltd. Sorel, Quebec./Baptême et mise en service de l'Huron, le 16 décembre 1972, aux chantiers de la Marine Industrie Limitée, Sorel, Québec. n.p.: n.d./s.l.: s.i., s.d. 1 vol., unpaged./1 tome, non-paginé. *Bilingual text./Texte bilingue.*

The Naming and Commissioning of HMCS Iroquois, 29 July 1972, at Marine Industries Ltd. Sorel, Quebec./Baptême et mise en service de l'Iroquois, le 29 juillet 1972, aux chantiers de la Marine Industrie Limitée, Sorel, Québec. n.p.: n.d./s.l.: s.i., s.d. 1 vol., unpaged./1 tome, non-paginé. *Bilingual text./Texte bilingue.*

The Naming and Commissioning of HMCS Nipigon, 30 May, 1964, at Marine Industries Limited, Sorel, Quebec./Baptême et mise en service du Nipigon, 30 mai 1964, à Marine Industries Limited, Sorel, Québec. n.p.: n.d./s.l.: s.i., s.d. 1 vol., unpaged./1 tome, non-paginé. *Bilingual text./Texte bilingue.*

Paré, Lorenzo. *Les canadiens français et l'organisation militaire.* (Oeuvre des tracts, 382.) Montréal: imprimé privé, [1951]. 16 pp.

* *"Pourquoi je sers ma patrie"*. (Actualités; revue destinée aux Forces canadiennes, vol. X, no. 15.) Ottawa: Imprimeur de la Reine, 1956. 26 pp.

Presentation of the Queen's Colour to the Royal Canadian Navy by Her Majesty the Queen, Halifax, Nova Scotia, Saturday, 1st August, 1959. n.p.: n.d. 1 vol., unpaged.

Preston, Richard A. *Canada's RMC; a History of the Royal Military College.* Toronto: Univ. of Toronto Press, 1969. 415 pp.

Puddester, J., ed. *The Crow's Nest (Officers Club); 30th Anniversary Souvenir, 1942-1972.* St. John's, Nfld.: privately printed, 1972. 51 pp.

Pugsley, William H. *Return to Sea; the Lower Deck of the Royal Canadian Navy Re-Visited Eleven Years after the 1945 Demobilization.* Toronto: Collins, 1960. 249 pp.

Robertson, Peter. *Irréductible vérité/Relentless Verity/les photographes militaires canadiens depuis 1885/Canadian Military Photographers since 1885.* (Les Archives publiques du Canada/ Public Archives of Canada Series.) Québec, P.Q.: Les Presses de l'Université Laval, 1973. 233 pp.
Texte bilingue./Bilingual text.

Royal Canadian Navy Monthly Review (R.C.N.M.R.). Ottawa: King's Printer, 1942-45, 1947-48.

Royal Canadian Navy, 1910-1960; the First Fifty Years. n.p.: 1960. v.p.

Royal Military College of Canada, Kingston, Ont. *The Cadet Handbook.* Kingston, Ont.: n.p., [1957?] 59 pp., looseleaf.

The Royal Military College of Canada Review. Vol. I- . Kingston, Ont.: privately printed, 1920-   .

* *Les services médicaux et dentaires pour les Forces armées.* (Actualités; revue destinée aux Forces canadiennes, vol. VI, no. 1.) Ottawa: Imprimeur de la Reine, 1954. 31 pp.

Smith, Waldo E.L. *The Navy Chaplain and his Parish.* Ottawa: Queen's Printer, 1967. 264 pp.

Snowy Owl; Journal of the Canadian Land Forces Command and Staff College. Kingston, Ont.: privately printed, 1952-73. 18 vols.
Title varies.

*Stacey, C.P., H.E.W. Strange and F.H. Hitchins. *Canada's Armed Forces Today.* (Current Affairs for the Canadian Forces, vol. II, no. 9.) Ottawa: Queen's Printer, 1952. 22 pp.

*Stacey, C.P., H.E.W. Strange et F.H. Hitchins. *Les Forces armées du Canada.* (Actualités; revue destinée aux Forces canadiennes, vol. II, no. 9.) Ottawa: Imprimeur de la Reine, 1952. 22 pp.

Supply Mercury; for the Supply Branch of the Royal Canadian Navy. Vol. I-X. Ottawa: Queen's Printer, 1950-59.

Swain, Hector. *History of the Naval Reserves in Newfoundland.* [St. John's, Nfld.: Provincial Archives, 1975.] 56 pp.

The Telescope; a Magazine of Current Information on the Royal Canadian Navy for Officers of the R.C.N.(R) and Members of the Naval Officers' Association. Vol. I-II. Ottawa: King's Printer, 1947-48.

**The Third Canadian Escort Squadron.* n.p.: [1958? 13 pp.]

Thompson, Roy J.C. *Wings of the Canadian Armed Forces, 1913-1972.* [Dartmouth], N.S.: n.p., 1973. 106 pp.

*Thorgrimsson, Thor, and E.C. Russell. *Canadian Naval Operations in Korean Waters, 1950-1955.* Ottawa: Queen's Printer, 1965. 167 pp.

*Thorgrimsson, Thor, et E.C. Russell. *Les opérations navales du Canada dans les eaux coréennes, 1950-1955.* Ottawa: Imprimeur de la Reine, 1965. 178 pp.

Thornton, J.M. *H.M.C.S. Discovery and Deadman's Island; a Brief History . . . .* n.p.: [197-?]. 52 pp.

**La troisième escadre d'escorte du Canada.* s.l.: s.i., [1958? 15 pp.]

Venturian; HMCS Venture, Esquimalt, B.C. Esquimalt, B.C.: privately printed, 1955-63.
Annual.

Vondette, H.W. *Athabaskan's Rescue.* Ottawa: Queen's Printer, 1964. 19 pp.

Wave Off. Vol. I-XIV? Ottawa: n.p., 1950-64?
Magazine of Inspectorate of Naval Flight Safety, RCN.

White Twist. n.p.: 1949-63?
Yearbook of the University Naval Training Divisions.

**"Why I Serve",* by the Serviceman. (Current Affairs for the Canadian Forces, vol. X, no. 15.) Ottawa: Queen's Printer, 1956. 26 pp.

D. LAND FORCES — FORCES DE TERRE

1867-1914

Adam, G. Mercer. *The Canadian North-West; its History and its Troubles from the Early Days of the Fur Trade to the Era of the Railway and the Settler; with Incidents of Travel in the Region, and the Narrative of Three Insurrections.* Toronto: Rose Pub. Co., 1885. 390 pp.

Anderson, Frank. *"1885"; the Riel Rebellion.* (Frontier Book, no. 3.) n.p.: n.d. 80 pp.

_____. *Riel's Manitoba Uprising.* (Frontier Book, no. 31.) Calgary, Alta.: Frontier Pub., 1974. 64 pp.

Armit, W.B. *Army Museum; Halifax Citadel, Halifax, Nova Scotia.* Kentville, N.S.: n.p., [1957?] 34 pp.

*L'Arsenal de Québec, 1880-1945. Québec, P.Q.: s.i., 1947. 166 pp.

Aston, Wm. H., comp. *History of the 21st Regiment, Essex Fusiliers of Windsor, Ontario, Canadian Militia, with a Brief History of the Essex Frontier, the War of 1812, Canadian Rebellion of 1837, Fenian Raids, War in South Africa, etc., Including an Account of the Different Actions in which the Militia of Essex have been Engaged.* Windsor, Ont.: Record Print. Co., 1902. 176 pp.

[Attwood, Peter Hinds.] *A Few Practical Hints to the Officers, N.C. Officers & Men of the 26th Battalion Relative to their Duties in Camp.* London, Ont.: Free Press Print. and Pub. Co., 1875. 15 pp.

Barnard, W.T. *The Queen's Own Rifles of Canada, 1860-1960; One Hundred Years of Canada.* Don Mills, Ont.: Ontario Pub. Co., 1960. 398 pp.

_____. *A Short History of the Queen's Own Rifles of Canada.* Toronto: MacKinnon & Atkins, n.d. 22 pp.

Barnes, C.H. *Colonel Colin Clarke Harbottle, C.M.G., D.S.O., V.D.* n.p.: [1958]. 20 pp.

Barnett, Donald C. *Poundmaker.* (The Canadians.) Don Mills, Ont.: Fitzhenry and Whiteside, 1976. 61 pp.

Baxter, John Babington Macaulay. *Historical Records of the New Brunswick Regiment Canadian Artillery.* St. John, N.B.: Sun Print., 1896. 259 pp.

[Baylay, George Taylor, ed.] *The Regimental History of the Governor General's Foot Guards.* Ottawa: privately printed, 1948. 268 pp.

[Beach, Thomas Miller.] *Twenty-Five Years in the Secret Service; the Recollections of a Spy,* by Major Henri Le Caron [*pseud.*] London: Heinemann, 1892. 311 pp.

Beattie, Kim. *48th Highlanders of Canada, 1891-1928.* Toronto: privately printed, 1932. 434 pp.

Beauregard, George. *Le 9me bataillon au Nord-Ouest (Journal d'un militaire).* Québec, P.Q.: J.G. Gingras, 1886. 100 pp.

Beck, Norman Edward, comp. *Souvenir Number of the Reveille, the Duke of Connaught's Own, the 158th (Overseas) Battalion.* Vancouver: privately printed, 1916. 20 pp.

Begg, Alexander, *Alexander Begg's Red River Journal and Other Papers Relative to the Red River Resistance of 1869-1870.* W.L. Morton, ed. (The Publications of the Champlain Society, XXXIV.) Toronto: Champlain Society, 1956. 636 pp.

_____. *The Creation of Manitoba or, a History of the Red River Troubles.* Toronto: A.H. Hovey, 1871. 408 pp.

Bellefeuille, E. Lef. de. *Le Canada et les zouaves pontificaux; memoires sur l'origine, l'enrôlement et l'expédition du contingent canadien à Rome, pendant l'année 1868.* Montréal: imprimé privé, [1868]. 263 pp.

Biggar, E.B. *The Boer War; its Causes and its Interest to Canadians with a Glossary of Cape Dutch and Kafir Terms.* Toronto: Bigger, Samuel, 1899, 38 pp.

Biggar, J. Lyons, *see* Canada. Dept. of Militia and Defence. *Manual for Use by the Canadian Army Service Corps . . . .*

Bindon, Kathryn M. *Queen's Men, Canada's Men; the Military History of Queen's University, Kingston.* [Kingston, Ont.]: privately printed, 1978. 180 pp.

Bird, Will R. *North Shore (New Brunswick) Regiment.* Fredericton, N.B.: Brunswick Press, 1963. 629 pp.

"Bluenose" [*pseud.*] *see* "How Not to Do It".

Boissonnault, Charles-Marie. *Histoire politico-militaire des Canadiens français (1763-1967).* Trois-Rivières, P.Q.: Editions du Bien public, 1967. 310 pp.

Boss, W. *The Stormont, Dundas and Glengarry Highlanders, 1783-1951.* Ottawa: Runge Press, 1952. 449 pp.

Boulton, [Charles Arkoll]. *Reminiscences of the North-West Rebellions; with a Record of the Raising of Her Majesty's 100th Regiment in Canada and a Chapter on Canadian Social and Political Life.* Toronto: Grip, 1886. 531 pp.

A Brief Account of the Fenian Raids on the Missisquoi Frontier, in 1866 and 1870. Montreal: "Witness" Steam Print. House, 1871. 32 pp.

A Brief Historical Sketch of the Lorne Scots (Peel, Dufferin and Halton Regiment). Brampton, Ont.: Charters Pub. Co., 1943. 24 pp.

A Brief Historical Sketch of the Queen's York Rangers, 1st American Regiment. Toronto: privately printed, 1942. 30 pp.

A Brief History of the Royal Regiment of Canada, [Allied with the King's Regiment (Liverpool)]. [Toronto: n.p., 1940.] 77 pp.

A Brief History of the Royal Regiment of Canada; Allied with the King's Regiment (Liverpool). [Toronto: n.p., 1948.] 135 pp.

Brough, H. Bruce. *Illustrated Historical Album of the Second Battalion the Queen's Own Rifles of Canada, 1856-1894.* Toronto: Toronto News Co., 1894. 80 pp.

Brown, Kingsley, *see* Greenhous, Brereton.

Brown, Stanley McKeown. *With the Royal Canadians.* Toronto: Publishers' Syndicate, 1900. 291 pp.

*Brown, W.J. *Les Cadets royaux de l'armée canadienne; cent ans d'exploits, 1879-1979.* s.l.: La Ligue des Cadets de l'Armée du Canada, [1979. 12 pp.]

*_____. *The Royal Canadian Army Cadets; a Century of Achievement, 1879-1979.* n.p.: The Army Cadet League of Canada, [1979. 12 pp.]

Bruce, Walter, H., and others, comps. *Historical Records of the Argyll and Sutherland Highlanders of Canada (Princess Louise's), Formerly 91st Regiment Canadian Highlanders, Canadian Militia, 1903-1928.* Hamilton, Ont.: R. Duncan, 1928. 99 pp.

Buchan, John, *see* Tweedsmuir, John Buchan, baron.

Buchan, Lawrence. *With the Infantry in South Africa; a Lecture Delivered at the Canadian Military Institute, 3rd February, 1902.* n.p.: n.d. 17 pp.

Bull, Wm. Perkins. *From Brock to Currie; the Military Development and Exploits of Canadians in General and of the Men of Peel in Particular, 1791-1930.* Toronto: G.J. McLeod, 1935. 772 pp.

Burnham, John Hampden. *Canadians in the Imperial Naval and Military Service Abroad.* Toronto: Williamson, 1891. 238 pp.

Butler, (Sir) W.F. *Sir William Butler; an Autobiography.* London: Constable, 1911. 476 pp.

The Cameron Highlanders of Ottawa; Standing Orders and Constitution and Rules of the Officers Mess. n.p.: [1934]. 88 pp.

Cameron, James M. *Pictonians in Arms; a Military History of Pictou County, Nova Scotia.* Fredericton, N.B.: privately printed, 1969. 301 pp.

Cameron, William Bleasdell. *The War Trail of Big Bear; being the Story of the Connection of Big Bear and Other Cree Indian Chiefs and their Followers with the Canadian North-West Rebellion of 1885, the Frog Lake Massacre and Events Leading up to and Following it and of Two Month's Imprisonment in the Camp of the Hostiles.* London: Duckworth, 1926. 256 pp.

Camp, A.D., comp. *7th Toronto Regiment, Royal Regiment of Canadian Artillery, 1866-1966.* n.p.: n.d. 33 pp.

Camp Stories; Hatley Squadron, 26th Stanstead Dragoons; Headquarters and Armoury, East Hatley, Que. n.p.: n.d. 16 pp.

Camp Valcartier, P.Q.; 1647 à 1957 en quelques lignes./Camp Valcartier P.Q.; a Short History, 1647-1957. s.l.: s.i./n.p.: 1957. 24 pp.
Texte bilingue./Bilingual text.

Campbell, Francis Wayland. *The Fenian Invasions of Canada of 1866 and 1870 and the Operations of the Montreal Militia Brigade in Connection Therewith; a Lecture Delivered before the Montreal Military Institute, April 23rd, 1898.* Montreal: J. Lovell, 1904. 55 pp.

Canada. Armée. Quartier général de l'Armée. Section historique. Introduction à l'étude de l'histoire militaire à l'intention des étudiants canadiens, [par C.P. Stacey]. Ottawa: [Imprimeur du Roi], 1951. 45 pp.
Editions subséquentes et révisées.

Canada. Armée. Régiment de la Chaudière. *Le Régiment de la Chaudière; notes historiques.* Québec, P.Q.: imprimé privé, 1955. 16 pp.

Canada. Army. Queen's Own Rifles of Canada. *Regimenal Catechism.* n.p.: n.d. 19 pp.

Canada. Army. Royal Canadian Army Service Corps. *RCASC Diamond Jubilee Year Book 1910-1961.* Ottawa: Queen's Printer, [1962]. 95 pp.

Canada. Army. Royal Winnipeg Rifles. *Seventy-fifth Anniversary, Royal Winnipeg Rifles, 1883-1958.* [Winnipeg: privately printed, 1958.] v.p.

*Canada. Army Headquarters. Historical Section. *Introduction to the Study of Military History for Canadian Students,* [by C. P. Stacey]. Ottawa: [King's Printer], 1951. 39 pp. *Many subsequent revised editions.*

_____. *The Regiments and Corps of the Canadian Army.* (The Canadian Army List, vol. 1.) Ottawa: Queen's Printer, 1964. 253 pp.

Canada. Commission to Inquire Into the Martineau Defalcation. *Report.* (Sessional Paper, no. 296.) Ottawa: King's Printer, 1903. 13 pp.

*Canada. Dept. of Militia and Defence. *Annual Report.* Ottawa: Queen's Printer, 1867-1922. *Title varies. Until 1883 was State of the Militia of the Dominion of Canada, with further variation in some years.*

_____. *Canadian Militia; Mobilization Regulations (Provisional), 1913.* Ottawa: King's Printer, 1912. 32 pp.

_____. *Cavalry Standing Orders.* Ottawa: Queen's Printer, 1884. v.p.

_____. *Cavalry Training, Canada, 1904.* Ottawa: King's Printer, 1904. 231 pp.

*_____. *Continuation of Appendix no. 4 to the Report of 18th May 1886, on Matters in Connection with the Suppression of the Rebellion in the North-West Territories, in 1885; Final Report of War Claims Commission.* (Sessional Paper, no. 9.) Ottawa: Queen's Printer, 1887. 80 pp.

_____. *The Department of Militia and Defence under the Honourable Sir Adolphe P. Caron, K.C.M.G.; and the Military Force of Canada.* Ottawa: Queen's Printer, 1887. 20 pp.

_____. *Dress Regulations for the Officers of the Canadian Militia.* Ottawa: King's Printer, 1907. 78 pp.

*_____. *Further Supplementary Report; Organization, Equipment, Despatch and Service of Canadian Contingents during the War in South Africa, 1899-1902.* (Sessional Paper, no. 35a.) Ottawa: King's Printer, 1903. 99 pp.

_____. *Guide for Paymasters of the Canadian Militia Consisting of the Financial Regulations (with the Exception of those of the Permanent Force) which have to do with the Canadian Militia, and a Few General Remarks on the Position of Paymaster and the Duties Pertaining Thereto,* by Edwyn R. Tooley. Ottawa: n.p., 1902. 31 pp.

Canada. Dept. of Militia and Defence. *Infantry Training, Canada, 1904.* Ottawa: King's Printer, 1904. 206 pp.

_____. *The King's Regulations and Orders for the Canadian Militia, 1910.* Ottawa: King's Printer, 1910. 378 pp.

_____. *The King's Regulations and Orders for the Militia of Canada, 1904.* Ottawa: King's Printer, 1904. 255 pp.

_____. *Manual for the Militia Artillery of Canada.* Quebec, P.Q.: Gunnery School Press, 1875-78. v.p.

_____. *Manual for Use by the Canadian Army Service Corps and Quartermasters of the Canadian Militia.* J. Lyons Biggar, comp. Ottawa: King's Printer, 1904. 98 pp.

_____. *Memorandum for Camps of Instruction.* Part 1: *Instructions for Training.* Ottawa: King's Printer, 1909?-28.
Title varies somewhat. Annual.

_____. *Memorandum Relating to Administration, Command and Staff for Camps of Training for the Canadian Militia, 1912.* Ottawa: King's Printer, 1912. 47 pp.

_____. *The Militia List.* Ottawa: Queen's Printer, 1867-1929.
Title and frequency vary, eg. — The Annual Volunteer and Service Militia List of Canada (1867); *The Quarterly Militia List of the Dominion of Canada* (1900).

_____. *Minutes of the Militia Council.* Ottawa: King's Printer, 1905-21. 23 vols.

_____. *Musketry Regulations for the Canadian Militia (Provisional).* Ottawa: King's Printer, 1904. 120 pp.

_____. *Pay and Allowance Regulations, 1912.* Ottawa: King's Printer, 1912. 107 pp.

_____. *Procedure in Regard to the Conduct of Business.* Ottawa: King's Printer, 1909. 14 pp.

_____. *Regimental Standing Orders of the Canadian Permanent Army Veterinary Corps and C.A.V.C.* Ottawa: King's Printer, 1912. 29 pp.

_____. *Regulations and Orders for the Active Militia, the Schools of Military Instruction, and the Reserve Militia (in the Cases therein Mentioned), of the Dominion of Canada./ Règlements et ordres pour la Milice active, les écoles d'instruction militaire et la Milice de réserve (dans les cas y mentionnés) de la Puissance du Canada.* Ottawa: Queen's Printer/Imprimeur de la Reine, 1870. 171 pp.
Bilingual text./Texte bilingue.

_____. *Regulations and Orders for the Militia of Canada, 1898.* Ottawa: Queen's Printer, 1898. 443 pp.

Canada. Dept. of Militia and Defence. *Regulations and Orders for the Militia of the Dominion of Canada.* Ottawa: Queen's Printer, 1879. 348 pp.

*_____. *Regulations and Orders for the Militia of the Dominion of Canada, 1st September, 1887.* Ottawa: Queen's Printer, 1887. 378 pp.
At head of title: Statutory Provisions.

_____. *Regulations and Orders for the Militia of the Dominion of Canada, 1883.* Ottawa: Queen's Printer, 1884. 318 pp.
At head of title: Statutory Provisions.

_____. *Regulations for Cadet Corps.* Ottawa: King's Printer, 1910. 19 pp.

_____. *Regulations for Canadian Ordnance Services (Part I).* Ottawa: King's Printer, 1908. 164 pp.

_____. *Regulations for Engineer Services, Canada, 1909.* Ottawa: King's Printer, 1908. 233 pp.

_____. *Regulations for Supply, Transport and Barrack Services for the Canadian Militia, 1909.* Ottawa: King's Printer, 1909. 75 pp.

_____. *Regulations for the Canadian Army Veterinary Service, 1912.* Ottawa: King's Printer, 1912. 49 pp.

_____. *Regulations for the Canadian Medical Service, 1910 (Approved by the Militia Council).* Ottawa: King's Printer, 1910. 66 pp.

_____. *Regulations for the Clothing of the Canadian Militia, 1909.* [Ottawa: King's Printer], 1909. 2 vols.

_____. *Regulations for the Corps of Guides, 1913.* Ottawa: King's Printer, 1913. 13 pp.

_____. *Regulations for the Equipment of the Canadian Militia.* Part 2, Section III: *Engineers Field Company; Permanent and Non-Permanent Units.* Ottawa: King's Printer, 1913. 19 pp.

_____. *Regulations for the Permanent Corps Active Militia.* Ottawa: Queen's Printer, 1889. 73 pp.

_____. *Regulations for the Permanent Corps, Active Militia, Canada, September 1886.* [Ottawa: Queen's Printer, 1886.] 37 pp.

_____. *Regulations for the Royal Military College of Canada, Kingston, Ontario (amended to 1st March, 1907).* Ottawa: King's Printer, 1907. 39 pp.

*Canada. Dept. of Militia and Defence. *Report of Lieutenant-Colonel W.H. Jackson, Deputy-Adjutant-General, Principal Supply, Pay and Transport Officer to the North-West Forces, and Chairman of War Claims Commission, on Matters in Connection with the Suppression of the Rebellion in the North-West Territories, in 1885.* (Sessional Paper, no. 9c.) Ottawa: Queen's Printer, 1887. 44 pp.

*_____. *Report of Major General Laurie, Commanding Bases and Lines of Communication, upon Matters in Connection with the Suppression of the Rebellion in the North-West Territories in 1885.* (Sessional Paper, no. 9d.) Ottawa: Queen's Printer, 1887. 39 pp.

_____. *Report of the Halifax Military Lands Board, 1915.* Ottawa: King's Printer, 1916. 171 pp.

*_____. *Report upon the Suppression of the Rebellion in the North-West Territories, and Matters in Connection Therewith, in 1885.* Ottawa: Queen's Printer, 1886. 384 pp.

_____. *Standing Orders of the Canadian Army Service Corps, 1910 (Published under the Authority of the Militia Council).* Ottawa: King's Printer, 1910. 44 pp.

_____. *Standing Orders of the Canadian Ordnance Corps, 1908.* Ottawa: King's Printer, 1908. 70 pp.

_____. *Standing Orders of the Canadian Permanent Army Service Corps (Approved by Militia Council) Published under, and Subject to the Conditions Laid Down in the K.R.&O. for the Militia, 1912.* Ottawa: King's Printer, 1912. 71 pp.

_____. *Standing Orders of the Royal Canadian Dragoons.* (Militia Book no. 2 (New Series).) Ottawa: King's Printer, 1907. 66 pp.

*_____. *Supplementary Report; Organization, Equipment, Despatch and Service of the Canadian Contingents during the War in South Africa, 1899-1900.* (Sessional Paper, no. 35a.) Ottawa: Queen's Printer, 1901. 192 pp.

*Canada. Dept. of Northern Affairs and National Resources. National Historic Sites Division. *Batoche National Historic Site.* Ottawa: Queen's Printer, 1960. 23 pp.

Canada. Dept. of the Secretary of State. *Correspondence Relating to the Fenian Invasion, and the Rebellion of the Southern States.* Ottawa: Queen's Printer, 1869. 176 pp.

Canada. Governor-General. *Fortifications and Defence, Arms &C; Laid before Parliament by Command of His Excellency the Governor-General.* Ottawa: Queen's Printer, [1869?] 15 pp.

Canada. Militia. Canadian Grenadier Guards. *Answers to Questions of the Day.* Montreal: Mortimer Press, [1916]. 15 pp.

Canada. Militia. Canadian Medical Service. *Manual of Establishments and Equipment.* Part I: *Peace.* Part II: *War; 1911 (Provisional).* n.p.: [1911?] 151 pp.

Canada. Militia. Queen's Own Rifles of Canada. *Officers.* n.p.: 1893. 1 vol., chiefly ports.

Canada. Militia Headquarters. *General Orders.* Ottawa: Queen's Printer, 1899-1946.
Superseded Militia General Orders. Frequency varies.

_____. *Militia General Orders.* Ottawa: Queen's Printer, 1867-99.
Frequency varies. Superseded by Militia Orders and General Orders.

_____. *Militia Orders.* Ottawa: Queen's Printer, 1899-1940.
Superseded Militia General Orders. Frequency varies.

*Canada. Ministère de la Milice et de la Défense. *Autre rapport supplémentaire; organisation, équipement, envoi et service de Contingents canadiens pendant la guerre sud-africaine, 1899-1902.* (Document de la session, no. 35a.) Ottawa: Imprimeur du Roi, 1903. 102 pp.

*_____. *Continuation de l'annexe no. 4 du rapport du 19 mai 1886 sur des matières relatives à la suppression de l'insurrection du Nord-Ouest en 1885; rapport final de la Commission des comptes de la guerre.* (Document de la session, no. 9b.) Ottawa: Imprimeur de la Reine, 1887. 80 pp.

*_____. *Rapport annuel.* Ottawa: Imprimeur de la Reine, 1867-1922.
Divergence du titre. Jusqu'à 1883 le titre était Rapport annuel sur l'état de la Milice de la Puissance du Canada; divers titres suivirent pendant quelques années.

*_____. *Rapport du Lieutenant-Colonel W.H. Jackson, aide adjudant-général, payeur et préposé-chef à l'approvisionnement et au transport des troupes expédiées au Nord-Ouest, et président de la commission des comptes de la guerre, sur les questions se rapportant à la répression de l'insurrection des territoires au Nord-Ouest en 1885.* (Document de la session, no. 9c.) Ottawa: Imprimeur de la Reine, 1887. 45 pp.

*_____. *Rapport du Major Général Laurie, commandant la base et les lignes de communication, sur des affaires relatives à la répression de l'insurrection soulevée dans les Territoires du Nord-Ouest.* (Document de la session, no. 9d.) Ottawa: Imprimeur de la Reine, 1887. 45 pp.

*Canada. Ministère de la Milice et de la Défense. *Rapport supplémentaire; organisation, équipement, envoi et service des contingents canadiens durant la guerre dans l'Afrique australe, 1899-1900.* (Document de la session, no. 35a.) Ottawa: Imprimeur de la Reine, 1901. 204 pp.

*_____. *Rapport sur la répression de l'insurrection dans les Territoires du Nord-Ouest, et autres choses s'y rattachant — 1885.* Ottawa: Imprimeur de la Reine, 1886. 126 pp.

*_____. *Règlements et ordonnances à l'usage de la Milice du Canada; 1er septembre 1887.* Ottawa: Imprimeur de la Reine, 1887. 387 pp.
En tête du titre: Dispositions statutaires.

_____. *Règles et règlements pour les écoles d'instruction militaire de la Puissance du Canada.* Ottawa: Imprimeur de la Reine, 1868. 15 pp.

*Canada. Ministère du nord canadien et des ressources nationales. Division des lieux historiques nationaux. *Lieu historique national de Batoche.* Ottawa: Imprimeur de la Reine, 1961. 24 pp.

*Canada. Parlement. *Collège militaire royal.* (Document de la session, no. 48, 48a.) Ottawa: Imprimeur de la Reine, 1900. 14 pp.

*_____. *Copies d'ordres en conseil, ordres généraux, nominations et ordres de la milice relatifs aux contingents et se rapportant à l'envoi de la force militaire coloniale dans le Sud-africain.* (Document de la session, no. 49.) Ottawa: Imprimeur de la Reine, 1900. 112 pp.

*_____. *Copies du décret en conseil nommant le major général comte de Dundonald commandant de la milice canadienne, 20 mai 1902, et du décret en conseil relevant le comte de Dundonald du commandement de la milice canadienne, 14 juin 1904, ainsi que de la correspondance et des autres documents s'y rattachant.* (Document de la session, no. 113, 113a.) Ottawa: Imprimeur du Roi, 1904. 42 pp.

*_____. [*Correspondance relative aux pensions et gratifications, rébellion Territoires du Nord-Ouest.*] (Document de la session, no. 80-80m.) Ottawa: Imprimeur de la Reine, 1886. 34 pp.

*_____. *Correspondance relative à l'envoi de contingents militaires coloniaux dans le Sud africain.* (Document de la session, no. 20, 20a.) Ottawa: Imprimeur de la Reine, 1900. 54 pp.

*_____. *Correspondance relative aux troubles qui ont lieu sur la ligne du Grand-Tronk sur 1er janvier 1877.* Ottawa: Imprimeur de la Reine, 1877. 53 pp.

*Canada. Parlement. *Déboursés faits sur le crédit de $2,300,000 ouvert pour couvrir dépenses et pertes occasionnées par les troubles du Nord-Ouest, du 1er juillet 1885 au 15 mars 1886; aussi, relevé supplémentaire pour les approvisionnements fournis par la Cie de la Baie d'Hudson, etc.* (Document de la session, no. 50.) Ottawa: Imprimeur de la Reine, 1886. 58 pp.

*_____. *Mémoire des Membres militaires du Conseil de la Milice au Ministre de la Milice et de la Défense; et aussi mémoire du Membre financier du dit Conseil concernant le budget de milice pour l'exercice 1905-1906.* (Document de la session, no. 130.) Ottawa: Imprimeur du Roi, 1905. 25 pp.

*_____. *Nominations au Ministère de la Milice.* (Documents parlementaire, no. 94.) Ottawa: Imprimeur du Roi, 1908. 51 pp.

*_____. *Rapport sur l'expédition de la Rivière rouge en 1870,* par S.J. Dawson. (Document de la session, no. 47.) Ottawa: Imprimeur de la Reine, 1871. 31 pp.

*_____. *Réponse à un ordre de la Chambre des Communes en date du 26 février 1900; copie de tous documents, de toute correspondance, etc., concernant le choix d'officiers de la Milice canadienne pour le cours d'instruction qui se donne actuellement à Kingston sur les devoirs d'état-major.* (Document de la session, no. 91.) Ottawa: Imprimeur de la Reine, 1900. 10 pp.

*_____. *Réponses à des adresses du Sénat et de la Chambre des Communes au sujet du retrait des troupes du Canada et de la défense du pays et rapport de l'honorable M. Campbell.* (Document de la session, no. 46.) Ottawa: Imprimeur de la Reine, 1871. 127 pp.

*Canada. Parliament. *Appointments to Militia Department.* (Sessional Paper, no. 94.) Ottawa: King's Printer, 1908. 51 pp.

*_____. *Copies of Orders in Council, General Orders, Appointments to Office and Militia Orders Affecting the Contingents, in Connection with the Despatch of the Colonial Military Force to South Africa.* (Sessional Paper, no. 49.) Ottawa: Queen's Printer, 1900. 107 pp.

*_____. *Copies of the Order in Council Appointing Major General, the Earl of Dundonald, to the Command of the Canadian Militia, 20th May, 1902, and the Order in Council Relieving from the Command of the Canadian Militia, 14th June, 1904, and also, Correspondence and Other Papers Connected Therewith.* (Sessional Paper, no. 113, 113a.) Ottawa: King's Printer, 1904. 41 pp.

*_____. [*Correspondence Concerning Militia Pensions and Medals in the Northwest Campaign.*] (Sessional Paper, no. 80-80m.) Ottawa: Queen's Printer, 1886. 34 pp.

*Canada. Parliament. *Correspondence Relating to the Despatch of Colonial Military Contingents to South Africa.* (Sessional Paper, no. 20, 20a.) Ottawa: Queen's Printer, 1900. 51 pp.

*_____. *Correspondence Respecting Disturbance on the Line of the Grand Trunk Railway, January 1st, 1877.* Ottawa: Queen's Printer, 1877. 53 pp.

*_____. *Expenditure Under Appropriation of $2,300,000 to Defray Expenses and Losses Arising Out of Troubles in the North-West Territories, from 1st July 1885, to 15th March, 1886; also Subsidiary Statement of Expenditure under Same Appropriation, &c., Hudson Bay Supplies, &c.* (Sessional Paper, no. 50.) Ottawa: Queen's Printer, 1886. 60 pp.

*_____. *Memorandum from the Military Members of the Militia Council to the Minister of Militia and Defence; and also Memorandum of the Finance Member of the Militia Council relating to the Militia Estimates for 1905-1906.* (Sessional Paper, no. 130.) Ottawa: King's Printer, 1905. 24 pp.

*_____. *Report on the Red River Expedition of 1870,* by S.J. Dawson. (Sessional Paper, no. 47.) Ottawa: Queen's Printer 1871. 31 pp.

_____. *Return to an Order of the House of Commons dated February 19, 1900, for Copies of all Correspondence, Telegrams, and Cablegrams that may have Passed between Major General Hutton and Lieutenant Colonel Samuel Hughes, M.P., or between these Officers and any Member of the Government of Canada or Others, Touching the Conduct of Lieutenant Colonel Hughes, M.P., in Connection with his Volunteering for Active Service in South Africa; these Papers to Include all Letters, Cablegrams and Telegrams Sent to South Africa, England or Elsewhere and Replies Received; also Any Report or Reports made by Major General Hutton on the Conduct of Lieut. Col. Hughes, M.P., in Connection with such Offer or Offers for Active Service.* (Sessional Paper, no. 77, 77a.) Ottawa: Queen's Printer, 1900. 32 pp.

*_____. *Return to an Order of the House of Commons, dated February 26, 1900, for a Return of All Papers and Correspondence etc., in Connection with the Selection of Officers of the Canadian Militia for the Course of Instruction in the Duties of General Staff now Being Carried out at Kingston.* (Sessional Paper, no. 91.) Ottawa: Queen's Printer, 1900. 10 pp.

*_____. *Returns to the Addresses of the Senate and House of Commons Relative to the Withdrawal of the Troops from the Dominion and on the Defence of the Country and Hon. Mr. Campbell's Report.* (Sessional paper, no. 46.) Ottawa: Queen's Printer, 1871. 127 pp.

*Canada. Parliament. *Royal Military College.* (Sessional Paper, no. 48, 48a.) Ottawa: Queen's Printer, 1894. 14 pp.

Canada in the Great World War; an Authentic Account of the Military History of Canada from the Earliest Days to the Close of the War of the Nations, by Various Authorities. Toronto: United Publishers, 1917-21. 6 vols.

The Canadian Artillerist; Journal of the Canadian Artillery Association. Vol. I. Kingston, Ont.: privately printed, 1905-06.

Canadian Artillery Association. *Annual Report.* n.p.: privately printed, 1876-   .
Not published 1940-46.

The Canadian Artillery Team at Shoeburyness, 1896; Extracts from the British Press. n.p.: n.d. 1 vol., unpaged.

Canadian Cavalry Association. *Proceedings.* n.p.: privately printed, 1913-   .
In 1943 became Canadian Armoured Association and in 1946 Royal Canadian Armoured Corps (Cavalry) Association. Title varies: also Annual Report *and* Information Digest and Annual Report.

The Canadian Fusiliers; City of London Regiment. n.p.: 1942. 12 pp.

Canadian Infantry Association. *Proceedings.* n.p.: privately printed, 1913-   .
Incorporated the Proceedings *of the Canadian Machine Gun Corps Association in 1936. Was the Infantry and Machine Gun Association of Canada, 1937-39. Not published 1940-45.*

Canadian Military Review./Revue militaire canadienne. Vol. I-II. Québec, P.Q.: privately printed/imprimé privé, 1880-81?

The Canadian Scottish Regiment. n.p.: n.d. 91 pp.

The Canadian United Service Magazine. Vol. I-IV? n.p.: privately printed 1894-98?
Title varies: Vols. I-II were titled The V.R.I. Magazine.

Canadians in Khaki; South Africa, 1899-1900; Nominal Rolls of the Officers, Non-Commissioned Officers & Men of the Canadian Contingent and Strathcona's Horse with Casualties to Date and also R.M.C. Graduates with the Army in South Africa. Montreal: Herald Pub. Co., 1900. 127 pp.

Capon, Alan R. *His Faults Lie Gently; the Incredible Sam Hughes.* Lindsay, Ont.: F.W. Hall, 1969. 159 pp.

Cavalry Standing Orders. Ottawa: printed by MacLean, Roger, 1887. 87 pp.

Cent ans d'histoire d'un régiment canadien-français; les Fusiliers Mont-Royal, 1869-1969. Montréal: Editions du Jour, 1971. 418 pp.

Centennial, 1863-1963; Presentation of Colours to the Princess of Wales' Own Regiment CA(M) by the Honourable W. Earle Rowe, P.C., Lieutenant-Governor of Ontario, Kingston, Ontario, Saturday 1st June 1963. [Kingston, Ont.: privately printed, 1963.] 15 pp.

Centennial Year, 1866-1966; 11th Field Artillery Regiment (M); 11th Field Artillery Regiment, Royal Regiment of Canadian Artillery, Canada's Oldest Artillery Regiment, Saturday, October 1, 1966. n.p.: n.d. 1 vol., unpaged.

Ceremony of Unveiling a Bronze Statue Erected on Major's Hill Park to the Memory of Ptes. Osgood and Rogers, of the Guards' Company Sharpshooters, who were Killed in the North West Rebellion in 1885. Ottawa: privately printed, 1889. 38 pp.

Chambers, Ernest J. *The Canadian Militia; a History of the Origin and Development of the Force.* Montreal: L.M. Fresco, 1907. 115 pp.

_____. *The Canadian Militia; and the Public Works Department; a History of the Origin and Development of the Force and Something about the Assistance Rendered by the Public Works Department.* Montreal: L.M. Fresco, 1907. 126 pp.

_____. *"The Duke of Cornwall's Own Rifles"; a Regimental History of the Forty-Third Regiment, Active Militia of Canada.* Ottawa: E.L. Ruddy, 1903. 82 pp.

_____. *The 5th Regiment Royal Scots of Canada Highlanders; a Regimental History.* Montreal: Guertin Print. Co., 1904. 90 pp.

_____. *The Governor-General's Body Guard; a History of the Origin, Development and Services of the Senior Cavalry Regiment in the Militia Service of the Dominion of Canada; with Some Information about the Martial Ancestry and Military Spirit of the Loyal Founders of Canada's Defensive Force.* Toronto: E.L. Ruddy, 1902. 168 pp.

_____. *Histoire du 65ème Régiment Carabiniers Mont-Royal.* Montréal: La Cie. d'Imprimerie Guertin, 1906. 151 pp.

_____. *The Montreal Highland Cadets; being a Record of the Organization and Development of a Useful and Interesting Corps.* Montreal: privately printed, 1901. 98 pp.

_____. *The 90th Regiment; Regimental History of the 90th Regiment Winnipeg Rifles.* n.p.: 1906. 99 pp.

Chambers, Ernest J. *The Origin and Services of The 3rd (Montreal) Field Battery of Artillery; with some Notes on the Artillery of By-Gone Days and a Brief History of the Development of Field Artillery.* Montreal: E.L. Ruddy, 1898. 84 pp.

_____. *The Origin and Services of the Prince of Wales Regiment; Including a Brief History of the Militia of French Canada and of the Canadian Militia Since Canada Became a British Colony; with an Account of the Different Actions in which they have Engaged, Including the North-West Rebellion of 1885.* Montreal: E.L. Ruddy, 1897. 99 pp.

_____. *The Queen's Own Rifles of Canada; a History of a Splendid Regiment's Origin, Development and Services, Including a Story of Patriotic Duties Well Performed in Three Campaigns.* Toronto: E.L. Ruddy, 1901. 156 pp.

_____. *The Royal Grenadiers; a Regimental History of the 10th Infantry Regiment of the Active Militia of Canada.* Toronto: E.L. Ruddy, 1904. 128 pp.

Champion, Thomas Edward. *History of the 10th Royals and of the Royal Grenadiers.* Toronto: Hunter, Rose, 1896. 279 pp.

[Chandler, C.M.] *The Militia in Durham County, 1812-1936; an Outline History of the Durham Regiment.* n.p.: privately printed, 1936. v.p.

50 ans d'activités avec le 6ᵉ Régiment d'artillerie, (Québec & Lévis), 1899-1949. Québec, P.Q.: Imprimerie Laflamme, 1949. 1 tome, non-paginé.

Clark, Lovell C. *The Guibord Affair.* (Canadian History through the Press.) Toronto: Holt, Rinehart & Winston, 1971. 126 pp.

Clint, H.C., comp. *A Short History of Artillery and of 57th Battery, R.C.A., 1855-1955; Formal Celebration and Reunion, Oct. 15th, 16th, 1955, Grande Allée Armouries, Quebec City.* Quebec, P.Q.: n.p., 1955. 48 pp.

Cochin, Louis. *Reminiscence of Louis Cochin, O.M.I.; a Veteran Missionary of the Cree Indians and a Prisoner in Poundmaker's Camp in 1885.* (Canadian North-West Historical Society Publications, vol. I, no. 2.) Battleford, Sask.: Star Pub. Co., 1927. 75 pp.

[Coffin, W.F.] *Thoughts on Defence; from a Canadian Point of View,* by a Canadian. Montreal: J. Lovell, 1870. 55 pp.

Le Corps de Santé royal canadien. Ottawa: Imprimeur de la Reine, 1954.. 11 pp.

The Corps of Royal Canadian Engineers. Ottawa: Queen's Printer, 1953. 21 pp.

The Corps of Royal Canadian Engineers; a Brief History. Ottawa: King's Printer, 1948. 56 pp.

Crook, E.D., and J.K. Marteinson, eds. *A Pictorial History of the 8th Canadian Hussars (Princess Louise's).* n.p.: privately printed, 1973. 343 pp.

Cross, Michael, and Robert Bothwell, eds. *Policy by Other Means; Essays in Honour of C.P. Stacey.* Toronto: Clarke, Irwin, 1972. 258 pp.

Cruikshank, E.A. *Camp Niagara; with a Historical Sketch of Niagara-on-the-Lake and Niagara Camp.* Niagara Falls, Ont.: F.H. Leslie, 1906. 1 vol., chiefly illus.

_____. *The Origin and Official History of the Thirteenth Battalion of Infantry; and a Description of the Work of the Early Militia of the Niagara Peninsula in the War of 1812 and the Rebellion of 1837.* Hamilton, Ont.: E.L. Ruddy, 1899. 88 pp.

Cunniffe, Dick. *Scarlet, Riflegreen and Khaki; the Military in Calgary.* Calgary: Century Calgary Publications, 1975. 40 pp.

Cunningham-Dunlop, C.J.A. *Mobility of the Modern Army; the Practical Use of Gig Infantry.* n.p.: n.d. 11 pp.

Curchin, Leonard A., and Brian D. Sim. *The Elgins; the Story of the Elgin Regt. (RCAC) and its Predecessors.* St. Thomas, Ont.: privately printed, 1977. 150 pp.

Cuthbertson-Muir, R. Major. *The Early Political and Military History of Burford.* Quebec, P.Q.: La Cie. d'imprimerie commerciale, 1913. 371 pp.

Daoust, Charles R. *Cent-vingt jours de service actif; récit historique très complet de la campagne du 65ème au Nord-Ouest.* Montréal: E. Sénécal, 1886. 242 pp.

Davidson, William McCartney. *The Life and Times of Louis Riel.* Calgary: Albertan Printers, [1952]. 114 pp.

_____. *Louis Riel, 1844-1885; a Biography.* Calgary: Albertan Pub. Co., 1955. 214 pp.

Davin, Nicholas Flood. *Strathcona Horse; Speech at Lansdowne Park, March 7th, A.D. 1900, on the Occasion of the First Parade of the Strathcona Horse when a Flag from the Town of Sudbury was Presented by Her Excellency the Countess of Minto.* Ottawa: J. Hope, 1900. 20 pp.

Davis, [Robert H.] *The Canadian Militia! Its Organization and Present Condition.* Caledonia, Ont.: T. Sawle, 1873. 16 pp.

Dawson, S.J., *see* Canada. Parliament. *Report on the Red River Expedition . . . .*

Dawson, S.J., *voir* Canada. Parlement. *Rapport sur l'expédition de la Rivière rouge . . . .*

De Malijay, Paul. *Le Colonel d'Orsonnens; considérations sur l'organisation militaire de la Confédération canadienne; observations critiques.* Montréal: Les Presses à vapeur du Franc-Parleur, 1874. 58 pp.

Denison, Frederick C. *Historical Record of the Governor-General's Body Guard and its Standing Orders.* Toronto: Hunter, Rose, 1876. 87 pp.

Denison, George T. *Soldiering in Canada; Recollections and Experiences.* Toronto: G.N. Morang, 1900. 364 pp.

[Denison, George T., comp.] *Reminiscences of the Red River Rebellion of 1869.* n.p.: n.d. 45 pp.

Denison, S.A. *Memoirs.* Toronto: T.H. Best Print. Co., 1927. 174 pp.

Desjardins, L.G. *Précis historique du 17ième batallion d'infanterie de Lévis, depuis sa formation en 1862 jusqu'à 1872, suivi des ordres permanents du même corps.* Lévis, P.Q.: Les Presses à Vapeur de "l'Echo de Lévis", 1872. 89 pp.

De Trémaudan, Auguste-Henri. *Histoire de la nation métisse dans l'ouest canadien.* Montréal: Editions A. Lévesque, 1935. 448 pp.

Dixon, F.E., comp. *The Volunteer's Active Service Manual; or, Internal Economy and Standing Orders for Volunteers when on Active Service with Bugle Calls and Forms of all Reports, Returns &c Necessary for the Government of a Volunteer Battalion and Shewing the Everyday Duties of the Various Grades of Rank and Command.* Toronto: G.M. Adam, 1867. 131 pp.

*The Dominion Arsenal at Quebec, 1880-1945. Quebec, P.Q.: n.p., 1947. 131 pp.

Dornbusch, C.E., comp. *The Canadian Army, 1855-1958; Regimental Histories and a Guide to the Regiments.* Cornwallville, N.Y.: Hope Farm Press, 1959. 216 pp.

_____. *The Canadian Army, 1855-1955; Regimental Histories and a Guide to the Regiments.* Cornwallville, N.Y.: n.p., 1957. 162 1.

_____. *The Canadian Army, 1855-1965; Lineages; Regimental Histories.* Cornwallville, N.Y.: Hope Farm Press, 1966. 179 pp.

_____. *Lineages of the Canadian Army, 1855-1961; Armour, Cavalry, Infantry.* Cornwallville, N.Y.: Hope Farm Press, 1961. 1 vol., unpaged.

D'Orsonnens, L.G. d'Odet. *Considérations sur l'organisation militaire de la Confédération canadienne.* Montréal: Typographie Duvernay, 1874. 70 pp.

Doward, Norman R. *The Queen's Own Rifles of Canada Buglers; Historical, Patriotic, Illustrated; Patriotic Souvenir.* Toronto: privately printed, 1915. 52 pp.

Drolet, Gustave A. *Zouaviana; étape de vingt-cinq ans, 1868-1893; lettres de Rome, souvenirs de voyage, études, etc.* Montréal: E. Sénécal, 1893. 460 pp.

Duguid, Archer Fortescue. *History of the Canadian Grenadier Guards, 1760-1964.* Montreal: Gazette Print. Co., 1965. 520 pp.

Dundonald, Douglas Mackinnon Baillie Hamilton Cochrane, 12th earl. *My Army Life.* London: E. Arnold, 1926. 342 pp.

Dunlevie, Horace G., comp. *Our Volunteers in the North-West; a Ready Reference Handbook.* Ottawa: Daily Free Press, 1885. 52 pp.

Egan, Thomas J. *History of the Halifax Volunteer Battalion and Volunteer Companies, 1859-1887.* Halifax: A. & W. Mackinlay, 1888. 182 pp.

Evans, W. Sanford. *The Canadian Contingents and Canadian Imperialism; a Story and a Study.* Toronto: Publishers' Syndicate, 1901. 352 pp.

Extracts from General Orders for the Guidance of Troops in Affording Aid to the Civil Power. Quebec, P.Q.: Daily Evening Mercury Office, 1868. 23 pp.

The Fenian Raid of 1870, by Reporters Present at the Scenes. Montreal: Witness Print. House, 1870. 73 pp.

Fetherstonhaugh, R.C. *A Short History of the Royal Canadian Dragoons.* Toronto: Southam Press, 1932. 52 pp.

Fetherstonhaugh, R.C., and G.R. Stevens. *The Royal Canadian Regiment.* Vol. I: Montreal: Gazette Print. Co., 1936. Vol. II: London, Ont.: privately printed, 1967. 2 vols.

A Few Practical Hints to the Officers . . . see Attwood, Peter Hinds.

A Few Words on Canada, by a Canadian. Ottawa: Hunter, Rose, 1871. 72 pp.

Fifth Military Tournament; to be Held in Conjunction with the Ninth Canadian Horse Show, Armouries, Toronto, Wednesday, Thursday, Friday, Saturday, April 29 and 30, May 1 and 2, 1903. n.p.: [1903]. 20 pp.

Fletcher, [Henry Charles]. *A Lecture Delivered at the Literary and Scientific Institute, Ottawa, by Col. Fletcher, Scots Fusilier Guards, Military Secretary, February, 1875.* Ottawa: n.p., n.d. 19 pp.

_____. *Memorandum on the Militia System of Canada.* Ottawa: Citizen Print. Co., 1873. 20 pp.

Flick, C.L. *A Short History of the 31st British Columbia Horse.* Victoria, B.C.: J.P. Buckle, 1922. 40 pp.

Fraser, Alexander. *The 48th Highlanders of Toronto; Canadian Militia; the Origin and History of this Regiment, and a Short History of the Highland Regiments from Time to Time Stationed in Canada.* Toronto: E.L. Ruddy, 1900. 128 pp.

Fraser, W.B. *Always a Strathcona.* Calgary: Comprint Pub. Co., 1976. 252 pp.

French, John Denton Pinkstone French, 1st earl of Ypres. *Report by General Sir John French, G.C.B., G.C.V.O., K.C.M.G., Inspector General of the Imperial Forces, upon his Inspection of the Canadian Military Forces.* (Sessional Paper, no. 35a.) Ottawa: King's Printer, 1910. 38 pp.

From Toronto to Fort Garry see Griffin, Justin A.

Gagan, David. *The Denison Family of Toronto, 1792-1925.* (Canadian Biographical Studies.) Toronto: Univ. of Toronto Press, 1973. 113 pp.

General Middleton's Defence see Middleton, (Sir) Fred.

*Le Génie royal canadien. Ottawa: Imprimeur de la Reine, 1954. 23 pp.

Goodspeed, D.J. *Battle Royal; a History of the Royal Regiment of Canada, 1862-1962.* Toronto: privately printed, 1962. 703 pp.

Governor General's Foot Guards, Ottawa; Seventy-Fifth Anniversary, June 8, 1872-1947. Ottawa: privately printed, 1947. 43 pp.

[Gowanlock, Theresa.] *Two Months in the Camp of Big Bear; the Life and Adventures of Theresa Gowanlock and Theresa Delaney.* Parkdale, Ont.: Times Office, 1885. 141 pp.

Granatstein, J.L., and R.D. Cuff, eds. *War and Society in North America.* Toronto: T. Nelson, 1971. 199 pp.

Gravel, Jean-Yves. *L'armée du Québec; un portrait social, 1868-1900.* Montréal: Les Editions du Boréal Express, 1974. 157 pp.

[Gt. Brit. Colonial Defence Committee Canada.] *Halifax Defence Scheme.* London: H.M. Stationery Office, 1904?-12? *Amended annually.*

Gt. Brit. Parliament. *Correspondence Relative to the Recent Expedition to the Red River Settlement; with Journal of Operations.* (Command Paper C298.) London: H.M. Stationery Office, 1871. 93 pp.

Gt. Brit. War Office. *Canadian Militia War Establishments (Provisional), 1912.* London: H.M. Stationery Office, 1911. 87 pp.

_____. *Regulations for the Clothing of the Canadian Militia (Permanent Units), Part I, 1909.* London: H.M. Stationery Office, 1909. 102 pp.

_____. *Regulations for the Equipment of the Canadian Militia.* London: H.M. Stationery Office, 1909. 38 pp.

Gt. Brit. War Office. General Staff. *Handbook of the Land Forces of British Dominions, Colonies and Protectorates (Other than India).* Part I: *The Dominion of Canada.* London: H.M. Stationery Office, 1908. 264 pp.

Greenhous, Brereton. *Semper Paratus; the History of the Royal Hamilton Light Infantry (Wentworth Regiment), 1862-1977,* by Kingsley Brown, Senior, Kingsley Brown, Junior, and Brereton Greenhous. Revised and edited by Brereton Greenhous. Hamilton, Ont.: privately printed, 1977. 446 pp.

Griesbach, W.A. *I Remember.* Toronto: Ryerson Press, 1946. 353 pp.

Griffin, Frederick. *Major-General Sir Henry Mill Pellatt, CVO, DCL, VD; a Gentleman of Toronto, 1859-1939.* Toronto: Ontario Pub. Co., 1939. 30 pp.

[Griffin, Justin A.] *From Toronto to Fort Garry; an Account of the Second Expedition to Red River; Diary of a Private Soldier.* Hamilton, Ont.: Evening Times, n.d. 64 pp.

Hamilton, Fred J. *The New Declaration; a Record of the Reception of the Sixth Fusiliers of Montreal, by the Citizens of St. Albans, Vt, July 4th, 1878; being the First Occasion on which British Armed Troops have Participated in the Declaration of American Independence.* Montreal: Dawson Bros., 1878. 53 pp.

Hamilton, (Sir) Ian. *Report on the Military Institutions of Canada.* Ottawa: King's Printer, 1913. 43 pp.

Hardy, René, *voir Les Zouaves pontificaux canadiens.*

Harker, Douglas E. *The Dukes; the Story of the Men who have Served in Peace and War with the British Columbia Regiment (D.C.O.), 1883-1973.* n.p.: privately printed, 1974. 438 pp.

Harman, S. Bruce. *'Twas 26 Years Ago; Narrative of the Red River Expedition, 1870.* Toronto: Toronto Mail and Empire, 1896. 31 pp.

Hart-McHarg, William. *From Quebec to Pretoria with the Royal Canadian Regiment.* Toronto: W. Briggs, 1902. 276 pp.

History of the Second Battalion, the "Queen's Own Rifles" of Toronto. n.p.: [189-?]. 1 vol., chiefly ports.

Hitsman, J. MacKay. *Safeguarding Canada, 1763-1871.* Toronto: Univ. of Toronto Press, 1968. 240 pp.

Holmes, J.G. *Dominion Artillery Association Prize Essay; on the Proportions of Artillery (Field, Siege and Garrison) Required for the Present Force of Active Militia of the Dominion, with Suggestions as to their Organization, Equipment and Localization.* Quebec, P.Q.: privately printed, 1878. 47 pp.

Houghton, C.F. *Houghton to Middleton; the Colonel with Vigor Replies to the General; Long but Interesting; Interesting Incidents of the Campaign of '85; Grave Charge Explained; Sir Fred. Middleton's Conduct towards his Second in Command as Seen by the Latter.* n.p.: 1894. 14 pp.

How, Douglas. *The 8th Hussars; a History of the Regiment.* Sussex, N.B.: Maritime Pub., 1964. 446 pp.

"How Not to Do It"; a Short Sermon on the Canadian Militia, by "Bluenose" [*pseud.*]. Quebec, P.Q.: Morning Chronicle, 1881. 29 pp.

Howard, Joseph Kinsey. *Strange Empire; a Narrative of the Northwest.* New York: Morrow, 1952. 601 pp.

Hubbell, E.L. *The Winnipeg Grenadiers.* n.p.: n.d. 16 pp.

Hubly, Russell C. *"G" Company, or Every-day Life of the R.C.R.; being a Descriptive Account of Typical Events in the Life of the First Canadian Contingent in South Africa.* St. John, N.B.: J. & A. McMillan, 1901. 109 pp.

Hughes, Stuart, ed. *The Frog Lake "Massacre"; Personal Perspectives on Ethnic Conflict.* (The Carleton Library, no. 97.) Toronto: McClelland and Stewart, 1976. 364 pp.

Hunter, A.T. *History of the 12th Regiment, York Rangers; with Some Account of the Different Raisings of Militia in the County of York, Ontario.* Toronto: Murray Print. Co., 1912. 90 pp.

Hutchison, Paul P. *A Short History of the Royal Highland Regiment the Black Watch, 1725-1948.* n.p.: 1948. 39 pp.

_____. *Canada's Black Watch; the First Hundred Years, 1862-1962.* Montreal: privately printed, [1962]. 340 pp.

Huyshe, G.L. *The Red River Expedition.* London: Macmillan, 1871. 276 pp.

Illustrated Historical Album of the 2nd Battalion, the Queen's Own Rifles of Canada, 1856-1894. Toronto: Toronto News Co., 1894. 80 pp.

The Illustrated War News; nos. 1 to 18 Inclusive; Containing All the Illustrations Referring to the North-West Rebellion of 1885, from its Outbreak to the Return and Disbanding of the Troops. Toronto: Grip, 1885. 152 pp.

L'Insurrection du Nord-Ouest, 1885. [Montréal]: Le Monde, s.d. 39 pp.

*L'Intendance royale canadienne. Ottawa: Imprimeur de la Reine, 1954. 12 pp.

Irvine, [M. Bell]. *Report on the Red River Expedition of 1870.* (Command Paper, C391.) London: H.M. Stationery Office, 1871. 16 pp.

Jackson, H.M. *Canadian Prime Ministers and the Canadian Militia.* n.p.: 1958. 11 pp.

_____. *The Princess Louise Dragoon Guards; a History.* n.p.: 1952. 306 pp.

_____. *The Roll of the Regiments (the Active Militia).* Ottawa: n.p., 1959. 176 pp.

_____. *The Roll of the Regiments (the Sedentary Militia).* n.p.: 1960. 100 pp.

_____. *The Royal Regiment of Artillery, Ottawa, 1855-1952; a History.* Montreal: privately printed, 1952. 418 pp.

_____. *The Sherbrooke Regiment (12th Armoured Regiment).* n.p.: 1958. 229 pp.

Jackson, Louis. *Our Caughnawagas in Egypt; a Narrative of What was Seen and Accomplished by the Contingent of North American Indian Voyageurs who Led the British Boat Expedition for the Relief of Khartoum up the Cataracts of the Nile.* Montreal: W.M. Drysdale, 1885. 35 pp.

Jamieson, F.C., ed. *The Alberta Field Force of 1885.* (Canadian North-West Historical Society Publications, vol. I, no. 7.) Battleford, Sask.: n.p., 1931. 53 pp.

Johnston, Stafford. *The Fighting Perths; the Story of the First Century in the Life of a Canadian County Regiment.* Stratford, Ont.: privately printed, 1964. 133 pp.

Kennedy, H.G., ed. *History of the 101st Regiment Edmonton Fusiliers; Allied with the Royal Munster Fusiliers, 1908-1913.* n.p.: Pierce & Kennedy, [1913]. 1 vol., unpaged.

Kennedy, Howard Angus. *The North-West Rebellion.* (The Ryerson Canadian History Readers.) Toronto: Ryerson Press, 1929. 32 pp.

Kerry, A.J., and W.A. McDill. *The History of the Corps of Royal Canadian Engineers.* Ottawa: privately printed, 1962. 2 vols.

King, Horatio C. *An Account of the Visit of the Thirteenth Regiment N.G.S.N.Y. to Montreal, Canada, May, 1879.* Brooklyn, N.Y.: privately printed, 1879. 68 pp.

King, W.D., comp. *A Brief History of Militia Units Established at Various Periods at Yarmouth, Nova Scotia, 1812-1947.* Yarmouth, N.S.: privately printed, 1947. 32 pp.

Kreutzweiser, Erwin E. *The Red River Insurrection; Its Causes and Events.* Gardenvale, P.Q.: Garden City Press, [1936]. 166 pp.

Labat, Gaston P. *Le Livre d'or (The Golden Book) of the Canadian Contingents in South Africa; with an Appendix on Canadian Loyalty, Containing Letters, Documents, Photographs.* Montreal: n.p., 1901. v.p.

_____. *Les voyageurs canadiens à l'expédition du Soudan; ou, quatre-vingt-dix jours avec les crocodiles.* Québec, P.Q.: L.J. Demers, 1886. 214 pp.

Lachance, François. *Prise de Rome; odyssée des Zouaves canadiens de Rome à Québec.* Québec, P.Q.: Léger Brousseau, 1870. 47 pp.

Laidlaw, Alexr. *From the St. Lawrence to the North Saskatchewan; being Some Incidents Connected with the Detachment of "A" Battery, Regt. Canadian Artillery, who Composed Part of the North West Field Force in the Rebellion of 1885.* Halifax, N.S.: n.p., 1885. 43 pp.

Lake, (Sir) P.H.N. *Memorandum by Major General P.H.N. Lake, C.B., C.M.G., Inspector General, upon that Portion of the Report of the Civil Service Commissioners, 1908, Which Deals with the Administration of the Militia.* Ottawa: King's Printer, 1908. 23 pp.

_____. *Report upon the Best Method of Giving Effect to the Recommendations of General Sir John French, Regarding the Canadian Militia.* (Sessional Paper, no. 35b.) Ottawa: King's Printer, 1910. 16 pp.

Lamontagne, Léopold. *Les archives régimentaires des Fusiliers du S.-Laurent.* Rimouski, P.Q.: s.i., 1943. 247 pp.

Laurie, R.C. *Reminiscences of Early Days in Battleford and with Middleton's Column.* Battleford, Sask.: privately printed, 1935. 140 pp.

Lavoie, Joseph A. *Le Régiment de Montmagny de 1869 à 1931.* s.l.: s.i., [1932]. 117 pp.

Le Caron, Henri, *see* Beach, Thomas Miller.

Leonard, R.W. *Gig Infantry.* St. Catharines, Ont.: n.p., 1908. 16 pp.

Lodolini, Ello, *voir Les Zouaves pontificaux canadiens.*

The Log; Containing an Account of the 7th Fusiliers' Trip from London, Ont., to Clark's Crossing, N.W.T.; also, the Official Reports of the Officers in Charge of Boats. London, Ont.: Free Press Print. Co., 1888. 47 pp.

Lord Dundonald; les motifs de sa révocation. s.l.: s.i., [1904?]. 16 pp.

Lord Dundonald; Orders in Council and Correspondence Showing Why he was Removed from Office; Attacked Canada's Government in Defiance of Military Regulations. (Political Pointers, no. 5.) n.p.: [1904]. 72 pp.

The Lorne Scots (Peel, Dufferin and Halton Regiment). Brampton, Ont.: privately printed, 1962. 47 pp.

Lyons, Herbert H. *6th Regiment, the Duke of Connaught's Own Rifles; Souvenir Edition.* Vancouver: privately printed, 1907. 1 vol., unpaged.

McAvity, J.M. *Lord Strathcona's Horse (Royal Canadians); a Record of Achievement.* Toronto: n.p., 1947. 280 pp.

McCormick, A.S. *The "Royal Canadians" in South Africa, 1899-1902.* n.p.: n.d. 13 pp.

McCourt, Edward. *Buckskin Brigadier; the Story of the Alberta Field Force.* Toronto: Macmillan, 1955. 150 pp.

_____. *Revolt in the West; the Story of the Riel Rebellion.* (Great Stories of Canada.) Toronto: Macmillan, 1958. 159 pp.

MacDermot, H.E. *Sir Thomas Roddick; his Work in Medicine and Public Life.* Toronto: Macmillan, 1938. 160 pp.

Macdonald, John A. *Troublous Times in Canada; a History of the Fenian Raids of 1866 and 1870.* Toronto: W.S. Johnston, 1910. 255 pp.

McGee, Robert. *The Fenian Raids on the Huntingdon Frontier 1866 and 1870; Centennial Issue.* n.p.: [1967]. 66 pp.

McGregor, F., ed. *LdSH (RC) '85-70'.* Winnipeg: privately printed, 1970. 62 pp.

McKee, Sandra Lynn, ed. *Gabriel Dumont; Indian Fighter.* (Frontier Books, no. 14.) [Calgary: Frontiers Unlimited, n.d.] 51 pp.

McKenzie, Thomas. *My Life as a Soldier.* St. John, N.B.: J. & A. McMillan, 1898. 202 pp.

Mackenzie-Naughton, J.D. *The Princess of Wales' Own Regiment (M.G.).* Kingston, Ont.: privately printed, 1946. 74 pp.

MacKinnon, Hedley V. *War Sketches; Reminiscences of the Boer War in South Africa, 1899-1900.* Charlottetown, P.E.I.: Examiner, 1900. 73 pp.

MacLaren, Roy. *Canadians on the Nile, 1882-1898; being the Adventures of the Voyageurs on the Khartoum Relief Expedition and Other Exploits.* Vancouver: Univ. of British Columbia Press, 1978. 184 pp.

MacLeod, [Elizabeth]. *For the Flag; or, Lays and Incidents of the South African War.* Charlottetown, P.E.I.: A. Irwin, 1901. 185 pp.

McMicken, Gilbert. *The Abortive Fenian Raid on Manitoba; Account by One who Knew its Secret History; a Paper Read before the Society May 11, 1888.* (Historical and Scientific Society of Manitoba Transactions, no. 32.) Winnipeg: Manitoba Free Press, 1888. 11 pp.

MacNachtan, Neil F., comp. *Guide for Duties of the Canadian Field Artillery.* Coburg, Ont.: n.p., 1904. 60 pp.

MacPherson, Pennington. *A Catechism on Military Law as Applicable to the Militia of Canada, Consisting of Questions and Answers on the Militia Act, 1883; Rules and Regulations for the Militia, 1883; The Army Act, 1881; Rules of Procedure, 1881; Queen's Regulations, 1883; Together with a Compilation of the Principal Points of the Law of Evidence.* Montreal: J. Lovell, 1886. 191 pp.

MacShane, J.R. *The Dominion Militia; Past and Present.* Halifax: J. Bowes, 1896. 40 pp.

Major, J.C. *The Red River Expedition.* Winnipeg: privately printed, 1870. 28 pp.

Manarey, R. Barrie. *The Canadian Bayonet.* Edmonton: Century Press, 1971. 51 pp.

Marraro, Howard R. *Canadian and American Zouaves in the Papal Army, 1868-1870.* n.p.: 1945. 22 pp.

Marquis, G.E. *Le Régiment de Lévis; historique et album.* Lévis, P.Q.: s.i., 1952. 292 pp.

Marquis T.G. *Canada's Sons on Kopje and Veldt; a Historical Account of the Canadian Contingents Based on the Official Despatches of Lieutenant-Colonel W.D. Otter and the Other Commanding Officers at the Front; on the Letters and Despatches of Such War Correspondents as C. Frederick Hamilton, S.C. Simonski, Stanley McKeown Brown, John Evans and W. Richmond Smith.* Toronto: The Canada's Sons Pub. Co., 1900. 490 pp.

Mazéas, Daniel. *Insignes armée canadienne, 1900-1914; Canadian Badges; supplément, 1920-1950.* Guincamp, France: privately printed, 1972. 116 pp.

Mellish, Annie Elizabeth. *Our Boys under Fire; or, Maritime Volunteers in South Africa.* Charlottetown, P.E.I.: privately printed, 1900. 120 pp.

Melrose, Wm. *The Stanstead Cavalry; History, Opportunities and Possibilities; Dedicated to the Young Men of Stanstead County and Those who Serve in the 26th Stanstead Dragoons.* [Hartford, Conn.: Plimpton Press], 1914. 52 pp.

Merritt, Wm. Hamilton. *Regimental Standing Orders of the Governor-General's Body Guard; with Prefatory Historical Summary and Lists of Officers and Sergeant-Majors.* Toronto: Hunter, Rose, 1910. 170 pp.

Middleton, (Sir) Fred. *General Middleton's Defence; as Contained in his Parting Address to the People of Canada.* Toronto: Evening Telegram, 1890. 14 pp.

_____. *Suppression of the Rebellion in the North West Territories of Canada, 1885.* G.H. Needler, ed. (University of Toronto Studies; History and Economics Series, vol. XI.) Toronto: Univ. of Toronto Press, 1948. 80 pp.

Mika, Nick, and Helma Mika, comps. *The Riel Rebellion, 1885.* Belleville, Ont.: Mika Silk Screening, [1972]. 354 pp.

The Militia in Durham County . . . see Chandler, C.M.

The Militia of Canada; from Letters to the Saturday's Special Military Column of the Empire upon Military Organization, by "The Odd File" [*pseud.*]. Toronto: Hunter, Rose, 1892. 24 pp.

Miller, Carman. *Canada and the Boer War./Le Canada et la guerre des Boers.* Ottawa: National Film Board of Canada/Office national du film du Canada, [1970]. 18 pp.
Bilingual text./Texte bilingue.

La Minerve, Montréal, P.Q. *Sir Adolphe Caron, G.C.M.G., Ministre de la Milice et ses détracteurs; ou huit années d'administration militaire.* Montréal: Cie. d'imprimerie et lithographie Gelhardt-Berthiaume, 1888. 34 pp.

Missisquoi County Historical Society. *The Fenian Raids 1866-1870; Missisquoi County.* Stanbridge East, P.Q.: privately printed, 1967. 88 pp.

Moir, J.S., ed. *History of the Royal Canadian Corps of Signals, 1903-1961.* Ottawa: privately printed, 1962. 336 pp.

Montizambert, C.E. *Dominion Artillery Association Prize Essay; on the Supply, Care and Repair of Artillery Materiel, Including Small Arms and Ammunition for Canadian Militia.* Quebec, P.Q.: Gunnery School Press, 1877. 38 pp.

Moogk, Peter N., and R.V. Stevenson. *Vancouver Defended; a History of the Men and Guns of the Lower Mainland Defences, 1859-1949.* Surrey, B.C.: Antonson Pub., 1978. 128 pp.

Moore, Alexander Huggins, comp. *Sketch of the XIII Battalion A.M. with a Statistical Record of the Officers.* Hamilton, Ont.: R. Raw, 1875. 60 pp.

Morice, A.G. *A Critical History of the Red River Insurrection, after Official Documents and non-Catholic Sources.* Winnipeg: Canadian Publishers, 1935. 375 pp.

Morrison, E.W.B. *With the Guns in South Africa.* Hamilton, Ont.: Spectator Print. Co., 1901. 307 pp.

Morton, Desmond. *The Canadian General, Sir William Otter.* (Canadian War Museum Historical Publication Number 9.) Toronto: Hakkert, 1974. 423 pp.

_____. *The Last War Drum; the North West Campaign of 1885.* (Canadian War Museum Publication, Number 5.) Toronto: Hakkert, 1972. 193 pp.

_____. *Ministers and Generals; Politics and the Canadian Militia, 1868-1904.* Toronto: Univ. of Toronto Press, 1970. 257 pp.

Morton, Desmond, and Reginald H. Roy, eds. *Telegrams of the North-West Campaign.* (Publications of the Champlain Society, XLVII.) Toronto: Champlain Society, 1972. 431 pp.

Mulvaney, Charles Pelham. *The History of the North-West Rebellion of 1885; Comprising a Full and Impartial Account of the Origin and Progress of the War, of the Various Engagements with the Indians and Half-Breeds, of the Heroic Deeds Performed by Officers and Men, and of Touching Scenes in the Field, the Camp and the Cabin; Including a History of the Indian Tribes of North-Western Canada, their Numbers, Modes of Living, Habits, Customs, Religious Rites and Ceremonies, with Thrilling Narratives of Captures, Imprisonments, Massacres and Hair-Breadth Escapes of White Settlers, etc.* Toronto: A.H. Hovey, 1885. 424 pp.

My Campaign at Niagara; being a very Veracious Account of Camp-Life and its Vicissitudes; and the Experiences, Triumphs, Trials and Sorrows of a Canadian Volunteer, by T.W. Toronto: "Pure Gold" Print. Establishment, [1871]. 95 pp.

Needler, G.H. *Louis Riel; the Rebellion of 1885.* Toronto: Burns & MacEachern, 1957. 81 pp.

Nelson, H.S. *Four Months under Arms; a Reminiscence of Events Prior to, and During, the Second Riel Rebellion.* Nelson, B.C.: Nelson Daily News, n.d. 20 pp.

Nicholson, G.W.L. *Canada's Nursing Sisters.* (Canadian War Museum Historical Publication Number 13.) Toronto: S. Stevens, Hakkert, 1975. 272 pp.

_____. *The Fighting Newfoundlanders; a History of the Royal Newfoundland Regiment.* St. John's, Nfld.: Govt. of Nfld., 1964. 614 pp.

_____. *The Gunners of Canada; the History of the Royal Regiment of Canadian Artillery.* Toronto: McClelland and Stewart, 1967-72. 2 vols.

_____. *Seventy Years of Service; a History of the Royal Canadian Army Medical Corps.* Ottawa: Borealis Press, 1977. 388 pp.

Nos Croisés; ou, histoire anecdotique de l'expédition des volontaires canadiens à Rome pour la défense de l'Eglise. Montréal: Fabre et Gravel, 1871. 338 pp.

Observations on the Armed Strength of Canada. n.p.: n.d. 12 pp.

"The Odd File" [*pseud.*] *see The Militia of Canada.*

The Officers Association of the Militia of Canada. [*Semi-Annual Meeting.* No. 1-2. Ottawa: n.p., 1898-99.]

Official Souvenir Programme; Queen's Own Rifles Semi-Centennial Reunion, Toronto, June 18th to 25th, 1910. Toronto: n.p., [1910]. 39 pp.

Once in the Queen's Own, Always in the Queen's Own. n.p.: privately printed, 1932. 70 pp.

[O'Neill, John.] *Official Report of Gen. John O'Neill, President of the Fenian Brotherhood; on the Attempt to Invade Canada, May 25th, 1870; the Preparations therefore, and the Cause of its Failure with a Sketch of his Connection with the Organization and the Motives which Led him to Join It; also a Report of the Battle of Ridgeway, Canada West, Fought June 2nd, 1866, by Colonel Booker, Commanding the Queen's Own, and other Canadian Troops, and Colonel John O'Neill, Commanding the Fenians.* New York: J.J. Foster, 1870. 62 pp.

Ontario. Legislative Assembly. *Documents and Correspondence Regarding Petawawa Camp and Proceedings in the Legislature.* Toronto: King's Printer, 1907. 14 pp.

Oppen, William A., comp. *The Riel Rebellions; a Cartographic History./Le récit cartographique des affaires Riel.* [Toronto]: Univ. of Toronto Press in association with the Public Archives of Canada and the Canadian Government Publishing Centre/ Univ. of Toronto Press avec la collaboration des Archives publiques du Canada et du Centre d'édition du gouvernement du Canada, 1979. 109 pp.
Bilingual text./Texte bilingue.

[Ord, Lewis Redman.] *Reminiscences of a Bungle, by one of the Bunglers.* Toronto: Grip, 1887. 66 pp.

Oswald, W.R. *The Canadian Militia; an Historical Sketch; a Lecture Delivered to the Young Men's Association of St. Paul's Church, Montreal, on 8th March, 1886.* n.p.: n.d. 14 pp.

Ottawa's Heroes; Portraits and Biographies of the Ottawa Volunteers Killed in South Africa. Ottawa: Reynolds, 1900. 49 pp.

Otter, W.D., comp. *The Guide; A Manual for the Canadian Militia (Infantry); Embracing the Interior Economy, Duties, Discipline, Dress, Books and Correspondence of a Regiment in Barracks, Camp or at Home, with Bugle Calls and Instructions for Transport, Pitching Tents, etc.* Toronto: Willing & Williamson, 1880. 246 pp.
Many subsequent editions.

Ouimet, Adolphe, et B.A.T. de Montigny. *La vérité sur la question métisse au Nord-Ouest,* par Adolphe Ouimet. *Biographie et récit de Gabriel Dumont sur les événements de 1885,* par B.A.T. de Montigny. Montréal: s.i., 1889. 400 pp.

Pelletier, Oscar C. *Mémoires, souvenirs de famille et récits.* Québec, P.Q.: s.i., 1940. 396 pp.

Pennefather, John P. *Thirteen Years on the Prairies; from Winnipeg to Cold Lake; Fifteen Hundred Miles.* London: K. Paul, Trench, Trubner, 1892. 127 pp.

Penny, Arthur G. *Royal Rifles of Canada, "Able and Willing" since 1862; a Short History.* n.p.: 1962. 62 pp.

Phillips, Roger, and Jerome J. Knap. *Sir Charles Ross and his Rifle.* (Historical Arms Series, no. 11.) Ottawa: Museum Restoration Service, 1969. 32 pp.

Preston, Richard A. *Canada and "Imperial Defense"; a Study of the Origins of the British Commonwealth's Defense Organization, 1867-1919.* (Duke University Commonwealth-Studies Center; Publication Number 29.) Durham, N.C.: Duke Univ. Press, 1967. 576 pp.

_____. *Canada's RMC; a History of the Royal Military College.* Toronto: Univ. of Toronto Press, 1969. 415 pp.

Prince Edward Island. Adjutant General's Office. *Militia List of the Local Forces of Prince Edward Island; Commissioned Officers of the Reserve Militia and Volunteer Corps.* Charlottetown, P.E.I.: Queen's Printer, 1869. 43 pp.

The Queen's Birth-Day in Montreal, 24th May, 1879; Orders for the Military Review and Sham-Fight, with a Field Sketch, Showing the Position of the Troops at Different Periods of the Day. Montreal: Dawson, 1879. 12 pp.

Queen's Own Rifles of Canada Association. [*Queen's Own Rifles of Canada; Book of Remembrance, 1866-1918.* n.p.: 1932.] 1 vol., unpaged.

Quigley, John Gordon. *A Century of Rifles, 1860-1960; the Halifax Rifles (RCAC)(M); "cede nullis".* Halifax: privately printed, 1960. 230 pp.

The Regimental History of the Governor General's Foot Guards see Baylay, George Taylor.

Reminiscences of a Bungle see Ord, Lewis Redman.

Reminiscences of the Red River Rebellion . . . see Denison, George T.

Reville, F. Douglas. *A Rebellion; a Story of the Red River Uprising.* Brantford, Ont.: Hurley Print. Co., 1912. 198 pp.

Riel, Louis. *L'amnistie aux métis de Manitoba; mémoire sur les causes des troubles du Nord-Ouest et sur les négociations qui ont amené leur règlement amiable.* Ottawa: s.i., 1874. 43 pp.

The Riel Rebellion, 1885. Montreal: Witness Print. House, nd.. 44 pp.

Ritchie, Mary Christine. *Major-General Sir Geoffrey Twining; a Biographical Sketch and the Story of his East African Diaries.* Toronto: Macmillan, 1972. 102 pp.

Robertson, F.A. *5th (B.C.) Regiment, Canadian Garrison Artillery, and Early Defences of B.C. Coast; Historical Record.* Victoria, B.C.: privately printed, 1925. 2 vols.

Robertson, Peter. *Irréductible vérité/Relentless Verity/les photographes militaires canadiens depuis 1885/Canadian Military Photographers since 1885.* (Les Archives publiques du Canada/Public Archives of Canada Series.) Québec, P.Q.: Les Presses de l'Université Laval, 1973. 233 pp.
Texte bilingue./Bilingual text.

Rocky Mountain Rangers; First Battalion C.A. — A.F., 1885-1941. New Westminster, B.C.: Columbian Co., 1941. 60 pp., chiefly illus.

Rogers, R.L. *History of the Lincoln and Welland Regiment.* n.p.: privately printed, 1954. 465 pp.

Ross, David. *The Journal of Moise Cormier, Zouaves Pontificaux, 1868-1870.* Winnipeg: Manitoba Museum of Man and Nature, 1975. 39 pp.

Rouleau, C.-E. *La papauté et les Zouaves pontificaux.* Québec, P.Q.: Le Soleil, 1905. 245 pp.

_____. *Souvenirs de voyage d'un soldat de Pie IX.* Québec, P.Q.: L.J. Demers, 1905. 245 pp.

_____. *Les Zouaves canadiens à Rome et au Canada.* Québec, P.Q.: Le Soleil, 1924. 83 pp.

_____. *Les Zouaves pontificaux; précis historique.* Québec, P.Q.: Le Soleil, 1924. 50 pp.

Roy, Pierre-Georges. *La Famille Panet.* Lévis, P.Q.: J.A.K. Laflamme, 1906. 212 pp.

Roy, R.H. *Sinews of Steel; the History of the British Columbia Dragoons.* Brampton, Ont.: privately printed, 1965. 468 pp.

The Royal Canadian Army Medical Corps. Ottawa: Queen's Printer, 1953. 10 pp.

Royal Canadian Army Pay Corps. Ottawa: Queen's Printer, 1953. 11 pp.

The Royal Canadian Army Service Corps. Ottawa: Queen's Printer, 1953. 11 pp.

The Royal Canadian Artillery. Ottawa: Queen's Printer, 1953. 10 pp.

Royal Canadian Horse Artillery; First Regiment, 1871-1971. Lahr, Ger.: privately printed, [1971]. 32 pp.

The Royal Canadian Ordnance Corps Diamond Jubilee Yearbook. n.p.: 1963. 106 pp.

The Royal Highlanders of Canada, Allied with the Black Watch (Royal Highlanders), Montreal, Canada. London: H. Rees, 1918. 30 pp.

Royal Military College Club of Canada. *Proceedings.* No. 1-30. Quebec, P.Q.: Chronicle Print. Co., 1891-1913.

_____. *Reference Book Containing Information Respecting the Graduates, Ex-Cadets and Gentlemen Cadets, of the Royal Military College of Canada.* Ernest F. Würtele, comp. n.p.: privately printed, 1892. 64 pp.

The Royal Military College of Canada, 1876-1919. Kingston, Ont.: n.p., 1919. 16 pp.

Royal Military College of Canada, Kingston, Ont. *General Regulations.* Ottawa: Queen's Printer, 1882. 24 pp.

_____. *General Regulations.* Ottawa: Queen's Printer, 1886. 33 pp.

The Royal Rifles of Canada, Allied with the King's Royal Rifle Corps, 1862-1937; Ypres 1915, Festubert, Mont Sorrel, Somme 1916, Arras 1917, Hill 70, Ypres 1917, Amiens; South Africa 1899-1900; Great War 1914-1918. n.p.: [1937]. 21 pp.

Rudbach, N.E. *The Halifax Rifles (23 Armoured Regiment) R.C.A.C.R.F.; "90th" Anniversary, 14th May 1860 — 14th May 1950.* Halifax: n.p., 1950. 20 pp.

Rundle, Edwin G. *A Soldier's Life; being the Personal Reminiscences of Edwin G. Rundle.* Toronto: W. Briggs, 1909. 127 pp.

Rutherford, Tom. *An Unofficial History of the Grey and Simcoe Foresters Regiment, 1866-1973.* n.p.: n.d. 88 pp.

Ryerson, George Sterling. *Looking Backward.* Toronto: Ryerson Press, 1924. 264 pp.

Schragg, Lex. *History of the Ontario Regiment, 1866-1951.* Oshawa, Ont.: privately printed, 1951. 286 pp.

Scoble, T.C. *The Utilization of Colonial Forces in Imperial Defence (Read before the Toronto (Canada) Militia Institute, on Saturday 25th October, 1879).* London: H.M. Stationery Office, n.d. 11 pp.

Scoble, T.C., comp. *The Canadian Volunteer's Hand Book for Field Service.* Toronto: H. Rowsell, 1868. 108 pp.

Service, G.T., and J.K. Marteinson. *The Gate; a History of the Fort Garry Horse.* Calgary: privately printed, 1971. 228 pp.

76th Anniversary, Her Majesty's Birthday, May 24th, 1895; Grand Military Review at London, Ontario; No. 1 Co'y R.R.C.I., 1st Hussars, London Field Battery, 7th Fusiliers, 13th Battalion, Hamilton, and Dufferin Rifles, Brantford. London, Ont.: London Print. and Lithographing Co., [1895]. 26 pp.

A Short History of the British Columbia Regiment; the "Dukes". n.p.: n.d. [11] pp.

Silver, A.I., and Marie-France Valleur. *The North-West Rebellion.* (Problems in Canadian History.) Toronto: Copp Clark, 1967. 68 pp.

Sinclair, J.D., comp. *The Queen's Own Cameron Highlanders of Canada; Twenty-Fifth Anniversary Souvenir.* Winnipeg: privately printed, 1935. 99 pp.

Sir Georges [sic] Cartier sur la défense du Canada. s.l.: s.i., [1909]. 13 pp.

[Slater, James.] *Three Years under the Canadian Flag as a Cavalry Soldier; a Peep behind the Scenes of Political, Municipal, Military, and Social Life in Canada.* n.p.: [1893]. 240 pp.

Souvenir de l'oeuvre des Zouaves pontificaux en Canada, Amérique du Nord. Montréal: Typ. du Nouveau Monde, [1868]. 26 pp.

Souvenir; Toronto Contingent of Volunteers for Service in Anglo-Boer War. [Toronto]: Toronto Print. Co., 1899. 1 vol., unpaged.

Stacey, C.P. *Canada and the British Army, 1846-1871; a Study in the Practice of Responsible Government.* (Royal Empire Society Imperial Studies Series, no. 11.) London: Longmans, Green, 1936. 287 pp.

Stacey, C.P., ed. *Records of the Nile Voyageurs, 1884-1885; the Canadian Contingent in the Gordon Relief Expedition.* (Publications of the Champlain Society, XXXVII.) Toronto: Champlain Society, 1959. 285 pp.

Standing Orders for the Regiment of Canadian Artillery. Ottawa: Queen's Printer, 1883. 42 pp.

Standing Orders [of the Fifth Regt. Royal Highlanders of Canada]. n.p.: 1912. 23 pp.

Standing Orders of the 1st or Prince of Wales Regt., Volunteer Rifles of Canadian Militia. Montreal: privately printed, 1878. 42 pp.

Standing Orders of the 43rd Battalion of Active Militia, the Ottawa and Carleton Rifles of Canada. Ottawa: privately printed, 1900. 35 pp.

Standing Orders of the Infantry School Corps, 1887. Ottawa: n.p., 1887. 79 pp.

Standing Orders of the Regiment of Canadian Artillery, March, 1887. Ottawa: printed by MacLean, Roger, 1887. 61 pp.

Standing Orders of the Royal Canadian Regiment. Ottawa: King's Printer, 1910. 46 pp.

Standing Orders of the Royal Regiment of Canadian Infantry. Ottawa: Queen's Printer, 1896. 42 pp.

Standing Orders of the 2nd Battalion Active Militia, the Queen's Own Rifles, of Canada. Toronto: Copp Clarke, 1883. 47 pp.

Standing Orders of the 2nd Battalion, Active Militia, the Queen's Own Rifles of Canada. Toronto: Brown, 1894. 32 pp.

Standing Orders of the 7th Regiment "Fusiliers". London, Ont.: n.p., 1906. 44 pp.

Standing Orders of the XIII Battalion A.M. of Canada; as Approved by His Excellency the Governor General, 23rd December, 1873. n.p.: [1873]. 12 pp.

Standing Orders of the 38th Battalion, the Dufferin Rifles. Brantford, Ont.: Watt & Shenston, 1886. 56 pp.

Standing Orders; Twenty-Third Battery, Canadian Field Artillery. n.p.: n.d. 16 pp.

Stanley, George F.G. *The Birth of Western Canada; a History of the Riel Rebellions.* London: Longmans, Green, 1936. 475 pp.

_____. *Canada's Soldiers, 1604-1954; the Military History of an Unmilitary People.* Toronto: Macmillan, 1954. 400 pp.

_____. *In the Face of Danger; the History of the Lake Superior Regiment.* Port Arthur, Ont.: privately printed, 1960. 357 pp.

Stanley, George F.G., and Richard A. Preston. *A Short History of Kingston as a Military and Naval Centre.* Kingston, Ont.: Queen's Printer, [195-?]. 33 pp.

Steele, Harwood. *The Long Ride; a Short History of the 17th Duke of York's Royal Canadian Hussars.* Montreal: Gazette Print. Co., 1934. 48 pp.

Steele, (Sir) Samuel Benfield. *Forty Years in Canada; Reminiscences of the Great Northwest with some Account of his Service in South Africa.* Mollie Glen Niblett, ed. Toronto: McClelland, Goodchild & Stewart, 1915. 428 pp.

Stewart, Charles H. *The Service of British Regiments in Canada and North America; a Resume, with a Chronological List of Uniforms Portrayed in Sources Consulted; Based on Regimental Histories Held in Department of National Defence Library.* (Department of National Defence Library Publication no. 1.) Ottawa: Queen's Printer, 1962. v.p.

Stewart, Charles H., comp. *The Concise Lineages of the Canadian Army, 1855 to Date.* Toronto: n.p., n.d. 161 pp.

Stirling, John. *The Colonials in South Africa, 1899-1902; their Record Based on the Despatches.* Edinburgh: Blackwood, 1907. 497 pp.

Strange, Thomas Bland. *Gunner Jingo's Jubilee.* London: Remington, 1893. 546 pp.

_____. *The Military Aspect of Canada; a Lecture Delivered at the Royal United Service Institution.* London: Harrison, [1879]. 66 pp.

Stuart, (Sir) Campbell. *Opportunity Knocks Once.* London: Collins, 1952. 248 pp.

Stubbs, Roy St. George. *Men in Khaki; Four Regiments of Manitoba.* Toronto: Ryerson Press, 1941. 72 pp.

Sturdee, E.T. *Historical Records of the 62nd St. John Fusiliers (Canadian Militia).* St. John, N.B.: J. & A. McMillan, 1888. 139 pp.

Sulte, Benjamin. *L'expédition militaire de Manitoba, 1870.* Montréal: E. Sénécal, 1871. 50 pp.

_____. *Histoire de la milice canadienne-française, 1760-1897.* Montréal: Desbarats, 1897. 147 pp.

Taché, Alexandre Antonin. *Fenian Raid; an Open Letter from Archbishop Taché to the Hon. Gilbert McMicken.* St. Boniface, Man.: n.p., 1888. 31 pp.

Tassie, W.T. *The Rights of the Militia; Address of Major W.T. Tassie, Delivered at Association Hall, at 8 p.m. February 14th 1902.* n.p.: n.d. 42 pp.

Tennant, Joseph F. *Rough Times, 1870-1920; a Souvenir of the 50th Anniversary of the Red River Expedition and the Formation of the Province of Manitoba.* n.p.: n.d. 271 pp.

Thompson, Roy J.C. *Cap Badges of the Canadian Officer Training Corps.* Dartmouth, N.S.: n.p., 1972. 68 pp.

Thoughts on Defence see Coffin, W.F.

Three Years under the Canadian Flag see Slater, James.

Tooley, Edwyn R., *see* Canada. Dept. of Militia and Defence. *Guide for Paymasters . . . .*

*La Trésorerie militaire royale canadienne. Ottawa: Imprimeur de la Reine, 1954. 12 pp.

[Tricoche, George Nestler.] *La vie militaire à l'étranger; les milices françaises et anglaises au Canada, 1627-1900.* Paris: H. Charles-Lavauzelle, [1902]. 317 pp.

Tweedsmuir, John Buchan, baron. *Lord Minto; a Memoir,* by John Buchan. London: T. Nelson, 1924. 352 pp.

Two Months in the Camp of Big Bear . . . see Gowanlock, Theresa.

Upper Canada Historical Arms Society. *The Military Arms of Canada.* (Historical Arms Series, 1.) West Hill, Ont.: Museum Restoration Service, 1963. 47 pp.

Upton, Terence B. *The Rocky Mountain Rangers, 1898-1944; a Short History.* n.p.: n.d. 13 pp.

Urquhart, Hugh M. *Arthur Currie; the Biography of a Great Canadian.* Toronto: Dent, 1950. 363 pp.

Van Der Schee, W. *A Short History of Lord Strathcona's Horse (Royal Canadians).* n.p.: 1973. 19 l.

Victoria Rifles of Canada, 1861-1951; Historical Notes. n.p.: n.d. 14 pp.

Victoria Rifles of Canada; Youth Trained in Mind and Body in a Great Regiment. n.p.: [ca. 1936]. 16 pp.

La vie militaire à l'étranger voir Tricoche, George Nestler.

Les Voltigeurs de Québec, 1862-1952; notes historiques. s.l.: s.i., 1952. 16 pp.

Les Voltigeurs de Québec, 1862-1962; album du centenaire, mai 1962. St-François, P.Q.: imprimé privé, 1962. 31 pp.

W.,T., see *My Campaign at Niagara.*

Wallace, N. Willoughby. *The Rebellion in the Red River Settlement, 1869-70; its Cause and Suppression; a Lecture Delivered at Clifton, October 25th, 1871.* Barnstaple, Eng.: H.T. Cook, 1872. 40 pp.

Ware, Francis B. *The Story of the Seventh Regiment Fusiliers of London, Canada, 1899 to 1914; with an Epilogue, "A Few Days with the Fusiliers at War".* London, Ont.: Hunter Print. Co., 1945. 190 pp.

Warren, Arnold. *Wait for the Waggon; the Story of the Royal Canadian Army Service Corps.* Toronto: McClelland and Stewart, 1961. 413 pp.

Warriors of the Ojibway Country; 97th Regiment Algonquin Rifles of Canada. n.p.: 1908. 40 pp.

Watson, W.S., and others, eds. *The Brockville Rifles, Royal Canadian Infantry Corps (Allied with the King's Royal Rifle Corps); Semper Paratus; an Unofficial History.* Brockville, Ont.: Recorder Print. Co., 1966. 138 pp.

Wicksteed, R.J. *The Canadian Militia.* Ottawa: MacLean, Roger, 1875. 139 pp.

Willcocks, K.D.H. *The Hastings and Prince Edward Regiment, Canada; a Short History.* Belleville, Ont.: n.p., 1967. 1 vol., unpaged.

Wilson, Barbara M., comp. *Military General Service, 1793-1814 (Canadian Recipients), Egypt Medal, 1882-1889 (Canadian Recipients), North West Canada, 1885; Index to the Medal Rolls.* London: Spink 1975. 191 pp.

The Winnipeg Rifles, 8th Battalion, C.E.F., Allied with the Rifle Brigade (Prince Consort's Own); Fiftieth Anniversary, 1883-1933. Winnipeg: privately printed, 1933. 59 pp.

Winter, Charles F. *Lieutenant-General the Hon. Sir Sam Hughes K.C.B., M.P.; Canada's War Minister, 1911-1916; Recollections of Service as Military Secretary at Headquarters, Canadian Militia, prior to and during the Early Stages of the Great War.* Toronto: Macmillan, 1931. 182 pp.

Wood, William. *The Fight for Canada; a Naval and Military Sketch from the History of the Great Imperial War.* Toronto: Musson Book Co., 1905. 370 pp.

Woodcock, George. *Gabriel Dumont; the Metis Chief and his Lost World.* Edmonton: Hurtig, 1975. 256 pp.

Worthington, Larry. *The Spur and the Sprocket; the Story of the Royal Canadian Dragoons.* Kitchener, Ont.: Reeve Press, 1968. 170 pp.

Wurtele, A.G.G. *The Non-Professional Notes of the Cadets' Tour of Instruction to Montreal, Quebec, Halifax and Minor Places and Forming an Interesting Supplement to the Published Official Reports.* Quebec, P.Q.: Morning Chronicle Office, 1881. 87 pp.

Würtele, Ernest F., *see* Royal Military College Club of Canada.

Ypres, John Pinkstone French, 1st earl *see* French, John Pinkstone French, 1st earl of Ypres.

Les Zouaves pontificaux canadiens; comprenant l'origine des Zouaves pontificaux canadiens, par René Hardy et *Les volontaires du Canada dans l'armée pontificale (1868-1870),* par Ello Lodolini. Traduit de l'Italien par le Bureau des traductions, Secrétariat d'état du Canada. (Musée national de l'homme; collection mercure; division de l'histoire dossier no. 19.) Ottawa: Imprimeur de la Reine, 1976. 161 pp.

Les Zouaves pontificaux de Québec, le 20 septembre, 1895. Québec, P.Q.: Imprimerie Proulx & Proulx, 1895. 19 pp.

1914-1918

Adami, George. *War Story of the Canadian Army Medical Corps.* London: Rolls House, 1918. 286 pp.

Aitken, William Maxwell, *see* Beaverbrook, William Maxwell Aitken, baron.

Album-souvenir publié par l'amicale du 22e, au profit des oeuvres de guerre du Royal 22e, des Fusiliers Mont-Royal et du Régiment de Maisonneuve, en service outre-mer à l'occasion du 25e anniversaire de la Bataille de Courcelette (15 septembre 1916) et du 26e anniversaire de l'arrivée du 22e bataillon canadien-français à Boulogne, France (15 septembre 1915). Montréal: imprimé privé, 1941. 1 tome, non-paginé.

[Allen, E.P.S.] *The 116th Battalion in France*, by the Adjutant. Toronto: privately printed, 1921. 111 pp.

Anderson, P. *I That's Me; Escape from German Prison Camp and Other Adventures.* Edmonton: Bradburn Printers, n.d. 174 pp.

Another Garland from the Front. Mark 1-4. London: G. Pulman, 1915-19.
Title varies. Annual.

Un aperçu historique et un régistre photographique du Bataillon "Acadien" d'outremer 165ième, F.E.C.; Lieut. Colonel L.C. D'Aigle, Officier Commandant. Ottawa: Mortimer, [1917]. 43 pp.

Argo, J.A. *The 2nd Can. Heavy Battery in the World War, 1914 to 1919; Record of the Battery from Mobilization in 1914 to Demobilization in 1919 Including Battle Engagements and Battery Positions; Chronology of World War, 1914 to 1919 and Miscellaneous Information; 2nd C.H.B. Old Boys Association: Constitution and Nominal Roll; also Maps of Western Front and Peace Proclamation Dated Mons, Nov 11, 1918.* [Montreal: n.p., 1932.] 117 pp., looseleaf.

Armit, W.B. *Army Museum; Halifax Citadel Halifax, Nova Scotia.* Kentville, N.S.: n.p., [1957?]. 34 pp.

*L'Arsenal de Québec, 1880-1945. Québec, P.Q.: s.i., 1947. 166 pp.

Art Gallery of Toronto. *Catalogue of an Exhibition of the Canadian War Memorials, October 1926.* Toronto: privately printed, [1926]. 21 pp.

At Duty's Call; Captain William Henry Victor van der Smissen; Queen's Own Rifles of Canada and 3rd Battalion (Toronto Regiment) Canadian Expeditionary Force; Born at Toronto the 6th of May, 1893, Killed on Mount Sorrel in Flanders the 13th of June, 1916. London: privately printed, n.d. 54 pp.

Babin, Lenard L., comp. *Cap Badges of the Canadian Expeditionary Forces 1914-1919, Illustrated.* John E. Snitzel, illus. Rochester, N.Y.: n.p., n.d. v.p.

Bagnall, F.W. *Not Mentioned in Despatches,* by Ex-Quaker. North Vancouver, B.C.: North Shore Press, 1933. 116 pp.

[Bailey, John Beswick.] *Cinquante-quatre; being a Short History of the 54th Canadian Infantry Battalion,* by One of Them. n.p.: [1919]. 108 pp.

Baldwin, Harold. *"Holding the Line".* Chicago: A.C. McClurg, 1918. 305 pp.

Bank of Montreal. *Memorial of the Great War, 1914-1918; a Record of Service.* Montreal: privately printed, 1921. 261 pp.

_____. *Victory; a Monument in Memory of the Men in the Service of the Bank of Montreal who Fell in the Great War.* n.p.: [1924]. 19 pp.

*Barnard, Leslie G. *La Guerre des nations; le meilleur souvenir illustré de la grande Guerre; décrivant spécialement le rôle du Canada et des Canadiens.* Montréal: Dodd-Simpson, 1914-15. 2 tomes.

*_____. *The War Pictorial; the Leading Pictorial Souvenir of the Great War; Depicting Especially the Part Played by Canada and Canadians.* Montreal: Dodd-Simpson, 1914-15. 2 vols.

Barnard, W.T. *The Queen's Own Rifles of Canada, 1860-1960; One Hundred Years of Canada.* Don Mills, Ont.: Ontario Pub. Co., 1960. 398 pp.

_____. *A Short History of the Queen's Own Rifles of Canada.* Toronto: MacKinnon & Atkins, n.d. 22 pp.

Barnes, C.H. *Colonel Colin Clarke Harbottle, C.M.G., D.S.O., V.D.* n.p.: [1958]. 20 pp.

The Barrage. Vol. I-? n.p.: privately printed, 1917-?
Journal of the Canadian Reserve Artillery.

Barry, A.L. *Batman to Brigadier.* n.p.: n.d. 90 pp.

[Baylay, George Taylor], ed. *The Regimental History of the Governor General's Foot Guards.* Ottawa: privately printed, 1948. 268 pp.

Beattie, Kim. *48th Highlanders of Canada, 1891-1928.* Toronto: privately printed, 1932. 434 pp.

*Beaverbrook, William Maxwell Aitken, baron. *Les Canadiens en Flandre.* (Relation officielle des opérations du Corps expéditionnaire canadien.) Montréal: Beauchemin, 1916. 248 pp.

Beaverbrook, William Maxwell Aitken, baron, and Charles G.D. Roberts. *Canada in Flanders.* (The Official Story of the Canadian Expeditionary Force.) London: Hodder and Stoughton, 1916-18. 3 vols.

Beck, Norman Edward, comp. *Souvenir Number of the Reveille, the Duke of Connaught's Own, the 158th (Overseas) Battalion.* Vancouver: privately printed, 1916. 20 pp.

Béland, Henri. *Mille et un jours en prison à Berlin.* Beauceville, P.Q.: L'Eclaireur, 1919. 277 pp.

Bell, F. McKelvey. *The First Canadians in France; the Chronicle of a Military Hospital in the War Zone.* Toronto: McClelland, Goodchild & Stewart, 1917. 308 pp.

Bell, Ralph W. *Canada in War-Paint.* London: Dent, 1917. 208 pp.

Belton, James, and E.G. Odell. *Hunting the Hun.* New York: D. Appleton, 1918. 269 pp.

Bennett, S.G. *The 4th Canadian Mounted Rifles, 1914-1919.* Toronto: privately printed, 1926. 336 pp.

Biggs, E.R.J., comp. *Historical Record of the 76th Overseas Battalion of the Canadian Expeditionary Force, 1915-1916.* Toronto: Hunter, Rose, n.d. 73 pp.

Bindon, Kathryn M. *More than Patriotism.* (A Personal Library Publication.) Don Mills, Ont.: Nelson, 1979. 192 pp.

_____. *Queen's Men, Canada's Men; the Military History of Queen's University, Kingston.* [Kingston, Ont.]: privately printed, 1978. 180 pp.

Bird, C.W. *The Canadian Forestry Corps; its Inception, Development and Achievements.* London: H.M. Stationery Office, 1919. 51 pp.

Bird, Will R. *And We Go On.* Toronto: Hunter, Rose, 1930. 343 pp.

_____. *The Communication Trench.* Amherst, N.S.: privately printed, 1933. 336 pp.

_____. *Ghosts have Warm Hands.* Toronto: Clarke, Irwin, 1968. 254 pp.

_____. *North Shore (New Brunswick) Regiment.* Fredericton, N.B.: Brunswick Press, 1963. 629 pp.

_____. *Private Timothy Fergus Clancy.* Ottawa: Graphic Publishers, 1930. 325 pp.

_____. *The Story of Vimy-Ridge./La crête de Vimy,* version française de Paul de Saint-Jullien. Arras, France; I.N.S.A.P., 1932. 24 pp.

_____. *Thirteen Years After; the Story of the Old Front Revisited, Reprinted from MacLean's Magazine with Additions.* Toronto: MacLean Pub. Co., 1932. 180 pp.

Bishop, Charles W. *The Canadian Y.M.C.A. in the Great War.* n.p.: National Council of Young Men's Christian Associations of Canada, 1924. 446 pp.

Black, Ernest G. *I Want One Volunteer.* Toronto: Ryerson Press, 1965. 183 pp.

Boissonnault, Charles-Marie. *Histoire politico-militaire des Canadiens français (1763-1967).* Trois-Rivières, P.Q.: Editions du Bien public, 1967. 310 pp.

Boss, W. *The Stormont, Dundas and Glengarry Highlanders, 1783-1951.* Ottawa: Runge Press, 1952. 449 pp.

Boyd, William. *With a Field Ambulance at Ypres.* Toronto: Musson Book Co., 1916. 110 pp.

The Brazier; a Trench Journal Printed and Published at the Front by the Canadian Scottish for the Brigade. No. 1-9? Various places: n.p., 1916-17?
Subtitle varies. A later publication of the same title was published by the 16th Battalion Association at Moose Jaw, Sask., 1926-28.

The Brazier; Marking the 50th Anniversary of the Canadian Scottish (Princess Mary's), June 6, 1964. Victoria, B.C.: privately printed, 1964. 19 pp.

Breckon, Fred. *In the Hands of the Hun; being an Account of the Experiences of Private Fred Breckon, 8th Battalion, Canadian Expeditionary Force, during Three years and Eight Months in German Prison Camps.* Fort Francis, Ont.: privately printed, 1919. 92 pp.

A Brief Historical Sketch of the Lorne Scots (Peel, Dufferin and Halton Regiment). Brampton, Ont.: Charters Pub. Co., 1943. 24 pp.

A Brief Historical Sketch of the Queen's York Rangers, 1st American Regiment. Toronto: privately printed, 1942. 30 pp.

A Brief History of the Active Service Battalion of the Victoria Rifles; 24th Battalion, 5th Brigade, 2nd Division, Canadian Expeditionary Force, 1914-15. Montreal: privately printed, n.d. 1 vol., chiefly illus.

Brief History of the 52nd, by W.D. Brandon, Man.: privately printed, n.d. 15 pp.

A Brief History of the Royal Regiment of Canada, [*Allied with the King's Regiment (Liverpool)*]. [Toronto: n.p., 1940.] 77 pp.

A Brief History of the Royal Regiment of Canada; Allied with the King's Regiment (Liverpool). [Toronto: n.p., 1948.] 135 pp.

A Brief History of the 3rd Battalion C.E.F. (Toronto Regiment), Now the Toronto Regiment; (Allied with the King's Regiment (Liverpool)). n.p.: 1934. 47 pp.

A Brief History of the 3rd Canadian Battalion, Toronto Regiment. Toronto: Rous & Mann, [1919?]. 30 pp.

A Brief Outline of the Story of the Canadian Grenadier Guards and the First Months of the Royal Montreal Regiment in the Great War, Told in an Anthology of Verse and Prose, compiled by an Officer of the Guards. Montreal: privately printed, 1926. 75 pp.

Brindle, W. France & Flanders; Four Years Experience Told in Poem & Story. St. John, N.B.: S.K. Smith, 1919. 84 pp.

Brown, Kingsley, see Greenhous, Brereton.

*Brown, W.J. Les Cadets royaux de l'armée canadienne; cent ans d'exploits, 1879-1979. s.l.: La Ligue des Cadets de l'Armée du Canada, [1979. 12 pp.]

*_____. The Royal Canadian Army Cadets; a Century of Achievement, 1879-1979. n.p.: The Army Cadet League of Canada, [1979. 12 pp.]

Brown, Walter. To the Memory of Lieutenant-Colonel James Alexander Turner, D.S.O., M.C., a Gallant Soldier who served his Country in the Great War 1914-1918 and Fell in the Battle of Buzancy on July Twenty-six, Nineteen Eighteen. New York: privately printed, n.d. 55 pp.

Bruce, Constance. Humour in Tragedy; Hospital Life behind 3 Fronts by a Canadian Nursing Sister. London: Skeffington, n.d. 66 pp.

Bruce, Herbert A. Politics and the Canadian Army Medical Corps; a History of Intrigue, Containing Many Facts Omitted from the Official Records, Showing how Efforts at Rehabilitation were Baulked. Toronto: W. Briggs, 1919. 321 pp.

_____. Report on the Canadian Army Medical Service. London: [H.M. Stationery Office], 1916. 168 pp.

Bruce, Walter H., and others, comps. Historical Records of the Argyll and Sutherland Highlanders of Canada (Princess Louise's), Formerly 91st Regiment Canadian Highlanders, Canadian Militia, 1903-1928. Hamilton, Ont.: R. Duncan, 1928. 99 pp.

Bull, Wm. Perkins. From Brock to Currie; the Military Development and Exploits of Canadians in General and of the Men of Peel in Particular, 1791 to 1930. Toronto: G.J. McLeod, 1935. 772 pp.

Burns, E.L.M. General Mud; Memoirs of Two World Wars. Toronto: Clarke, Irwin, 1970. 254 pp.

Buswell, Leslie. Ambulance No. 10; Personal Letters from the Front. Toronto: T. Allen, 1916. 155 pp.

Calder, Donald George Scott. *The History of the 28th (Northwest) Battalion C.E.F. (October 1914 — June 1919); from the Memoirs of Brigadier-General Alexander Ross.* Regina: privately printed, 1961. 277 pp.

The Call to Arms; Montreal's Roll of Honour, European War, 1914. B.K. Sandwell, ed. Montreal: Southam Press, 1914. 209 pp.

Callan, John J. *With Guns and Wagons; a Day in the Life of an Artillery Chaplain.* Charles Lyons Foster and William Smith Duthie, eds. London: Society for Promoting Christian Knowledge, 1918. 24 pp.

The Cameron Highlanders of Ottawa; Standing Orders and Constitution and Rules of the Officers Mess. n.p.: [1934]. 88 pp.

Cameron, James M. *Pictonians in Arms; a Military History of Pictou County, Nova Scotia.* Fredericton, N.B.: privately printed, 1969. 301 pp.

Cameron, Kenneth. *History of No. 1 General Hospital, Canadian Expeditionary Force.* Sackville, N.B.: privately printed, 1938. 667 pp.

Camp, A.D., comp. *7th Toronto Regiment, Royal Regiment of Canadian Artillery, 1866-1966.* n.p.: n.d. 33 pp.

Camp Valcartier, P.Q.; 1647 à 1957 en quelques lignes./Camp Valcartier P.Q.; a Short History, 1647-1957. s.l.: s.i./n.p.: 1957. 24 pp.
Texte bilingue./Bilingual text.

*Canada. Armée. Quartier général de l'Armée. Section Historique. *Introduction à l'étude de l'histoire militaire à l'intention des étudiants canadiens,* [par C.P. Stacey]. Ottawa: [Imprimeur du Roi], 1951. 45 pp.
Editions subséquentes et révisées.

*_____. *La 1ère Brigade d'infanterie canadienne, 1914-1954.* (Actualités; revue destinée aux Forces canadiennes, vol. VII, no. 3.) Ottawa: Imprimeur de la Reine, 1954. 31 pp.

*_____. *La 1re Division d'infanterie canadienne, 1915-1955.* (Actualités; revue destinée aux Forces canadiennes, vol. IX, no. 1.) Ottawa: Imprimeur de la Reine, 1955. 31 pp.

Canada. Armée. Régiment de la Chaudière. *Le Régiment de la Chaudière; notes historiques.* Québec, P.Q.: imprimé privé, 1955. 16 pp.

Canada. Army. Queen's Own Rifles of Canada. *Regimental Catechism.* n.p.: n.d. 19 pp.

Canada. Army. Royal Canadian Army Service Corps. *RCASC Diamond Jubilee Year Book, 1910-1961.* Ottawa: Queen's Printer, [1962]. 95 pp.

Canada. Army. Royal Winnipeg Rifles. *Seventy-fifth Anniversary, Royal Winnipeg Rifles, 1883-1958.* [Winnipeg: privately printed, 1958.] v.p.

*Canada. Army Headquarters. Historical Section. *The 1st Canadian Infantry Brigade, 1914-1954.* (Current Affairs for the Canadian Forces, vol. VII, no. 3,) Ottawa: Queen's Printer, 1954. 31 pp.

*_____. *Introduction to the Study of Military History for Canadian Students,* [by C.P. Stacey]. Ottawa: [King's Printer], 1951. 39 pp.
Many subsequent revised editions.

*_____. *The Old Red Patch; the 1st Canadian Infantry Division, 1915-1955.* (Current Affairs for the Canadian Forces, vol. IX, no. 1.) Ottawa: Queen's Printer, 1955. 31 pp.

_____. *The Regiments and Corps of the Canadian Army.* (The Canadian Army List, vol. 1.) Ottawa: Queen's Printer, 1964. 253 pp.

*Canada. Dept. of Militia and Defence. *Annual Report.* Ottawa: Queen's Printer, 1867-1922.
Title varies. Until 1883 was State of the Militia of the Dominion of Canada, with further variation in some years.

_____. *Canadian Expeditionary Force Units; Instructions Governing Organization and Administration.* Ottawa: King's Printer, 1916. 109 pp.

_____. *Canadian Militia; Financial Instructions, 1914, and Standing Orders, Canadian Army Pay Corps.* Ottawa: King's Printer, 1915. 97 pp.

_____. *Canadian Militia; Pay and Allowance Regulations, 1914.* Ottawa: King's Printer, 1915. 115 pp.

_____. *Canadian Militia War Establishments (Provisional), 1914.* n.p.: n.d. 104 pp.

_____. *European War; Memorandum no. 5 Respecting Work of the Department of Militia and Defence from January 1, 1918, to October 31, 1918.* [Ottawa: King's Printer, 1919.] 103 pp.

_____. *European War; Memorandum no. 4 Respecting Work of the Department of Militia and Defence from January 1, 1917, to December 31, 1917.* [Ottawa: King's Printer, 1918.] 31 pp.

_____. *European War; Memorandum no. 6 Respecting Work of the Department of Militia and Defence from November 1, 1918, to October 31, 1919.* [Ottawa: King's Printer, 1920.] 102 pp.

Canada. Dept. of Militia and Defence. *European War; Memorandum no. 3 Respecting Work of the Department of Militia and Defence, from February 1, 1916, to December 31, 1916.* Ottawa: King's Printer, 1917. 83 pp.

_____. *Financial Instructions and Allowances for the Canadian Expeditionary Force, 1916.* Ottawa: King's Printer, 1916. 141 pp.

_____. *Historical Summary; Canadian Expeditionary Force.* [Ottawa: King's Printer, 1918.] v.p.

_____. *How to Qualify; a Short Guide for Officers and Non-Commissioned Officers of the Cavalry and Infantry, Canadian Militia.* Ottawa: King's Printer, 1915. 15 pp.

_____. *The King's Regulations and Orders for the Canadian Militia, 1917.* Ottawa: King's Printer, 1917. 422 pp.

_____. *Memoranda Respecting Work of the Department of Militia and Defence; European War, 1914-15.* Ottawa: King's Printer, 1915. 72 pp.

_____. *Memorandum for Camps of Instruction.* Part 1: *Instructions for Training.* Ottawa: King's Printer, 1909?-28.
Title varies somewhat. Annual.

_____. *Memorandum Showing Rates of Pay and Allowances Authorized for the Canadian Expeditionary Force, the Active Militia on Home Guard Duty, and the Active Militia Called Out for Active Service, together with Rates of Pensions Applicable in the Case of Death or Disability Incurred on Services.* n.p.: 1916. 20 pp.

_____. *The Militia List.* Ottawa: Queen's Printer, 1867-1929.
Title and frequency vary, eg. — The Annual Volunteer and Service Militia List of Canada (1867); The Quarterly Militia List of the Dominion of Canada (1900).

_____. *Minutes of the Militia Council.* Ottawa: King's Printer, 1905-21. 23 vols.

_____. *Regulations for the Cadet Services of Canada, 1915.* Ottawa: King's Printer, 1915. 14 pp.

_____. *Regulations for the Canadian Army Veterinary Service, 1916.* Ottawa: King's Printer, 1916. 51 pp.

_____. *Regulations for the Canadian Medical Service, 1914 (Approved by the Militia Council).* Ottawa: King's Printer, 1915. 62 pp.

_____. *Regulations for the Canadian Officers Training Corps, 1916.* n.p.: 1916. 26 pp.

Canada. Dept. of Militia and Defence. *Report of the Halifax Military Lands Board, 1915.* Ottawa: King's Printer, 1916. 171 pp.

_____. *The Return of the Troops; a Plain Account of the Demobilization of the Canadian Expeditionary Force.* Ottawa: King's Printer, 1920.

_____. *Returned Soldiers' Handbook; Containing Instructions and Information dealing with Returned Warrant Officers, Non-Commissioned Officers and Men of the Canadian Expeditionary Force.* [Ottawa: King's Printer,] 1918. 84 pp.

_____. *Revised Instructions for Dealing with Deserters and Absentees without Leave.* Ottawa: King's Printer, 1918. 60 pp.

_____. *Standing Orders for the Permanent Army Medical Corps (and for the Army Medical Corps on Mobilization), 1918.* Ottawa: King's Printer, 1918. 83 pp.

Canada. Director of Public Information. *Canada's Part in the Great War.* Ottawa: n.p., 1919. 64 pp.
Also issued by Information Branch, Dept. of External Affairs.

_____. *Canada's War Effort, 1914-1918.* Ottawa: King's Printer, 1918. 31 pp.

Canada. Dept. of Veterans Affairs. *60th Anniversary; Vimy Ridge, 1917 — April 9 — 1977./Soixantième anniversaire; la crête de Vimy, 1917 — le 9 avril — 1977.* n.p./s.l.: s.i., [1977]. 14 pp.
Bilingual text./Texte bilingue.

Canada. Militia. Canadian Expeditionary Force. *Routine Orders.* Ottawa: n.p., ?-1920.
Supplements also issued.

Canada. Militia. Canadian Expeditionary Force. 11th Canadian Field Ambulance. *Diary of the Eleventh; being a Record of the XIth Canadian Field Ambulance (Western Universities) Feb. 1916 — May 1919.* n.p.: n.d. 128 pp.

Canada. Militia. Canadian Expeditionary Force. 1st Canadian Contingent. *Gradation List & List of Appointments, Staff & Units.* n.p.: n.d. 118 pp.

Canada. Militia. Canadian Expeditionary Force. 1st Canadian Contingent. Pay and Record Office, comp. *List of Officers and Men Serving in the First Canadian Contingent of the British Expeditionary Force, 1914.* London: H.M. Stationery Office, [1915]. 353 pp.

Canada. Militia. Canadian Grenadier Guards. *Answers to Questions of the Day.* Montreal: Mortimer Press, [1916]. 15 pp.

Canada. Militia. Military District No. 2. *Manual for Chaplains of the Canadian Expeditionary Force.* Toronto: n.p., 1916. 134 pp.

Canada. Militia Headquarters. *Canadian Expeditionary Force Nominal Rolls.* Ottawa: King's Printer, 1915-18. 13 vols.
Issued with Militia Orders. Number of volumes may vary.

_____. *General Orders.* Ottawa: Queen's Printer, 1899-1946.
Superseded Militia General Orders. Frequency varies.

_____. *Militia Orders.* Ottawa: Queen's Printer, 1899-1940.
Superseded Militia General Orders. Frequency varies.

_____. *Official List of Casualties to Members of the Canadian Expeditionary Force* . . . . Ottawa: King's Printer, 1914-19. 5 vols.
Issued with Militia Orders. Number of volumes may vary.

Canada. Ministère de la Milice et de la Défense. *Avantages qu'il y a dans la force permanente; conditions sous lesquelles les jeunes gens sont invités à entrer dans les troupes permanentes du Canada.* s.l.: s.i., 1914. 18 pp.

*_____. *Rapport annuel.* Ottawa: Imprimeur de la Reine, 1867-1922.
Divergence du titre. Jusqu'à 1883 le titre était Rapport annuel sur l'état de la Milice de la Puissance du Canada; divers titres suivirent pendant quelques années.

Canada. Ministry of Overseas Military Forces of Canada. *Memorandum from the Department of the Ministry of Overseas Military Forces of Canada on the Subject of Overseas Forces of Canada.* n.p.: 1918. 53 pp.

_____. *Report of the Ministry; Overseas Military Forces of Canada, 1918.* London: H.M. Stationery Office, 1919. 533 pp.

_____. *Routine Orders.* London: Canadian Print. and Stationery Services, H.M. Stationery Office, 1917-20.

*Canada. Parlement. *Correspondance concernant la discontinuation de l'usage de la carabine Ross dans l'armée canadienne.* (Document parlementaire, no. 44.) Ottawa: Imprimeur du Roi, 1917. 12 pp.

*_____. *Correspondance entre l'Auditeur général et le Ministère de la Milice relative aux dépenses en vertu de la Loi des crédits de la guerre.* (Document parlementaire, no. 122.) Ottawa: Imprimeur du Roi, 1915. 47 pp.

*_____. *Liste des décorations et des médailles décernées aux membres du Corps expéditionnaire canadien et aux officiers de la Milice canadienne jusqu'au 17 mars 1916.* (Document parlementaire, no. 259.) Ottawa: Imprimeur du Roi, 1916. 18 pp.

*Canada. Parlement. *Pensions et allocations accordées aux membres des troupes expéditionnaires canadiennes depuis le commencement de la guerre jusqu'au 16 février 1916.* (Document parlementaire, no. 185.) Ottawa: Imprimeur du Roi, 1916. 84 pp.

*_____. *Réponse à une adresse de la Chambre des Communes en date du 3 février 1916, donnant une copie de tous les décrets du conseil édictés depuis le 4 août 1914, relatifs aux soldats des Corps expéditionnaires canadiens, quant aux sujets suivants: pensions décretées pour soldats en partie ou totalement invalidés, ou pour ceux dont ils étaient les soutiens; gratifications en argent ou autres aides déterminées pour le support ou le soin des soldats revenus du front en partie ou totalement invalidés; et solde, allocations ou autres gratifications accordées aux personnes dépendant des soldats durant leur service actif, et après leur retour du service, pas suite d'invalidité, quelle qu'en soit la cause.* (Document parlementaire, no. 150.) Ottawa: Imprimeur du Roi, 1916. 11 pp.

*Canada. Parliament. *Correspondence between Auditor General and Militia Department Referring to Expenditure under War Appropriation Act.* (Sessional Paper, no. 122.) Ottawa: King's Printer, 1915. 44 pp.

*_____. *Correspondence Relating to the Withdrawal of the Ross Rifle from the Canadian Army Corps.* (Sessional Paper, no. 44.) Ottawa: King's Printer, 1917. 12 pp.

*_____. *List of Decorations and Medals Awarded to Members of the Canadian Expeditionary Force and Officers of the Canadian Militia to 17th March, 1916.* (Sessional Paper, no. 259.) Ottawa: King's Printer, 1916. 17 pp.

_____. *Parliamentary Memoir of George Harold Baker, Lieut.-Colonel, Fifth Canadian Mounted Rifles, Killed in Action, June 2, 1916.* Ottawa: King's Printer, 1924. 22 pp.

*_____. *Pensions Granted and Money Allowances Made to Members of Canadian Expeditionary Forces since Beginning of War to February 16, 1916.* (Sessional Paper, no. 185.) Ottawa: King's Printer, 1916. 83 pp.

*Canada. Parliament. *Return to an Address of the House of Commons, dated the 3rd February, 1916, Showing a Copy of all Orders in Council Passed since August 4, 1914, Dealing with Members of the Canadian Expeditionary Forces in the Following Particulars; Pensions to Partially or Totally Disabled Soldiers or their Dependents; Money Allowances or Other Provisions Made for the Support or Care of Partially or Totally Disabled Returned Soldiers; and Pay Allowances or Other Consideration to Dependents of Soldiers while on Active Service, and After their Return from Active Service because of Disablement from any Cause.* (Sessional Paper, no. 150.) Ottawa: King's Printer, 1916. 10 pp.

Canada. Parliament. House of Commons. Special Committee on Battlefield Memorials. *Battlefields Memorials; Report of the Special Committee Appointed to Consider and Report Upon the Question of What Memorials, if Any, Should be Erected in the Battlefields of the Late War to Commemorate the Gallantry of the Canadian Troops; with Statements and Evidence Attached Thereto.* Ottawa: King's Printer, 1920. 18 pp.

Canada. Parliament. House of Commons. Special Committee on Boot Inquiry. *Proceedings and Evidence.* Ottawa: King's Printer, 1915.

Canada. Royal Commission Concerning Purchase of War Supplies and Sale of Small Arms Ammunition. *Evidence.* The Honourable Sir Charles Davidson, Commissioner. Ottawa: King's Printer, 1917. 3 vols.

Canada. Royal Commission on Purchase of Surgical Field Dressings and Other Surgical Supplies. *Report of the Commissioner.* The Honourable Sir Charles Davidson, Commissioner. Ottawa: King's Printer, 1917. 28 pp.

[Canada. Royal Commission to Inquire into the Purchase by and on Behalf of the Government of the Dominion of Canada, of Arms, Munitions, Implements, Materials, Horses, Supplies, and Other Things for the Purpose of the Present War.] *Report of the Commissioner Concerning Sale of Small Arms Ammunition.* Sir Charles Davidson, Commissioner. Ottawa: King's Printer, 1917. 56 pp.

Canada and Her Soldiers. London: St. Clements Press, 1919. 48 pp.

Canada in Khaki. No. 1-3. London: Pictorial Newspaper Co. (1910), 1917-19.

Canada in the Great World War; an Authentic Account of the Military History of Canada from the Earliest Days to the Close of the War of the Nations, by Various Authorities. Toronto: United Publishers, 1917-21. 6 vols.

Canada in the Great War; an Illustrated Record of the Canadian Army in France and Flanders during the Years 1915-1918. Ottawa: Heliotype Co., 1919. 1 vol., chiefly illus.

Canada Victory Souvenir. London: Canada Newspaper Co., 1919. 72 pp.

Canada's Effort in the Great War to March, 1917. Moose Jaw, Sask.: privately printed, [1917]. 79 pp.

Canada's Heroes in the Great War; Cornwall, Alexandria, Vankleek Hill, Hawkesbury, and Intermediate Points. Vol. I. Noah J. Gareau, ed. With an historical narrative by Lt-Col. F. McKelvey Bell. Ottawa: War Publications, 1921. v.p.

Canadian Artillery Association. *Annual Report.* n.p.: privately printed, 1876- .
Not published 1940-46.

_____. *Officers who Served Overseas in the Great War with the Canadian Artillery, 1914-1919.* Ottawa: n.p., 1922. 258 pp.

Canadian Bank of Commerce. *Letters from the Front; being a Record of the Part Played by Officers of the Bank in the Great War, 1914-1919.* Toronto: privately printed, n.d. 2 vols.

Canadian Battlefields Memorials Commission. *Canadian Battlefield Memorials.* Ottawa: King's Printer, 1929. 84 pp.

Canadian Broadcasting Corporation. *Flanders' Fields.* n.p.: [1964]. 1 vol., unpaged.

Canadian Cavalry Association. *Proceedings.* n.p.: privately printed, 1913- .
In 1943 became Canadian Armoured Association and in 1946 Royal Canadian Armoured Corps (Cavalry) Association. Title varies; also Annual Report and Information Digest and Annual Report.

Canadian Corps Championships; France, Dominion Day, 1918. London: privately printed, [1918]. 31 pp.

Canadian Corps Trench Standing Orders. n.p.: [1918]. 24 pp.

Canadian Field Comforts Commission. *With the First Canadian Contingent.* Toronto: Hodder & Stoughton, 1915. 119 pp.

The Canadian Fusiliers; City of London Regiment. n.p.: 1942. 12 pp.

Canadian Infantry Association. *Proceedings.* n.p.: privately printed, 1913- .
Incorporated the Proceedings of the Canadian Machine Gun Corps Association in 1936. Was the Infantry and Machine Gun Association of Canada, 1937-39. Not published 1940-45.

The Canadian Machine Gunner. Vol. I-II. [Seaford, Eng.]: privately printed, 1917-19.

Canadian Officers Training Corps, University of Toronto Contingent. [Toronto?]: n.p., 1937. 32 pp.

Canadian Pacific Railway Co. *Their Glory Cannot Fade.* n.p.: 1918. [15] pp.

The Canadian Scottish Regiment. n.p.: n.d. 91 pp.

A Canadian Subaltern; Billy's Letters to his Mother. London: Constable, 1917. 128 pp.
    Toronto ed. titled: <u>A Sunny Subaltern; Billy's Letters from Flanders</u>.

Canadian Veteran Associates. *The Story of the Canadian Corps, 1914-1954; a Record of the Canadian Corps Re-Union, August 4, 5, 6, 1954, Toronto, Canada; the Story of Canada in the Great War of 1914-1918, as Recorded on the Walls of the Memorial Chamber in the Peace Tower at Ottawa.* Toronto: privately printed, 1934. 87 pp.

Canadian War Contingent Association. *Field Comforts for Fighting Canadians.* No. 1. Toronto: privately printed, 1917.

Canadian War Memorials Painting Exhibition, 1920; New Series; the Last Phase. n.p.: n.d. 25 pp.

[Canadian War Museum.] *La coopération canada-polonaise au cours des deux guerres mondiales./Polish-Canadian Co-operation in the Two World Wars.* Ottawa: n.p., 1973. 36 pp.
    Texte bilingue./Bilingual text.

Canadian War Records Office. *Art and war; Canadian War Memorials; a Selection of the Works Executed for the Canadian War Memorials Fund to Form a Record of Canada's Part in the Great War and a Memorial to those Canadians who have Made the Great Sacrifice.* London: n.p., 1919. 1 vol., unpaged.

_____. *Canadian War Memorials Exhibition, [New York] 1919.* n.p.: n.d. 48 pp.

_____. *Canadian War Memorials Exhibition, Royal Academy, Piccadilly, W., 1918.* n.p.: n.d. 42 pp.

_____. *Souvenir; New Exhibition of Canadian Official War Photographs in Colour.* London: n.p., 1919. 16 pp., chiefly illus.

_____. *Thirty Canadian V.C.'s; 23rd April 1915 to 20th March 1918.* London: Skeffington, n.d. 96 pp.

Capon, Alan R. *His Faults Lie Gently; the Incredible Sam Hughes.* Lindsay, Ont.: F.W. Hall, 1969. 159 pp.

Carrel, Frank. *Impressions of War.* Quebec, P.Q.: Telegraph Print. Co., 1919. 248 pp.

Catalogue of the Canadian Official War Photographs Exhibition; for the Benefit of the Canadian War Memorials Fund. Toronto: privately printed, [1916?]. 14 pp.

Catalogue of Canadian War Trophies; Including Field Guns, Surrendered and Captured Planes, Flags, Uniforms, Helmets, Swords, Posters, Proclamations, Prints, etc., National Exhibition, Toronto, August 23 to September 6, 1919. n.p.: [1919]. 64 pp.

Catalogue of Canadian War Trophies; Including Field Guns, Surrendered and Captured Planes, Flags, Uniforms, Helmets, Swords, Posters, Proclamations, Prints, etc., The Armouries, Hamilton, November 3 to November 15, 1919. n.p.: [1919]. 64 pp.

Cave, Joy B. *What Became of Corporal Pittman?* Portugal Cove, Nfld.: Breakwater Books, 1976. v.p.

Cent ans d'histoire d'un régiment canadien-français; les Fusiliers Mont-Royal, 1869-1969. Montréal: Editions du Jour, 1971. 418 pp.

Centennial, 1863-1963; Presentation of Colours to the Princess of Wales' Own Regiment CA(M) by the Honourable W. Earle Rowe, P.C., Lieutenant-Governor of Ontario, Kingston, Ontario, Saturday 1st June 1963. [Kingston, Ont.: privately printed, 1963.] 15 pp.

Centennial Year, 1866-1966; 11th Field Artillery Regiment (M); 11th Field Artillery Regiment, Royal Regiment of Canadian Artillery, Canada's Oldest Artillery Regiment, Saturday, October 1, 1966. n.p.: n.d. 1 vol., unpaged.

Chaballe, Joseph. *Histoire du 22e Bataillon canadien-français.* Tome I: *1914-1919.* Montréal: Les Editions Chantecler, 1952. 412 pp.

[Chandler, C.M.] *The Militia in Durham County, 1812-1936; an Outline History of the Durham Regiment.* n.p.: privately printed, 1936. v.p.

Chassé, Noël. *Avant la poussée finale.* Québec, P.Q.: Imprimerie "L'événement", 1918. 98 pp.

[Chattan Club, Toronto, Ont.] *War Record of Chattan Men.* n.p.: n.d. [34] pp.

Chute, Arthur Hunt. *The Real Front.* New York: Harper, 1918. 309 pp.

50 ans d'activités avec le 6e Régiment d'artillerie, (Québec & Lévis), 1899-1949. Québec, P.Q.: Imprimerie Laflamme, 1949. 1 tome, non-paginé.

Cinquante-quatre see Bailey, John Beswick.

Clark, Gregory. *War Stories.* Toronto: Ryerson Press, 1964. 171 pp.

Clark, H.D., comp. *Extracts from the War Diary and Official Records of the Second Canadian Divisional Ammunition Column.* St. John, N.B.: privately printed, 1921. 166 pp.

Claxton, Brooke. *War Diary, 10th Canadian Siege Battery, 1917-1919.* n.p.: n.d. 32 pp.

Clint, H.C., comp. *A Short History of Artillery and of 57th Battery, R.C.A., 1855-1955; Formal Celebration and Reunion, Oct. 15th, 16th, 1955, Grande Allée Armouries, Quebec City.* Quebec, P.Q.: n.p., 1955. 48 pp.

Clint, M.B. *Our Bit; Memories of War Service by a Canadian Nursing Sister.* Montreal: Barwick, 1934. 177 pp.

Clyne, Henry Randolph Notman. *Vancouver's 29th; a Chronicle of the 29th in Flanders Fields.* Vancouver: privately printed, 1964. 166 pp.

Coleman, Frederic. *From Mons to Ypres with the French; a Personal Narrative; Attached to Sir John French's Headquarters during the Retreat from Mons, and the 2nd Cavalry Brigade Headquarters during the Advance across the Marne and Aisne, to the 1st Cavalry Division Headquarters during the Fighting on the Lys, at Ploegsteert, Messines, and Ypres and at the Front in France and Flanders until June, 1915.* London: Sampson, Low, Marston, 1916. 324 pp.

Commemorative Number of the Western Scot; Yukon, Cariboo, Vancouver Island, 67th Pioneer Battalion, 4th Canadian Division. n.p.: n.d. 72 pp.

Commonwealth War Graves Commission. *The War Dead of the Commonwealth; the Register of the Names of Those who Fell in the Great War of 1914-1918 and are Buried in Cemeteries in France; Canadian Cemetery No. 2 Neuville-St. Vaast.* London: H.M. Stationery Office, 1967. 38 pp.

Cooper, J.A., comp. *Fourth Canadian Infantry Brigade; History of Operations, April 1915 to Demobilization.* London: Charles, n.d. 54 pp.

Corneloup, Claudius. *L'épopée du vingt-deuxième.* Montréal: La Presse, 1919. 150 pp.

Corporation of British Columbia Land Surveyors. *Roll of Honour; British Columbia Land Surveyors; 1914 the Great War 1918.* n.p.: privately printed, n.d. 1 vol., unpaged.

*Le Corps blindé royal canadien. Ottawa: Imprimeur de la Reine, 1954. 11 pp.

*Le Corps de Santé royal canadien. Ottawa: Imprimeur de la Reine, 1954. 11 pp.

*The Corps of Royal Canadian Engineers. Ottawa: Queen's Printer, 1953. 21 pp.

The Corps of Royal Canadian Engineers; a Brief History. Ottawa: King's Printer, 1948. 56 pp.

Corrigall, D.J. *The History of the Twentieth Battalion (Central Ontario Regiment), Canadian Expeditionary Force in the Great War, 1914-18.* Toronto: privately printed, 1935. 268 pp.

Cosgrave, L. Moore. *Afterthoughts of Armageddon; the Gamut of Emotions Produced by the War, Pointing a Moral that is not too Obvious.* Toronto: S.B. Gundy, 1919. 35 pp.

Coyne, F.W., comp. *Illustrated Souvenir; Dominion Orthopaedic Hospital, Christie Street, Toronto; Containing Photo Groups of Officers, Nursing Sisters, Patients, Hospital Celebrities, Distinguished Visitors and Others; Alphabetical List of Over 3000 Names of All Patients, Past and Present, Together with Present Addresses; also Names and Addresses of Officers, Nursing Sisters and Others.* Toronto: privately printed, n.d. 104 pp.

Cramm, Richard. *The First Five Hundred; being a Historical Sketch of the Military Operations of the Royal Newfoundland Regiment in Gallipoli and on the Western Front during the Great War (1914-1918).* New York: Williams, n.d. 315 pp.

Creed, Catherine. *"Whose Debtors We Are."* (Niagara Historical Society, 34.) Niagara, Ont.: Niagara Historical Society, 1922. 116 pp.

Critchley, A. *Critch! The Memoirs of Brigadier-General A.C. Critchley.* London: Hutchinson, 1961. 256 pp.

Crook, E.D., and J.K. Marteinson, eds. *A Pictorial History of the 8th Canadian Hussars (Princess Louise's).* n.p.: privately printed, 1973. 343 pp.

Cross, Michael, and Robert Bothwell, eds. *Policy by Other Means; Essays in Honour of C.P. Stacey.* Toronto: Clarke, Irwin, 1972. 258 pp.

Cunliffe, J.W. *A Canadian Soldier; George Harold Baker, M.P., Lieutenant-Colonel 5th C.M.R., Killed in Action at Ypres, June 2nd, 1916.* New York: privately printed, [1917]. 83 pp.

Cunniffe, Dick. *Scarlet, Riflegreen and Khaki; the Military in Calgary.* Calgary: Century Calgary Publications, 1975. 40 pp.

Curchin, Leonard A., and Brian D. Sim. *The Elgins; the Story of the Elgin Regt. (RCAC) and its Predecessors.* St. Thomas, Ont.: privately printed, 1977. 150 pp.

Currie, (Sir) Arthur W. *The Canadian Corps and its Part in the War* [and] *Uncle Sam and John Bull,* by Frederic William Wile. n.p.: [1920?]. 24 pp.

_____. *Canadian Corps Operations during the Year 1918; Interim Report.* Ottawa: King's Printer, 1919. 94 pp.

Currie, J.A. *"The Red Watch"; with the First Canadian Division in Flanders.* Toronto: McClelland, Goodchild & Stewart, 1916. 308 pp.

Curry, Frederic C. *From the St. Lawrence to the Yser with the 1st Canadian Brigade.* Toronto: McClelland, Goodchild & Stewart, 1916. 167 pp.

D., W., *see Brief History of the 52nd.*

Dafoe, John W. *Over the Canadian Battlefields; Notes of a Little Journey in France in March, 1919.* Toronto: T. Allen, 1919. 89 pp.

Daniel, I.J.E., and D.A. Casey. *A History of the Canadian Knights of Columbus, Catholic Army Huts.* n.p.: 1922. 214 pp.

Davidson, (Sir) Charles, *see* Canada. Royal Commission . . .

Dawson, Coningsby. *Carry On; Letters in Wartime.* New York: J. Lane, 1917. 133 pp.
London ed. titled: Khaki Courage; Letters in Wartime.

_____. *The Glory of the Trenches; an Interpretation.* Toronto: S.B. Gundy, 1918. 141 pp.

_____. *Living Bayonets; a Record of the Last Push.* New York: J. Lane, 1919. 221 pp.

De Saint-Jullien, Paul, *see* Bird, Will R.

De Verneuil, Marcel. *Croquis de guerre, 1915-1917.* Montréal: Editions de la Revue moderne, 1921. 84 pp.

De Wolfe, J.H., comp. *Our Heroes in the Great World War; Giving Facts and Details on Canada's Part in the Greatest War in History.* Ottawa: Patriotic Pub. Co., 1919. 415 pp.

The Diary of the 61st Battery, Canadian Field Artillery. London: Canada Newspaper Co., n.d. 99 pp.

Dinesen, Thomas. *Merry Hell! A Dane with the Canadians.* London: Jarrolds, 1929. 254 pp.

*The Dominion Arsenal at Quebec, 1880-1945. Quebec, P.Q.: n.p., 1947. 131 pp.

Dominion of Canada Roll of Honor; a Directory of Casualties (Deaths Only) of the World's Greatest War, 1914-1918, of the City of Toronto; Dedicated to Perpetuate Those who Made the Supreme Sacrifice, "They Shall Not be Forgotten". n.p.: C. McAlpine, 1919. 28 1.

Dornbusch, C.E., comp. The Canadian Army, 1855-1958; Regimental Histories and a Guide to the Regiments. Cornwallville, N.Y.: Hope Farm Press, 1959. 216 pp.

_____. The Canadian Army, 1855-1955; Regimental Histories and a Guide to the Regiments. Cornwallville, N.Y.: n.p., 1957. 162 1.

_____. The Canadian Army, 1855-1965; Lineages; Regimental Histories. Cornwallville, N.Y.: Hope Farm Press, 1966. 179 pp.

_____. Lineages of the Canadian Army, 1855-1961; Armour, Cavalry, Infantry. Cornwallville, N.Y.: Hope Farm Press, 1961. 1 vol., unpaged.

Douglas, J. Harvey. Captured; Sixteen Months as a Prisoner of War. Toronto: McClelland, Goodchild & Stewart, 1918. 195 pp.

Doward, Norman R. The Queen's Own Rifles of Canada Buglers; Historical, Patriotic, Illustrated; Patriotic Souvenir. Toronto: privately printed, 1915. 52 pp.

Drage, Charles. The Life and Times of General Two-Gun Cohen. New York: Funk & Wagnalls, 1954. 312 pp.
London ed. titled: Two-Gun Cohen.

Drysdale, A.M. Canada to Ireland; the Visit of the "Duchess of Connaught's Own". London: T.F. Unwin, 1917. 20 pp.

Duguid, Archer Fortescue. The Canadian Forces in the Great War, 1914-1919; the Record of Five Years of Active Service. Ottawa: King's Printer, 1947. 14 pp.

*_____. Histoire officielle de l'armée canadienne dans la grande Guerre, 1914-1919. Vol. I. Ottawa: Imprimeur du Roi, 1947. 1 tome en 2 vol.

_____. History of the Canadian Grenadier Guards, 1760-1964. Montreal: Gazette Print. Co., 1965. 520 pp.

*_____. Official History of the Canadian Forces in the Great War, 1914-1919. Vol. I. Ottawa: King's Printer, 1938. 1 vol. in 2.

Duguid, Archer Fortescue, see also The Memorial Chamber in the Peace Tower . . . .

Duncan-Clark, S.J., and W.R. Plewman. *Pictorial History of the Great War, [including] Canada in the Great War,* by W.S. Wallace. Toronto: J.L. Nichols, 1919. 2 vols. in 1.

Dunwoody, James M. *The Colonel; Some Reminiscences.* n.p.: [1972?]. 36 pp.

Edwards, E.W. *The Last Hundred Days of the War.* n.p.: privately printed, [1931]. 1 vol., unpaged.

Ellis, W.D., ed. *Saga of the Cyclists in the Great War, 1914-1918.* Toronto: privately printed, 1965. 93 pp.

Engineer's Annual. Vol. I-? North Vancouver, B.C.: privately printed, 1914-?
Published by the non-commissioned officers of the 6th Field Company, Canadian Engineers.

Fallis, George O. *A Padre's Pilgrimmage.* Toronto: Ryerson Press, 1953. 166 pp.

Fetherstonhaugh, R.C. *McGill University at War, 1914-1918; 1939-1945.* Montreal: McGill Univ., 1947. 437 pp.

_____. *The Royal Montreal Regiment, 14th Battalion, C.E.F., 1914-1925.* Montreal: privately printed, 1927. 334 pp.

_____. *A Short History of the Royal Canadian Dragoons.* Toronto: Southam Press, 1932. 52 pp.

_____. *The 13th Battalion Royal Highlanders of Canada, 1914-1919.* Montreal: privately printed, 1925. 344 pp.

Fetherstonhaugh, R.C., comp. *No. 3 Canadian General Hospital (McGill), 1914-1919.* Montreal: Gazette Print. Co., 1928. 274 pp.

_____. *The 24th Battalion, C.E.F., Victoria Rifles of Canada, 1914-1919.* Montreal: Gazette Print. Co., 1930. 318 pp.

Fetherstonhaugh, R.C., and G.R. Stevens. *The Royal Canadian Regiment.* Vol. I: Montreal: Gazette Print, Co., 1936. Vol. II: London, Ont.: privately printed, 1967. 2 vols.

The 58th Regiment Westmount Rifles; Canada Militia 1914. [Montreal?: privately printed, 1970?] 12 pp.

Fighters for Freedom; Honor Roll of Halifax; the Great War, 1914-1919. Halifax: Service Pub. Co., [1919]. 191 pp.

Filteau, Gérard. *Le Québec, le Canada et la guerre, 1914-1918.* Montréal: Editions de l'Aurore, 1977. 231 pp.

The 1st Canadian Division in the Battles of 1918. London: Barr, 1919. 55 pp.

Firth, L.M. *6th Battery, 2nd Brigade, C.F.A.* Bonn, Ger.: privately printed, 1919. 53 pp.

Flahaut, Jean. *Par mon hublot; reflets du temps héroïque, 1914-1918.* Montréal: Beauchemin, 1931. 185 pp.

Flick, C.L. *"Just What Happened"; a Diary of the Mobilization of the Canadian Militia, 1914.* London: privately printed, 1917. 99 pp.

_____. *A Short History of the 31st British Columbia Horse.* Victoria, B.C.: J.P. Buckle, 1922. 40 pp.

41st Battalion French Canadians. Bramshott, Eng.: privately printed, 1915. [52] pp.

47th Battalion Yearbook, 1917. London: Jordan-Gashell, 1918. 63 pp.

The Fortyniner. Vol. I. In the field: n.p., 1915-18?
Magazine of the 49th Canadian Battalion, CEF. A magazine of the same title was published by the Forty-Ninth Battalion, the Loyal Edmonton Regiment Association beginning about 1929.

Fourth Anniversary of the Eleventh Battery, C.F.A., in France, February 1919. n.p.: 1919. 27 pp.

4th Canadian Division Standing Orders (War), 1916. London: Page & Thomas, 1916. 25 pp.

Fox, Henry L., ed. *What the "Boys" Did Over There,* by "Themselves". New York: Allied Overseas Veterans Stories Co., 1918. 165 pp.

Fraser, W.B. *Always a Strathcona.* Calgary: Comprint Pub. Co., 1976. 252 pp.

Frost, Leslie M. *Fighting Men.* Toronto: Clarke, Irwin, 1967. 262 pp.

Gallishaw, John. *Trenching at Gallipoli; the Personal Narrative of a Newfoundlander with the Ill-fated Dardanelles Expedition.* Toronto: S.B. Gundy, 1916. 241 pp.

[Garvin, Amelia Beers (Warnock).] *Canada's Peace Tower and Memorial Chamber, Designed by John A. Pearson, D. Arch., F.R.A.I.C., F.R.I.B.A., A.R.C.A., G.D.I.A., a Record and Interpretation by Katherine Hale [pseud.] Dedicated by the Architect to the Veterans of the Great War.* Toronto: Mundy-Goodfellow Print. Co., 1935. 29 pp.

*Le Génie royal canadien. Ottawa: Imprimeur de la Reine, 1954. 23 pp.

Gibbons, Arthur. *A Guest of the Kaiser; the Plain Story of a Lucky Soldier.* Toronto: Dent, 1919. 198 pp.

[Gibson, George Herbert Rae.] *Maple Leaves in Flanders Fields,* by Herbert Rae [pseud.] London: Smith, Elder, 1916. 268 pp.

Gibson, W.L., comp. *Records of the Fourth Canadian Infantry Battalion in the Great War, 1914-1918.* Toronto: MacLean Pub. Co., 1924. 274 pp.

Godenrath, Percy F. *Lest We Forget; a Record in Art of the Dominion's Part in the War (1914-1918) and a Memorial to those Canadians who Made the Great Sacrifice, being the Gift of the Over-Seas Military Forces to the Nation; a Brief History of the Collection of War Paintings, Etchings and Sculpture, Made Possible by the Work of the Canadian War Memorials Fund and the Canadian War Record Office.* Ottawa: n.p., 1934. 46 pp.

The Gold Stripe; a Tribute to the British Columbia Men who have been Killed, Crippled and Wounded in the Great War. No. 1-3. Vancouver: n.p., 1918-19.
  Title varies. No. 3: The Gold Stripe; a Tribute to Those who were Killed, Maimed and Wounded in the Great War; a Book, One of Many Efforts to Re-Establish Some Back in Civil Life.

Goodspeed, D.J. *Battle Royal; a History of the Royal Regiment of Canada, 1862-1962.* Toronto: privately printed, 1962. 703 pp.

_____. *The Road Past Vimy; the Canadian Corps, 1914-1918.* Toronto: Macmillan, 1969. 185 pp.

Gould, L. McLeod. *From B.C. to Baisieux; being the Narrative History of the 102nd Canadian Infantry Battalion.* Victoria, B.C.: privately printed, 1919. 134 pp.

Gould, R.W., and S.K. Smith. *The Glorious Story of the Fighting 26th; New Brunswick's One Infantry Unit in the Greatest War of all the Ages.* n.p.: n.d. 48 pp.

Governor General's Foot Guards, Ottawa; Seventy-Fifth Anniversary, June 8, 1872-1947. Ottawa: privately printed, 1947. 43 pp.

Grafton, C.S. *The Canadian "Emma Gees"; a History of the Canadian Machine Gun Corps.* London, Ont.: privately printed, 1938. 218 pp.

Granatstein, J.L., and R.D. Cuff, eds. *War and Society in North America.* Toronto: T. Nelson, 1971. 199 pp.

Grant, Reginald. *S.O.S. Stand To!* New York: D. Appleton, 1918. 296 pp.

The Great Adventure with the 4th Battery, C.F.A., B.E.F. n.p.: n.d. 70 pp.

Gt. Brit. Imperial War Graves Commission. *Beaumont-Hamel (Newfoundland) Memorial; bearing the Names of those Sailors, Soldiers and Merchant Seamen from Newfoundland who Fell in the Great War and have no Known Graves.* London: H.M. Stationery Office, 1929. 45 pp.

Gt. Brit. Imperial War Graves Commission. *Introduction to the Register of the Vimy Memorial.* London: H.M. Stationery Office, 1931. 14 pp.

_____. *Memorials Erected at Halifax, Nova Scotia, and Victoria, British Columbia, Canada, bearing the Name of those Sailors, Soldiers and Merchant Seamen of Canada who Fell in the Great War and have no Known Graves.* London: H.M. Stationery Office, 1930. 24 pp.

_____. *The Register of the Names of Soldiers of the Overseas Military Forces of Canada who Fell in France in the Great War, whose Graves are not Known, and who are Commemorated on the Vimy Memorial, France.* London: H.M. Stationery Office, 1930. 8 vols.

_____. *The War Graves of the British Empire; the Register of the Names of Those who Fell in the Great War and are Buried in Adanac Military Cemetery, Miraumont and Pys, France.* London: H.M. Stationery Office, 1925. 67 pp.

_____. *The War Graves of the British Empire; the Register of the Names of Those who Fell in the Great War and are Buried in Aix-Noulette Communal Cemetery and Extension, France.* London: H.M. Stationery Office, 1928. 38 pp.

_____. *The War Graves of the British Empire; the Register of the Names of Those who Fell in the Great War and are Buried in Barlin Communal Cemetery Extension, Barlin, France.* London: H.M. Stationery Office, 1922. 54 pp.

_____. *The War Graves of the British Empire; the Register of the Names of Those who Fell in the Great War and are Buried in Bois-Carré British Cemetery, Lichfield Crater and Zivy Crater, Thélus, Givenchy Road Canadian Cemetery, Neuville-St. Vaast, and Vimy Communal Cemetery, Farbus, France.* London: H.M. Stationery Office, 1930. 44 pp.

_____. *The War Graves of the British Empire; the Register of the Names of Those who Fell in the Great War and are Buried in Canada Cemetery, Tilloy-lès-Cambrai, Ramillies and Proville British Cemeteries, Crest Cemetery, Fontaine-Notre Dame and Neuville-St. Remy Churchyard, France.* London: H.M. Stationery Office, 1925. 39 pp.

_____. *The War Graves of the British Empire; the Register of the Names of Those who Fell in the Great War and are Buried in Cemeteries and Churchyards in Nova Scotia, Prince Edward Island and New Brunswick, Canada.* London: H.M. Stationery Office, 1931. 92 pp.

Gt. Brit. Imperial War Graves Commission. *The War Graves of the British Empire; the Register of the Names of Those who Fell in the Great War and are Buried in Cemeteries in Newfoundland.* London: H.M. Stationery Office, 1930. 19 pp.

_____. *The War Graves of the British Empire; the Register of the Names of Those who Fell in the Great War and are Buried in Cemeteries in the Province of British Columbia, Canada.* London: H.M. Stationery Office, 1931. 48 pp.

_____. *The War Graves of the British Empire; the Register of the Names of Those who Fell in the Great War and are Buried in Cemeteries in the Province of Manitoba, Canada.* London: H.M. Stationery Office, 1931. 48 pp.

_____. *The War Graves of the British Empire; the Register of the Names of Those who Fell in the Great War and are Buried in Cemeteries in the Province of Ontario, Canada.* London: H.M. Stationery Office, 1931. 2 vols.

_____. *The War Graves of the British Empire; the Register of the Names of Those who Fell in the Great War and are Buried in Cemeteries in the Province of Quebec, Canada.* London: H.M. Stationery Office, 1931. 64 pp.

_____. *The War Graves of the British Empire; the Register of the Names of Those who Fell in the Great War and are Buried in Cemeteries in the Provinces of Saskatchewan and Alberta, Canada.* London: H.M. Stationery Office, 1931. 63 pp.

_____. *The War Graves of the British Empire; the Register of the Names of Those who Fell in the Great War and are Buried in Courcelette British Cemetery, France.* London: H.M. Stationery Office, 1926. 42 pp.

_____. *The War Graves of the British Empire; the Register of the Names of Those who Fell in the Great War and are Buried in Ecoivres Military Cemetery, Mont-St. Eloy, France.* London: H.M. Stationery Office, 1922. 82 pp.

_____. *The War Graves of the British Empire; the Register of the Names of Those who Fell in the Great War and are Buried in Fosse No. 10 Communal Cemetery and Extension, Sains-en-Gohelle, Beuvry Communal Cemetery and Extension, Quatre-Vents Military Cemetery, Estrée-Cauchy, Verquignel Communal Cemetery and Gouy-Servins Communal Cemetery, France.* London: H.M. Stationery Office, 1928. 51 pp.

Gt. Brit. Imperial War Graves Commission. *The War Graves of the British Empire; the Register of the Names of Those who Fell in the Great War and are Buried in Hawthorn Ridge Cemeteries No. 1 and No. 2, Auchonvillers, Hunter's Cemetery, Beaumont-Hamel, Mesnil Ridge Cemetery, Miraumont Communal Cemetery, and Sunken Road and 2nd Canadian Cemeteries, Contalmaison.* London: H.M. Stationery Office, 1930. 45 pp.

_____. *The War Graves of the British Empire; the Register of the Names of Those who Fell in the Great War and are Buried in Haynecourt British Cemetery and Cantimpré Canadian Cemetery, Sailly (Nord), France.* London: H.M. Stationery Office, 1924. 31 pp.

_____. *The War Graves of the British Empire; the Register of the Names of Those who Fell in the Great War and are Buried in Iwuy Communal Cemetery, Niagara Cemetery, Iwuy, and the Communal Cemeteries at Noyelles-sur-Selle, Hordain and Thunl'Evèque, France.* London: H.M. Stationery Office, 1929. 25 pp.

_____. *The War Graves of the British Empire; the Register of the Names of Those who Fell in the Great War and are Buried in La Chaudière Military Cemetery, Vimy, France.* London: H.M. Stationery Office, 1923. 33 pp.

_____. *The War Graves of the British Empire; the Register of the Names of Those who Fell in the Great War and are Buried in La Targette British Cemetery (Aux-Rietz) and Petit-Vimy British Cemetery, France.* London: H.M. Stationery Office, 1926. 36 pp.

_____. *The War Graves of the British Empire; the Register of the Names of Those who Fell in the Great War and are Buried in Ligny-St. Flochel British Cemetery, Averdoingt, France.* London: H.M. Stationery Office, 1922. 35 pp.

_____. *The War Graves of the British Empire; the Register of the Names of Those who Fell in the Great War and are Buried in Ontario Cemetery, Inchy-lès-Marquion, Triangle Cemetery, Inchy-en-Artois, Sucerie British Cemetery, Graincourt-lès-Havrincourt, and Moeuvres British Cemetery, France.* London: H.M. Stationery Office, 1928. 35 pp.

_____. *The War Graves of the British Empire; the Register of the Names of Those who Fell in the Great War and are Buried in Passchendaele New British Cemetery, Belgium.* London: H.M. Stationery Office, 1928. 28 pp.

Gt. Brit. Imperial War Graves Commission. *The War Graves of the British Empire; the Register of the Names of Those who Fell in the Great War and are Buried in Quarry Cemetery, Marquion, Chapel Corner Cemetery, Sauchy-Lestrée and Sains-lès-Marquion British Cemetery, France.* London: H.M. Stationery Office, 1926. 30 pp.

_____. *The War Graves of the British Empire; the Register of the Names of Those who Fell in the Great War and are Buried in Quéant Communal Cemetery British Extension, Dominion and Upton Wood Cemeteries, Hendecourt-lès-Cagnicourt, Croisilles Railway Cemetery, and Ecoust Military Cemetery, Ecoust-St. Mein, France.* London: H.M. Stationery Office, 1928. 56 pp.

_____. *The War Graves of the British Empire; the Register of the Names of Those who Fell in the Great War and are Buried in Ribécourt British Cemetery, Ribécourt Road Cemetery, Trescault, Trescault Communal Cemetery, Quarry Wood Cemetery, Sains-lès-Marquion, and Bourlon Wood Cemetery, France.* London: H.M. Stationery Office, 1928. 58 pp.

_____. *The War Graves of the British Empire; the Register of the Names of Those who Fell in the Great War and are Buried in Rosières Communal Cemetery, Communal Cemetery Extension and British Cemetery, Caix Communal and British Cemeteries, Lihons French National Cemetery, Framerville Communal Cemetery, Herleville Churchyard and Proyart Communal Cemetery, France.* London: H.M. Stationery Office, 1928. 46 pp.

_____. *The War Graves of the British Empire; the Register of the Names of Those who Fell in the Great War and are Buried in Sancourt British Cemetery, Porte-de-Paris Cemetery, Cambrai, Mill Switch British Cemetery, Tilloy-lès-Cambrai, St. Olle British and Communal Cemeteries, Raillencourt, Cantaing British Cemetery and Fontaine-Notre Dame Communal Cemetery, France.* London: H.M. Stationery Office, 1928. 39 pp.

_____. *The War Graves of the British Empire; the Register of the Names of Those who Fell in the Great War and are Buried in Sucerie Cemetery, Ablain-St. Nazaire, and Givenchy-en-Gohelle Canadian Cemetery and Zouave Valley Cemetery, Souchez, France.* London: H.M. Stationery Office, 1928. 39 pp.

_____. *The War Graves of the British Empire; the Register of the Names of Those who Fell in the Great War and are Buried in Sun Quarry and Quebec Cemeteries, Cherisy, Quebec Cemetery, Orange Trench Cemetery, Monchy-le-Preux, Happy Valley British Cemetery, Fampoux, and Valley Cemetery, Vis-en-Artois, France.* London: H.M. Stationery Office, 1927. 38 pp.

Gt. Brit. Imperial War Graves Commission. *The War Graves of the British Empire; the Register of the Names of Those who Fell in the Great War and are Buried in the Domart-sur-la-Luce Group of Cemeteries, France.* London: H.M. Stationery Office, 1928. 39 pp.

_____. *The War Graves of the British Empire; the Register of the Names of Those who Fell in the Great War and are Buried in the Fouquescourt Group of Cemeteries, France.* London: H.M. Stationery Office, 1928. 32 pp.

_____. *The War Graves of the British Empire; the Register of the Names of Those who Fell in the Great War and are Buried in Thelus Military Cemetery and Nine Elms Military Cemetery, Thelus, France.* London: H.M. Stationery Office, 1928.

_____. *The War Graves of the British Empire; the Register of the Names of Those who Fell in the Great War and are Buried in Villers Station Cemetery, Villers-au-Bois, France.* London: H.M. Stationery Office, 1924. 62 pp.

_____. *The War Graves of the British Empire; the Register of the Names of Those who Fell in the Great War and are Buried in Wailly Orchard Cemetery and Le Fremont Military Cemetery, Rivière, France.* London: H.M. Stationery Office, 1925. 29 pp.

The Great War and Canadian Society; an Oral History. Daphne Read, ed. Toronto: New Hogtown Press, 1978. 223 pp.

Green, F.G. *A History of the 6th Canadian Siege Battery; France, Belgium and Germany, 1916-1919.* n.p.: privately printed, n.d. 70 pp.

Greenhous, Brereton. *Semper Paratus; the History of the Royal Hamilton Light Infantry (Wentworth Regiment), 1862-1977,* by Kingsley Brown, Senior, Kingsley Brown, Junior, and Brereton Greenhous. Revised and edited by Brereton Greenhous. Hamilton, Ont.: privately printed, 1977. 446 pp.

Gregory, William T. *From Camp to Hammock with the Canadian Scottish Borderers.* [Leamington, Ont.]: n.p., 1917. 35 pp.

Griesbach W.A. *I Remember.* Toronto: Ryerson Press, 1946. 353 pp.

_____. *Observations on Cavalry Duties; Hints for Western Canadian Cavalry Men.* Edmonton: Edmonton Law Stationers, 1914. 38 1.

Griffin, Frederick. *Major-General Sir Henry Mill Pellatt, CVO, DCL, VD; a Gentleman of Toronto, 1859-1939.* Toronto: Ontario Pub. Co., 1939. 30 pp.

Groves, Hubert, comp. *Toronto Does Her "Bit".* Toronto: Municipal Intelligence Bureau, 1918. 72 pp.

Gunn, J.N., and E.E. Dutton. *Historical Records of No. 8 Canadian Field Ambulance; Canada, England, France, Belgium, 1915-1919.* Toronto: Ryerson Press, 1920. 169 pp.

H., J.A., *voir Les poilus canadiens.*

Hahn, E. *The Intelligence Service within the Canadian Corps, 1914-1918.* Toronto: Macmillan, 1930. 263 pp.

Hale, Katherine, [*pseud.*] *see* Garvin, Amelia Beers (Warnock).

Hamilton, J.H., comp. *Vancouver's Contribution to the Empire; a Souvenir of the First Overseas Contingent who Volunteered for Foreign Service from the Regiments of Vancouver and District.* Vancouver: privately printed, 1914. 32 pp.

Harker, Douglas E. *The Dukes; the Story of the Men who have Served in Peace and War with the British Columbia Regiment (D.C.O.), 1883-1973.* n.p.: privately printed, 1974. 438 pp.

Hayes, Joseph. *The Eighty-Fifth in France and Flanders.* Halifax: privately printed, 1920. 362 pp.
85th Battalion, C.E.F.

Herrington, Walter S., and A.J. Wilson. *The War Work of the County of Lennox and Addington.* Napanee, Ont.: Beaver Press, 1922. 278 pp.

Hewitt, G.E. *The Story of the Twenty-Eighth (North-West) Battalion, 1914-1917.* London: Charles, n.d. 24 pp.

Hezzelwood, Oliver, *see* Trinity Methodist Church, Toronto, Ont.

Historical Calendar; 21st Canadian Infantry Battalion (Eastern Ontario Regiment); Belgium — France — Germany, 1915-1919. Aldershot, Eng.: privately printed, 1919. 72 pp.

Historical Record of the No. 54 District Canadian Forestry Corps, 1916-1919. London: Bassano, 1919. 35 pp.

An Historical Sketch of the Seventy-Seventh Battalion, Canadian Expeditionary Force; Having Particular Reference to the Military Record of the Members of this Battalion, with Three Pictorial Sections, i.e., Personal Portraits, Battalion Portraits, War Views. Ottawa: War Publications, 1926. v.p.

A History of No. 7 (Queen's) Canadian General Hospital, March 26th, 1915 — Nov. 15th, 1917. London: privately printed, [1917]. 66 pp.

Hodder-Williams, Ralph, G.R. Stevens, and R.B. Mainprize. *Princess Patricia's Canadian Light Infantry.* London: Hodder and Stoughton, 1923-[57?]. 4 vols.

Holland, J.A. *The Story of the Tenth Canadian Battalion, 1914-1917.* London: Charles, n.d. 35 pp.

Holyoak, F.G. *The History of the 39th Battery, Canadian Field Artillery.* n.p.: 1919. 1 vol., unpaged.

Hopkins, J. Castell. *Canada at War; a Record of Heroism and Achievement, 1914-1918, Containing also a Story of Five Cities,* by Rev. Robert Renison. Toronto: Canadian Annual Review, 1919. 448 pp.

How, Douglas. *The 8th Hussars; a History of the Regiment.* Sussex, N.B.: Maritime Pub., 1964. 446 pp.

Howard, Fred. *On Three Battle Fronts.* New York: V. Waring, 1918. 177 pp.

Howard, Gordon L. *The Memories of a Citizen Soldier, 1914-1945.* n.p.: n.d. 114 pp.

_____. *Sixty Years of Centennial in Saskatchewan, 1906-1968.* n.p.: n.d. 140 pp.

Hubbell, E.L. *The Winnipeg Grenadiers.* n.p.: n.d. 16 pp.

Hundevad, John, ed. *Guide Book of the Pilgrimmage to Vimy and the Battlefields, July-August, 1936.* Ottawa: privately printed, [1936]. 136 pp.

Hunt, M.S., comp. *Nova Scotia's Part in the Great War.* Halifax: Veteran Pub., 1920. 466 pp.

Hutchison, Paul P. *Canada's Black Watch; the First Hundred Years, 1862-1962.* Montreal: privately printed, [1962]. 340 pp.

_____. *Five Strenuous Years; the McGill Chapter of Alpha Delta Phi during the Great War.* Toronto: privately printed, n.d. 292 pp.

_____. *A Short History of the Royal Highland Regiment the Black Watch, 1725-1948.* n.p.: 1948. 39 pp.

*L'Intendance royale canadienne. Ottawa: Imprimeur de la Reine, 1954. 12 pp.

The Irish-Canadian Rangers. Montreal: privately printed, 1916. 57 pp.

Jackson, H.M. *Canadian Prime Ministers and the Canadian Militia.* n.p.: 1958. 11 pp.

_____. *The 127th Battalion, C.E.F.; 2nd Battalion, Canadian Railway Troops.* Montreal: privately printed, n.d. 186 pp.

_____. *The Princess Louise Dragoon Guards; a History.* n.p.: 1952. 306 pp.

_____. *The Roll of the Regiments (the Active Militia).* Ottawa: n.p.: 1959. 176 pp.

Jackson, H.M. *The Royal Regiment of Artillery, Ottawa, 1855-1952; a History.* Montreal: privately printed, 1952. 418 pp.

_____. *The Sherbrooke Regiment (12th Armoured Regiment).* n.p.: 1958. 229 pp.

_____. *The Story of the Royal Canadian Dental Corps.* Ottawa: privately printed, 1956. 475 pp.

James, F. Treve, and Thos. Johnston, ed. *Bruce in Khaki; Containing a History of the 160th Overseas Bruce Battalion and Complete Nominal Roll of All Men who were at any Time on the Strength of the Battalion.* Chesley, Ont.: privately printed, 1934. 1 vol., unpaged.

James, Fred. *Canada's Triumph; Amiens — Arras — Cambrai; August — September — October, 1918.* London: Charles, n.d. 63 pp.

Jeffery, R.A. *Catholic Army Huts; Progress Report to June 1st, 1918, and Recommendations for this Year's Campaign; Presented at the Ontario State Convention of the Knights of Columbus Held in Windsor, Ontario, on June 4th and 5th, 1918.* Windsor, Ont.: n.p., 1918. 11 pp.

Johnston, G. Chalmers. *The 2nd Canadian Mounted Rifles (British Columbia Horse) in France and Flanders.* From the records of Lieutenant-Colonel G. Chalmers Johnston. M.V. McGuire and others, eds. Vernon, B.C.: privately printed, n.d. 174 pp.

Johnston, Stafford. *The Fighting Perths; the Story of the First Century in the Life of a Canadian County Regiment.* Stratford, Ont.: privately printed, 1964. 133 pp.

Jones, G.C. *Interim Report of Surgeon-General G.C. Jones, Director Medical Services, Canadians, in Reply to the Report on the Candian Army Medical Service, by Colonel Herbert A. Bruce, Special Inspector-General, Medical Services, Canadian Expeditionary Force.* London: n.p., 1916. 163 pp.

Jones, William R. *Fighting the Hun from Saddle and Trench, by Sgt Major William R. Jones, Known among his Comrades as "Lucky Bill", no. 59 of the Royal Canadian Dragoons.* Albany, N.Y.: Aiken Book Co., 1918. 281 pp.

Kay, Hugh R. *The History of the Forty-Third Battery, C.F.A.* Niagara Falls, Ont.: privately printed, [1955?]. 23 pp.

_____. *The History of the Forty-Third Battery, C.F.A.* Vol. I. Edinburgh: privately printed, 1918. 47 pp.

Kay, Hugh R., George Magee, and F.A. MacLennan. *Battery Action; the Story of the 43rd Battery, C.F.A.* Toronto: Warrick & Rutter, n.d. 304 pp.

Keene, Louis. *"Crumps"; the Plain Story of a Canadian who Went.* Boston: Houghton Mifflin, 1917. 156 pp.

Kerr, Wilfred Brenton. *Arms and the Maple Leaf; Memories of Canada's Corps, 1918.* Seaforth, Ont.: Huron Expositor, 1943. 90 pp.

_____. *"Shrieks and Crashes"; being Memories of Canada's Corps, 1917.* Toronto: Hunter, Rose, 1929. 218 pp.

Kerry, A.J., and W.A. McDill. *The History of the Corps of Royal Canadian Engineers.* Ottawa: privately printed, 1962. 2 vols.

Kimball, Harold G. *The 104th New Brunswick Battalion in the First World War, 1915-1918.* Fredericton, N.B.: privately printed, 1962. 20 pp.

King, W.D., comp. *A Brief History of Militia Units Established at Various Periods at Yarmouth, Nova Scotia, 1812-1947.* Yarmouth, N.S.: privately printed, 1947. 32 pp.

L., R.A., see *Letters of a Canadian Stretcher Bearer.*

Laflamme, Jean. *Les camps de détention au Québec durant la première guerre mondiale.* Montréal: s.i., 1973. 49 pp.

Laird, Donald Harry. *Prisoner Five-One-Eleven.* Toronto: Ontario Press, [191-?]. 115 pp.

Lamontagne, Léopold. *Les archives régimentaires des Fusiliers du S.-Laurent.* Rimouski, P.Q.: s.i., 1943. 247 pp.

*Lapointe, Arthur J. *Souvenirs et impressions de ma vie de soldat (1916-1919); Vingt-deuxième Bataillon (1917-1918).* St-Ulric, P.Q.: s.i., 1919. 109 pp.

*_____. *Soldier of Quebec (1916-1919).* R.C. Fetherstonhaugh, tr. Montreal: Garand, 1931. 116 pp.

La Presse, Montreal, P.Q. *Our Volunteer Army; Facts and Figures.* Montreal: La Presse, 1916. 38 pp.

Lavoie, Joseph A. *Le Régiment de Montmagny de 1869 à 1931.* s.l.: s.i., [1932]. 117 pp.

_____. *Une unité canadienne; "coq-à-l'âne" sériocomique,* par E.I. Oval [*pseud.*] et E. Rastus [*pseud.* Québec, P.Q.: M. E. Martin], 1920. 162 pp.

Leash, Homer E. *131st Westminster Overseas Battalion, 1916; Headquarters, New Westminster, British Columbia.* Vancouver: n.p., 1916. 1 vol., unpaged.

Letters of a Canadian Stretcher Bearer, by R.A.L. Anna Chapin Ray, ed. Boston: Little, Brown, 1918. 288 pp.

Lewis, R. *Over the Top with the 25th; Chronicle of Events at Vimy Ridge and Courcelette.* Halifax: H.H. Marshall, 1918. 59 pp.

Lind, [Francis Thomas]. *The Letters of Mayo Lind.* Introd. by J. Alex. Robinson. St. John's, Nfld.: Robinson, 1919. 175 pp.

Lindsey, C.B., comp. *The Story of the Fourth Canadian Division, 1916-1919.* Aldershot, Eng.: Gale & Polden, n.d. 51 pp.

The Listening Post. No. 1-32. [Bailleul, Bel.]: n.p., 1915-18.
  Journal of the 7th Battalion, C.E.F. A veteran's journal of the same title was published in Montreal beginning in 1923.

Livesay, J.F.B. *Canada's Hundred Days; with the Canadian Corps from Amiens to Mons, Aug 8 — Nov 11, 1918.* Toronto: Allen, 1919. 421 pp.

Logan, H.T. *History of the Canadian Machine Gun Corps, C.E.F.* n.p.: 1919. 3 vols.

The Lorne Scots (Peel, Dufferin and Halton Regiment). Brampton, Ont.: privately printed, 1962. 47 pp.

Lynch, Alex. *Dad, the Motors and the Fifth Army Show.* Westport, Ont.: privately printed, 1978. 1 vol., unpaged.
  1st Canadian Motor Machine Gun Brigade.

Lynch, John William. *Princess Patricia's Canadian Light Infantry, 1917-1919.* Hicksville, N.Y.: Exposition Press, 1976. 208 pp.

MacArthur, D.C. *The History of the Fifty-Fifth Battery, C.F.A.* Hamilton, Ont.: H.S. Longhurst, 1919. 94 pp.

McAvity, J.M. *Lord Strathcona's Horse (Royal Canadians); a Record of Achievement.* Toronto: n.p., 1947. 280 pp.

McBride, Herbert W. *The Emma Gees.* Indianapolis, In.: Bobbs-Merrill, 1918. 219 pp.

_____. *A Rifleman Went to War; being a Narrative of the Author's Experiences and Observations while with the Canadian Corps in France and Belgium, September 1915 — April 1917, with Particular Emphasis upon the Use of the Military Rifle in Sniping, its Place in Modern Armament, and the Work of the Individual Soldier.* Marines, N.C.: Small Arms Technical Pub. Co., 1935. 398 pp.

McClintock, Alexander. *Best o'Luck; How a Fighting Canadian Won the Thanks of Britain's King.* Toronto: McClelland, Goodchild & Stewart, 1917. 171 pp.

McClung, Nellie L., *see* Simmons, Mervin C.

Macdermot, T.W.L. *The Seventh.* Montreal: privately printed, n.d. 144 pp.
  7th Battalion, C.E.F.

MacDonald. Frank C. *The Kaiser's Guest*. Garden City, N.Y.: privately printed, 1918. 250 pp.

MacDonald, J.A. *Gun-Fire; an Historical Narrative of the 4th Bde C.F.A. in the Great War (1914-18)*. Toronto: privately printed, 1929. 264 pp.

McEvoy, Bernard, and A.H. Finlay, comps. *History of the 72nd Canadian Infantry Battalion, Seaforth Highlanders of Canada*. Vancouver: Cowan and Brookhouse, 1920. 311 pp.

McGill Univ., Montreal, P.Q. *A Memorial Service for the McGill Men and Women who Gave Their Lives during the First and Second World Wars*. n.p.: [1946]. 1 vol., unpaged.

McGregor, F., ed. *LdSH (RC) '85-70'*. Winnipeg: privately printed, 1970. 62 pp.

Macintyre, D.E. *Canada at Vimy*. Toronto: P. Martin, 1967. 229 pp.

McKean, G.B. *Scouting Thrills*. New York: Macmillan, 1919. 235 pp.

McKee, A. *Vimy Ridge*. London: Souvenir Press, 1966. 242 pp.
New York ed. titled: The Battle of Vimy Ridge.

McKenzie, F.A. *Canada's Day of Glory*. Toronto: W. Briggs, 1918. 342 pp.

_____. *Through the Hindenburg Line; Crowning Days on the Western Front*. London: Hodder and Stoughton, 1918. 429 pp.

Mackenzie, J.J. *Number 4 Canadian Hospital; the Letters of Professor J.J. Mackenzie from the Salonika Front; with a Memoir by his Wife Kathleen Cuffe Mackenzie*. Toronto: Macmillan, 1933. 247 pp.

Mackenzie-Naughton, J.D. *The Princess of Wales' Own Regiment (M.G.)*. Kingston, Ont.: privately printed, 1946. 74 pp.

McKeown, J.D. *From Otterpool to the Rhine with the 23rd Battery, Canadian Field Artillery, via Caestre, St. Eloi, Ypres, The Somme, Vimy, Hill 70, Cinnibar Trench, Passchendaele, Arras, Amiens, Cambria [sic], Valenciennes, Mons*. London: Charles, n.d. 48 pp.

Macksey, Kenneth. *The Shadow of Vimy Ridge*. Toronto: Ryerson Press, 1965. 264 pp.

_____. *Vimy Ridge*. (Pan/Ballantine Illustrated History of the First World War, no. 6.) New York: Pan/Ballantine, 1972. 160 pp.

MacLaren, Roy. *Canadians in Russia, 1918-1919.* Toronto: Macmillan, 1976. 301 pp.

MacLeod, John N. *A Pictorial Record and Original Muster Roll, 29th Battalion.* Vancouver: privately printed, 1919. 64 pp.

McMullen, Fred, and Jack Evans. *Out of the Jaws of Hunland; the Stories of Corporal Fred McMullen, Sniper, Private Jack Evans, Bomber, Canadian Soldiers, Three Times Captured and Finally Escaped from German Prison Camps.* Toronto: W. Briggs, 1918. 248 pp.

MacPhail, (Sir) Andrew. *The Medical Services.* (Official History of the Canadian Forces in the Great War, 1914-19.) Ottawa: King's Printer, 1925. 428 pp.

McWilliams, James L., and R. James Steele. *The Suicide Battalion.* Edmonton. Hurtig Publishers, 1978. 226 pp.
46th Battalion (South Saskatchewan), C.E.F.

Machum, George C. *The Story of the 64th Battalion, c.e.f., 1915-16.* Montreal: privately printed, 1956. 94 pp.

Major J.M. Langstaff, F.I.A., F.A.S., C.A., Barrister-at-Law; a Memorial. Toronto: Press of Miln-Bingham Co., n.d. 77 pp.

Manarey, R. Barrie. *The Canadian Bayonet.* Edmonton: Century Press, 1971. 51 pp.

Manion, R.J. *A Surgeon in Arms.* New York: D. Appleton, 1918. 310 pp.

Marquis, G.E. *Le Régiment de Lévis; historique et album.* Lévis, P.Q.: s.i., 1952. 292 pp.

Martin, Stuart. *The Story of the Thirteenth Battalion, 1914-1917.* London: Charles, [1918]. 19 pp.

Mazéas, Daniel. *Insignes armée canadienne, 1900-1914; Canadian Badges; supplément, 1920-1950.* Guincamp, France: privately printed, 1972. 116 pp.

Meek, John F. *Over the Top; the Canadian Infantry in the First World War.* Orangeville, Ont.: privately printed, 1971. 188 pp.

Meighen, F.S., ed. *Photographic Record and Souvenir of the Canadian Grenadier Guards Overseas Battalion, "Eighty Seventh".* Montreal: privately printed, 1916. 55 pp.

The Memorial Chamber in the Peace Tower, Houses of Parliament, Ottawa, Canada, [by A.F. Duguid]. Ottawa: Photogelatine Engraving Co., n.d. [34] pp.

Memorial of the 27th Battery, Canadian Field Artillery. London: McCorquodale, 1919. 27 pp.

Menzies, J.H. *Canada and the War; the Promise of the West.* Toronto: Copp Clark, 1916. 117 pp.

Merritt, Wm. Hamilton. *Canada and National Service.* Toronto: Macmillan, 1917. 247 pp.

The Message from Mars; being a Christmas Greeting from the Officers, Non-Commissioned Officers and Men of the 4th Canadian Division, B.E.F., to Friends the World Over. London: Carlton Studio, 1918. 60 pp.

Metson, Graham, comp. *The Halifax Explosion, December 6, 1917.* Toronto: McGraw-Hill Ryerson, n.d. 173 pp.

Military Vaudeville by 144th Overseas Battalion, C.E.F.; 3rd Battalion 90th Winnipeg Rifles, Under the Patronage of His Honor the Lieutenant-Governor, Sir Douglas Cameron and the District Officer Commanding M.D. No. 10, Col. H.N. Ruttan, Winnipeg Theatre, Winnipeg, March 9th, 10th, 11th, 1916. Winnipeg: privately printed, 1916. 95 pp.

The Militia in Durham County . . . see Chandler, C.M.

Millar, W.C. *From Thunder Bay through Ypres with the Fighting Fifty-Second.* n.p.: [ca. 1918]. 101 pp.

Miller, James Martin, and H.S. Canfield. *The People's War Book; History, Encyclopedia and Chronology of the Great World War; and Canada's Part in the War,* by W.R. Plewman. Toronto: Imperial Pub. Co., 1919. 520 pp.

Milsom, H.G. *Sunset, Night and Dawn.* [Camden, N.J.: Magrath Print. House, 1918?] 60 pp.

Moir, J.S., ed. *History of the Royal Canadian Corps of Signals, 1903-1961.* Ottawa: privately printed, 1962. 336 pp.

Monaghan, Hugh B. *The Big Bombers of World War I; a Canadian's Journal.* Burlington, Ont.: R. Gentle Communications, n.d. 101 pp.

Montagu-Marsden, M. *A Short History of Captured Guns, the Great European War, 1914-1918; the British Columbia Regiment (7th Bn., C.E.F.), the Seaforth Highlanders of Canada (72nd Bn., C.E.F.).* Vancouver: privately printed, n.d. 1 vol., unpaged.

The Montreal Standard. *Canada's Aid to the Allies, and Peace Memorial.* Frederic Yorston, ed. Montreal: Standard Pub. Co., 1918, 1 vol., unpaged, chiefly illus.

Moogk, Peter N., and R.V. Stevenson. *Vancouver Defended; a History of the Men and Guns of the Lower Mainland Defences, 1859-1949.* Surrey, B.C.: Antonson Pub., 1978. 128 pp.

Moore, Mary Macleod. *The Maple Leaf's Red Cross; the War Story of the Canadian Red Cross Overseas.* London: Skeffington, n.d. 223 pp.

More Letters From Billy; by the Author of "A Sunny Subaltern; Billy's Letters from Flanders". Toronto: McClelland, Goodchild & Stewart, 1917. 121 pp.

Morley, A.W. *Standing Orders, 144th Overseas Battalion, C.E.F., Winnipeg Rifles.* n.p.: 1916. 45 pp.

Morton, Desmond. *The Canadian General, Sir William Otter.* (Canadian War Museum Historical Publication Number 9.) Toronto: Hakkert, 1974. 423 pp.

Munroe, Jack. *A Dog Story of the Princess "Pats"; Mopping Up! Through the Eyes of Bobbie Burns, Regimental Mascot.* New York: H.K. Fly, [1918]. 319 pp.

Murdoch, B.J. *The Red Vineyard.* Cedar Rapids, Iowa: Torch Press, 1923. 313 pp.
Memoirs of a CEF chaplain.

Murray, W.W. *Five Nines and Whiz Bangs,* by "the Orderly Sergeant". Ottawa: The Legionary, 1937. 224 pp.

_____. *The History of the 2nd Canadian Battalion (East. Ontario Regiment) Canadian Expeditionary Force in the Great War, 1914-1918.* Ottawa: n.p., 1947. 408 pp.

Murray, W.W., ed. *The Epic of Vimy.* Ottawa: The Legionary, [1936]. 223 pp.

N.R.E.F., 16th Brigade C.F.A., 67th and 68th Batteries in North Russia, September 1918 to June 1919. n.p.: n.d. 55 pp.

Nasmith, George Gallie. *Canada's Sons in the World War; a Complete and Authentic Story of the Commanding Part Played by Canada and the British Empire in the World's Greatest War.* Toronto: J.C. Winston, 1919. 2 vols.

Nicholson, G.W.L. *Canada's Nursing Sisters.* (Canadian War Museum Historical Publication Number 13.) Toronto: S. Stevens, Hakkert, 1975. 272 pp.

*_____. *Canadian Expeditionary Force, 1914-1919.* (Official History of the Canadian Army in the First World War.) Ottawa: Queen's Printer, 1962. 621 pp.

*_____. *Corps expéditionnaire canadien, 1914-1919.* (Histoire officielle de la participation de l'Armée canadienne à la première guerre mondiale.) Ottawa: Imprimeur de la Reine, 1963. 671 pp.

_____. *The Fighting Newfoundlanders; a History of the Royal Newfoundland Regiment.* St. John's, Nfld.: Govt. of Nfld., 1964. 614 pp.

Nicholson, G.W.L. *The Gunners of Canada; the History of the Royal Regiment of Canadian Artillery.* Toronto: McClelland and Stewart, 1967-72. 2 vols.

_____. "Nous nous souviendrons . . ."; mémoriaux outremer aux morts de guerre du Canada. Ottawa: Imprimeur de la Reine, 1973. 118 pp.

_____. *Seventy Years of Service; a History of the Royal Canadian Army Medical Corps.* Ottawa: Borealis Press, 1977. 388 pp.

_____. "We will Remember . . ."; Overseas Memorials to Canada's War Dead. Ottawa: Queen's Printer, 1973. 110 pp.

The 9th Mississauga Horse; and its Contribution to the Canadian Expeditionary Force. [Toronto]: n.p., n.d. 36 pp.

Norris, Armine. *"Mainly for Mother."* Toronto: Ryerson Press, n.d. 219 pp.

Noyes, Frederick W. *Stretcher Bearers . . . at the Double!* Toronto: Hunter, Rose, 1937. 315 pp.

No. 3 Canadian General Hospital . . . see Pirie, Alexander Howard.

O'Brien, Jack. *Into the Jaws of Death.* New York: Dodd, Mead, 1919. 295 pp.

Odds and Ends from a Regimental Diary. n.p.: n.d. 30 pp.

Officers' Gradation List; Canadian Expeditionary Force (Revised to 1st November 1915). n.p.: n.d. 234 pp.

Ogle, Robert J. *The Faculties of Canadian Military Chaplains; a Commentary on the Faculty Sheet of December, 1955, and the Directives for Holy Week Promulgated March 14, 1956.* Ottawa: n.p., 1956. 267 pp.

O'Gorman, J.R. *Soldiers of Christ; Canadian Catholic Chaplains, 1914-1918.* Toronto: privately printed, 1936. 72 pp.

O'Gorman, J.R., comp. *The War and the 7th Bn. C.R.T.* n.p.: [1920]. 67 pp.

Oh, Canada; a Medley of Stories, Verse, Pictures and Music, Contributed by Members of the Canadian Expeditionary Force. London: Simpkin, Marshall, Hamilton, Kent, 1916. 95 pp.

On the Roll of Honour, G.L.B. Mackenzie, Lieutenant in the Third Battalion, Toronto Regiment, 1st Division, Canadian Expeditionary Force, 4th January, 1892 — 7th June, 1916. n.p.: privately printed, [1916]. 64 pp.

Once in the Queen's Own, Always in the Queen's Own. n.p.: privately printed, 1932. 70 pp.

101st Overseas Battalion, W.L.I., C.E.F.; Souvenir Programme.
Winnipeg: privately printed, 1916. 88 pp.

The 116th Battalion in France see Allen, E.P.S.

Ontario. Dept. of Education. *Annals of Valour; Empire Day, Friday, May 23rd, 1919.* Toronto: King's Printer, 1919. 165 pp.

_____. *Canada's Part in the Present War; Empire Day, Thursday, May 23rd, 1918.* Toronto: King's Printer, 1918. 95 pp.

_____. *The Roll of Honour of the Ontario Teachers who Served in the Great War, 1914-1918.* Toronto: Ryerson Press, 1922. 72 pp.

Ontario Agricultural College, Guelph, Ont. *Ontario Agricultural College Honor and Service Rolls.* n.p.: n.d. 1 vol., unpaged.

Oval, E.I., [*pseud.*] *voir* Lavoie, Joseph A.

Overseas Service of the 18th Battery, Canadian Field Artillery. n.p.: [1919]. 26 pp.

Parkdale Collegiate Institute, Toronto, Ont. *Roll of Service in the Great War, 1914-1919.* n.p.: n.d. 22 pp.

_____. *Their Name Liveth; a Memoir of the Boys of Parkdale Collegiate Institute who Gave their Lives in the Great War.* Toronto: privately printed, n.d. 177 pp.

Peace Souvenir; Activities of Waterloo County in the Great War, 1914-1918. Kitchener, Ont.: Kitchener Daily Telegraph, 1919. 70 pp.

Pearson, George. *The Escape of a Princess Pat; Being the Full Account of the Capture and Fifteen Months' Imprisonment of Corporal Edwards, of the Princess Patricia's Canadian Light Infantry, and his Final Escape from Germany into Holland.* Toronto: McClelland, Goodchild & Stewart, 1918. 227 pp.

Peat, Harold R. *Private Peat.* Indianapolis, In.: Bobbs-Merrill, 1917. 235 pp.

Pedley, James H. *Only This; a War Retrospect.* Ottawa: Graphic Publishers, 1927. 371 pp.

Penny, Arthur G. *Royal Rifles of Canada, "Able and Willing" Since 1862; a Short History.* n.p.: 1962. 62 pp.

Peterson, W.G. *Silhouettes of Mars.* London: J. Lane, 1920. 266 pp.

Peterson, (Sir) William. *"A Canadian Hospital in France."* n.p.: 1915. 12 pp.
At head of title: McGill University, Montreal, Annual University Lecture.

Phillips, Roger, and Jerome J. Knap. *Sir Charles Ross and his Rifle.* (Historical Arms Series, no. 11.) Ottawa: Museum Restoration Service, 1969. 32 pp.

[Pirie, Alexander Howard, comp.] *No. 3 Canadian General Hospital (McGill) in France (1915, 1916, 1917); Views Illustrating Life and Scenes in the Hospital, with a Short Description of its Origin, Organisation and Progress.* Middlesbrough, Eng.: Hood, 1918. 1 vol., unpaged.

Plewman, W.R., *see* Miller, James Martin.

Plummer, Mary. *With the First Canadian Contingent.* London: Hodder & Stoughton, 1916. 118 pp.

Les poilus canadiens; le roman du vingt-deuxième bataillon canadien-français, par J.A.H. s.l.: s.i., s.d. 47 pp.

Pontifex, Bryan, comp. *Canadian Army Service Corps, 2nd Divisional Train; Record of Service of Officers, 1914-1919.* Toronto: Carswell, 1920. 42 pp.

Pope, Maurice A. *Soldiers and Politicians; the Memoirs of Lt.-Gen. Maurice A. Pope, C.B., M.C.* Toronto: Univ. of Toronto Press, 1962. 462 pp.

Preston, Richard A. *Canada and "Imperial Defense"; a Study of the Origins of the British Commonwealth's Defense Organization, 1867-1919.* (Duke University Commonwealth-Studies Center; Publication Number 29.) Durham, N.C.: Duke Univ. Press, 1967. 576 pp.

_____. *Canada's RMC; a History of the Royal Military College.* Toronto: Univ. of Toronto Press, 1969. 415 pp.

Princess Patricia's Canadian Light Infantry Recruit's Book. [Winnipeg: n.p., 1946.] 24 pp.

Programme souvenir; publié à l'occasion du retour d'outre-mer du 22eme Bataillon (Canadien-français), mai, 1919. Québec, P.Q.: s.i., [1919]. 32 pp.

Queen's Own Rifles of Canada Association. *A Brief Resumé of the Activities of the Queen's Own Rifles of Canada Association, 1914-1932.* Toronto: privately printed, 1932. 70 pp.

_____. [*Queen's Own Rifles of Canada; Book of Remembrance, 1866-1918.* n.p.: 1932.] 1 vol., unpaged.

Queen's Univ., Kingston, Ont. *Overseas Record; Record of Graduates, Alumni, Members of Staff, and Students of Queen's University on Active Military (Overseas) Service (to June 1st, 1917), 1914-1917.* n.p.: [1917?]. 44 pp.

Quigley, John Gordon. *A Century of Rifles, 1860-1960; the Halifax Rifles (RCAC)(M); "cede nullis".* Halifax: privately printed, 1960. 230 pp.

Rabjohn, R.H. *A Diary; a Story of My Experience: in France, and Belgium, during the World War, 1914-1918.* Burlington, Ont.: CDM Business Services, 1977. 1 vol., chiefly illus.

Rae, Herbert, [*pseud.*] *see* Gibson, George Herbert Rae.

Ralphson, George H. *Over There, with the Canadians at Vimy Ridge.* Chicago: M.A. Donohue, 1919. 221 pp.

Rawlinson, James H. *Through St. Dunstan's to Light.* Toronto: T. Allen, 1919. 86 pp.

The Regimental History of the Governor General's Foot Guards see Baylay, George Taylor.

A Remembrance from the Survivors, All Ranks, of the 16th Battalion (the Canadian Scottish) C.E.F., 1914-1919, to All Ranks now Serving in the Canadian Scottish Regiment, which Regiment Perpetuates the 16th. n.p.: n.d. 91 pp.

Renison, Robert, *see* Hopkins, J. Castell.

A Report Addressed to the Canadian Hierarchy on the Organization and Work of the Canadian Catholic Chaplains Overseas, for the Year 1917. London: privately printed, 1918. 16 pp.

Richards, R. *The Story of the Princess Patricia's Canadian Light Infantry, 1914-1917.* London: Charles, 1918. 23 pp.

Robertson, F.A. *5th (B.C.) Regiment, Canadian Garrison Artillery, and Early Defences of B.C. Coast; Historical Record.* Victoria, B.C.: privately printed, 1925. 2 vols.

Robertson, Heather, [comp.] *A Terrible Beauty; the Art of Canada at War.* Toronto: J. Lorimer, 1977. 239 pp.

Robertson, Peter. *Irréductible vérité/Relentless Verity/les photographes militaires canadiens depuis 1885/Canadian Military Photographers since 1885.* (Les Archives publiques du Canada/Public Archives of Canada Series.) Québec, P.Q.: Les Presses de l'Université Laval, 1973. 233 pp.
Texte bilingue./Bilingual text.

Rocky Mountain Rangers; First Battalion, C.A. — A.F., 1885-1941. New Westminster, B.C.: Columbian Co., 1941. 60 pp., chiefly illus.

Rogers, R.L. *History of the Lincoln and Welland Regiment.* n.p.: privately printed, 1954. 465 pp.

Roll Call of Canadian Irish. Toronto: n.p., 1916. 32 pp.

Rossiter, Ivan. *In Kultured Kaptivity; Life and Death in Germany's Prison Camps and Hospitals.* Indianapolis, In.: Bobbs-Merrill, 1918. 244 pp.

Roy, R.H. *For Most Conspicuous Bravery; a Biography of Major-General George R. Pearkes, V.C., through Two World Wars.* Vancouver: Univ. of British Columbia Press, 1977. 388 pp.

_____. *Ready for the Fray (Deas Gu Cath); the History of the Canadian Scottish Regiment (Princess Mary's), 1920-1955.* Vancouver: privately printed, 1958. 509 pp.

_____. *The Seaforth Highlanders of Canada, 1919-1965.* Vancouver: privately printed, 1969. 559 pp.

_____. *Sinews of Steel; the History of the British Columbia Dragoons.* Brampton, Ont.: privately printed, 1965. 468 pp.

*The Royal Canadian Armoured Corps. Ottawa: Queen's Printer, 1953. 11 pp.

*The Royal Canadian Army Medical Corps. Ottawa: Queen's Printer, 1953. 10 pp.

*Royal Canadian Army Pay Corps. Ottawa: Queen's Printer, 1953. 11 pp.

*The Royal Canadian Army Service Corps. Ottawa: Queen's Printer, 1953. 11 pp.

The Royal Canadian Artillery. Ottawa: Queen's Printer, 1953. 10 pp.

Royal Canadian Horse Artillery; First Regiment, 1871-1971. Lahr, Ger.: privately printed, [1971]. 32 pp.

Royal Canadian Military Institute, Toronto, Ont. *The Golden Book.* Toronto: privately printed, 1927. 1 vol., unpaged.

The Royal Canadian Ordnance Corps Diamond Jubilee Yearbook. n.p.: 1963. 106 pp.

The Royal Highlanders of Canada, Allied with the Black Watch (Royal Highlanders), Montreal, Canada. London: H. Rees, 1918. 30 pp.

The Royal Military College of Canada, 1876-1919. Kingston: n.p., 1919. 16 pp.

Royal Military College of Canada, Kingston, Ont. *Regulations for the Royal Military College of Canada, Kingston, Ont.; Amended to May 1917.* Ottawa: King's Printer, 1917. 25 pp.

_____. *The Stone Frigate.* Kingston, Ont.: privately printed, 1914. 301 pp.

The Royal Rifles of Canada, Allied with the King's Royal Rifle Corps, 1862-1937; Ypres 1915, Festubert, Mont Sorrel, Somme 1916, Arras 1917, Hill 70, Ypres 1917, Amiens; South Africa 1899-1900; Great War 1914-1918. n.p.: [1937]. 21 pp.

Rudbach, N.E. *The Halifax Rifles (23 Armoured Regiment) R.C.A.C.R.F.; "90th" Anniversary, 14th May 1860 — 14th May 1950.* Halifax: n.p., 1950. 20 pp.

Russenholt, E.S., comp. *Six Thousand Canadian Men; being the History of the 44th Battalion Canadian Infantry, 1914-1919.* Winnipeg: privately printed, 1932. 364 pp.

Rutherford, Tom. *An Unofficial History of the Grey and Simcoe Foresters Regiment, 1866-1973.* n.p.: n.d. 88 pp.

Rutledge, Stanley A. *Pen Pictures from the Trenches.* Toronto: W. Briggs, 1918. 159 pp.

Ryerson, George Sterling. *Looking Backward.* Toronto: Ryerson Press, 1924. 264 pp.

Santor, Donald M. *Canadians at War, 1914-1918.* (Canadiana Scrapbook.) Scarborough, Ont.: Prentice-Hall, 1978. 48 pp.

Schragg, Lex. *History of the Ontario Regiment, 1866-1951.* Oshawa, Ont.: privately printed, 1951. 286 pp.

Scott, Frederic George. *The Great War as I Saw It.* Toronto: Goodehill, 1922. 327 pp.

Scudamore, T.V. *Lighter Episodes in the Life of a Prisoner of War.* Aldershot, Eng.: Gale & Polden, 1933. 92 pp.

_____. *A Short History of the 7th Battalion, C.E.F.* Vancouver: privately printed, 1930. 1 vol., unpaged.

Second Contingent, Military District No. 10, 1915; in Commemoration of the Second Contingent Going to the Front from Military District No. 10, Canada, 1915. [Winnipeg: n.p., 1915.] 1 vol., chiefly illus.

Service, G.T., and J.K. Marteinson. *The Gate; a History of the Fort Garry Horse.* Calgary: privately printed, 1971. 228 pp.

78th Overseas Battalion (Winnipeg Grenadiers). Winnipeg: Advance Photo Co., 1916. 35 pp., chiefly illus.

75th Battalion; Book of the Battalion. Toronto: privately printed, [1916]. 36 pp.

77th Overseas Battalion, Canadian Expeditionary Force, Ottawa. Ottawa: privately printed, [1916]. 1 vol., chiefly illus.

Sheldon-Williams, Ralf Frederic Lardy. *The Canadian Front in France and Flanders.* Inglis Sheldon-Williams, illus. London: A. and C. Black, 1920. 208 pp.

A Short History and Photographic Record of 106th Overseas Battalion, C.E.F., Nova Scotia Rifles, Lieut. Col. Robert Innes, Commanding Officer. [Ottawa]: Mortimer, 1916. 47 pp.

A Short History & Photographic Record of the Nova Scotia Overseas Highland Brigade, C.E.F., Composed of the 85th Nova Scotia Highlanders, 193rd Nova Scotia Highlanders, 219th Overseas Highland Battalion, Lieut. Col. A.H. Borden, Brigadier. Halifax: Mortimer, 1916. v.p.

A Short History and Photographic Record of the 73rd Battalion, Canadian Expeditionary Force, Royal Highlanders of Canada; Allied with the Black Watch. Ottawa: privately printed, n.d. 47 pp.

A Short History of the British Columbia Regiment; the "Dukes". n.p.: n.d. [11] pp.

Short Memoirs of the Third Canadian Divisional Mechanical Transport Company; Organized April 14th, 1918, Demobilized May 1st, 1919. London, privately printed, [1919]. 34 pp.

Sifton, C., comp. *The Diary of the 13th Battery, Canadian Field Artillery, 1914-1919.* London: privately printed, 1919. 47 pp.

Sime, J.G. *Canada Chaps.* Toronto: S.B. Gundy, 1917. 270 pp.

Simmons, [Mervin C.] *Three Times Out,* told by Private Simmons, written by Nellie L. McClung. Toronto: T. Allen, 1918. 247 pp.

Sinclair, J.D., comp. *The Queen's Own Cameron Highlanders of Canada; Twenty-fifth Anniversary Souvenir.* Winnipeg: privately printed, 1935. 99 pp.

Singer, H.C., and A.A. Peebles. *History of Thirty-First Battalion C.E.F. from its Organization, November, 1914, to its Demobilization, June, 1919.* Calgary: privately printed, [1939]. 515 pp.

Six Bits. Vol. I, no. 1-7. Toronto: privately printed, 1919-20. Published by the 75th Battalion Overseas Association.

The 60th C.F.A. Battery Book, 1916-1919. London: Canada Newspaper Co., [1919]. 190 pp.

60th Canadian Battalion B.E.F. (Victoria Rifles of Canada). n.p.: [1917. 10 pp.]

Smith, G. Oswald, *see University of Toronto . . . .*

Smith, Joseph S. *Over There and Back in Three Uniforms; being the Experiences of an American Boy in the Canadian, British and American Armies at the Front and through No Man's Land.* New York: Dutton, 1917. 244 pp.

Snell, A.E. *The C.A.M.C., with the Canadian Corps during the Last Hundred Days of the Great War.* Ottawa: King's Printer, 1924. 292 pp.

Social Service Council of Canada. *Moral Conditions among our Soldiers Overseas; Official and other Reliable Evidence.* Toronto: privately printed, [191-?]. 12 pp.

Souvenir Book of the 79th Cameron Highlanders of Canada. Winnipeg: n.p., 1916. 32 pp.

Souvenir, 231st Overseas Battalion, C.E.F., 3rd Battn., 72nd Seaforth Highlanders of Canada. Vancouver: n.p., 1917. 41 pp.

Speaight, Robert. *Vanier; Soldier, Diplomat and Governor General.* Toronto: Collins, 1970. 488 pp.

Stanley, George F.G. *Canada's Soldiers, 1604-1954; the Military History of an Unmilitary People.* Toronto: Macmillan, 1954. 400 pp.

_____. *In the Face of Danger; the History of the Lake Superior Regiment.* Port Arthur, Ont.: privately printed, 1960. 357 pp.

Stanley, George, F.G., and Richard A. Preston. *A Short History of Kingston as a Military and Naval Centre.* Kingston, Ont.: Queen's Printer, [195-?]. 33 pp.

Steele, Harwood. *The Canadians in France, 1915-1918.* Toronto: Copp Clark, 1920. 364 pp.

_____. *The Long Ride; a Short History of the 17th Duke of York's Royal Canadian Hussars.* Montreal: Gazette Print. Co., 1934. 48 pp.

Steven, Walter T. *In this Sign.* Toronto: Ryerson Press, 1948. 182 pp.

Stevens, G.R. *A City Goes to War.* Brampton, Ont.: Charters Pub., 1964. 431 pp.

Stewart, Charles H., comp. *The Concise Lineages of the Canadian Army, 1855 to Date.* Toronto: n.p., n.d. 163 pp.

_____. *"Overseas"; the Lineages and Insignia of the Canadian Expeditionary Force, 1914-1919.* Toronto: Little and Stewart, 1970. 167 pp.

The Story of the Sixty-Sixth C.F.A. Edinburgh: Turnbull & Spears, 1919. 148 pp.

The Strathconian. Calgary: n.p., 1914-?, 1927-38, 1947-   .
Regimental journal of the Lord Strathcona's Horse (Royal Canadians). Re-numbered from no. 1 after each gap in publication.

Stuart, (Sir) Campbell. *Opportunity Knocks Once.* London: Collins, 1952. 248 pp.

Stubbs, Roy St. George. *Men in Khaki; Four Regiments of Manitoba.* Toronto: Ryerson Press, 1941. 72 pp.

A Sunny Subaltern; Billy's Letters from Flanders. Toronto: McClelland, Goodchild & Stewart, 1916. 175 pp.
London ed. titled: *A Canadian Subaltern; Billy's Letters to his Mother.*

Swettenham, John. *Allied Intervention in Russia, 1918-1919; and the Part Played by Canada.* Toronto: Ryerson Press, 1967. 315 pp.

_____. *Canada and the First World War.* Toronto: Ryerson Press, 1969. 160 pp.

_____. *Canada and the First World War./La participation du Canada à la première guerre mondiale.* Ottawa: Canadian War Museum/Musée de guerre, n.d./s.d. 56/63 pp.
Bilingual text./Texte bilingue.

_____. *McNaughton.* Toronto: Ryerson Press, 1968-69. 3 vols.

_____. *To Seize the Victory; the Canadian Corps in World War I.* Toronto: Ryerson Press, 1965. 265 pp.

T., R.H., *see* Tupper, Reginald H.

Tamblyn, D.S. *The Horse in War, and Famous Canadian War Horses.* Kingston, Ont.: Jackson Press, n.d. 120 pp.

3rd Contingent from 1st & 2nd Divisions, Ontario; in Commemoration of the 3rd Contingent Going to the Front from the 1st and 2nd Divisions, Ontario ... 1915. n.p.: G.R. Gibbons, n.d. 1 vol., chiefly illus.

Thomas, Hartley Munro. *UWO Contingent COTC; the History of the Canadian Officers' Training Corps at the University of Western Ontario.* London, Ont.: Univ. of Western Ontario, 1956. 422 pp.

Thompson, Roy J.C. *Cap Badges of the Canadian Officer Training Corps.* Dartmouth, N.S.: n.p., 1972. 68 pp.

_____. *Wings of the Canadian Armed Forces, 1913-1972.* [Dartmouth], N.S.: n.p., 1973. 106 pp.

Thorburn, Ella M., and Charlotte Whitton. *Canada's Chapel of Remembrance.* Toronto: British Book Service (Canada), 1961. 68 pp.

Thorn, J.C. *Three Years a Prisoner in Germany; the Story of Major J.C. Thorn, a First Canadian Contingent Officer, who was Captured by the Germans at Ypres on April 24th, 1915; Relating his many Attempts to Escape (once Disguised as a Widow) and Life in the Various Camps and Fortresses.* n.p.: 1919. 152 pp.

Topp, C. Beresford. *The 42nd Battalion, C.E.F., Royal Highlanders of Canada in the Great War.* Montreal: privately printed, 1931. 412 pp.

Toronto's Roll of Honour Fighting the Empire's Battles; an Alphabetical Directory of the Toronto Members of the First and Second Contingents. Toronto: Stevenson & Hevey, 1915. 120 pp.

*La Trésorerie militaire royale canadienne. Ottawa: Imprimeur de la Reine, 1954. 12 pp.

Tributes to the Memory of Corp. G. Gordon Galloway, B.A., 26th Battery, C.F.A., Killed in Action in Flanders, Feb. 10, 1916; Aged 21 yrs. 8 mos. n.p.: n.d. 27 pp.

Trinity Methodist Church, Toronto, Ont. *Trinity War Book; a Recital of Service and Sacrifice in the Great War.* Oliver Hezzelwood, comp. Toronto: privately printed, 1921. 368 pp.

Tucker, A.B. *The Battle Glory of Canada; being the Story of the Canadians at the Front, Including the Battle of Ypres.* London: Cassell, [1915]. 168 pp.

[Tupper, Reginald H.] *Victor Gordon Tupper; a Brother's Tribute,* by R.H.T. London: privately printed, 1921. 66 pp.

Turner, H.S., *With the Tenth Field Company, Canadian Engineers, C.E.F.* [Goderich, Ont.: n.p., 1936-41.] 3 vols.

Twenty-Third Battery, Field Artillery; Active Service, 1915. London: Roberts & Leete, [1915. 31 pp.]

226th Overseas Battalion, C.E.F., North-Western Manitoba. Winnipeg: privately printed, n.d. 60 pp.

Univ. of British Columbia. *Record of Service, 1914-1918; University of British Columbia, McGill British Columbia, Vancouver College.* Vancouver: privately printed, 1924. 142 pp.

Univ. of Manitoba. *Roll of Honour, 1914-1918.* Winnipeg: privately printed, 1923. 150 pp.

Univ. of Toronto. Victoria College. *Acta Victoriana; War Supplement.* [Toronto]: n.p., 1919. 128 pp.

University of Toronto; Roll of Service, 1914-1918. G. Oswald Smith, ed. Toronto: Univ. of Toronto Press, 1921. 603 pp.

Unknown Soldiers, by One of Them. New York: Vantage Press, 1959. 170 pp.

Upper Canada Historical Arms Society. *The Military Arms of Canada.* (Historical Arms Series, 1.) West Hill, Ont.: Museum Restoration Service, 1963. 47 pp.

Upton, Terence B. *The Rocky Mountain Rangers, 1898-1944; a Short History.* n.p.: n.d. 13 pp.

Urquhart, Hugh M. *Arthur Currie; the Biography of a Great Canadian.* Toronto: Dent, 1950. 363 pp.

_____. *The History of the 16th Battalion (the Canadian Scottish) Canadian Expeditionary Force in the Great War, 1914-1919.* Toronto: Macmillan, 1932. 853 pp.

The Vancouver Battalion. Vol. I, no. 1. Vancouver: privately printed, 1915. 34 pp.
  Journal of the 29th (Vancouver) Battalion, CEF. Apparently no further numbers were published.

Van Der Schee, W. *A Short History of Lord Strathcona's Horse (Royal Canadians).* n.p.: 1973. 19 1.

Victoria Rifles of Canada, 1861-1951; Historical Notes. n.p.: n.d. 14 pp.

Victoria Rifles of Canada; Youth Trained in Mind and Body in a Great Regiment. n.p.: [ca. 1936]. 16 pp.

Les Voltigeurs de Québec, 1862-1952; notes historiques. s.l.: s.i., 1952. 16 pp.

Les Voltigeurs de Québec, 1862-1962; album du centenaire, mai 1962. St-François, P.Q.: imprimé privé, 1962. 31 pp.

War Record of Chattan Men see Chattan Club, Toronto, Ont.

War Record of McGill Chapter of Delta Upsilon. Montreal: n.p., 1919. 47 pp.

Ware, Francis B. *The Story of the Seventh Regiment Fusiliers of London, Canada, 1899 to 1914; with an Epilogue, "A Few Days with the Fusiliers at War".* London, Ont.: Hunter Print. Co., 1945. 190 pp.

Warren, Arnold. *Wait for the Waggon; the Story of the Royal Canadian Army Service Corps.* Toronto: McClelland and Stewart, 1961. 413 pp.

Watson, W.S., and others, eds. *The Brockville Rifles, Royal Canadian Infantry Corps (Allied with the King's Royal Rifle Corps); Semper Paratus; an Unofficial History.* Brockville, Ont.: Recorder Print. Co., 1966. 138 pp.

Weatherbe, K., comp. *From the Rideau to the Rhine; the 6th Field Co. and Battalion Canadian Engineers in the Great War; a Narrative.* Toronto: Hunter-Rose Co., 1928. 519 pp.

Wells, Clifford Almon. *From Montreal to Vimy Ridge and Beyond; the Correspondence of Lieut. Clifford Almon Wells, B.A., of 8th Battalion Canadians, B.E.F., November, 1915 — April, 1917.* O.C.S. Wallace, ed. Toronto: McClelland, Goodchild & Stewart, 1917. 321 pp.

Willcocks, K.D.H. *The Hastings and Prince Edward Regiment, Canada; a Short History.* Belleville, Ont.: n.p., 1967. 1 vol., unpaged.

Williams, Jeffery. *Princess Patricia's Canadian Light Infantry.* (Famous Regiments.) London: L. Cooper, 1972. 110 pp.

Williams, S.H. *Stand to Your Horses; through the First World War, 1914-1918, with the Lord Strathcona's Horse (Royal Canadians).* Winnipeg: privately printed, 1961. 308 pp.

Willson, Gordon Beckles. *From Quebec to Picadilly and Other Places; some Anglo-Canadian Memories.* London: J. Cape, 1929. 366 pp.

_____. *In the Ypres Salient; the Story of a Fortnight's Canadian Fighting, June 2-16, 1916.* London: W. Cloes, n.d. 79 pp.

Wilson, Barbara M., ed. *Ontario and the First World War, 1914-1918; a Collection of Documents.* (The Publications of the Champlain Society; Ontario Series, X.) Toronto: Champlain Society, 1977. 201 pp.

Winnington-Ingram, Arthur F. *'Life for Ever and Ever'; Preached by the Right Hon. and Right Rev. Arthur F. Winnington-Ingram, D.D., Lord Bishop of London, at the Canadian Memorial Service, St. Paul's Cathedral, May 10th, 1915.* London: Wells Gardner, Darton, n.d. 19 pp.

Winnipeg Grain Exchange Honor Roll; Resident Members and Employees who Enlisted and Fought in the Great War, August 4th, 1914 — November 11th, 1918. n.p.: n.d. 1 vol., unpaged.

The Winnipeg Rifles, 8th Battalion, C.E.F., Allied with the Rifle Brigade (Prince Consort's Own); Fiftieth Anniversary, 1883-1933. Winnipeg: privately printed, 1933. 59 pp.

Winter, Charles F. *Lieutenant-General the Hon. Sir Sam Hughes K.C.B., M.P.: Canada's War Minister, 1911-1916; Recollections of Service as Military Secretary at Headquarters, Canadian Militia, prior to and during the Early Stages of the Great War.* Toronto: Macmillan, 1931. 182 pp.

With the 4th Canadian Div'l Signal Coy C.E. on Active Service. n.p.: n.d. 111 pp.

Wodehouse, R.F. *A Check List of the War Collections of World War I, 1914-1918, and World War II, 1939-1945.* Ottawa: Queen's Printer, 1968. 239 pp.

Wood, Herbert Fairlie. *Vimy!* Toronto: Macmillan, 1967. 186 pp.

Worthington, Larry. *Amid the Guns Below; the Story of the Canadian Corps, 1914-1919.* Toronto: McClelland and Stewart, 1965. 171 pp.

Worthington, Larry. *The Spur and the Sprocket; the Story of the Royal Canadian Dragoons.* Kitchener, Ont.: Reeve Press, 1968. 170 pp.

_____. *"Worthy"; a Biography of Major-General F.F. Worthington, C.B., M.C., M.M.* Toronto: Macmillan, 1961. 236 pp.

Young, A.H., and W.A. Kirkwood, eds. *The War Memorial Volume of Trinity College, Toronto.* [Toronto]: Printers Guild, 1922. 165 pp.

Young, A.H., ed. *The War Book of Upper Canada College, Toronto.* Toronto: privately printed, 1923. 322 pp.

Young Men's Christian Associations, Canada. *The Camera with the Canadian Forestry Corps in Great Britain.* London: n.p., n.d. 24 pp., chiefly illus.

Young Men's Christian Associations, Canada. National Council. *The Achievements of the Young Men's Christian Associations in the Great War.* Toronto: privately printed, [1935]. 20 pp.

_____. *On Leave; How the Red Triangle Club, Toronto, Provides for the Soldier while Off Duty.* Toronto: privately printed, 1917. 1 vol., unpaged.

1919-1945

Abautret, René. *Dieppe, le sacrifice des Canadiens, 19 août 1942.* Paris: R. Laffont, 1969. 250 pp.

Active Service Canteen, Toronto, 1939-1945. Toronto: n.p., 1945. 1 vol., unpaged.

Adleman, Robert H., and George Walton. *The Devil's Brigade.* Philadelphia, Pa.: Chilton Books, 1966. 259 pp.

Aernoudts, Karel. *Waar de rode klaproos bloeit; een episode uit de Tweede Wereldoorlog; strijd om de vrijmaking van de linker Scheldemonding, september, oktober, november 1944.* Oostburg, Neth.: W.J. Pieters, 1972. 201 pp.

Alexander, G.M., ed. *4th Canadian Armoured Brigade.* [Mitcham, Eng.: privately printed, n.d.] 47 pp.

Allister, William. *A Handful of Rice.* London: Secker and Warburg, 1961. 288 pp.

Armit, W.B. *Army Museum; Halifax Citadel Halifax, Nova Scotia.* Kentville, N.S.: n.p., [1957?]. 34 pp.

*L'Arsenal de Québec, 1880-1945. Québec, P.Q.: s.i., 1947. 166 pp.

Austin, A.B. *We Landed at Dawn; the Story of the Dieppe Raid.* New York: Harcourt, Brace, 1943. 217 pp.

B.M.A. Blitz. Vol. I-IV. Brockville, Ont.: privately printed, 1942-45. *Journal of the Officers' Training Centre, Brockville.*

Bank of Montreal. *Field of Honour; the Second World War, 1939-1945.* Montreal: n.p., 1950. 1 vol., unpaged.

Barnard, W.T. *The Queen's Own Rifles of Canada, 1860-1960; One Hundred Years of Canada.* Don Mills, Ont.: Ontario Pub. Co., 1960. 398 pp.

_____. *A Short History of the Queen's Own Rifles of Canada.* Toronto: MacKinnon & Atkins, n.d. 22 pp.

Barnes, C.H. *Colonel Colin Clarke Harbottle, C.M.G., D.S.O., V.D.* n.p.: [1958]. 20 pp.

Barrass, R., and T.J.H. Sloan. *The Story of 657 Air O.P. Squadron R.A.F., January 31st, 1943, to May 8th, 1945.* London: Whitefriars Press, n.d. 96 pp.

Barrett, W.W. *The History of 13 Canadian Field Regiment, Royal Canadian Artillery, 1940-1945.* n.p.: n.d. 188 pp.

Bartlett, Jack Fortune. *1st Battalion, the Highland Light Infantry of Canada, 1940-1945.* Galt, Ont.: privately printed, n.d. 126 pp.

Bates, Maxwell. *A Wilderness of Days; an Artist's Experiences as a Prisoner of War in Germany.* Victoria, B.C.: Sono Nis Press, 1978. 133 pp.

[Baylay, George Taylor], ed. *The Regimental History of the Governor General's Foot Guards.* Ottawa: privately printed, 1948. 268 pp.

Beattie, Kim. *Dileas; History of the 48th Highlanders of Canada, 1929-1956.* Toronto: privately printed, 1957. 847 pp.

_____. *48th Highlanders of Canada, 1891-1928.* Toronto: privately printed, 1932. 434 pp.

Beckles, Gordon, [*pseud.*] *see* Willson, Gordon Beckles.

Bell, G.K. *Curtain Call.* Toronto: Intaglio Gravure, 1953. 136 pp.

Bell, J. Mackintosh. *Sidelights on the Siberian Campaign.* Toronto: Ryerson Press, 1923. 132 pp.

Bell, K., and C.P. Stacey. *Not in Vain.* Toronto: Univ. of Toronto Press, 1973. 143 pp.

Bell, T.J. *Into Action with the 12th Field.* T.E. Jarvis, ed. n.p.: n.d. 159 pp.

Bezeau, M.V. *University of Ottawa Contingent, Canadian Officers Training Corps.* n.p.: 1968. 15 pp.

Bindon, Kathryn M. *Queen's Men, Canada's Men; the Military History of Queen's University, Kingston.* [Kingston, Ont.]: privately printed, 1978. 180 pp.

Bird, Will R. *No Retreating Footsteps; the Story of the North Nova Scotia Highlanders.* Kentville, N.S.: privately printed, n.d. 399 pp.

_____. *North Shore (New Brunswick) Regiment.* Fredericton, N.B.: Brunswick Press, 1963. 629 pp.

_____. *The Two Jacks; the Amazing Adventures of Major Jack M. Veness and Major Jack L. Fairweather.* Toronto: Ryerson Press, 1954. 209 pp.

Birney, Earle, ed. *Record of Service in the Second World War; the University of British Columbia; a Supplement to the University of British Columbia War Memorial Manuscript Record.* Vancouver: privately printed, 1955. 46 pp.

Boissonnault, Charles-Marie. *Histoire du Royal 22e Régiment.* Québec, P.Q.: Editions du pélican, 1964. 414 pp.

_____. *Histoire politico-militaire des Canadiens français (1763-1967).* Trois-Rivières, P.Q.: Editions du Bien public, 1967. 310 pp.

Boss, W. *The Stormont, Dundas and Glengarry Highlanders, 1783-1951.* Ottawa: Runge Press, 1952. 449 pp.

Bowering, Clifford H. *Service; the Story of the Canadian Legion, 1925-1960.* Ottawa: privately printed, 1960. 240 pp.

Bowman, Phylis. *We Skirted the War!* Prince Rupert, B.C.: privately printed, 1975. 133 pp.

The Brazier; Marking the 50th Anniversary of the Canadian Scottish (Princess Mary's), June 6, 1964. Victoria, B.C.: privately printed, 1964. 19 pp.

A Brief Historical Sketch of the Lorne Scots (Peel, Dufferin and Halton Regiment). Brampton, Ont.: Charters Pub. Co., 1943. 24 pp.

A Brief Historical Sketch of the Queen's York Rangers, 1st American Regiment. Toronto: privately printed, 1942. 30 pp.

A Brief History of the Royal Regiment of Canada, [Allied with the King's Regiment (Liverpool)]. [Toronto: n.p., 1940.] 77 pp.

A Brief History of the Royal Regiment of Canada; Allied with the King's Regiment (Liverpool). [Toronto: n.p., 1948.] 135 pp.

A Brief History of the 3rd Battalion C.E.F. (Toronto Regiment), Now the Toronto Regiment; (Allied with the King's Regiment (Liverpool)). n.p.: 1934. 47 pp.

The Brigade. Vol. I-III? Winnipeg: privately printed, 1942-46? *Journal of the 38th Reserve Brigade.*

British Great War Veterans of America, Inc. *Official Souvenir Book in Commemoration of the Visit to New York of the Fifth Royal Highlanders of Canada, the "Black Watch" of Montreal on Memorial Day, 1925.* New York: n.p., 1925. 1 vol., unpaged.

Broadfoot, Barry. *Six War Years, 1939-1945; Memories of Canadians at Home and Abroad.* Toronto: Doubleday Canada, 1974. 417 pp.

Brock, Thomas Leith. *Fight the Good Fight; Looking in on the Recruit Class at the Royal Military College of Canada during a Week in February, 1931.* Montreal: privately printed, 1964. 30 pp.

Brown, Kingsley, *see* Greenhous, Brereton.

*Brown, W.J. *Les Cadets royaux de l'armée canadienne; cent ans d'exploits, 1879-1979.* s.l.: La Ligue des Cadets de l'Armée du Canada, [1979. 12 pp.]

* _____. *The Royal Canadian Army Cadets; a Century of Achievement, 1879-1979.* n.p.: The Army Cadet League of Canada, [1979. 12 pp.]

Bruce, Walter H., and others, comps. *Historical Records of the Argyll and Sutherland Highlanders of Canada (Princess Louise's), Formerly 91st Regiment Canadian Highlanders, Canadian Militia, 1903-1928.* Hamilton, Ont.: R. Duncan, 1928. 99 pp.

Buchanan, G.B. *The March of the Prairie Men; a Story of the South Saskatchewan Regiment.* Weyburn, Sask.: privately printed, [1957?]. 75 pp.

Buckingham, N.A. *A Brief History of the 4th Canadian Armoured Brigade in Action July 1944 — May 1945.* n.p.: privately printed, 1945. 47 pp.

Bull, Wm. Perkins. *From Brock to Currie; the Military Development and Exploits of Canadians in General and of the Men of Peel in Particular, 1791 to 1930.* Toronto: G.J. McLeod, 1935. 772 pp.

Burch, E.T. *"So, I Said to the Colonel."* Toronto: Ryerson Press, 1941. 72 pp.

Burhans, R.D. *The First Special Service Force; a War History of the North Americans, 1942-1944.* Washington: Infantry Journal Press, 1947. 376 pp.

Burns, E.L.M. *General Mud; Memoirs of Two World Wars.* Toronto: Clarke, Irwin, 1970. 254 pp.

_____. *Manpower in the Canadian Army, 1939-1945.* Toronto: Clarke, Irwin, 1956. 184 pp.

CAM. Vol. I-II. Ottawa: King's Printer, 1943-45.
Journal of the Directorate of Mechanical Maintenance, National Defence Headquarters.

The Calgary Regiment. n.p.: n.d. 17 pp.

Callan, Les. *From "D" Day to Victory, Normandy and On with the Fighting Canadians.* Toronto: Longmans, Green, 1945. 126 pp.

The Cameron Highlanders of Ottawa: Standing Orders and Constitution and Rules of the Officers Mess. n.p.: [1934]. 88 pp.

Cameron, James M. *Pictonians in Arms; a Military History of Pictou County, Nova Scotia.* Fredericton, N.B.: privately printed, 1969. 301 pp.

Camp, A.D., comp. *7th Toronto Regiment, Royal Regiment of Canadian Artillery, 1866-1966.* n.p.: n.d. 33 pp.

Camp Valcartier, P.Q.; 1647 à 1957 en quelques lignes./Camp Valcartier P.Q.; a Short History, 1647-1957. s.l.: s.i./n.p.: 1957. 24 pp.
Texte bilingue./Bilingual text.

Canada. Armée. Quartier général de l'Armée. Section Historique. Introduction à l'étude de l'histoire militaire à l'intention des étudiants canadiens, [par C.P. Stacey]. Ottawa: [Imprimeur du Roi], 1951. 45 pp.
Editions subséquentes et révisées.

_____. La 1ère Brigade d'infanterie canadienne, 1914-1954. (Actualités; revue destinée aux Forces canadiennes, vol. VII, no. 3.) Ottawa: Imprimeur de la Reine, 1954. 31 pp.

_____. La 1re Division d'infanterie canadienne, 1915-1955. (Actualités; revue destinée aux Forces canadiennes, vol. IX, no. 1.) Ottawa: Imprimeur de la Reine, 1955. 31 pp.

Canada. Armée. Régiment de la Chaudière. *Le Régiment de la Chaudière; notes historiques.* Québec, P.Q.: imprimé privé, 1955. 16 pp.

Canada. Armée. Service féminin de l'Armée canadienne. CWAC-compact; vue d'ensemble sur le CWAC. s.l.: s.i., s.d. 32 pp.

[Canada. Army.] *The Man in Battledress.* n.p.: [1941]. 41 pp.

Canada. Army. Canadian Military Headquarters. *Canadian Army (Overseas) Routine Orders.* London: n.p., 1940-47.
Title varies. Issued as Canadian Active Service Force (Overseas) Routine Orders until December 1940. Supplements also issued.

Canada. Army. Canadian Scottish Regiment (Princess Mary's). *History of the Regiment from Mobilization to Present Day.* Utrecht, Neth.: privately printed, [1945]. 31 pp.

*Canada. Army. Canadian Women's Army Corps. *CWAC Digest; Facts about the C.W.A.C.* n.p.: n.d. 32 pp.

Canada. Army. 1st Canadian Armoured Carrier Regiment. *The History of the Kangaroos.* n.p.: Imit Hergelo, 1945. 11 pp.

Canada. Army. 1st Canadian Army Headquarters. Supplies and Transport Branch. *An Account of Operations of Supplies and Transport Service, First Canadian Army, France and Belgium, 23 July 44 — 31 Oct 44.* Printed in the field, 1944. 254 pp.

Canada. Army. First Canadian Army Headquarters and Gt. Brit. Air Force. 35 Reconnaissance Wing. *Air Recce.* London: n.p., n.d. 66 pp.

Canada. Army. 1 Canadian Special Wireless Group. *1 Canadian Special Wireless Group; Royal Canadian Corps of Signals; Souvenir Booklet, 1944-45.* n.p.: privately printed, [1945]. 32 pp.

Canada. Army. 19 Canadian Army Field Regiment. *Regimental History, September 1941 — July 1945.* Deventer, Neth.: privately printed, 1945. 131 pp.

Canada. Army. Queen's Own Rifles of Canada. *Regimental Catechism.* n.p.: n.d. 19 pp.

Canada. Army. Royal Canadian Army Service Corps. *RCASC Diamond Jubilee Year Book, 1910-1961.* Ottawa: Queen's Printer, [1962]. 95 pp.

Canada. Army. Royal Canadian Engineers. 2nd Battalion. *The Story of 2 Bn R.C.E.* Zwolle, Neth.: privately printed, 1945. 1 vol., unpaged.

Canada. Army. Royal Canadian Engineers. 3rd Field (Reproduction) Survey Company. *432; 3rd Field (Reproduction) Survey Company, Royal Canadian Engineers, 1939-1945 (on Active Service).* [n.p.: 1945?] 1 vol., unpaged.

Canada. Army. Royal Canadian Engineers. 23 Field Company. *The Twenty-Third Story.* [London, Ont.: n.p., 1947.] 86 pp.

Canada. Army. Royal Winnipeg Rifles. *Seventy-Fifth Anniversary, Royal Winnipeg Rifles, 1883-1958.* [Winnipeg: privately printed, 1958.] v.p.

Canada. Army. Victoria Rifles of Canada. *The Victorian, 1st Battalion, 1940-1941.* n.p.: [1941]. 36 pp.

Canada. Army Headquarters. Director of Artillery. *Standing Orders for the Royal Regiment of Canadian Artillery.* Don Mills, Ont.: T.H. Best, 1963. 62 pp.

*Canada. Army Headquarters. Historical Section. *The 1st Canadian Infantry Brigade, 1914-1954.* (Current Affairs for the Canadian Forces, vol. VII, no. 3.) Ottawa: Queen's Printer, 1954. 31 pp.

*_____. *Introduction to the Study of Military History for Canadian Students,* [by C.P. Stacey]. Ottawa: [King's Printer], 1951. 39 pp.
Many subsequent revised editions.

*_____. *The Old Red Patch; the 1st Canadian Infantry Division, 1915-1955.* (Current Affairs for the Canadian Forces, vol. IX, no. 1.) Ottawa: Queen's Printer, 1955. 31 pp.

_____. *The Regiments and Corps of the Canadian Army.* (The Canadian Army List, vol. 1.) Ottawa: Queen's Printer, 1964. 253 pp.

*Canada. Commission royale sur le Corps expéditionnaire canadien envoyé dans la Colonie de la Couronne de Hong-Kong. *Rapport,* par Sir Lyman P. Duff, commissaire royal. Ottawa: Imprimeur du Roi, 1942. 64 pp.

*Canada. Dept. of Militia and Defence. *Annual Report.* Ottawa: Queen's Printer, 1867-1922.
Title varies.

_____. *Memorandum for Camps of Instruction.* Part 1: *Instructions for Training.* Ottawa: King's Printer, 1909?-28.
Title varies somewhat. Annual.

_____. *The Militia List.* Ottawa: Queen's Printer, 1867-1929.
Title and frequency vary. Superseded by Defence Forces List, Canada.

_____. *Minutes of the Militia Council.* Ottawa: King's Printer, 1905-21. 23 vols.

_____. *Pay and Allowance Regulations for the Permanent Force and Non-Permanent Active Militia, 1920.* Ottawa: King's Printer, 1920. 170 pp.
Reprinted with amendments, 1924, 1927, 1937.

_____. *The Return of the Troops; a Plain Account of the Demobilization of the Canadian Expeditionary Force.* Ottawa: King's Printer, 1920. 180 pp.

Canada. Dept. of National Defence. *The Canadian Army List.* Ottawa: King's Printer, 1940-66.
Title varies, eg. — Gradation List, Canadian Army Active (1940-45); Canadian Army (Regular) List (1959-66).

_____. *Canadian Prisoners of War and Missing Personnel in the Far East.* Ottawa: King's Printer, 1945. 59 1.

*_____. *The Canadians in Britain, 1939-1944.* (The Canadian Army at War, no. 1.) Ottawa: King's Printer, [1945]. 172 pp.

_____. *Defence Forces List, Canada (Naval, Military and Air Forces).* Ottawa: King's Printer, 1930-39.
Title varies somewhat. Superseded The Militia List. Superseded by The Canadian Navy List, The Canadian Army List and The Royal Canadian Air Force List.

_____. *Digest of Opinions and Rulings; Ottawa; March 31, 1944; Compiled from the Records of the Office of the Judge Advocate-General, at National Defence Headquarters.* n.p.: [1944]. 353 pp., looseleaf.

_____. *Dress Regulations for the Officers of the Canadian Militia.* Ottawa: King's Printer, 1932. [50] pp.

_____. *50 Questions and Answers about CWAC.* Ottawa: King's Printer, 1944. 13 pp.

_____. *Financial Regulations and Instructions for the Canadian Active Service Force (Canada).* Ottawa: King's Printer, 1939. 87 pp.

_____. *Financial Regulations and Instructions for the Canadian Active Service Force (Overseas).* Ottawa: King's Printer, 1939. 123 pp.

*_____. *From Pachino to Ortona; the Canadian Campaign in Sicily and Italy, 1943.* (The Canadian Army at War, no. 2.) Ottawa: King's Printer, [1945]. 160 pp.

_____. *Instructions for Engineer Services, Canada, 1936.* Ottawa: King's Printer, 1936. 152 pp.

_____. *Instructions for the Royal Canadian Army Medical Corps and the Canadian Army Dental Corps, 1937.* Ottawa: King's Printer, 1937. 162 pp.

_____. *Instructions for the Royal Canadian Army Pay Corps, 1938.* Ottawa: King's Printer, 1938. 68 pp.

_____. *The King's Regulations and Orders for the Canadian Militia.* Ottawa: King's Printer, 1939. 409 pp.

_____. *The King's Regulations and Orders for the Canadian Militia, 1926.* Ottawa: King's Printer, 1926. 477 pp.

Canada. Dept. of National Defence. *Memorandum on Training of the Canadian Militia.* Ottawa: King's Printer, 1934. 200 pp.

_____. *Regulations and Instructions for the Clothing of the Non-Permanent Active Militia, 1928.* Ottawa: King's Printer, 1928.

_____. *Regulations and Instructions for the Equipment of the Canadian Militia.* Ottawa: King's Printer, 1930. 227 pp.

_____. *Regulations for the Cadet Services of Canada, 1942.* Ottawa: King's Printer, 1942. 56 pp.

*_____. *Regulations for the Cadet Services of Canada, 1928.* Ottawa: King's Printer, 1928. 53 pp.

_____. *Regulations for the Canadian Medical Service, 1923 (Approved by the Defence Council).* Ottawa: King's Printer, 1923. 118 pp.

_____. *Regulations for the Clothing of the Canadian Militia.* Part I: *Permanent Active Militia.* Ottawa: King's Printer, 1935. 83 pp.

_____. *Regulations for the Clothing of the Canadian Militia.* Part I: *Permanent Active Militia.* Ottawa: King's Printer, 1924. 77 pp.

*_____. *Report.* Ottawa: King's Printer, 1923-59.
Title varies. Annual most years.

_____. *War Dress Regulations for the Officers and Other Ranks of the Canadian Army (1943).* Ottawa: King's Printer, 1943. 85 pp.

_____. *Where Do We Go From Here? Facts for the Guidance of Canadian Army Personnel.* n.p.: [1945]. 28 pp.

Canada. Dept. of National War Services. *Annual Report.* Ottawa: King's Printer, 1945. 3 vols.

Canada. Dept. of Veterans Affairs. *30th Anniversary of the D-Day Landings in Normandy, 1944 — June 6 — 1974./30e anniversaire des débarquements en Normandie au jour J, 1944 — le 6 juin — 1974.* n.p./s.l.: s.i., 1974. 22 pp.
Bilingual text./Texte bilingue.

_____. *30th Anniversary of the Dieppe Raid, 19 August 1942./ Le trentième anniversaire du Raid de Dieppe (19 août 1942).* n.p./s.l.: s.i., 1972. [16] pp.
Bilingual text./Texte bilingue.

_____. *35th Anniversary; the Raid on Dieppe, 1942 August 19 1977./35ième anniversaire; le coup de main de Dieppe, 1942 le 19 août 1977.* n.p./s.l.: s.i., [1977]. 14 pp.
Bilingual text./Texte bilingue.

*Canada. Director of Public Information. *Canada at War.* No. 1-45. Ottawa: King's Printer, 1941-45.

Canada. Militia. Canadian Machine Gun Corps. *Canadian Machine Gun Corps; Organization, Administration and Duties.* London: Page and Thomas, 1919. 129 pp.

Canada. Militia. Canadian Expeditionary Force. *Routine Orders.* Ottawa: n.p., ?-1920.
Supplements also issued.

Canada. Militia Headquarters. *General Orders.* Ottawa: Queen's Printer, 1899-1946.
Superseded Militia General Orders. Frequency varies.

——————. *Militia Orders.* Ottawa: Queen's Printer, 1899-1940.
Superseded Militia General Orders. Frequency varies.

*Canada. Ministère de la Défense nationale. *Les Canadiens en Grande-Bretagne, 1939-1944.* (L'Armée canadienne à la Guerre, no. 1.) Ottawa: Imprimeur du Roi, 1946. 188 pp.

*——————. *De Pachino à Ortona; la campagne des Canadiens en Sicile et en Italie, 1943.* (L'Armée canadienne à la Guerre, no. 2.) Ottawa: Imprimeur du Roi, 1946. 168 pp.

*——————. *Rapport.* Ottawa: Imprimeur du Roi, 1923-59.
Divergence du titre. Annuel, la plupart des années.

——————. *Règlement et instructions d'ordre financier applicables à l'armée active (Canada).* Ottawa: Imprimeur du Roi, 1942. 114 pp.

*——————. *Règlements concernant les services du cadets du Canada, 1928.* Ottawa: Imprimeur du Roi, 1928. 53 pp.

*Canada. Ministère de la Milice et de la Défense. *Rapport annuel.* Ottawa: Imprimeur de la Reine, 1867-1922.
Divergence du titre.

Canada. Ministry of Overseas Military Forces of Canada. *Routine Orders.* London: Canadian Print. and Stationery Services, H.M. Stationery Office, 1917-20.

*Canada. National Defence Headquarters. *Canadian Army Orders.* [Ottawa: King's Printer], 1941-64.
From 1947 issued as a non-chronological series, with orders being discarded when obsolete. Supplements also issued from 1947.

——————. *Canadian Army Routine Orders.* Ottawa: n.p., 1939-46.
Title varies. Issued as Canadian Active Service Force Routine Orders until December 1940. Supplements also issued.

Canada. National Gallery. *Exhibition of Canadian War Art.* Ottawa: King's Printer, 1945. 22 pp.

Canada. National Research Council. *Medical Research and Development in the Canadian Army During World War II, 1942-1946.* n.p.: n.d. v.p.

*Canada. Parlement. Chambre des Communes. Comité spécial d'enquête sur les distinctions honorifiques et les décorations. *Procès-verbaux et témoignages.* No. 1-6. Ottawa: Imprimeur du Roi, 1942.

Canada. Parliament. House of Commons. Special Committee on Canteen Funds. *Minutes of Proceedings and Evidence.* No. 1-11. Ottawa: King's Printer, 1942.

*Canada. Parliament. House of Commons. Special Committee on Honours and Decorations. *Minutes of Proceedings and Evidence.* No. 1-6. Ottawa: King's Printer, 1942.

*Canada. Quartier général de la Défense nationale. *Ordres de l'Armée canadienne.* [Ottawa: Imprimeur du Roi], 1941-64.
Publiés en série de façon non chronologique, à partir de 1947; les ordres périmés sont remplacés. Des suppléments sont également publiés à partir de 1947.

Canada. Royal Commission on the Bren Machine Gun Contract. *Report.* Henry Hague Davis, Commissioner. Ottawa: King's Printer, 1939. 52 pp.

*Canada. Royal Commission on the Canadian Expeditionary Force to the Crown Colony of Hong Kong. *Report,* by Sir Lyman P. Duff, Royal Commissioner. Ottawa: King's Printer, 1942. 61 pp.

Canada. Royal Commission to Conduct an Inquiry into Certain Disorders Occurring May 7-8, 1945, in the City of Halifax. *Report on the Halifax Disorders, May 7th-8th, 1945.* Hon. Mr. Justice R.L. Kellock, Royal Commissioner. Ottawa: King's Printer, 1945. 61 pp.

*Canada. Service de l'Information. *Le Canada en guerre.* No. 1-45. Ottawa: Imprimeur du Roi, 1941-45.

Canadian Armoured Association *see* Canadian Cavalry Association.

*_Canadian Army Training Memorandum._ No. 1-72. Ottawa: King's Printer, 1941-47.

Canadian Artillery Association. *Annual Report.* n.p.: privately printed, 1876-   .
Not published 1940-46.

_____. *Artillery Summary.* Vol. I-XIII. n.p.: privately printed, 1921-42.

Canadian Bank of Commerce. *War Service Records, 1939-1945; an Account of the War Service of Members of the Staff during the Second World War.* D.P. Wagner and C.G. Siddall, eds. Toronto: Rous & Mann, 1947. 331 pp.

Canadian Broadcasting Corporation. Publications Branch. *We have been There; Authoritative Reports by Qualified Observers who have Returned from the War Zones, as Presented Over the CBC National Network.* Toronto: Canadian Broadcasting Corporation, 1941-42. 2 vols.

Canadian Cavalry Association. *Proceedings.* n.p.: privately printed, 1913- .
In 1943 became Canadian Armoured Association and in 1946 Royal Canadian Armoured Corps (Cavalry) Association. Title varies: also Annual Report and Information Digest and Annual Report.

Canadian Defence Quarterly. Vol. I-XVI. Ottawa: privately printed, 1923-39.

The Canadian Fusiliers; City of London Regiment. n.p.: 1942. 12 pp.

Canadian Infantry Association. *Proceedings.* n.p.: privately printed, 1913- .
Incorporated the Proceedings of the Canadian Machine Gun Corps Association in 1936. Was the Infantry and Machine Gun Association of Canada, 1937-39. Not published 1940-45.

Canadian Jewish Congress. *Canadian Jews in World War II.* Montreal: privately printed, 1947-48. 2 vols.

Canadian Legion War Services, Inc. *A Year of Service; a Summary of Activities on Behalf of His Majesty's Canadian Forces Rendered during Nineteen-Forty.* n.p.: n.d. 1 vol., unpaged.

Canadian Machine Gun Corps Association. *Proceedings.* n.p.: privately printed, 1928-35.
Superseded by Infantry and Machine Gun Association of Canada Proceedings.

Canadian Officers Training Corps, University of Toronto Contingent. [Toronto?]: n.p., 1937. 32 pp.

The Canadian Provost Corps; Silver Jubilee, 1940-1965. Ottawa: privately printed, 1965. 96 pp.

The Canadian Scottish Regiment. n.p.: n.d. 91 pp.

[Canadian War Museum.] *La coopération canada-polonaise au cours des deux guerres mondiales./Polish-Canadian Co-operation in the Two World Wars.* Ottawa: n.p., 1973. 36 pp.
Texte bilingue./Bilingual text.

Capon, Alan R. *Mascots of the Hastings and Prince Edward Regiment*. Picton, Ont.: Picton Gazette, 1977. 31 pp.

Cash, Gwen. *A Million Miles from Ottawa*. Toronto: Macmillan, 1942. 152 pp.

Cassidy, G.L. *Warpath; the Story of the Algonquin Regiment, 1939-1945*. Toronto: Ryerson Press, 1948. 372 pp.

Cent ans d'histoire d'un régiment canadien-français; les Fusiliers Mont-Royal, 1869-1969. Montréal: Editions du Jour, 1971. 418 pp.

Centennial, 1863-1963; Presentation of Colours to the Princess of Wales' Own Regiment CA(M) by the Honourable W. Earle Rowe, P.C., Lieutenant-Governor of Ontario, Kingston, Ontario, Saturday 1st June 1963. [Kingston, Ont.: privately printed, 1963.] 15 pp.

Centennial Year, 1866-1966; 11th Field Artillery Regiment (M); 11th Field Artillery Regiment, Royal Regiment of Canadian Artillery, Canada's Oldest Artillery Regiment, Saturday, October 1, 1966. n.p.: n.d. 1 vol., unpaged.

Chambers, Robert W. *Halifax in Wartime; a Collection of Drawings*. Halifax; The Halifax Herald and the Halifax Mail, 1943. 1 vol., unpaged.

[Chandler, C.M.] *The Militia in Durham County, 1812-1936; an Outline History of the Durham Regiment*. n.p.: privately printed, 1936. v.p.

*Chevaliers de Colomb. *Services de guerre des Chevaliers de Colomb canadiennes, 1939-1947; l'oeuvre des huttes militaires des Chevaliers de Colomb*. Montréal: s.i., 1948. 280 pp.

50 ans d'activités avec le 6e Régiment d'artillerie, (Québec & Lévis), 1899-1949. Québec, P.Q.: Imprimerie Laflamme, 1949. 1 tome, non-paginé.

Clark, Gregory. *War Stories*. Toronto: Ryerson Press, 1964. 171 pp.

Claude-Laboissière, Alphonse. *Journal d'un aumônier militaire canadien, 1939-1945*. Montréal: Editions françaises, 1948. 330 pp.

Claxton, Brooke. *Notes on Military Law and Discipline for Canadian Soldiers*. n.p.: [1939]. 37 pp.

Clegg, Howard. *A Canuck in England; Journal of a Canadian Soldier*. Toronto: Harrap, 1942. 160 pp.

Clint, H.C., comp. *A Short History of Artillery and of 57th Battery, R.C.A., 1855-1955; Formal Celebration and Reunion, Oct. 15th, 16th, 1955, Grande Allée Armouries, Quebec City*. Quebec, P.Q.: n.p., 1955. 48 pp.

Colton, E. Bert, comp. *History of the 42nd. Infantry Reserve Company, Veterans Guard of Canada, Attached to the Black Watch (RHR) of Canada during the Period of World War II.* Montreal: privately printed, 1947. 28 pp.

Comfort, Charles Fraser. *Artist at War.* Toronto: Ryerson Press, 1956. 187 pp.

Commonwealth War Graves Commission. *The War Dead of the Commonwealth; the Register of the Names of Those who Fell in the 1939-1945 War and are Buried; Cemeteries in Canada; Cemeteries in Ontario.* London: H.M. Stationery Office, 1961. 2 vols.

_____. *The War Dead of the Commonwealth; the Register of the Names of Those who Fell in the 1939-1945 War and are Buried in Cemeteries in Canada; Cemeteries in British Columbia, Yukon Territory and Alberta.* Maidenhead, Eng.: [H.M. Stationery Office], 1972. 82 pp.

_____. *The War Dead of the Commonwealth; the Register of the Names of Those who Fell in the 1939-1945 War and are Buried in Cemeteries in Canada; Cemeteries in New Brunswick, Nova Scotia, Newfoundland and Prince Edward Island.* London: H.M. Stationery Office, 1962. 81 pp.

_____. *The War Dead of the Commonwealth; the Register of the Names of Those who Fell in the 1939-1945 War and are Buried in Cemeteries in Canada; Cemeteries in Quebec.* London: H.M. Stationery Office, 1962. 63 pp.

_____. *The War Dead of the Commonwealth; the Register of the Names of Those who Fell in the 1939-1945 War and are Buried in Cemeteries in Canada; Cemeteries in Saskatchewan and Manitoba.* London: [H.M. Stationery Office], 1963. 79 pp.

_____. *The War Dead of the Commonwealth; the Register of the Names of Those who Fell in the 1939-1945 War and Have no known Grave; the Halifax Memorial.* London: [H.M. Stationery Office], 1968. 2 vols.

The Connecting File. Vol. I- . London, Ont.: privately printed, 1921-   .
Journal of the Royal Canadian Regiment.

Cornelius, J.R. *Cadet Training as a National Wealth.* Ottawa: King's Printer, 1923. 12 pp.

*Le Corps blindé royal canadien. Ottawa: Imprimeur de la Reine, 1954. 11 pp.

*Le Corps de Santé royal canadien. Ottawa: Imprimeur de la Reine, 1954. 11 pp.

*The Corps of Royal Canadian Engineers. Ottawa: Queen's Printer, 1953. 21 pp.

The Corps of Royal Canadian Engineers; a Brief History. Ottawa: King's Printer, 1948. 56 pp.

[Corrigan, Cecil Edwin.] *Tales of a Forgotten Theatre,* by "Pooch" [*pseud.*] Winnipeg: Day Publishers, 1969. 223 pp.

Couffon, Claude. *A Caen avec les Canadiens.* (Collections "Patrie".) Paris: Rouff, 1949. 24 pp.

Coughlin, Bing. *Herbie.* n.p.: T. Nelson, 1946. 190 pp.

_____. *This Army; a Portfolio of Cartoons Drawn on the Italian Battle Front especially for the Maple Leaf, Canadian Army Newspaper.* Rome: No. 2 Cdn Public Relns Group, 1944. 2 vols., chiefly illus.

Coursaget, A.C., comp. *Histoire d'une petite plage normande devenue grande dans le souvenir des français par l'heroïsme du "Royal Regiment of Canada".* Paris: R. Girard, 1946. 1 tome, en majeure partie ill.

Couture, Claude-Paul. *Operation "Jubilee", Dieppe, 19 août 1942.* Paris: Editions France-Empire, 1969. 662 pp.

*[Cras, Hervé.] *Dieppe; the Dawn of Decision,* by Jacques Mordal [*pseud.*] Mervyn Savill, tr. Toronto: Ryerson Press, 1963. 285 pp.

* _____. *Les Canadiens à Dieppe,* par Jacques Mordal [*pseud.*] Paris: Presses de la Cité, 1962. 343 pp.

Crook, E.D., and J.K. Marteinson, eds. *A Pictorial History of the 8th Canadian Hussars (Princess Louise's).* n.p.: privately printed, 1973. 343 pp.

Cunniffe, Dick. *Scarlet, Riflegreen and Khaki; the Military in Calgary.* Calgary: Century Calgary Publications, 1975. 40 pp.

Curchin, Leonard A., and Brian D. Sim. *The Elgins; the Story of the Elgin Regt. (RCAC) and its Predecessors.* St. Thomas, Ont.: privately printed, 1977. 150 pp.

Darby, H., and M. Cunliffe. *A Short Story of 21 Army Group; the British and Canadian Armies in the Campaigns in North West Europe, 1944-1945.* Aldershot, Eng.: Gale and Polden, 1949. 147 pp.

Davis, Henry Hague, *see* Canada. Royal Commission on the Bren Gun Contract.

Desjardins, Maurice. *Momo s'en va-t-en guerre.* Montréal: Ferron Editeur, 1973. 159 pp.

The Dominion Arsenal at Quebec, 1880-1945. Quebec, P.Q.: n.p., 1947. 131 pp.

Dornbusch, C.E., comp. *The Canadian Army, 1855-1958; Regimental Histories and a Guide to the Regiments.* Cornwallville, N.Y.: Hope Farm Press, 1959. 216 pp.

_____. *The Canadian Army, 1855-1955; Regimental Histories and a Guide to the Regiments.* Cornwallville, N.Y.: n.p., 1957. 162 1.

_____. *The Canadian Army, 1855-1965; Lineages; Regimental Histories.* Cornwallville, N.Y.: Hope Farm Press, 1966. 179 pp.

_____. *Lineages of the Canadian Army, 1855-1961; Armour, Cavalry, Infantry.* Cornwallville, N.Y.: Hope Farm Press, 1961. 1 vol., unpaged.

Douglas, W.A.B., and Brereton Greenhous. *Out of the Shadows; Canada in the Second World War.* Toronto: Oxford Univ. Press, 1977. 288 pp.

Drage, Charles. *The Life and Times of General Two-Gun Cohen.* New York: Funk & Wagnalls, 1954. 312 pp.
London ed. titled: Two-Gun Cohen.

Drive to the Rhine; the First Canadian Army in Action; Dispatches by CP Correspondents. [Toronto: Canadian Press, 1945.] 21 pp.

Duff, (Sir) Lyman P., *see* Canada. Royal Commission on the Canadian Expeditionary Force to the Crown Colony of Hong Kong.

Duff, (Sir) Lyman P. *voir* Canada. Commission royale sur le Corps expéditionnaire canadien envoyé dans la Colonie de la Couronne de Hong-Kong.

Duguid, Archer Fortescue. *History of the Canadian Grenadier Guards, 1760-1964.* Montreal: Gazette Print. Co., 1965. 520 pp.

Dumais, Lucien A. *Un Canadien français à Dieppe.* Paris: Editions France-Empire, 1968. 283 pp.

_____. *Un Canadien français face à la Gestapo.* Montréal: Editions du Jour, 1969. 280 pp.

Dumais, Lucien A., and Hugh Popham. *The Man Who Went Back.* London: L. Cooper, 1975. 213 pp.

Duncan, Donald Albert. *Some Letters and Other Writings.* Halifax: Imperial Pub. Co., 1945. 199 pp.

Dunkelman, Ben. *Dual Allegiance; an Autobiography.* Toronto: Macmillan, 1976. 336 pp.

Dunwoody, James M. *The Colonel; Some Reminiscences.* n.p.: [1972?]. 36 pp.

Edelstein, H. *All Quiet in Canada — and Why; "Cpl. Ray's" Pen and Camera Pictures of the War (1939-1944) with Verse Comment and Later Poems.* Ottawa: privately printed, 1944. 41 pp.

Einer kam durch see/voir Werra, Franz von.

Ellis, Chris, and Peter Chamberlain. *Ram and Sexton* (AFV, no. 13.) Windsor, Eng.: Profile Publications, n.d. 20 pp.

Ellis, Jean M., and Isabel Dingman. *Face Powder and Gunpowder.* Toronto: S.J.R. Saunders, 1947. 229 pp.

Ettenger, G.H. *History of the Associate Committee on Medical Research, Ottawa, 1938-1946.* Ottawa: n.p., n.d. 46 pp.

Falardeau, Victor, et Jean Parent. *La musique du Royal 22e Régiment; 50 ans d'histoire, 1922-1972.* Québec, P.Q.: Editions Garneau, 1976. 243 pp.

Fallis, George O. *A Padre's Pilgrimmage.* Toronto: Ryerson Press, 1953. 166 pp.

Farran, Roy. *The History of the Calgary Highlanders, 1921-54.* n.p.: Bryant Press, [1954]. 222 pp.

Farrel, J.C., and others. *Memoirs of 4 Canadian Armoured Troops Workshop, Royal Canadian Electrical and Mechanical Engineers.* Enschede, Neth.: n.p., 1945. 74 pp.

Feasby, W.R. *Official History of the Canadian Medical Services, 1939-1945.* Ottawa: Queen's Printer, 1956. 2 vols.

Fetherstonhaugh, R.C. *McGill University at War, 1914-1918; 1939-1945.* Montreal: McGill Univ., 1947. 437 pp.

_____. *The Royal Montreal Regiment, 14th Battalion, C.E.F., 1914-1925.* Montreal: privately printed, 1927. 334 pp.

_____. *The Royal Montreal Regiment, 1925-1945.* Westmount, P.Q.: privately printed, 1949. 298 pp.

_____. *A Short History of the Royal Canadian Dragoons.* Toronto: Southam Press, 1932. 52 pp.

Fetherstonhaugh, R.C., and G.R. Stevens. *The Royal Canadian Regiment.* Vol. I: Montreal: Gazette Print. Co., 1936. Vol. II: London, Ont.: privately printed, 1967. 2 vols.

First Battalion, Rocky Mountain Rangers. n.p.: [1944?]. 13 pp.

First Battalion the Canadian Scottish Regiment, Victoria, B.C. . . . Souvenir Programme of the Civic Welcome Extended by the Citizens of Victoria, B.C., on the Homecoming of Vancouver Island's Own Regiment, December, 1945. Victoria, B.C.: Economy Press, 1945. 32 pp.

1st Battalion, the Saskatoon Light Infantry (M.G.), Canadian Army Overseas; Honour Roll, 10th July 1943 to 8th May, 1945, Sicily, Italy, Holland. n.p.: privately printed, n.d. 15 pp.

Flatt, S.A. *History of the 6th Field Company, Royal Canadian Engineers, 1939-1945.* Vancouver: privately printed, n.d. 141 pp.

*Florentin, Eddy. *Battle of the Falaise Gap.* Mervyn Savill, tr. London: Elek Books, 1965. 336 pp.

*_____. *Stalingrad en Normandie.* Paris: Presses de la Cité, 1964. 389 pp.

Forbes, D.F. *North Nova Scotia Highlanders.* Varel, Ger.: n.p., [1945]. 32 pp.

The Fort Garry Horse, C.A.S.F. (Allied with 4th/7th Dragoon Guards). Winnipeg: n.p., 1939. 47 pp.

Fraser, W.B. *Always a Strathcona.* Calgary: Comprint Pub. Co., 1976. 252 pp.

Galloway, Strome. *"55 Axis"; with the Royal Canadian Regiment, 1939-1945.* Montreal: Provincial Pub. Co., 1946. 232 pp.
Reprinted in 1979, titled: A Regiment at War; the Story of the Royal Canadian Regiment, 1939-1945.

*_____. *30th Anniversary; the Canadians in Italy, April 22 to May 3, 1975.* n.p.: [1975]. 28 pp.

*_____. *Trentième anniversaire; les Canadiens en Italie, du 22 avril au 3 mai 1975.* s.l.: s.i., [1975]. 31 pp.

Gavin, T.M. ed. *The Story of 1 Canadian Survey Regiment, RCA, 1939-1945.* n.p.: privately printed, 1945. 99 pp.

[General Motors of Canada, Limited.] *Achievement.* n.p.: [1943]. 74 pp.

Le Génie royal canadien. Ottawa: Imprimeur de la Reine, 1954. 23 pp.

The Goat see The Springbok.

Goodspeed, D.J. *Battle Royal; a History of the Royal Regiment of Canada, 1862-1962.* Toronto: privately printed, 1962. 703 pp.

Gouin, Jacques. *Lettres de guerre d'un Québecois, 1942-1945.* Montréal: Editions du Jour, 1975. 341 pp.

_____. *Par la bouche de nos canons; histoire du 4e Régiment d'artillerie moyenne/4th Cdn Medium Regt RCA/1941-1945.* [Montréal]: Gasparo, 1970. 248 pp.

Governor General's Foot Guards, Ottawa; Seventy-Fifth Anniversary, June 8, 1872-1947. Ottawa: privately printed, 1947. 43 pp.

The Governor General's Horse Guards, 1939-1945. Toronto: Canadian Military Journal, [1953]. 243 pp.

Grafton, C.S. *The Canadian "Emma Gees"; a History of the Canadian Machine Gun Corps.* London, Ont.: privately printed, 1938. 218 pp.

Granatstein, J.L., and R.D. Cuff, eds. *War and Society in North America.* Toronto: T. Nelson, 1971. 199 pp.

Grant, D.W. *"Carry On"; the History of the Toronto Scottish Regiment (M.G.), 1939-1945.* Toronto: privately printed, 1949. 177 pp.

Gt. Brit. Army. British Army of the Rhine, and Canada. Army Headquarters. Historical Section. *British Army of the Rhine; Battlefield Tour, Second Day; 2 Canadian Corps Operations Astride the Road Caen-Falaise, 7-8 August, 1944 (Operation Totalize).* n.p.: 1947. 71 pp.

Gt. Brit. Army. 21 Army Group Headquarters. Canadian Section. *Canadian Routine Orders (21 Army Group).* n.p.: 1944-45. *Title varies. Issued as* Canadian Routine Orders (British Army of the Rhine) *from August 1945.*

Gt. Brit. Imperial War Graves Commission. *The War Dead of the British Commonwealth and Empire; the Register of the Names of Those who Fell in the 1939-1945 War and are Buried in Cemeteries and Churchyards in Surrey; Brookwood Military Cemetery, Woking.* London: [H.M. Stationery Office], 1958. 3 vols.

_____. *The War Dead of the British Commonwealth and Empire; the Register of the Names of Those who Fell in the 1939-1945 War and are Buried in Cemeteries in Belgium; Adegem Canadian War Cemetery.* London: H.M. Stationery Office, 1956. 42 pp.

_____. *The War Dead of the British Commonwealth and Empire; the Register of the Names of Those who Fell in the 1939-1945 War and are Buried in Cemeteries in France; Beny-sur-mer Canadian War Cemetery.* London: H.M. Stationery Office, 1955. 2 vols.

_____. *The War Dead of the British Commonwealth and Empire; the Register of the Names of Those who Fell in the 1939-1945 War and are Buried in Cemeteries in France; Bretteville-sur-Laize Canadian War Cemetery.* London: H.M. Stationery Office, 1955. 3 vols.

_____. *The War Dead of the British Commonwealth and Empire; the Register of the Names of Those who Fell in the 1939-1945 War and are Buried in Cemeteries in France; Calais War Cemetery, Calais Canadian War Cemetery.* London: H.M. Stationery Office, 1956. 43 pp.

Gt. Brit. Imperial War Graves Commission. *The War Dead of the British Commonwealth and Empire; the Register of the Names of Those who Fell in the 1939-1945 War and are Buried in Cemeteries in France; Dieppe Canadian War Cemetery; Janval Cemetery, Dieppe.* London: H.M. Stationery Office, 1956. 40 pp.

_____. *The War Dead of the British Commonwealth and Empire; the Register of the Names of Those who Fell in the 1939-1945 War and are Buried in Cemeteries in Hong Kong.* London: H.M. Stationery Office, 1956-58. 2 vols.

_____. *The War Dead of the British Commonwealth and Empire; the Register of the Names of Those who Fell in the 1939-1945 War and are Buried in Cemeteries in Italy; Agira Canadian War Cemetery, Sicily.* London: H.M. Stationery Office, 1953. 29 pp.

_____. *The War Dead of the British Commonwealth and Empire; the Register of the Names of Those who Fell in the 1939-1945 War and are Buried in Cemeteries in Italy; Argenta Gap War Cemetery; Bologna War Cemetery; Villanova Canadian War Cemetery.* London: H.M. Stationery Office, 1953. 70 pp.

_____. *The War Dead of the British Commonwealth and Empire; the Register of the Names of Those who Fell in the 1939-1945 War and are Buried in Cemeteries in Italy; Moro River Canadian War Cemetery, Ortona.* London: H.M. Stationery Office, 1954. 2 vols.

_____. *The War Dead of the British Commonwealth and Empire; the Register of the Names of Those who Fell in the 1939-1945 War and are Buried in Cemeteries in Italy; Ravenna War Cemetery.* London: [H.M. Stationery Office], 1956. 44 pp.

_____. *The War Dead of the British Commonwealth and Empire; the Register of the Names of Those who Fell in the 1939-1945 War and are Buried in Cemeteries in the Netherlands; Bergen-Op-Zoom Canadian War Cemetery.* London: H.M. Stationery Office, 1957. 50 pp.

_____. *The War Dead of the British Commonwealth and Empire; the Register of the Names of Those Who Fell in the 1939-1945 War and are Buried in Cemeteries in the Netherlands; Groesbeek Canadian War Cemetery, Nijmegen.* London: H.M. Stationery Office, 1956. 2 vols.

_____. *The War Dead of the British Commonwealth and Empire; the Register of the Names of Those who Fell in the 1939-1945 War and are Buried in Cemeteries in the Netherlands; Holten Canadian War Cemetery; Holten General Cemetery.* London: H.M. Stationery Office, 1956. 64 pp.

Greenhous, Brereton. *Semper Paratus; the History of the Royal Hamilton Light Infantry (Wentworth Regiment), 1862-1977,* by Kingsley Brown, Senior, Kingsley Brown, Junior, and Brereton Greenhous. Revised and edited by Brereton Greenhous. Hamilton, Ont.: privately printed, 1977. 446 pp.

Griffin, Frederick. *Major-General Sir Henry Mill Pellatt, CVO, DCL, VD; a Gentleman of Toronto, 1859-1939.* Toronto: Ontario Pub. Co., 1939. 30 pp.

Gutta Percha and Rubber, Limited. *A Selection of Badge Designs of the Canadian Forces.* Toronto: n.p., n.d. 16 pp., chiefly illus.

Halton, Matthew. *Ten Years to Alamein.* Toronto: S.J.R. Saunders, 1944. 319 pp.

Harker, Douglas E. *The Dukes; the Story of the Men Who have Served in Peace and War with the British Columbia Regiment (D.C.O.), 1883-1973.* n.p.: privately printed, 1974. 438 pp.

_____. *The Story of the British Columbia Regiment, 1939-1945.* [Vancouver: n.p., 1950.] 1 vol., unpaged.

Heaps, Leo. *Escape from Arnhem; a Canadian Among the Lost Paratroops.* Toronto: Macmillan, 1945. 159 pp.

_____. *The Evaders.* New York: W. Morrow, 1976. 245 pp. *London ed. titled:* The Grey Goose of Arnhem.

Hello, Canada! Canada's Mackenzie Papineau Battalion, 1837-1937; 15th Brigade I.B.; "Fascism Shall be Destroyed". n.p.: n.d. 46 pp.

Henry, C.E. *Regimental History of the 18th Armoured Car Regiment (XII Manitoba Dragoons).* Deventer, Neth.: privately printed, n.d. 151 pp.

Hermann, J. Douglas. *Report to the Minister of Veterans Affairs of a Study on Canadians who were Prisoners of War in Europe during World War II./Rapport présenté au Ministre des affaires des anciens combattants au sujet d'une enquête portant sur les Canadiens prisonniers de guerre en Europe au cours de la seconde guerre mondiale.* Ottawa: Queen's Printer/Imprimeur de la Reine, 1973. 56/60 pp. *Bilingual text./Texte bilingue.*

Hickey, R.M. *The Scarlet Dawn.* Campbellton, N.B.: Tribune Publishers, 1949. 277 pp.

Hill, B. Kirkbride, comp. *The Price of Freedom.* Toronto: Ryerson Press, 1942-44. 2 vols.

Hillsman, John Burwell. *Eleven Men and a Scalpel.* Winnipeg: Columbia Press, 1948. 144 pp.

History; 49th Battalion (C.E.F.), the Loyal Edmonton Regiment. Edmonton: Bradburn Printers, n.d. 16 pp.

History of 17th Field Regiment, Royal Canadian Artillery, 5th Canadian Armoured Division. Groningen, Neth.: J. Niemeijer, 1946. 107 pp.

The History of the 8th Canadian Light Anti-Aircraft Regiment, R.C.A. Amersfoort, Neth.: n.p., 1945. 124 pp.

A History of the First Hussars Regiment. London, Ont.: privately printed, 1951. 172 pp.

A History of the 7th Anti-Tank Regiment, Royal Canadian Artillery, n.p.: n.d. 22 pp.

History of the 7th Canadian Medium Regiment . . . see Lockwood, A.M.

History of the 6th. Canadian Anti-Tank Regiment, Royal Canadian Artillery, 1st April 1942 — 24th June 1945. n.p.: n.d. 38 pp.

The History of the 65th Canadian Anti-Tank Battery, Royal Canadian Artillery, 9 September 1941 — 20 September 1945. Lochem, Neth.: privately printed, 1945. 36 pp.

The History of the Third Canadian Light Anti-Aircraft Regiment from 17 Aug '40 to 7 May '45; World War II. Deventer, Neth.: privately printed, [1945]. 50 pp.
Reprinted in Calgary, 1955.

The History of the 23rd Field Regiment . . . see Smith, Lawrence N.

History, 1 Anti-Tank Regiment, RCA, 5 Sep. '39 - 31 Jul. '45; World War II. n.p.: [1945]. v.p.

Hoar, Victor. *The Mackenzie-Papineau Battalion; Canadian Participation in the Spanish Civil War.* [Toronto]: Copp, Clark, 1969. 285 pp.

Hodder-Williams, Ralph, G.R. Stevens and R.B. Mainprize. *Princess Patricia's Canadian Light Infantry.* London: Hodder and Stoughton, 1923-[57?] 4 vols.

Hodgins, J. Herbert, and others, comps. *Women at War.* Montreal: MacLean Pub., 1943. 190 pp.

Hopkins, Anthony. *Songs from the Front & Rear; Canadian Servicemen's Songs of the Second World War.* Edmonton: Hurtig Publishers, 1979. 192 pp.

How, Douglas. *The 8th Hussars; a History of the Regiment.* Sussex, N.B.: Maritime Pub., 1964. 446 pp.

Howard, Gordon L. *The Memories of a Citizen Soldier, 1914-1945.* n.p.: n.d. 114 pp.

Howard, Gordon L. *Sixty Years of Centennial in Saskatchewan, 1906-1968.* n.p.: n.d. 140 pp.

Hubbell, E.L. *The Winnipeg Grenadiers.* n.p.: n.d. 16 pp.

Hutchison, Paul P. *Canada's Black Watch; the First Hundred Years, 1862-1962.* Montreal: privately printed, [1962]. 340 pp.

_____. *A Short History of the Royal Highland Regiment the Black Watch, 1725-1948.* n.p.: 1948. 39 pp.

In Memoriam; the Perth Regiment, 4th September 1939 to 8th May 1945. n.p.: [1945]. 20 pp.

L'Intendance royale canadienne. Ottawa: Imprimeur de la Reine, 1954. 12 pp.

The Irish Regiment of Canada; Memorial Service to Honour our Gallant Dead, Canada, England, Italy, Holland, June 1940 - to - May 1945, Heerenveen, Holland, Sunday, July 1st, 1945. Groningen, Neth.: privately printed, 1945. 1 vol., unpaged.

Jackson, H.M. *Canadian Prime Ministers and the Canadian Militia.* n.p.: 1958. 11 pp.

_____. *The Princess Louise Dragoon Guards; a History.* n.p.: 1952. 306 pp.

_____. *The Roll of the Regiments (the Active Militia).* Ottawa: n.p., 1959. 176 pp.

_____. *The Royal Regiment of Artillery, Ottawa, 1855-1952; a History.* Montreal: privately printed, 1952. 418 pp.

_____. *The Sherbrooke Regiment (12th Armoured Regiment).* n.p.: 1958. 229 pp.

_____. *The Story of the Royal Canadian Dental Corps.* Ottawa: privately printed, 1956. 475 pp.

Jackson, H.M., ed. *The Argyll and Sutherland Highlanders of Canada (Princess Louise's), 1928-1953.* Montreal: privately printed, 1953. 497 pp.

Johnson, Charles Monroe. *Action With the Seaforths.* New York: Vantage Press, 1954. 342 pp.

Johnston, Stafford. *The Fighting Perths; the Story of the First Century in the Life of a Canadian County Regiment.* Stratford, Ont.: privately printed, 1964. 133 pp.

Jones, William. *Twelve Months with Tito's Partisans.* Bedford, Eng.: Bedford Books, 1946. 128 pp.

Journal of the Edmonton Military Institute. Vol. I-IV? Edmonton: Edmonton Military Institute, 1937-46?

Joy, Edward H. *Gentlemen from Canada.* London: Hodder & Stoughton. 1943. 92 pp.

Kardash, William. *I Fought for Canada in Spain . . . .* (Timely Topics, no. 3.) Toronto: New Era Publishers, n.d. 30 pp.

Kelsey Club, Winnipeg, Man. *Canadian Defence; What We have to Defend; Various Defence Policies.* Toronto: T. Nelson, 1937. 98 pp.

Kellock, R.L., *see* Canada. Royal Commission to Conduct an Inquiry into Certain Disorders Occurring May 7-8, 1945, in the City of Halifax.

Kembar, A.K., and W.T. Gundy. *The Six Years of 6 Canadian Field Regiment, Royal Canadian Artillery; September 1939 — September 1945.* n.p.: privately printed, 1945. 128 pp.

Kerr, John. *A Souvenir War History of the 8th Canadian Field Squadron, Royal Canadian Engineers.* Zutphen, Neth.: privately printed, n.d. 1 vol., unpaged.

Kerry, A.J., and W.A. McDill. *The History of the Corps of Royal Canadian Engineers.* Ottawa: privately printed, 1962. 2 vols.

King, W.D., comp. *A Brief History of Militia Units Established at Various Periods at Yarmouth, Nova Scotia, 1812-1947.* Yarmouth, N.S.: privately printed, 1947. 32 pp.

*Knights of Columbus. *War Services of Canadian Knights of Columbus, 1939-1947; a History of the Work of the Knights of Columbus Canadian Army Huts.* Montreal: privately printed, 1948. 260 pp.

Laing, Gertrude. *A Community Organized for War; the Story of the Greater Winnipeg Co-ordinating Board for War Services and Affiliated Organizations, 1939-1946.* Winnipeg: n.p., 1948. 103 pp.

Lamontagne, Léopold. *Les archives régimentaires des Fusiliers du S.-Laurent.* Rimouski, P.Q.: s.i., 1943. 247 pp.

Lavoie, Joseph A. *Le Régiment de Montmagny de 1869 à 1931.* s.l.: s.i., [1932]. 117 pp.

Leasor, James. *Green Beach.* London: Heinemann, 1975. 250 pp.

Lindsay, Oliver. *The Lasting Honour; the Fall of Hong Kong, 1941.* London: H. Hamilton, 1978. 226 pp.

[Lockwood, A.M., comp.] *History of the 7th Canadian Medium Regiment, R.C.A.; from 1st September, 1939 to 8th June, 1945.* n.p.: n.d. 111 pp.

Londerville, J.D. *The Pay Services of the Canadian Army Overseas in the War of 1939-45.* Ottawa: privately printed, 1950. 315 pp.

The Lorne Scots (Peel, Dufferin and Halton Regiment). Brampton, Ont.: privately printed, 1962. 47 pp.

The Loyal Edmonton Regiment Memorial Booklet Including the Memorial Service, a Short History of the Regiment, the Roll of Honour. Nijkerk, Neth.: privately printed, 1945. 38 pp.

Lucas, James S., and James Barker. *The Killing Ground; the Battle of the Falaise Gap, August 1944.* London: Batsford, 1978. 176 pp.

Luxton, E.C. *1st Battalion, the Regina Rifle Regiment, 1939-1946.* n.p.: n.d. 70 pp.

Lyman, Tom. *5 LAA W/S RCEME; Unit History, 1943-1945.* n.p.: 1945. 1 vol., unpaged.

McAvity, J.M. *Lord Strathcona's Horse (Royal Canadians); a Record of Achievement.* Toronto: n.p., 1947. 280 pp.

Macbeth, John Douglas. *Somewhere in England; War Letters of a Canadian Officer on Overseas Service.* (Macmillan War Pamphlets; Canadian Series, no. 4.) Toronto: Macmillan, 1941. 32 pp.

Macdonald, B.J S. *The Trial of Kurt Meyer.* Toronto: Clarke, Irwin, 1954. 216 pp.

Macdonald, Grant. *Our Canadian Armed Services,* sketches by Grant Macdonald. Montreal: Gazette, 1943. 1 vol., chiefly illus.

Macdougall, G.L. *A Short History of the 29 Cdn Armd Recce Regt (South Alberta Regiment).* Amsterdam: Spin's Pub. Co., [1945?]. 87 pp.

McGill Univ., Montreal, P.Q. *A Memorial Service for the McGill Men and Women who Gave Their Lives during the First and Second World Wars.* n.p.: [1946]. 1 vol., unpaged.

McGregor, F., ed. *LdSH (RC) '85-70'.* Winnipeg: privately printed, 1970. 62 pp.

McKee, Alexander. *Caen, Anvil of Victory.* London: Souvenir Press, 1964. 368 pp.

Mackenzie-Naughton, J.D. *The Princess of Wales' Own Regiment (M.G.).* Kingston, Ont.: privately printed, 1946. 74 pp.

MacLaren, Roy. *Canadians in Russia, 1918-1919.* Toronto: Macmillan, 1976. 301 pp.

Maguire, E. *Dieppe, August 19.* London: Cape, 1963. 205 pp.

Malone, Dick. *Missing from the Record.* Toronto: Collins, 1946. 227 pp.

Maltby, R.G. *The Calgary Regiment.* Hilversum, Neth.: privately printed, 1945. 17 pp.

Manarey, R. Barrie. *The Canadian Bayonet.* Edmonton: Century Press, 1971. 51 pp.

Marcotte, Jean-Marie. *Mektoub! C'était écrit; "les récits du capitaine".* Montréal: Editions Lumen, 1946. 204 pp.

Marquis, G.E. *Le Régiment de Lévis; historique et album.* Lévis, P.Q.: s.i., 1952. 292 pp.

Maule, Henry. *Caen; the Brutal Battle and Break-out from Normandy.* Newton Abbot, Eng.: David & Charles, 1976. 176 pp.

Mazéas, Daniel. *Croquis d'insignes armée canadienne, 1920-1950; Canadian Badges.* Guincamp, France: privately printed, 1970. 64 pp.

_____. *Insignes armée canadienne, 1900-1914; Canadian Badges; supplément, 1920-1950.* Guincamp, France: privately printed, 1972. 116 pp.

Meanwell, R.W. *1 Battalion, the Essex Scottish Regiment (Allied with the Essex Regiment), 1939-1945; a Brief Narrative.* Aldershot, Eng.: Gale & Polden, 1946. 95 pp.

Mellor, John. *Forgotten Heroes; the Canadians at Dieppe.* Toronto: Methuen, 1975. 163 pp.

Memorandum sur l'instruction de l'Armée canadienne. No. 1-72. Ottawa: Imprimeur du Roi, 1941-47.

The Militia in Durham County . . . see Chandler, C.M.

Mitchell, Steve. *They were Invincible; Dieppe and After.* Bracebridge, Ont.: Herald-Gazette, 1976. 132 pp.

Miville-Deschênes, Charles. *Souvenirs de guerre.* Québec, P.Q.: s.i., 1946. 128 pp.

Moir, J.S., ed. *History of the Royal Canadian Corps of Signals, 1903-1961.* Ottawa: privately printed, 1962. 336 pp.

Moogk, Peter N., and R.V. Stevenson. *Vancouver Defended; a History of the Men and Guns of the Lower Mainland Defences, 1859-1949.* Surrey, B.C.: Antonson Pub., 1978. 128 pp.

Mordal, Jacques, [*pseud.*] see/voir Cras, Hervé.

Morton, Desmond. *The Canadian General, Sir William Otter.* (Canadian War Museum Historical Publication Number 9.) Toronto: Hakkert, 1974. 423 pp.

Mowat, Farley. *And No Birds Sang.* Toronto: McClelland and Stewart, 1979. 250 pp.

_____. *The Regiment.* Toronto: McClelland and Stewart, 1955. 312 pp.
The Hastings and Prince Edward Regiment in World War II.

Munro, Ross. *Gauntlet to Overlord; the Story of the Canadian Army.* Toronto: Macmillan, 1946. 477 pp.

_____. *Red Patch in Sicily; the Story of the 1st Canadian Division in Action; Dispatches by Ross Munro.* Toronto: Canadian Press, 1943. 13 pp.

N.R.E.F. 16th Brigade C.F.A., 67th and 68th Batteries in North Russia, September 1918 to June 1919. n.p.: n.d. 55 pp.

Nicholson, G.W.L. *Canada's Nursing Sisters.* (Canadian War Museum Historical Publication Number 13.) Toronto: S. Stevens, Hakkert, 1975. 272 pp.

*_____. *The Canadians in Italy, 1943-1945.* (Official History of the Canadian Army in the Second World War, vol. II.) Ottawa: Queen's Printer, 1956. 807 pp.

*_____. *Les Canadiens en Italie, 1943-1945.* (Histoire officielle de l'Armée canadienne dans la seconde guerre mondiale, vol. II.) Ottawa: Imprimeur de la Reine, 1960. 851 pp.

_____. *The Gunners of Canada; the History of the Royal Regiment of Canadian Artillery.* Toronto: McClelland and Stewart, 1967-72. 2 vols.

_____. *More Fighting Newfoundlanders; a History of Newfoundland's Fighting Forces in the Second World War.* [St. John's, Nfld.]: Govt. of Nfld., 1969. 621 pp.

*_____. *"Nous nous souviendrons . . ."; mémoriaux outremer aux morts de guerre du Canada.* Ottawa: Imprimeur de la Reine, 1973. 118 pp.

_____. *Seventy Years of Service; a History of the Royal Canadian Army Medical Corps.* Ottawa: Borealis Press, 1977. 388 pp.

*_____. *"We Will Remember . . ."; Overseas Memorials to Canada's War Dead.* Ottawa: Queen's Printer, 1973. 110 pp.

Noblston, Allen. *5 Canadian Light Anti-Aircraft Regiment; Regimental History; World War II (1 March 1941 — 8 May 1945).* Groningen, Neth.: privately printed, 1945. 64 pp.

*Nord, Max, comp. *Merci Canada.* Afdeling, Neth.: Stichting Wereldtentoon-stelling, 1967. 192 pp.

*_____. *Thank You, Canada.* Afdeling, Neth.: Stichting Wereldtentoon-stelling, 1967. 192 pp.

Nova Scotia. *Nova Scotia Helps the Fighting Man.* n.p.: [1942]. 32 pp.

Officers' Directory 1st Cdn armd Bde., Holland, June 7, 1945. n.p.: 1945. 25 1.

Ogle, Robert J. *The Faculties of Canadian Military Chaplains; a Commentary on the Faculty Sheet of December, 1955 and the Directives for Holy Week Promulgated March 14, 1956.* Ottawa: n.p., 1956. 267 pp.

Oldfield, J.E. *The Westminsters' War Diary; an Unofficial History of the Westminster Regiment (Motor) in World War II.* New Westminster, B.C.: privately printed, 1964. 209 pp.

Once in the Queen's Own, Always in the Queen's Own. n.p.: privately printed, 1932. 70 pp.

Osler, John G. *2nd Canadian Medium Regiment, R.C.A.; Regimental History, 18 January 1942 — 30 June 1945.* Deventer, Neth.: privately printed, 1945. 119 pp.

Paterson, R.A. *A History of the 10th Canadian Infantry Brigade.* n.p.: privately printed, 1945. 78 pp.

Pavey, Walter G. *An Historical Account of the 7th Canadian Reconnaissance Regiment (17th Duke of York's Royal Canadian Hussars) in the World War, 1939-1945.* Montreal: privately printed, [1948]. 139 pp.

Pearce, Donald. *Journal of a War, North-West Europe, 1944-1945.* Toronto: Macmillan, 1965. 188 pp.

Pellatt, Reginald. *A Guide to Riflemen of the Queen's Own Rifles of Canada.* Toronto: privately printed, 1924. 40 pp.

_____. *Standing Orders of the Queen's Own Rifles of Canada.* [Toronto: n.p., 1925.] 77 pp.

Penny, Arthur G. *Royal Rifles of Canada, "Able and Willing" Since 1862; a Short History.* n.p.: 1962. 62 pp.

Pepin, J.C. *Mes cinq ans à la Légion; histoire véridique vécue par l'auteur lui-même.* Beauceville, P.Q.: L'Eclaireur, 1932. 150 pp.

Phillips, Norman, and J. Nikerk. *Holland and the Canadians.* Amsterdam: Contact Pub., 1945. 72 pp.

A Pictorial Review of Military District No. 10, 1939-1940. Winnipeg: Winnipeg Saturday Post, [1940?]. 100 pp., chiefly illus.

Pipet, Albert. *Mourir à Caen.* Paris: Presses de la Cité, 1974. 249 pp.

"Pooch" [*pseud.*] *see* Corrigan, Cecil Edwin.

Pope, Maurice A. *Soldiers and Politicians; the Memoirs of Lt.-Gen. Maurice A. Pope, C.B., M.C.* Toronto: Univ. of Toronto Press, 1962. 462 pp.

Poulin, J.G. *696 heures d'enfer avec le Royal 22e Régiment; récit vécu et inspiré d'un journal tenu tant bien que mal au front.* Montréal: Beauchemin, 1946. 181 pp.

Pouliot, Henri. *Légionnaire! Histoire véridique et vécue d'un Québe-cois simple soldat à la Légion étrangère.* Québec, P.Q.: Impri-merie le "Soleil", 1931. 300 pp.

Powley, A.E. *Broadcast from the Front; Canadian Radio Overseas in the Second World War.* (Canadian War Museum Historical Publication Number 11.) Toronto: Hakkert, 1975. 189 pp.

Presentation of Colours by His Excellency the Earl of Bessborough; the 1st (13th) and 2nd (42nd) Battalions, the Black Watch (Royal Highlanders) of Canada; at the McGill Stadium, Montreal, May 28th, 1931; Programme of Ceremonies. n.p.: n.d. 18 pp.

Presentation of Colours to 1st Battalion, the Royal Regiment of Canada, and the South Saskatchewan Regiment, by His Majesty the King, at Witley, Surrey, England, 16th July, 1943. Alder-shot, Eng.: privately printed, [1943]. 1 vol., chiefly illus.

Presentation of Colours to the Carleton & York Regiment and the Edmonton Regiment by His Majesty the King at Caterham, Surrey, England, Dominion Day, 1st July, 1941. Aldershot, Eng.: privately printed, [1941]. 1 vol., chiefly illus.

Presentation of Colours to the First Battalion the Saskatoon Light Infantry by Her Majesty the Queen, at Caterham, Surrey, England, 24th October, 1941. Aldershot, Eng.: privately printed, [1941]. 1 vol., unpaged.

Presentation of Colours to the Toronto Scottish Regiment (M.G.) by Her Majesty the Queen, Colonel-in-Chief, the Toronto Scottish Regiment (M.G.), Monday, May 22nd, 1939, in the Forenoon on the Grounds of the University of Toronto. [n.p.: 1939. 18 pp.]

Preston, Richard A. *Canada's RMC; a History of the Royal Military College.* Toronto: Univ. of Toronto Press, 1969. 415 pp.

Princess Patricia's Canadian Light Infantry Recruit's Book. [Winni-peg: n.p., 1946.] 24 pp.

Programme-souvenir; le Régiment de Hull, mai 1964; publication autorisée par le Lt-Col. Guy de Marlis, C.D., Commandant, le Régiment de Hull; programme-souvenir publié pour marquer le 50e anniversaire du Régiment de Hull et le 25e anniversaire du manège de Salaberry. Hull, P.Q.: imprimé privé, [1964]. 60 pp.

Proulx, Benjamin A. *Underground from Hongkong.* New York: Dutton, 1943. 214 pp.

Queen's Own Rifles of Canada Association. *A Brief Resumé of the Activities of the Queen's Own Rifles of Canada Association, 1914-1932.* Toronto: privately printed, 1932. 70 pp.

_____. *Yearbook.* [Toronto: n.p.], 1923-47. 18 vols. *Not issued 1939-44, 1946.*

Queen-Hughes, R.W. *Whatever Men Dare; a History of the Queen's Own Cameron Highlanders of Canada, 1935-1960.* Winnipeg: privately printed, 1960. 247 pp.

Quigley, John Gordon. *A Century of Rifles, 1860-1960; the Halifax Rifles (RCAC)(M); "cede nullis".* Halifax: privately printed, 1960. 230 pp.

RCCS; Second Canadian Armoured Brigade Signals. n.p.: n.d. 40 pp.

Raddall, Thomas H. *West Novas; a History of the West Nova Scotia Regiment.* Toronto: privately printed, 1947. 326 pp.

The Rally Magazine. Vol. I-? Wrecclesham, Eng.: n.p., 1939?-? *A monthly magazine for Canadian Active Service Forces.*

The Ranger. Vol. I-V. Vancouver: privately printed, 1942-45. *Journal of the Pacific Coast Militia Rangers.*

Reader's Digest. *The Canadians at War, 1939/45.* Montreal: Reader's Digest, 1969. 2 vols.

_____. *The Tools of War, 1939/45, and a Chronology of Important Events.* Montreal: Reader's Digest, 1969. 96 pp.

Regimental History, 85 Cdn Bridge Coy, June, 1941 — May, 1945. [Zwolle, Neth.: n.p., 1945.] 82 pp.

The Regimental History of the Governor General's Foot Guards see Baylay, George Taylor.

Regimental Standing Orders of the Royal Canadian Army Service Corps, 1925. Ottawa: King's Printer, 1925. 162 pp.

Reyburn, Wallace. *Glorious Chapter; the Canadians at Dieppe.* Toronto: Oxford Univ. Press, 1943. 165 pp. *London ed. titled: Rehearsal for Invasion.*

Reynolds, Quentin. *Dress Rehearsal; the Story of Dieppe.* New York: London House, 1943. 278 pp.

Robertson, F.A. *5th (B.C.) Regiment, Canadian Garrison Artillery, and Early Defences of B.C. Coast; Historical Record.* Victoria, B.C.: privately printed, 1925. 2 vols.

Robertson, Heather, [comp.] *A Terrible Beauty; the Art of Canada at War.* Toronto: J. Lorimer, 1977. 239 pp.

Robertson, Peter. *Irréductible vérité/Relentless Verity/les photographes militaires canadiens depuis 1885/Canadian Military Photographers since 1885.* (Les Archives publiques du Canada/ Public Archives of Canada Series.) Québec, P.Q.: Les Presses de l'Université Laval, 1973. 233 pp. *Texte bilingue./Bilingual text.*

*Robertson, Terence. *Dieppe; journée de honte, journée de gloire.* R. Jouan, tr. Paris: Presses de la Cité, 1963. 379 pp.

*Robertson, Terence. *The Shame and the Glory; Dieppe.* Toronto: McClelland and Stewart, 1962. 432 pp.

Rocky Mountain Rangers; First Battalion C.A. — A.F., 1885-1941. New Westminster, B.C.: Columbian Co., 1941. 60 pp., chiefly illus.

Roe, Kathleen Robson. *War Letters from the C.W.A.C. (Canadian Women's Army Corp)* [*sic*]. Toronto: Kakabeka Pub. Co., 1976. 169 pp.

Rogers, R.L. *History of the Lincoln and Welland Regiment.* n.p.: privately printed, 1954. 465 pp.

Rollifson, M.O. *Green Route Up; Fourth Canadian Armoured Division.* The Hague, Neth.: Mouton, 1945. 119 pp.

Ross, Armand, et Michel Gauvin. *Le geste du Régiment de la Chaudière.* B.J. Van Der Velde, ed. Rotterdam: imprimé privé, 1945. 179 pp.

Ross, Richard M. *The History of the 1st Battalion Cameron Highlanders of Ottawa (M.G.).* Ottawa: privately printed, 1946. 96 pp.

Roy, R.H. *For Most Conspicuous Bravery; a Biography of Major-General George R. Pearkes, V.C., through Two World Wars.* Vancouver: Univ. of British Columbia Press, 1977. 388 pp.

_____. *Ready for the Fray (Deas Gu Cath); the History of the Canadian Scottish Regiment (Princess Mary's), 1920-1955.* Vancouver: privately printed, 1958. 509 pp.

_____. *The Seaforth Highlanders of Canada, 1919-1965.* Vancouver: privately printed, 1969. 559 pp.

_____. *Sinews of Steel; the History of the British Columbia Dragoons.* Brampton, Ont.: privately printed, 1965. 468 pp.

The Royal Canadian Armoured Corps. Ottawa: Queen's Printer, 1953. 11 pp.

The Royal Canadian Army Medical Corps. Ottawa: Queen's Printer, 1953. 10 pp.

Royal Canadian Army Pay Corps. Ottawa: Queen's Printer, 1953. 11 pp.

The Royal Canadian Army Service Corps. Ottawa: Queen's Printer, 1953. 11 pp.

The Royal Canadian Artillery. Ottawa: Queen's Printer, 1953. 10 pp.

Royal Cdn. Artillery; History of the 4th Cdn. Anti-Tank Battery, June 1940 — July 1945. n.p.: [1945]. 60 pp.

Royal Canadian Dragoons, 1939-1945. Montreal: privately printed, 1946. 233 pp.

Royal Canadian Horse Artillery; First Regiment, 1871-1971. Lahr, Ger.: privately printed, [1971]. 32 pp.

The Royal Canadian Ordnance Corps Diamond Jubilee Yearbook. n.p.: 1963. 106 pp.

Royal Military College of Canada, Kingston, Ont. *Regulations and Calendar of the Royal Military College of Canada, 1922.* Ottawa: King's Printer, 1923. 68 pp.

_____. *Standing Orders, Amended to January, 1924.* Ottawa: King's Printer, 1924. 120 pp.

_____. *Standing Orders, Amended to January, 1926.* Ottawa: King's Printer, 1926. 105 pp.

_____. *Standing Orders; the Royal Military College of Canada, 1938.* Ottawa: King's Printer, 1938. 67 pp.

The Royal Military College of Canada Review. Vol. I- . Kingston, Ont.: privately printed, 1920- .

The Royal Rifles of Canada, Allied with the King's Royal Rifle Corps, 1862-1937; Ypres 1915, Festubert, Mont Sorrel, Somme 1916, Arras 1917, Hill 70, Ypres 1917, Amiens; South Africa 1899-1900; Great War 1914-1918. n.p.: [1937]. 21 pp.

Le Royal 22e Régiment armée active du Canada, Londres, du 17 au 21 avril, mil neuf cent quarante. Aldershot, Angleterre: imprimé privé, 1940. [20] pp.

Rudbach, N.E. *The Halifax Rifles (23 Armoured Regiment) R.C.A.C.R.F.; "90th" Anniversary, 14th May 1860 — 14th May 1950.* Halifax: n.p., 1950. 20 pp.

Rudler, Raymond. *Le jubilé des Canadiens.* Paris: Presses de la Cité, 1972. 309 pp.

Ruffee, G.E.M., and J.B. Dickie. *The History of the 14th Field Regiment, Royal Canadian Artillery, 1940-1945.* Amsterdam: Wereldbibliotheek N.V., 1945. 61 pp.

Russell, W.S. *The History of the 8th Canadian Light Anti-Aircraft Regiment, R.C.A.* Amersfoort, Neth.: privately printed, 1945. 124 pp.

Rutherford, T.H., comp. *Honour Roll; Royal Canadian Armoured Corps; World War II.* Oromocto, N.B.: privately printed, 1972. 1 vol., unpaged.

Rutherford, Tom. *An Unofficial History of the Grey and Simcoe Foresters Regiment, 1866-1973.* n.p.: n.d. 88 pp.

Sabourin, J. Armand. *This Was Dieppe.* n.p.: National War Finance Committee of the Province of Quebec, n.d. 1 vol., unpaged.

Sallans, G.H. *With Canada's Fighting Men.* Ottawa: King's Printer, 1941. 46 pp.

The Salute; Official Organ of the 103rd C.A.(B)T.C., Fort Garry, Manitoba. Vol. I-III. n.p.: privately printed, 1942-45.

Savage, J.M. *The History of the 5th Canadian Anti-Tank Regiment, 10 Sept. 1941 — 10 June 1945.* John P. Claxton, ed. Lochem, Neth.: privately printed, [1945]. 83 pp.

*Savard, Adjutor. *The Defence of Our Land.* n.p.: 1943. 12 pp.

*_____. *La défense du territoire.* s.l.: s.i., 1943. 11 pp.

Scislowski, Stanley. *Return to Italy, 1975; a Modern-Day Pilgrimage.* n.p.: [1977]. 73 pp.

Schragg, Lex. *History of the Ontario Regiment, 1866-1951.* Oshawa, Ont.: privately printed, 1951. 286 pp.

Service, G.T., and J.K. Marteinson. *The Gate; a History of the Fort Garry Horse.* Calgary: privately printed, 1971. 228 pp.

Le Service Jociste du Soldat. *Nos Canadiens en service; sous les drapeaux.* Montréal: Les Editions Ouvrières, 1943. 142 pp.

Sévigny, Pierre. *Face à l'ennemi.* Montréal: Beauchemin, 1946. 176 pp.

Shapiro, L.S.B. *They Left the Back Door Open; a Chronicle of the Allied Campaign in Sicily and Italy.* Toronto: Ryerson Press, 1944. 191 pp.

Shea, A.A., and E. Estoriak. *Canada and the Short-Wave War.* (Behind the Headlines, vol. III.) Toronto: Canadian Institute of International Affairs, 1942. 36 pp.

A Short History of the British Columbia Regiment; the "Dukes". n.p.: n.d. [11] pp.

The Signalman. Vol. I-IV? Kingston, Ont.: King's Printer, 1942-46?

Simonds, Peter. *Maple Leaf Up Maple Leaf Down; the Story of the Canadians in the Second World War.* New York: Island Press, 1946. 356 pp.

Sinclair, J.D., comp. *The Queen's Own Cameron Highlanders of Canada; Twenty-Fifth Anniversary Souvenir.* Winnipeg: privately printed, 1935. 99 pp.

Singer, Burrell M., and R.J.S. Langford. *Handbook of Canadian Military Law.* Toronto: Copp Clark, 1941. 272 pp.

Slinger, J.E., and D. McNichol. *History of the 11th Canadian Armoured Regiment (the Ontario Regiment) in the Field, 1939-1945.* Harlingen, Neth.: Flevo Press, 1945. 44 pp.

Smith, Doug. *Bless 'em All.* Vancouver: privately printed, 1967. 152 pp.

_____. *Memoirs of an Old Sweat.* Vancouver: privately printed, 1961. 154 pp.

[Smith, Lawrence N.] *The History of the 23rd Field Regiment (SP) R.C.A., World War II.* St. Catharines, Ont.: privately printed, n.d. 81 pp.

Smith, Waldo E.L. *What Time the Tempest; an Army Chaplain's Story.* Toronto: Ryerson Press, 1953. 305 pp.

South Saskatchewan Regiment; Welcome Home, Weyburn, November 1945. Estevan, Sask.: Mercury Print, n.d. 12 pp.

Speaight, Robert. *Vanier; Soldier, Diplomat and Governor General.* Toronto: Collins, 1970. 488 pp.

Spencer, R.A. *History of the Fifteenth Canadian Field Regiment; Royal Canadian Artillery, 1941 to 1945.* Amsterdam: Elsevier, 1945. 302 pp.

The Springbok. Various places: n.p., 1923-   .
Regimental journal of the Royal Canadian Dragoons. Title varies: <u>The Goat</u> (1923-36).

*Stacey, C.P. *L'Armée canadienne, 1939-1945; résumé historique officiel.* Ottawa: Imprimeur du Roi, 1949. 364 pp.

*_____. *Armes, hommes et gouvernements; les politiques de guerre du Canada, 1939-1945.* Ottawa: Imprimeur de la Reine, 1970. 747 pp.

*_____. *Arms, Men and Governments; the War Policies of Canada, 1939-1945.* Ottawa: Queen's Printer, 1970. 681 pp.

*_____. *La campagne de la victoire; les opérations dans le Nord-Ouest de l'Europe, 1944-45.* (Histoire officielle de la participation de l'Armée canadienne à la seconde guerre mondiale, vol. III.) Ottawa: Imprimeur de la Reine, 1960. 837 pp.

*_____. *Canada's Battle in Normandy; the Canadian Army's Share in the Operations 6 June — 1 September, 1944.* (The Canadian Army at War, no. 3.) Ottawa: King's Printer, 1946. 159 pp.

*_____. *The Canadian Army 1939-1945; an Official Historical Summary.* Ottawa: King's Printer, 1948. 312 pp.

*Stacey, C.P. *Les Canadiens dans la bataille de Normandie; la partici-pation de l'Armée canadienne aux opérations du 6 juin au 1er septembre 1944.* (L'Armée canadienne à la Guerre, no. 3.) Ottawa: Imprimeur du Roi, 1946. 159 pp.

*_____. *Six années de guerre; l'Armée au Canada, en Grande-Bretagne et dans le Pacifique.* (Histoire officielle de la participa-tion de l'Armée canadienne à la seconde guerre mondiale, vol. I.) Ottawa: Imprimeur de la Reine, 1957. 652 pp.

*_____. *Six Years of War; the Army in Canada, Britain and the Pacific.* (Official History of the Canadian Army in the Second World War, vol. I.) Ottawa: Queen's Printer, 1955. 629 pp.

*_____. *The Victory Campaign; the Operations in North West Europe, 1944-45.* (Official History of the Canadian Army in the Second World War, vol. III.) Ottawa: Queen's Printer, 1960. 770 pp.

Stalmann, Reinhart. *Die Ausbrecherkönige von Kanada.* [Hamburg, Ger.]: Sternbücher, 1958. 191 pp.

Standing Orders of Princess Patricia's Canadian Light Infantry. Ottawa: King's Printer, 1920. 42 pp.

Standing Orders of the Royal Canadian Regiment. Ottawa: T. Mulvey, [1920?]. 78 pp.

Stanley, George F.G. *Canada's Soldiers, 1604-1954; the Military History of an Unmilitary People.* Toronto: Macmillan, 1954. 400 pp.

_____. *In the Face of Danger; the History of the Lake Superior Regiment.* Port Arthur, Ont.: privately printed, 1960. 357 pp.

Stanley, George F.G., and Richard A. Preston. *A Short History of Kingston as a Military and Naval Centre.* Kingston, Ont.: Queen's Printer, [195-?]. 33 pp.

Steele, Harwood. *The Long Ride; a Short History of the 17th Duke of York's Royal Canadian Hussars.* Montreal: Gazette Print. Co., 1934. 48 pp.

Steven, Walter T. *In this Sign.* Toronto: Ryerson Press, 1948. 182 pp.

Stevens, G.R. *A City Goes to War.* Brampton, Ont.: Charters Pub., 1964. 431 pp.

_____. *The Sun is Setting on the Paleface Brave or Down the Drain a Billion a Year Goes.* Montreal: privately printed, [1968]. 16 pp.

Stewart, Charles H., comp. *The Concise Lineages of the Canadian Army, 1855 to Date.* Toronto: n.p., n.d. 163 pp.

Stormont, Dundas and Glengarry Highlanders; a Brief History, 1784-1945; Presented to Members of the First Battalion upon their Return from Overseas. Cornwall, Ont.: n.p., [1945]. 39 pp.

The Story of the 69th Light Anti-Aircraft Battery, R.C.A. Toronto: T.H. Best Print. Co., n.d. 179 pp.

The Strathconian. Calgary: n.p., 1914-?, 1927-38, 1947-   .
Regimental journal of the Lord Strathcona's Horse (Royal Canadians). Re-numbered from no. 1 after each gap in publication.

Stuart, (Sir) Campbell. *Opportunity Knocks Once.* London: Collins, 1952. 248 pp.

Stubbs, Roy St. George. *Men in Khaki; Four Regiments of Manitoba.* Toronto: Ryerson Press, 1941. 72 pp.

Stursberg, Peter. *Journey into Victory; up the Alaska Highway and to Sicily and Italy.* London: Harrap, 1944. 160 pp.

Swettenham, John. *Allied Intervention in Russia, 1918-1919; and the Part Played by Canada.* Toronto: Ryerson Press, 1967. 315 pp.

_____. *D-Day./Jour-J.* Jacques Gouin, tr. Ottawa: National Museum of Man/Le Musée national de l'homme, [1970]. 27/30 pp.
Bilingual text./Texte bilingue.

_____. *McNaughton.* Toronto: Ryerson Press, 1968-69. 3 vols.

Thomas, Hartley Munro. *UWO Contingent COTC; the History of the Canadian Officers' Training Corps at the University of Western Ontario.* London, Ont.: Univ. of Western Ontario, 1956. 422 pp.

Thompson, R.W. *Dieppe at Dawn; the Story of the Dieppe Raid.* London: Hutchinson, 1956. 215 pp.
New York ed. titled: At Whatever Cost.

_____. *The Eighty-Five Days; the Story of the Battle of the Scheldt.* London: Hutchinson, 1957. 235 pp.

Thompson, Roy J.C. *Cap Badges of the Canadian Officer Training Corps.* Dartmouth, N.S.: n.p., 1972. 68 pp.

_____. *Wings of the Canadian Armed Forces, 1913-1972.* [Dartmouth], N.S.: n.p., 1973. 106 pp.

*La Trésorerie militaire royale canadienne. Ottawa: Imprimeur de la Reine, 1954. 12 pp.

Trinity College School Old Boys at War, 1899-1902, 1914-1918, 1939-1945. Port Hope, Ont.: privately printed, 1948. 245 pp.

Turner, T.H. *Mechanics to Mars; the Story of the Canadian Ordnance Corps Training Centre at Barriefield, Ontario.* Barriefield, Ont.: n.p., n.d. 16 pp.

The 23rd Canadian Field Regiment (S.P.) Royal Canadian Artillery; a Compilation of All the Photos used to Illustrate the Featured Articles of the "S.P." Paper. n.p.: n.d. 72 pp.

The University of Alberta in the War of 1939-45. Edmonton: n.p., 1948. 70 pp.

Upper Canada Historical Arms Society. *The Military Arms of Canada.* (Historical Arms Series, 1.) West Hill, Ont.: Museum Restoration Service, 1963. 47 pp.

Upton, Terence B. *The Rocky Mountain Rangers, 1898-1944; a Short History.* n.p.: n.d. 13 pp.

Urquhart, Hugh M. *Arthur Currie; the Biography of a Great Canadian.* Toronto: Dent, 1950. 363 pp.

Vallée, Pierre. *Prisonnier à l'Oflag 79.* Montréal: Editions de l'homme, 1964. 123 pp.

Van Der Schee, W. *A Short History of Lord Strathcona's Horse (Royal Canadians).* n.p.: 1973. 19 1.

Vanguard; the Fort Garry Horse in the Second World War. Doetinchem, Neth.: privately printed, 1945. 196 pp.

Vanier, Georges-P. *Paroles de guerre.* Montréal: Beauchemin, 1944. 148 pp.

Victoria Rifles of Canada, 1861-1951; Historical Notes. n.p.: n.d. 14 pp.

Victoria Rifles of Canada; Youth Trained in Mind and Body in a Great Regiment. n.p.: [ca. 1936]. 16 pp.

Les Voltigeurs de Québec, 1862-1952; notes historiques. s.l.: s.i., 1952. 16 pp.

Les Voltigeurs de Québec, 1862-1962; album du centenaire, mai 1962. St-François, P.Q.: imprimé privé, 1962. 31 pp.

Walker, D.E., comp. *A Resume of the Story of 1st Battalion the Saskatoon Light Infantry (MG), Canadian Army, Overseas.* Saskatoon, Sask.: privately printed, n.d. 139 pp.

Walmsley, R.Y., and B.J.P. Whalley. *The History of the First Med. Regt., 1940-1945.* Amsterdam: Spin's Pub. Co., 1945. 121 pp.

Wamper, Hans. *Dieppe; Die Bewährung des Küstenwestwalles.* Berlin: E.S. Mittler, 1943. 97 pp.

Warren, Arnold. *Wait for the Wagon; the Story of the Royal Canadian Army Service Corps.* Toronto: McClelland and Stewart, 1961. 413 pp.

Watson, W.S., and others, eds. *The Brockville Rifles, Royal Canadian Infantry Corps (Allied with the King's Royal Rifle Corps); Semper Paratus; an Unofficial History.* Brockville, Ont.: Recorder Print. Co., 1966. 138 pp.

Watts, E.M. *Some Soldiers; the Story of 80(R) Company, Veteran's Guard of Canada.* Brampton, Ont.: privately printed, 1960. 24 pp.

Welcome Home, 14th C.A.(T.)R. Calgary Regiment (Tank). [Calgary: n.p., 1945.] 14 pp.

Wentzel, Fritz. *Single or Return? The Story of a German P.O.W. in British Camps, and the Escape of Lieutenant Franz von Werra.* Edward Fitzgerald, tr. London: W. Kimber, 1954. 172 pp.

[Werra, Franz von.] *Einer kam durch; Fluchtbericht des Fliegerleutnants Franz von Werra.* Hamburg, Ger.: Verlag der Sternbücher, [1959]. 244 pp.

*Whitcombe, Fred, and Blair Gilmour. *L'histoire illustrée de L'Armée canadienne outre-mer, 1939-1945.* Placide Labelle, tr. Montréal: Whitcombe Gilmour, s.d. 280 pp.

*_____. *The Pictorial History of Canada's Army Overseas, 1939-1945.* Montreal: Whitcombe Gilmour, 1947. 262 pp.

Whitehead, William. *Dieppe, 1942; Echoes of Disaster.* Terence Macartney-Filgate, ed. (A Personal Library Publication.) Don Mills, Ont.: Nelson, 1979. 187 pp., chiefly illus.

Whitton, Charlotte. *Canadian Women in the War Effort.* Toronto: Macmillan, 1942. 56 pp.

Wilkinson, Arthur Campbell. *Ottawa to Caen; Letters.* Alta R. Wilkinson, ed. Ottawa: Tower Books, 1947. 122 pp.

Willcocks, K.D.H. *The Hastings and Prince Edward Regiment, Canada; a Short History.* Belleville, Ont.: n.p., 1967. 1 vol., unpaged.

Williams, Jeffery. *Princess Patricia's Canadian Light Infantry.* (Famous Regiments.) London: L. Cooper, 1972. 110 pp.

[Willson, Gordon Beckles.] *Canada Comes to England,* by Gordon Beckles [*pseud.*] London: Hodder and Stoughton, 1941. 166 pp.

Wilson, J.E., and others. *A History of 2 Cdn H.A.A. Regt.* Soesterberg, Neth.: privately printed, 1945. 59 pp.

Windsor, John. *Blind Date.* Sidney, B.C.: Gray's Pub., 1962. 192 pp.

_____. *The Mouth of the Wolf.* Sidney, B.C.: Gray's Pub., 1967. 224 pp.

The Winnipeg Rifles, 8th Battalion, C.E.F., Allied with the Rifle Brigade (Prince Consort's Own); Fiftieth Anniversary, 1883-1933. Winnipeg: privately printed, 1933. 59 pp.

Wodehouse, R.F. *A Check List of the War Collections of World War I, 1914-1918, and World War II, 1939-1945.* Ottawa: Queen's Printer, 1968. 239 pp.

Women in Khaki. n.p.: n.d. 32 pp.

Wood, Alan. *The Falaise Road.* Toronto: Macmillan, 1944. 64 pp.

Wood, Gordon. *The Story of the Irish Regiment of Canada, 1939-1945.* Heerenveen, Neth.: privately printed, 1945. 87 pp.

Wood, J.E.R., ed. *Detour; the Story of Oflag IV C.* J.F. Watton, illus. London: Falcon Press, 1946. 183 pp.

Worthington, Larry. *The Spur and the Sprocket; the Story of the Royal Canadian Dragoons.* Kitchener, Ont.: Reeve Press, 1968. 170 pp.

_____. *"Worthy"; a Biography of Major-General F.F. Worthington, C.B., M.C., M.M.* Toronto: Macmillan, 1961. 236 pp.

The York Ranger. No. 1. [Toronto]: n.p., 1922.
Only one number published.

Young, C.R. *Notes on Elementary Military Law for Canadian Officers.* [Toronto]: Univ. of Toronto Press, 1939. 70 pp.

Young Men's Christian Associations, Canada. *The 1st Year; a War Service Record of the Canadian Y.M.C.A. from the Outbreak of the War.* n.p.: [1940]. 23 pp.

Young Men's Christian Associations, Canada. National Council. War Services Executive. *With Arthur Jones through 5 Years of War; a Report of Canadian Y.M.C.A. War Services.* n.p.: n.d. 1 vol., unpaged.

Young, Scott. *Red Shield in Action; a Record of Canadian Salvation Army War Services in the Second Great War.* Toronto: F.F. Clarke, 1949. 149 pp.

Zepeda Turcios, Roberto. *Caminos de Renuncicion.* Tegucigalpa, Honduras: Talles Tipograficos de la Imprenta Caldéron, 1947. 244 pp.

1946-1967

Air Force College Journal. Toronto: privately printed, 1956-64. 9 vols.
Title varies.

L'Amicale du 22e. Vol. I-XVIII. Québec, P.Q.: imprimé privé, 1947-64.
Remplacé par La Citadelle.

Barnard, W.T. *The Queen's Own Rifles of Canada, 1860-1960; One Hundred Years of Canada.* Don Mills, Ont.: Ontario Pub. Co., 1960. 398 pp.

_____. *A Short History of the Queen's Own Rifles of Canada.* Toronto: MacKinnon & Atkins, n.d. 22 pp.

*Barton, William H. *Science and the Armed Services.* (Current Affairs for the Canadian Forces, vol. II, no. 1.) Ottawa: King's Printer, 1952. 22 pp.

*_____. *La science et les Services armés.* (Actualités; revue destinée aux Forces canadiennes, vol. II, no. 1.) Ottawa: Imprimeur du Roi, 1952. 22 pp.

Beattie, Kim. *Dileas; History of the 48th Highlanders of Canada, 1929-1956.* Toronto: privately printed, 1957. 847 pp.

Bezeau, M.V. *University of Ottawa Contingent, Canadian Officers Training Corps.* n.p.: 1968. 15 pp.

Bindon, Kathryn M. *Queen's Men, Canada's Men; the Military History of Queen's University, Kingston.* [Kingston, Ont.]: privately printed, 1978. 180 pp.

Bird, Will R. *North Shore (New Brunswick) Regiment.* Fredericton, N.B.: Brunswick Press, 1963. 629 pp.

Boissonault, Charles-Marie. *Histoire politico-militaire des Canadiens français (1763-1967).* Trois-Rivières, P.Q.: Editions du Bien public, 1967. 310 pp.

Boss, W. *The Stormont, Dundas and Glengarry Highlanders, 1783-1951.* Ottawa: Runge Press, 1952. 449 pp.

Bowering, Clifford H. *Service; the Story of the Canadian Legion, 1925-1960.* Ottawa: privately printed, 1960. 240 pp.

The Brazier; Marking the 50th Anniversary of the Canadian Scottish (Princess Mary's), June 6, 1964. Victoria, B.C.: privately printed, 1964. 19 pp.

A Brief History of the Royal Regiment of Canada; Allied with the King's Regiment (Liverpool). [Toronto: n.p., 1948.] 135 pp.

Brown, Kingsley, *see* Greenhous, Brereton.

*Brown, W.L. *Les Cadets royaux de l'armée canadienne; cent ans d'exploits, 1879-1979.* s.l.: La Ligue des Cadets de l'Armée du Canada, [1979. 12 pp.]

*Brown, W.L. *The Royal Canadian Army Cadets; a Century of Achievement, 1879-1979.* n.p.: The Army Cadet League of Canada, [1979. 12 pp.]

Burns, E.L.M. *Between Arab and Israeli.* Toronto: Clarke, Irwin, 1962. 336 pp.

Cameron, James M. *Pictonians in Arms; a Military History of Pictou County, Nova Scotia.* Fredericton, N.B.: privately printed, 1969. 301 pp.

Camp, A.D., comp. *7th Toronto Regiment, Royal Regiment of Canadian Artillery, 1866-1966.* n.p.: n.d. 33 pp.

Camp Valcartier, P.Q.; 1647 à 1957 en quelques lignes./Camp Valcartier P.Q.; a Short History 1647-1957. s.l.: s.i./n.p.: 1957. 24 pp.
Texte bilingue./Bilingual text.

*Canada. Armée. Quartier général de l'Armée. Section historique. *L'Armée canadienne en Corée; les opérations des Nations unies (1950-1953) et leurs répercussions; court récit officiel.* Ottawa: Imprimeur de la Reine, 1956. 118 pp.

*_____. *La 1re Division d'infanterie canadienne, 1915-1955.* (Actualités; revue destinée aux Forces canadiennes, vol. IX, no. 1.) Ottawa: Imprimeur de la Reine, 1955. 31 pp.

Canada. Armée. Régiment de la Chaudière. *Le Régiment de la Chaudière; notes historiques.* Québec, P.Q.: imprimé privé, 1955. 16 pp.

Canada. Army. *Army Life.* Ottawa: Queen's Printer, [195-?]. 1 vol., unpaged.

Canada. Army. The Black Watch (Royal Highland Regiment) of Canada. *The Black Watch (Royal Highland Regiment) of Canada; the Regimental Book.* Montreal: privately printed, 1965. 1 vol., unpaged, looseleaf.

Canada. Army. Canadian Guards. 2nd Battalion. *Changing the Guard, by 2nd Battalion, the Canadian Guards on Parliament Hill, Ottawa, Canada.* n.p.: n.d. 16 pp.

Canada. Army. Canadian Military Headquarters. *Canadian Army (Overseas) Routine Orders.* London: n.p., 1940-47.
Title varies. Issued as Canadian Active Service Force (Overseas) Routine Orders until December 1940. Supplements also issued.

Canada. Army. Canadian Officers Training Corps. Carleton Univ. Contingent. *Unit Notes.* n.p.: 1966. 53 pp.

Canada. Army. Queen's Own Rifles of Canada. *Regimental Catechism.* n.p.: n.d. 19 pp.

Canada. Army. Royal Canadian Army Service Corps. *RCASC Diamond Jubilee Year Book, 1910-1961.* Ottawa: Queen's Printer, [1962]. 95 pp.

Canada. Army. Royal Winnipeg Rifles. *Seventy-fifth Anniversary, Royal Winnipeg Rifles, 1883-1958.* [Winnipeg: privately printed, 1958.] v.p.

Canada. Army Headquarters. Director of Artillery. *Standing Orders for the Royal Regiment of Canadian Artillery.* Don Mills, Ont.: T. H. Best, 1963. 62 pp.

Canada. Army Headquarters. Directorate of Manning. *Canadian Army Manual for the Canadian Officers Training Corps (Short Title: COTC Manual), 1962.* Ottawa: n.p., [1962]. 1 vol., looseleaf.

_____. *The Canadian Regular Army.* Ottawa: Queen's Printer, 1955. 49 pp.

*Canada. Army Headquarters. Historical Section. *Canada's Army in Korea; the United Nations Operations, 1950-53, and their Aftermath; a Short Official Account.* Ottawa: Queen's Printer, 1956. 108 pp.

*_____. *The Old Red Patch; the 1st Canadian Infantry Division, 1915-1955.* (Current Affairs for the Canadian Forces, vol. IX, no. 1.) Ottawa: Queen's Printer, 1955. 31 pp.

_____. *The Regiments and Corps of the Canadian Army.* (The Canadian Army List, vol. 1.) Ottawa: Queen's Printer, 1964. 253 pp.

Canada. Canadian Forces Headquarters. *Canadian Forces Administrative Orders.* Ottawa: n.p., 1965-71.
Issued as a non-chronological sequence in which orders were discarded when obsolete. Superseded by a bilingual format in 1972.

Canada. Court Martial Appeal Board. *Court Martial Appeal Reports.* Ottawa: Queen's Printer, 1957-73. 3 vols.

Canada. Dept. of National Defence. *The Canadian Army List.* Ottawa: King's Printer, 1940-66.
Title varies, eg. — Gradation List, Canadian Army Active (1940-45); Canadian Army (Regular) List (1959-66).

*_____. *The Defence Research Board, Canada.* n.p.: n.d. 1 vol., unpaged.

_____. *Defence Research Board; the First Twenty-five Years./ Conseil de recherches pour la défense; les 25 premières années.* Ottawa: Queen's Printer/Imprimeur de la Reine, 1972. 46 pp. *Bilingual text./Texte bilingue.*

Canada. Dept. of National Defence. *The King's Regulations and Orders for the Canadian Army.* Ottawa: King's Printer, 1951. 3 vols. in 1.

_____. *Manual of the Canadian Forces Medical Service in the Field, 1959.* Ottawa: Queen's Printer, 1959. 324 pp., looseleaf.

_____. *Pay and Allowance Regulations for the Canadian Army, 1946.* Ottawa: King's Printer, 1946. 1 vol., looseleaf.

*_____. *The Queen's Regulations and Orders for the Cadet Services of Canada and the Royal Canadian Army Cadets, 1956.* Ottawa: Queen's Printer, 1956. 1 vol., looseleaf.

_____. *The Queen's Regulations and Orders for the Canadian Army.* Ottawa: Queen's Printer, 1959. 3 vols., looseleaf.

*_____. *The Queen's Regulations and Orders for the Canadian Army.* Ottawa: Queen's Printer, 1952. 3 vols., looseleaf.

*_____. *The Queen's Regulations and Orders for the Canadian Forces.* Ottawa: Queen's Printer, 1965. 3 vols., looseleaf.

*_____. *Queen's Regulations for the Canadian Services Colleges.* Ottawa: Queen's Printer, 1958. 1 vol., unpaged.

_____. *Regulations for the Organization and Control of the Royal Canadian Army Cadets, 1948.* Ottawa: King's Printer, 1949. 41 pp.

*_____. *Report.* Ottawa: King's Printer, 1923-59.
Title varies. Annual most years.

*_____. *White Paper on Defence.* Ottawa: Queen's Printer, 1964. 30 pp.

Canada. Dept. of National Defence. Defence Research Board. *Annual Review./Revue annuelle.* n.p./s.l.: s.i., 1966-   .
Bilingual text./Texte bilingue.

Canada. Dept. of Veterans Affairs. *Commemoration; Canadians in Korea, 1978./Souvenir; Canadiens en Corée, 1978.* n.p./s.l.: s.i., [1978. 14 pp.]
Bilingual text./Texte bilingue.

Canada. Militia Headquarters. *General Orders.* Ottawa: Queen's Printer, 1899-1946.
Superseded Militia General Orders*. Frequency varies.*

*Canada. Ministère de la Défense nationale. *Le Conseil de recherches pour la défense, Canada.* s.l.: s.i., s.d. 1 tome, non-paginé.

*_____. *Livre blanc sur la défense.* Ottawa: Imprimeur de la Reine, 1964. 34 pp.

*Canada. Ministère de la Défense nationale. *Ordonnances et règlements royaux applicables à l'Armée canadienne.* Ottawa: Imprimeur de la Reine, 1953. 3 tomes, feuilles mobiles.

*_____. *Ordonnances et règlements royaux applicables aux Forces canadiennes.* Ottawa Imprimeur de la Reine, 1965. 3 tomes, feuilles mobiles.

*_____. *Ordonnances et règlements royaux applicables aux Services des Cadets du Canada et au Corps royal des Cadets de l'Armée canadienne, 1956.* Ottawa: Imprimeur de la Reine, 1957. 1 tome, feuilles mobiles.

*_____. *Rapport.* Ottawa: Imprimeur du Roi, 1923-59.
Divergence du titre. Annuel, la plupart des années.

*_____. *Règlements royaux applicables aux Collèges des services armés du Canada.* Ottawa: Imprimeur de la Reine, 1958. 1 tome, non-paginé.

*Canada. National Defence Headquarters. *Canadian Army Orders.* [Ottawa: King's Printer], 1941-64.
From 1947 issued as a non-chronological series, with orders being discarded when obsolete. Supplements also issued from 1947.

Canada. National Defence Headquarters. *Canadian Army Routine Orders.* Ottawa: n.p., 1939-46.
Title varies. Issued as <u>Canadian Active Service Force Routine Orders</u> until December 1940. Supplements also issued.

Canada. Parliament. House of Commons. Special Committee on Canteen Funds. *Minutes of Proceedings and Evidence.* No. 1-10. Ottawa: King's Printer, 1947.

*Canada. Quartier général de la Défense nationale. *Ordres de l'Armée canadienne.* [Ottawa: Imprimeur du Roi], 1941-64.
Publiés en série de façon non chronologique, à partir de 1947; les ordres périmés sont remplacés. Des suppléments sont également publiés à partir de 1947.

**The Canadian Army Journal.* Vol. I-XIX. Ottawa: King's Printer, 1947-65.

**Canadian Army Training Memorandum.* No. 1-72. Ottawa: King's Printer, 1941-47.

Canadian Artillery Association. *Annual Report.* n.p.: privately printed, 1876-   .
Not published 1940-46.

Canadian Cavalry Association. *Proceedings.* n.p.: privately printed, 1913-   .
In 1943 became Canadian Armoured Association and in 1946 Royal Canadian Armoured Corps (Cavalry) Association. Title varies: also Annual Report and Information Digest and Annual Report.

Canadian Defence Quarterly./Revue canadienne de défense. Vol. I-   . Toronto: Baxter Pub., 1971-   .

The Canadian Guardsman. n.p.: privately printed, 1956-69.

The Canadian Gunner. Vol. I-   . n.p.: privately printed, 1965-   .

Canadian Infantry Association. *Proceedings.* n.p.: privately printed, 1913-   .
Incorporated the Proceedings of the Canadian Machine Gun Corps Association in 1936. Was the Infantry and Machine Gun Association of Canada, 1937-39. Not published 1940-45.

The Canadian Intelligence Quarterly; the Journal of the Canadian Intelligence Corps. Vol. I-VI. n.p.: privately printed, 1963-68.

The Canadian Provost Corps; Silver Jubilee, 1940-1965. Ottawa: privately printed, 1965. 96 pp.

The Canadian Scottish Regiment. n.p.: n.d. 91 pp.

Capon, Alan R. *Mascots of the Hastings and Prince Edward Regiment.* Picton, Ont.: Picton Gazette, 1977. 31 pp.

Castonguay, Jacques. *Les bataillons et le dépôt du Royal 22e Régiment; vingt ans d'histoire, 1945-1965.* Québec, P.Q.: imprimé privé, 1974. 284 pp.

Cent ans d'histoire d'un régiment canadien-français; les Fusiliers Mont-Royal, 1869-1969. Montréal: Editions du Jour, 1971. 418 pp.

Centennial, 1863-1963; Presentation of Colours to the Princess of Wales' Own Regiment CA(M) by the Honourable W. Earle Rowe, P.C., Lieutenant-Governor of Ontario, Kingston, Ontario, Saturday 1st June 1963. [Kingston, Ont.: privately printed, 1963.] 15 pp.

Centennial Year, 1866-1966; 11th Field Artillery Regiment (M); 11th Field Artillery Regiment, Royal Regiment of Canadian Artillery, Canada's Oldest Artillery Regiment, Saturday, October 1, 1966. n.p.: n.d. 1 vol., unpaged.

The Ceremony of Trooping the Colour of the Second Battalion, the Royal Canadian Regiment; Taking the Salute, General C. Foulkes, Chairman Chiefs of Staff Committee, London, Ontario, 27th October 1956. n.p.: [1956]. 1 vol., unpaged.

50 ans d'activités avec le 6e Régiment d'artillerie, (Québec & Lévis), 1899-1949. Québec, P.Q.: Imprimerie Laflamme, 1949. 1 tome, non-paginé.

La Citadelle. Vol. I- . Québec, P.Q.: s.i., 1965- .
   Bimestriel. La revue de l'Association du 22e, Inc. Remplace L'Amicale du 22e.

Clint, H.C., comp. *A Short History of Artillery and of 57th Battery, R.C.A., 1855-1955; Formal Celebration and Reunion, Oct. 15th, 16th, 1955, Grande Allée Armouries, Quebec City.* Québec, P.Q.: n.p., 1955. 48 pp.

Collège militaire royal de Saint-Jean. *Ouverture officielle./Official Opening.* s.l.: s.i., s.d./n.p.: n.d. 27 pp.
   Texte bilingue./Bilingual text.

The Connecting File. Vol. I- . London, Ont.: privately printed, 1921- .
   Journal of the Royal Canadian Regiment.

*Le Corps blindé royal canadien. Ottawa: Imprimeur de la Reine, 1954. 11 pp.

*Le Corps de Santé royal canadien. Ottawa: Imprimeur de la Reine, 1954. 11 pp.

*The Corps of Royal Canadian Engineers. Ottawa: Queen's Printer, 1953. 21 pp.

Coup d'oeil sur le Collège militaire royal de Saint-Jean. Ottawa: Imprimeur de la Reine, 1959. 20 pp.

Crook, E.D., and J.K. Marteinson, eds. *A Pictorial History of the 8th Canadian Hussars (Princess Louise's).* n.p.: privately printed, 1973. 343 pp.

Cross, Michael, and Robert Bothwell, eds. *Policy by Other Means; Essays in Honour of C.P. Stacey.* Toronto: Clarke, Irwin, 1972. 258 pp.

Cunniffe, Dick. *Scarlet, Riflegreen and Khaki; the Military in Calgary.* Calgary: Century Calgary Publications, 1975. 40 pp.

Curchin, Leonard A., and Brian D. Sim. *The Elgins; the Story of the Elgin Regt. (RCAC) and its Predecessors.* St. Thomas, Ont.: privately printed, 1977. 150 pp.

Le Défilé; la revue du Collège militaire royal de Saint-Jean. St-Jean, P.Q.: imprimé privé, 1952- .
   Divergence du titre.

Dornbusch, C.E., comp. *The Canadian Army, 1855-1958; Regimental Histories and a Guide to the Regiments.* Cornwallville, N.Y.: Hope Farm Press, 1959. 216 pp.

Dornbusch, C.E., comp. *The Canadian Army, 1855-1955; Regimental Histories and a Guide to the Regiments.* Cornwallville, N.Y.: n.p., 1957. 162 1.

_____. *The Canadian Army, 1855-1965; Lineages; Regimental Histories.* Cornwallville, N.Y.: Hope Farm Press, 1966. 179 p.

_____. *Lineages of the Canadian Army, 1855-1961; Armour, Cavalry, Infantry.* Cornwallville, N.Y.: Hope Farm Press, 1961. 1 vol., unpaged.

Duguid, Archer Fortescue. *History of the Canadian Grenadier Guards, 1760-1964.* Montreal: Gazette Print. Co., 1965. 520 pp.

Dunkelman, Ben. *Dual Allegiance; an Autobiography.* Toronto: Macmillan, 1976. 336 pp.

Falardeau, Victor, et Jean Parent. *La musique du Royal 22e Régiment; 50 ans d'histoire, 1922-1972.* Québec, P.Q.: Editions Garneau, 1976. 243 pp.

Farran, Roy. *The History of the Calgary Highlanders, 1921-54.* n.p.: Bryant Press, [1954]. 222 pp.

Fetherstonhaugh, R.C., and G.R. Stevens. *The Royal Canadian Regiment.* Vol. I: Montreal: Gazette Print. Co., 1936. Vol. II: London, Ont.: privately printed, 1967. 2 vols.

First Battalion, Princess Patricia's Canadian Light Infantry and the King's Own Calgary Regiment; the Ceremony of Presentation of Colours by Her Majesty Queen Elizabeth II, Beacon Hill Park, Victoria, British Columbia, Friday, July 17th, 1959. Victoria, B.C.: privately printed, [1959]. 16 pp.

Fraser, W.B. *Always a Strathcona.* Calgary: Comprint Pub. Co., 1976. 252 pp.

The Gauntlet; RCAC School COTC. Camp Borden, Ont.: privately printed, 1953?-59?
Annual.

Le Génie royal canadien. Ottawa: Imprimeur de la Reine, 1954. 23 pp.

Goodspeed, D.J. *Battle Royal; a History of the Royal Regiment of Canada, 1862-1962.* Toronto: privately printed, 1962. 703 pp.

_____. *A History of the Defence Research Board of Canada.* Ottawa: Queen's Printer, 1958. 259 pp.

Granatstein, J.L., and R.D. Cuff, eds. *War and Society in North America.* Toronto: T. Nelson, 1971. 199 pp.

Greenhous, Brereton. *Semper Paratus; the History of the Royal Hamilton Light Infantry (Wentworth Regiment), 1862-1977,* by Kingsley Brown, Senior, Kingsley Brown, Junior, and Brereton Greenhous. Revised and edited by Brereton Greenhous. Hamilton, Ont.: privately printed, 1977. 446 pp.

Harker, Douglas E. *The Dukes; the Story of the Men who have Served in Peace and War with the British Columbia Regiment (D.C.O.), 1883-1973.* n.p.: privately printed, 1974. 438 pp.

Hodder-Williams, Ralph, G.R. Stevens and R.B. Mainprize. *Princess Patricia's Canadian Light Infantry.* London: Hodder and Stoughton, 1923-[57?]. 4 vols.

How, Douglas. *The 8th Hussars; a History of the Regiment.* Sussex, N.B.: Maritime Pub., 1964. 446 pp.

Hubbell, E.L. *The Winnipeg Grenadiers.* n.p.: n.d. 16 pp.

Hutchison, Paul P. *Canada's Black Watch; the First Hundred Years, 1862-1962.* Montreal: privately printed, [1962]. 340 pp.

*L'Intendance royale canadienne. Ottawa: Imprimeur de la Reine, 1954. 12 pp.

Jackson, H.M. *Canadian Prime Ministers and the Canadian Militia.* n.p.: 1958. 11 pp.

_____. *The Roll of the Regiments (the Active Militia).* Ottawa: n.p., 1959. 176 pp.

_____. *The Royal Regiment of Artillery, Ottawa, 1855-1952; a History.* Montreal: privately printed, 1952. 418 pp.

_____. *The Sherbrooke Regiment (12th Armoured Regiment).* n.p.: 1958. 229 pp.

_____. *The Story of the Royal Canadian Dental Corps.* Ottawa: privately printed, 1956. 475 pp.

Jackson, H.M., ed. *The Argyll and Sutherland Highlanders of Canada (Princess Louise's), 1928-1953.* Montreal: privately printed, 1953. 497 pp.

Johnston, Stafford. *The Fighting Perths; the Story of the First Century in the Life of a Canadian County Regiment.* Stratford, Ont.: privately printed, 1964. 133 pp.

*Journal de l'Armée canadienne. Vol. I-XIX. Ottawa: Imprimeur du Roi, 1947-65.

Kerry, A.J., and W.A. McDill. *The History of the Corps of Royal Canadian Engineers.* Ottawa: privately printed, 1962. 2 vols.

King, W.D., comp. *A Brief History of Militia Units Established at Various Periods at Yarmouth, Nova Scotia, 1812-1947.* Yarmouth, N.S.: privately printed, 1947. 32 pp.

The Link. Vol. I-IV? Rivers, Man.: privately printed, 1948-51?
Journal of Canadian Joint Air Training Centre, Rivers, Man.

The Log; Royal Roads Military College. Vol. V- . Victoria, B.C.:
privately printed, 1942- .

The Lorne Scots (Peel, Dufferin and Halton Regiment). Brampton,
Ont.: privately printed, 1962. 47 pp.

*McCracken, George W. *Votre armée*. (Actualités; revue destinée aux
Forces canadiennes, vol. IV, no. 10.) Ottawa: Imprimeur de la
Reine, 1953. 31 pp.

*_____. *Your Army*. (Current Affairs for the Canadian Forces,
vol. IV, no. 10.) Ottawa: Queen's Printer, 1953. 31 pp.

McGregor, F., ed. *LdSH (RC) '85-70'*. Winnipeg: privately printed,
1970. 62 pp.

Mackenzie-Naughton, J.D. *The Princess of Wales' Own Regiment
(M.G.)*. Kingston, Ont.: privately printed, 1946. 74 pp.

McKeown, Michael G. *Kapyong Remembered; Anecdotes from
Korea; Second Battalion, Princess Patricia's Canadian Light
Infantry; Korea, 1950-1951*. n.p.: [1976]. 40 pp.

Manarey, R. Barrie. *The Canadian Bayonet*. Edmonton: Century
Press, 1971. 51 pp.

Maple Leaf Services Serving the Canadian Army. Ottawa: Queen's
Printer, 1958. 18 pp.

Marcoux, Jules, éd. *CMR, 1952-1977; album du 25e anniversaire./
25th anniversary album*. St-Jean, P.Q.: s.i./n.p., 1977. 62 pp.
Texte bilingue./Bilingual text.

Marquis, G.E. *Le Régiment de Lévis; historique et album*. Lévis,
P.Q.: s.i., 1952. 292 pp.

Martin, Paul. *Canada and the Quest for Peace*. New York: Columbia
Univ. Press, 1967. 93 pp.

Mazéas, Daniel. *Croquis d'insignes armée canadienne, 1920-1950;
Canadian Badges*. Guincamp, France: privately printed, 1970.
64 pp.

_____. *Insignes armée canadienne, 1900-1914; Canadian
Badges; supplément, 1920-1950*. Guincamp, France: privately
printed, 1972. 116 pp.

The Medical and Dental Services of the Canadian Forces. (Current
Affairs for the Canadian Forces, vol. VI, no. 1.) Ottawa:
Queen's Printer, 1954. 31 pp.

Memorandum sur l'instruction de l'Armée canadienne. No. 1-72.
Ottawa: Imprimeur du Roi, 1941-47.

Moir, J.S., ed. *History of the Royal Canadian Corps of Signals, 1903-1961.* Ottawa: privately printed, 1962. 336 pp.

Moogk, Peter N., and R.V. Stevenson. *Vancouver Defended; a History of the Men and Guns of the Lower Mainland Defences, 1859-1949.* Surrey, B.C.: Antonson Pub., 1978. 128 pp.

Nicholson, G.W.L. *Canada's Nursing Sisters.* (Canadian War Museum Historical Publication Number 13.) Toronto: S. Stevens, Hakkert, 1975. 272 pp.

_____. *The Gunners of Canada; the History of the Royal Regiment of Canadian Artillery.* Toronto: McClelland and Stewart, 1967-72. 2 vols.

_____. *Seventy Years of Service; a History of the Royal Canadian Army Medical Corps.* Ottawa: Borealis Press, 1977. 388 pp.

The Northwest Highway System; Canadian Army, General Information, Camp Takhini, Whitehorse, Y.T. Ottawa: Queen's Printer, 1961. 25 pp.

Ogle, Robert J. *The Faculties of Canadian Military Chaplains; a Commentary on the Faculty Sheet of December, 1955 and the Directives for Holy Week Promulgated March 14, 1956.* Ottawa: n.p., 1956. 267 pp.

Paré, Lorenzo. *Les canadiens français et l'organisation militaire.* (Oeuvre des tracts, 382.) Montréal: imprimé privé, [1951]. 16 pp.

The Patrician. Vol. I- . Edmonton: privately printed, 1948- .
Regimental journal of the Princess Patricia's Canadian Light Infantry.

Penny, Arthur G. *Royal Rifles of Canada, "Able and Willing" Since 1862; a Short History.* n.p.: 1962. 62 pp.

"Pourquoi je sers ma patrie". (Actualités; revue destinée aux Forces canadiennes, vol. X, no. 15.) Ottawa: Imprimeur de la Reine, 1956. 26 pp.

The Powder Horn; Chronicle of the Queen's Own Rifles of Canada. Calgary, Alta., Victoria, B.C.: privately printed, 1960-70.

Presentation of Colours by Her Majesty Queen Elizabeth II, to Canadian Grenadier Guards (6th Battalion, Canadian Guards), 48th Highlanders of Canada, the Argyll and Sutherland Highlanders of Canada (Princess Louise's.) Ottawa: n.p., 1959. 20 pp.

Presentation of Colours by His Excellency Major-General Georges P. Vanier, D.S.O., M.C., E.D., the Governor-General of Canada to the Royal Hamilton Light Infantry (Wentworth Regiment), Hamilton, Ontario, 30th June, 1962. n.p.: [1962]. 20 pp.

Presentation of Colours to the Second Battalion, the Royal Canadian Regiment, by Field-Marshal His Royal Highness the Duke of Edinburgh, Colonel-in-Chief of the Regiment, Nominated by Her Majesty the Queen to Make this Presentation, Fort York, Germany, 17th October 1955. Aldershot, Eng.: privately printed, 1955. [12] pp.

Presentation of Guidons and Colours by Her Majesty Queen Elizabeth II to 1st Battalion, the Canadian Guards, the Ontario Regiment, the Sherbrooke Hussars, 1st Hussars, the Cameron Highlanders of Ottawa, Ottawa, 5 July 1967. Ottawa: Queen's Printer, 1967. 1 vol., unpaged.

Presentation of New Colours to the Highland Light Infantry of Canada by Her Royal Highness the Princess Margaret, C.I., G.C.V.O., Colonel-in-Chief of the Regiment, Nominated by Her Majesty the Queen to Make this Presentation, Hamilton, Ontario, August 1st, 1958. Ottawa: Queen's Printer, 1958. 1 vol., unpaged.

Preston, Richard A. *Canada's RMC; a History of the Royal Military College.* Toronto: Univ. of Toronto Press, 1969. 415 pp.

Programme-souvenir; le Régiment de Hull, mai 1964; publication autorisée par le Lt-Col. Guy de Marlis, C.D., Commandant, le Régiment de Hull; programme-souvenir publié pour marquer le 50e anniversaire du Régiment de Hull et le 25e anniversaire du manège de Salaberry. Hull, P.Q.: imprimé privé, [1964]. 60 pp.

The Queen's Own Rifles of Canada Association. *Yearbook.* [Toronto: n.p.], 1923-47. 18 vols.
Not issued 1939-44, 1946.

Queen-Hughes, R.W. *Whatever Men Dare; a History of the Queen's Own Cameron Highlanders of Canada, 1935-1960.* Winnipeg: privately printed, 1960. 247 pp.

Quigley, John Gordon. *A Century of Rifles, 1860-1960; the Halifax Rifles (RCAC)(M); "cede nullis".* Halifax: privately printed, 1960. 230 pp.

R.C.E.M.E. Quarterly. Vol. I-V. Ottawa: King's Printer, 1949-53.

The RCOC Quarterly. Vol. I-VII. Ottawa: n.p., 1947-54?

Review of the Regiment and Presentation of New Colours to the First and Third Battalions by the Colonel-in-Chief His Royal Highness the Prince Philip, Duke of Edinburgh, London, Ontario, 2nd July 1959. n.p.: [1959]. 1 vol., unpaged.
Royal Canadian Regiment.

La Revue régimentaire; le Régiment de Maisonneuve. Vol. I-VIII. Montréal: imprimé privé, 1960-72.

Robertson, Peter. *Irréductible vérité/Relentless Verity/les photographes militaires canadiens depuis 1885/Canadian Military Photographers since 1885.* (Les Archives publiques du Canada/Public Archives of Canada Series.) Québec, P.Q.: Les Presses de l'Université Laval, 1973. 233 pp.
Texte bilingue./Bilingual text.

Rosner, Gabriella. *The U.N. Emergency Force.* New York: Columbia Univ. Press, 1963. 294 pp.

Roy, R.H. *Ready for the Fray (Deas Gu Cath); the History of the Canadian Scottish Regiment (Princess Mary's), 1920-1955.* Vancouver: privately printed, 1958. 509 pp.

_____. *The Seaforth Highlanders of Canada, 1919-1965.* Vancouver: privately printed, 1969. 559 pp.

_____. *Sinews of Steel; the History of the British Columbia Dragoons.* Brampton, Ont.: privately printed, 1965. 468 pp.

*The Royal Canadian Armoured Corps. Ottawa: Queen's Printer, 1953. 11 pp.

Royal Canadian Armoured Corps (Cavalry) Association *see* Canadian Cavalry Association.

*The Royal Canadian Army Medical Corps. Ottawa: Queen's Printer, 1953. 10 pp.

*Royal Canadian Army Pay Corps. Ottawa: Queen's Printer, 1953. 11 pp.

*The Royal Canadian Army Service Corps. Ottawa: Queen's Printer, 1953. 11 pp.

The Royal Canadian Artillery. Ottawa: Queen's Printer, 1953. 10 pp.

Royal Canadian Horse Artillery; First Regiment, 1871-1971. Lahr, Ger.: privately printed, [1971]. 32 pp.

The Royal Canadian Ordnance Corps Diamond Jubilee Yearbook. n.p.: 1963. 106 pp.

Royal Canadian Signals Quarterly. Vol. I-II? Ottawa: King's Printer, 1951-52?

Royal Military College of Canada, Kingston, Ont. *The Cadet Handbook.* Kingston: n.p., [1957?]. 59 pp., looseleaf.

The Royal Military College of Canada Review. Vol. I- . Kingston, Ont.: privately printed, 1920-   .

Le Royal 22ᵉ Régiment; remise de nouveaux drapeaux aux 1er, 2eme et 3eme bataillons par Sa Majesté la Reine Elizabeth II; les plaines d'Abraham, le 23 juin 1959. Aldershot, Angleterre: imprimé privé, 1959. [16] pp.

Rudbach, N.E. *The Halifax Rifles (23 Armoured Regiment) R.C.A.C.R.F.; "90th" Anniversary, 14th May 1860 — 14th May 1950.* Halifax: n.p., 1950. 20 pp.

Rutherford, Tom. *An Unofficial History of the Grey and Simcoe Foresters Regiment, 1866-1973.* n.p.: n.d. 88 pp.

Schragg, Lex. *History of the Ontario Regiment, 1866-1951.* Oshawa: Ont.: privately printed, 1951. 286 pp.

Service, G.T., and J.K. Marteinson. *The Gate; a History of the Fort Garry Horse.* Calgary: privately printed, 1971. 228 pp.

*Les services medicaux et dentaires pour les Forces armées. (Actualités; revue destinée aux Forces canadiennes, vol. VI, no. 1.) Ottawa: Imprimeur de la Reine, 1954. 31 pp.

A Short History of the British Columbia Regiment; the "Dukes". n.p.: n.d. [11] pp.

The Signalman. Vol. I-IV? Kingston, Ont.: King's Printer, 1942-46?

Snowy Owl; Journal of the Canadian Land Forces Command and Staff College. Kingston, Ont.: privately printed, 1952-73. 18 vols.
Title varies.

The Springbok. Various places: n.p., 1923-   .
Regimental journal of the Royal Canadian Dragoons. Title varies: The Goat (1923-36).

*Stacey, C.P., H.E.W. Strange and F.H. Hitchins. *Canada's Armed Forces Today.* (Current Affairs for the Canadian Forces, vol. II, no. 9.) Ottawa: Queen's Printer, 1952. 22 pp.

*Stacey, C.P., H.E.W. Strange et F.H. Hitchins. *Les Forces armées du Canada.* (Actualités; revue destinée aux Forces canadiennes, vol. II, no. 9.) Ottawa: Imprimeur de la Reine, 1952. 22 pp.

Stanley, George F.G. *Canada's Soldiers, 1604-1954; the Military History of an Unmilitary People.* Toronto: Macmillan, 1954. 400 pp.

_____. *In the Face of Danger; the History of the Lake Superior Regiment.* Port Arthur, Ont.: privately printed, 1960. 357 pp.

Stanley, George F.G., and Richard A. Preston. *A Short History of Kingston as a Military and Naval Centre.* Kingston, Ont.: Queen's Printer, [195-?]. 33 pp.

Stefaniuk, M.E. *8th Canadian Hussars (Princess Louise's), 1957-1967.* n.p.: privately printed, 1967. 154 pp.

Steven, Walter T. *In this Sign.* Toronto: Ryerson Press, 1948. 182 pp.

Stevens, G.R. *The Sun Is Setting on the Paleface Brave or Down the Drain a Billion a Year Goes.* Montreal: privately printed, [1968]. 16 pp.

Stewart, Charles H., comp. *The Concise Lineages of the Canadian Army, 1855 to Date.* Toronto: n.p., n.d. 163 pp.

The Strathconian. Calgary: n.p., 1914-?, 1927-38, 1947- .
Regimental journal of the Lord Strathcona's Horse (Royal Canadians). Re-numbered from no. 1 after each gap in publication.

Stuart, (Sir) Campbell. *Opportunity Knocks Once.* London: Collins, 1952. 248 pp.

Tackaberry, R.B. *Keeping the Peace; a Canadian Military Viewpoint on Peace-Keeping Operations.* (Behind the Headlines, vol. XXVI.) Toronto: Canadian Institute of International Affairs, 1966. 26 pp.

Taylor, Alastair, David Cox and J.L. Granatstein. *Peacekeeping; International Challenge and Canadian Response.* (Contemporary Affairs, no. 39.) [Toronto]: Canadian Institute of International Affairs, 1968. 211 pp.

Thompson, Roy J.C. *Canadian Army Cap Badges, 1953-1973.* [Dartmouth], N.S.: n.p., 1973. 215 pp.

_____. *Cap Badges of the Canadian Officer Training Corps.* Dartmouth, N.S.: n.p., 1972. 68 pp.

_____. *Wings of the Canadian Armed Forces, 1913-1972.* [Dartmouth], N.S.: n.p., 1973. 106 pp.

The Toronto Scottish Regimental Gazette. Vol. I. n.p.: privately printed, 1946-50.

La Trésorerie militaire royale canadienne. Ottawa: Imprimeur de la Reine, 1954. 12 pp.

Upper Canada Historical Arms Society. *The Military Arms of Canada.* (Historical Arms Series, 1.) West Hill, Ont.: Museum Restoration Service, 1963. 47 pp.

Van Der Schee, W. *A Short History of Lord Strathcona's Horse (Royal Canadians).* n.p.: 1973. 19 1.

Victoria Rifles of Canada, 1861-1951; Historical Notes. n.p.: n.d. 14 pp.

Les Voltigeurs de Québec, 1862-1952; notes historiques. s.l.: s.i., 1952. 16 pp.

Les Voltigeurs de Québec, 1862-1962; album du centenaire, mai 1962. St-François, P.Q.: imprimé privé, 1962. 31 pp.

Vox Pat. Vol. I-IV? n.p.: privately printed, 1954-57?
   Title varies, vol. I, no. 1-2 titled: 2 VP; You Name It. Journal of 2nd Battalion, Princess Patricia's Canadian Light Infantry.

Warren, Arnold. *Wait for the Wagon; the Story of the Royal Canadian Army Service Corps.* Toronto: McClelland and Stewart, 1961. 413 pp.

Watson, W.S., and others, eds. *The Brockville Rifles, Royal Canadian Infantry Corps (Allied with the King's Royal Rifle Corps); Semper Paratus; an Unofficial History.* Brockville, Ont.: Recorder Print. Co., 1966. 138 pp.

*"Why I Serve", by the Serviceman. (Current Affairs for the Canadian Forces, vol. X, no. 15.) Ottawa: Queen's Printer, 1956. 26 pp.

Willcocks, K.D.H. *The Hastings and Prince Edward Regiment, Canada; a Short History.* Belleville, Ont.: n.p., 1967. 1 vol., unpaged.

Williams, Jeffery. *Princess Patricia's Canadian Light Infantry.* (Famous Regiments.) London: L. Cooper, 1972. 110 pp.

*Wood, Herbert Fairlie. *Singulier champ de bataille; les opérations en Corée et leurs effets sur la politique de défense du Canada.* (Histoire officielle de l'armée canadienne.) Ottawa; Imprimeur de la Reine, 1966. 354 pp.

*_____. *Strange Battleground; the Operations in Korea and their Effects on the Defence Policy of Canada.* (Official History of the Canadian Army.) Ottawa: Queen's Printer, 1966. 317 pp.

Worthington, Larry. *The Spur and the Sprocket; the Story of the Royal Canadian Dragoons.* Kitchener, Ont.: Reeve Press, 1968. 170 pp.

_____. *"Worthy"; a Biography of Major-General F.F. Worthington, C.B., M.C., M.M.* Toronto: Macmillan, 1961. 236 pp.

E. AIR FORCES — FORCES DE L'AVIATION

1867-1918

Air Heroes in the Making; the Imperial Royal Flying Corps. n.p.: n.d. 19 pp.

Art Gallery of Toronto. *Catalogue of an Exhibition of the Canadian War Memorials, October 1926.* Toronto: privately printed, [1926]. 21 pp.

Bank of Montreal. *Memorial of the Great War, 1914-1918; a Record of Service.* Montreal: privately printed, 1921. 261 pp.

_____. *Victory; a Monument in Memory of the Men in the Service of the Bank of Montreal who Fell in the Great War.* n.p.: [1924]. 19 pp.

Bindon, Kathryn M. *More than Patriotism.* (A Personal Library Publication.) Don Mills, Ont.: Nelson, 1979. 192 pp.

Bishop, William A. *Winged Peace.* New York: Viking Press, 1944. 175 pp.

_____. *Winged Warfare.* Toronto: McClelland, Goodchild and Stewart, 1918. 272 pp.

Bishop, William Arthur. *The Courage of the Early Morning; a Son's Biography of a Famous Father; the Story of Billy Bishop.* Toronto: McClelland & Stewart, 1965. 211 pp.

The C.A.H.S. Journal. Vol. I- . Willowdale, Ont.: Canadian Aviation Historical Society, 1963- .

Canada. Air Force. *Canada's Air Heritage.* Ottawa: King's Printer, 1941. 23 pp.

Canada. Air Force Headquarters. Air Historical Section. *RCAF Logbook; a Chronological Outline of the Origin, Growth and Achievement of the Royal Canadian Air Force.* Ottawa: King's Printer, 1949. 96 pp.

Canada. Director of Public Information. *Canada's Part in the Great War.* Ottawa: n.p., 1919. 64 pp.
Also issued by Information Branch, Dept. of External Affairs.

Canada. Ministry of Overseas Military Forces of Canada. *Report of the Ministry; Overseas Military Forces of Canada, 1918.* London: H.M. Stationery Office, 1919. 533 pp.

Canada in the Great World War; an Authentic Account of the Military History of Canada from the Earliest Days to the Close of the War of the Nations, by Various Authorities. Toronto: United Publishers, 1917-21. 6 vols.

Canadian Bank of Commerce. *Letters from the Front; being a Record of the Part Played by Officers of the Bank in the Great War, 1914-1919.* Toronto: privately printed, n.d. 2 vols.

Canadian Broadcasting Corporation. *Flanders' Fields.* n.p.: [1964]. 1 vol., unpaged.

Canadian Pacific Railway Co. *Their Glory Cannot Fade.* n.p.: 1918. [15] pp.

Canadian War Memorials Painting Exhibition, 1920; New Series; the Last Phase. n.p.: n.d. 25 pp.

Canadian War Records Office. *Art and war; Canadian War Memorials; a Selection of the Works Executed for the Canadian War Memorials Fund to Form a Record of Canada's Part in the Great War and a Memorial to those Canadians who have Made the Great Sacrifice.* London: n.p., 1919. 1 vol., unpaged.

_____. *Canadian War Memorials Exhibition, [New York] 1919.* n.p.: n.d. 48 pp.

_____. *Thirty Canadian V.C.'s; 23rd April 1915 to 20th March 1918.* London: Skeffington, n.d. 96 pp.

Carisella, P.J., and James W. Ryan. *Who Killed the Red Baron; the Final Answer.* Wakefield, Mass.: Daedalus, 1969. 254 pp.

Carr, William Guy. *Out of the Mists.* London: Hutchinson, n.d. 176 pp.

Castonguay. Jacques. *Unsung Mission; History of the Chaplaincy Service (RC) of the R.C.A.F.* Montreal: Institut de Pastorale, 1968. 173 pp.

Catalogue of Canadian War Trophies; Including Field Guns, Surrendered and Captured Planes, Flags, Uniforms, Helmets, Swords, Posters, Proclamations, Prints, etc., National Exhibition, Toronto, August 23 to September 6, 1919. n.p.: [1919]. 64 pp.

Catalogue of Canadian War Trophies; Including Field Guns, Surrendered and Captured Planes, Flags, Uniforms, Helmets, Swords, Posters, Proclamations, Prints, etc., The Armouries, Hamilton, November 3 to November 15, 1919. n.p.: [1919]. 64 pp.

Clark, Don. *Wild Blue Yonder; an Air Epic.* Seattle, Wash.: Superior, 1972. 172 pp.

Collishaw, Raymond, and R.V. Dodds. *Air Command; a Fighter Pilot's Story.* London: W. Kimber, 1973. 256 pp.

Corporation of British Columbia Land Surveyors. *Roll of Honour; British Columbia Land Surveyors; 1914 the Great War 1918.* n.p.: privately printed, n.d. 1 vol., unpaged.

Cosgrove, Edmund. *Canada's Fighting Pilots.* (Canadian Portraits.) Toronto: Clarke, Irwin, 1965. 190 pp.

Creed, Catherine. *"Whose Debtors We Are".* (Niagara Historical Society, 34.) Niagara, Ont.: Niagara Historical Society, 1922. 116 pp.

Critchley, A. *Critch! The Memoirs of Brigadier-General A.C. Critchley.* London: Hutchinson, 1961. 256 pp.

Cross, Michael, and Robert Bothwell, eds. *Policy by Other Means; Essays in Honour of C.P. Stacey.* Toronto: Clarke, Irwin, 1972. 258 pp.

Dominion of Canada Roll of Honor; a Directory of Casualties (Deaths Only) of the World's Greatest War, 1914-1918, of the City of Toronto; Dedicated to Perpetuate Those who Made the Supreme Sacrifice, "They Shall Not be Forgotten". n.p.: C. McAlpine, 1919. 28 1.

Drew, George A. *Canada's Fighting Airmen.* Toronto: MacLean Pub. Co., 1930. 305 pp.

Duguid, Archer Fortescue. *The Canadian Forces in the Great War, 1914-1919; the Record of Five Years of Active Service.* Ottawa: King's Printer, 1947. 14 pp.

Duguid, Archer Fortescue, *see also The Memorial Chamber in the Peace Tower . . . .*

Duncan-Clark, S.J., and W.R. Plewman. *Pictorial History of the Great War,* [including] *Canada in the Great War,* by W.S. Wallace. Toronto: J.L. Nichols, 1919. 2 vols. in 1.

Ellis, Frank H. *Canada's Flying Heritage.* Toronto: Univ. of Toronto Press, 1954. 398 pp.

_____. *Fifty Years of Adventure and Progress in Canadian Skies.* Toronto: Ryerson Press, 1959. 230 pp.

Fetherstonhaugh, R.C. *McGill University at War, 1914-1918; 1939-1945.* Montreal: McGill Univ., 1947. 437 pp.

Fighters for Freedom; Honor Roll of Halifax; the Great War, 1914-1919. Halifax: Service Pub. Co., [1919]. 191 pp.

[Garvin, Amelia Beers (Warnock).] *Canada's Peace Tower and Memorial Chamber, Designed by John A. Pearson, D. Arch., F.R.A.I.C., F.R.I.B.A., A.R.C.A., G.D.I.A., a Record and Interpretation by Katherine Hale* [*pseud.*] *Dedicated by the Architect to the Veterans of the Great War.* Toronto: Mundy-Goodfellow Print. Co., 1935. 29 pp.

Godenrath, Percy F. *Lest We Forget; a Record in Art of the Dominion's Part in the War (1914-1918) and a Memorial to those Canadians who Made the Great Sacrifice, being the Gift of the Over-Seas Military Forces to the Nation; a Brief History of the Collection of War Paintings, Etchings and Sculpture, Made Possible by the Work of the Canadian War Memorials Fund and the Canadian War Record Office.* Ottawa: n.p., 1934. 46 pp.

Gordon, John. . . .*Of Men and Planes.* Ottawa: Love Print., 1968. 3 vols.

_____. *Winged Sentries./Sentinelles de l'air.* Claude Rousseau, illus. n.p./s.l.: s.i., 1963. 104 pp.
Bilingual text./Texte bilingue.

Graves, Sandham. *The Lost Diary.* Victoria, B.C.: C.F. Banford, 1941. 131 pp.

Gt. Brit. Imperial War Graves Commission. *The War Graves of the British Empire; the Register of the Names of Those who Fell in the Great War and are Buried in Cemeteries and Churchyards in Nova Scotia, Prince Edward Island and New Brunswick, Canada.* London: H.M. Stationery Office, 1931. 92 pp.

_____. *The War Graves of the British Empire; the Register of the Names of Those who Fell in the Great War and are Buried in Cemeteries in Newfoundland.* London: H.M. Stationery Office, 1930. 19 pp.

_____. *The War Graves of the British Empire; the Register of the Names of Those who Fell in the Great War and are Buried in Cemeteries in the Province of British Columbia, Canada.* London: H.M. Stationery Office, 1931. 48 pp.

_____. *The War Graves of the British Empire; the Register of the Names of Those who Fell in the Great War and are Buried in Cemeteries in the Province of Manitoba, Canada.* London: H.M. Stationery Office, 1931. 48 pp.

_____. *The War Graves of the British Empire; the Register of the Names of Those who Fell in the Great War and are Buried in Cemeteries in the Province of Ontario, Canada.* London: H.M. Stationery Office, 1931. 2 vols.

Gt. Brit. Imperial War Graves Commission. *The War Graves of the British Empire; the Register of the Names of Those who Fell in the Great War and are Buried in Cemeteries in the Province of Quebec, Canada.* London: H.M. Stationery Office, 1931. 64 pp.

_____. *The War Graves of the British Empire; the Register of the Names of Those who Fell in the Great War and are Buried in Cemeteries in the Provinces of Saskatchewan and Alberta, Canada.* London: H.M. Stationery Office, 1931. 63 pp.

Groves, Hubert, comp. *Toronto Does Her "Bit".* Toronto: Municipal Intelligence Bureau, 1918. 72 pp.

Hale, Katherine, [*pseud.*] *see* Garvin, Amelia Beers (Warnock).

[Hallam, T. Douglas.] *The Spider Web; the Romance of a Flying-Boat Flight,* by P.I.X. [*pseud.*] Edinburgh: W. Blackwood, 1919. 278 pp.

Halliday, H.A. *Chronology of Canadian Military Aviation.* (National Museum of Man Mercury Series; Canadian War Museum Paper, no. 6.) Ottawa: [Queen's Printer], 1975. 168 pp.

Harris, John Norman. *Knights of the Air; Canadian Aces of World War I.* (Great Stories of Canada, no. 18.) Toronto: Macmillan, 1958. 156 pp.

Hartney, Harold E. *Up and at 'em.* Stanley M. Ulanoff, ed., (Air Combat Classics.) Garden City, N.Y.: Doubleday, 1971. 360 pp.

Herrington, Walter S., and A.J. Wilson. *The War Work of the County of Lennox and Addington.* Napanee, Ont.: Beaver Press, 1922. 278 pp.

Hezzelwood, Oliver, *see* Trinity Methodist Church, Toronto, Ont.

The Illustrated Review of Aviation in Canada; Celebrating the Golden Anniversary of Powered Flight in Canada. Montreal: privately printed, [1959]. 1 vol., unpaged.

*Kealy, J.D.F., and E.C. Russell. *A History of Canadian Naval Aviation, 1918-1962.* Ottawa: Queen's Printer, 1965. 164 pp.

*Kealy, J.D.F., et E.C. Russell. *Histoire de l'aéronavale canadiennc, 1918-1962.* Ottawa: Imprimeur de la Reine, 1965. 185 pp.

McGill Univ., Montreal, P.Q. *A Memorial Service for the McGill Men and Women who Gave Their Lives during the First and Second World Wars.* n.p.: [1946]. 1 vol., unpaged.

Main, J.R.K. *Voyageurs of the Air; a History of Civil Aviation in Canada.* Ottawa: Queen's Printer, 1967. 397 pp.

Mazéas, Daniel. *Insignes armée canadienne, 1900-1914; Canadian Badges; supplément, 1920-1950.* Guincamp, France: privately printed, 1972. 116 pp.

The Memorial Chamber in the Peace Tower, Houses of Parliament, Ottawa, Canada, [by A.F. Duguid.] Ottawa: Photogelatine Engraving Co., n.d. [34] pp.

Milberry, Larry. *Aviation in Canada.* Toronto: McGraw-Hill Ryerson, 1979. 272 pp.

Miller, James Martin, and H.S. Canfield. *The People's War Book; History, Encyclopedia and Chronology of the Great World War; and Canada's Part in the War,* by W.R. Plewman. Toronto: Imperial Pub. Co., 1919. 520 pp.

Monaghan, Hugh B. *The Big Bombers of World War I; a Canadian's Journal.* Burlington, Ont.: R. Gentle Communications, n.d. 101 pp.

Myles, Eugenie Louise. *Airborne from Edmonton.* Toronto: Ryerson Press, 1959. 280 pp.

National Aeronautical Collection. Ottawa: Queen's Printer, 1967. 36 pp.

National Aeronautical Collection./Collection aéronautique nationale. n.p.: n.d./s.l.: s.i., s.d. 36 pp. *Bilingual text./Texte bilingue.*

Ontario. Dept. of Education. *The Roll of Honour of the Ontario Teachers who Served in the Great War, 1914-1918.* Toronto: Ryerson Press, 1922. 72 pp.

Ontario Agricultural College, Guelph, Ont. *Ontario Agricultural College Honor and Service Rolls.* n.p.: n.d. 1 vol., unpaged.

P.I.X. [*pseud.*] *see* Douglas, T. Hallam.

Parkdale Collegiate Institute, Toronto, Ont. *Roll of Service in the Great War, 1914-1919.* n.p.: n.d. 22 pp.

_____. *Their Name Liveth; a Memoir of the Boys of Parkdale Collegiate Institute who Gave their Lives in the Great War.* Toronto: privately printed, n.d. 177 pp.

Peace Souvenir; Activities of Waterloo County in the Great War, 1914-1918. Kitchener, Ont.: Kitchener Daily Telegraph, 1919. 70 pp.

Plewman, W.R., *see* Miller, James Martin.

Queen's Univ., Kingston, Ont. *Overseas Record; Record of Graduates, Alumni, Members of Staff, and Students of Queen's University on Active Military (Overseas) Service (to June 1st, 1917) 1914-1917.* n.p.: [1917?]. 44 pp.

Roberts, Leslie. *There Shall be Wings; a History of the Royal Canadian Air Force.* Toronto: Clarke, Irwin, 1959. 250 pp.

Robertson, Heather, [comp.] *A Terrible Beauty; the Art of Canada at War.* Toronto: J. Lorimer, 1977. 239 pp.

Royal Canadian Military Institute, Toronto, Ont. *The Golden Book* Toronto: privately printed, 1927. 1 vol., unpaged.

Sandwell, A.H. *Planes over Canada.* London: T. Nelson, 1938 120 pp.

Santor, Donald M. *Canadians at War, 1914-1918.* (Canadiana Scrap book.) Scarborough, Ont.: Prentice-Hall, 1978. 48 pp.

Smith, G. Oswald, *see University of Toronto . . . .*

Stedman, Ernest W. *From Boxkite to Jet; Memoirs of Air Vice-Marshall Ernest W. Stedman.* [Toronto]: Univ. of Toronto Press, 1963. 1 vol., unpaged.
Reprints of articles from Canadian Aviation. *An enlarged edition was published as* From Boxkite to Jet; the Memoirs of an Aeronautical Engineer. *(National Museum of Man Mercury Series; Canadian War Museum Paper, no. 1.) Ottawa: Queen's Printer, 1972.*

Sullivan, Alan. *Aviation in Canada, 1917-1918; being a Brief Account of the Work of the Royal Air Force Canada, the Aviation Department of the Imperial Munitions Board and the Canadian Aeroplanes Limited.* Toronto: Rous & Mann, 1919. 318 pp.

Swettenham, John. *Canada and the First World War.* Toronto: Ryerson Press, 1969. 160 pp.

_____. *Canada and the First World War./La participation du Canada à la première guerre mondiale.* Ottawa: Canadian War Museum/Musée de guerre, n.d./s.d. 56/63 pp.
Bilingual text./Texte bilingue.

Thompson, Roy J.C. *Wings of the Canadian Armed Forces, 1913-1972.* [Dartmouth], N.S.: n.p., 1973. 106 pp.

Thorburn, Ella M., and Charlotte Whitton. *Canada's Chapel of Remembrance.* Toronto: British Book Service (Canada), 1961. 68 pp.

Trinity Methodist Church, Toronto, Ont. *Trinity War Book; a Recital of Service and Sacrifice in the Great War.* Oliver Hezzelwood, comp. Toronto: privately printed, 1921. 368 pp.

Univ. of British Columbia. *Record of Service, 1914-1918; University of British Columbia, McGill British Columbia, Vancouver College.* Vancouver: privately printed, 1924. 142 pp.

Univ. of Manitoba. *Roll of Honour, 1914-1918.* Winnipeg: privately printed, 1923. 150 pp.

Univ. of Toronto. Victoria College. *Acta Victoriana; War Supplement.* [Toronto]: n.p., 1919. 128 pp.

University of Toronto: Roll of Service, 1914-1918. G. Oswald Smith, ed. Toronto: Univ. of Toronto Press, 1921. 603 pp.

Wallace, W.S., *see* Duncan-Clark, S.J.

War Record of McGill Chapter of Delta Upsilon. Montreal: n.p., 1919. 47 pp.

Wilson, J.A. *Development of Aviation in Canada, 1879-1948.* Ottawa: Dept. of Transport Air Services Branch, n.d. 105 pp.

Wodehouse, R.F. *A Check List of the War Collections of World War I, 1914-1918, and World War II, 1939-1945.* Ottawa: Queen's Printer, 1968. 239 pp.

*_____. *Aviation Paintings from the Art Collection of the Canadian War Museum.* Ottawa: [Queen's Printer], 1972. 84 pp.

*_____. *Tableaux de l'aviation militaire; provenant de la Collection d'art du Musée de guerre canadien.* Ottawa: [Imprimeur de la Reine], 1972. 84 pp.

X., P.I., [*pseud.*] *see* Hallam, T. Douglas.

Young, A.H., and W.A. Kirkwood, eds. *The War Memorial Volume of Trinity College, Toronto.* [Toronto]: Printers Guild, 1922. 165 pp.

1919-1945

Active Service Canteen, Toronto, 1939-1945. Toronto: n.p., 1945. 1 vol., unpaged.

The Adastrian; being the Journal of No. 31 E.F.T.S. Royal Air Force, De Winton, Alberta, Canada. No. 1-? De Winton, Alta.: n.p., 1942-?

Adelberg, Philip, ed. *414 Squadron (1941-1975); a Short History.* n.p.: 1975. 1 vol., unpaged.

The Adventura; Magazine of the Royal Air Force Station Pennfield, New Brunswick. n.p.: ?-1944.

Aer-Log. Vol. I-? Brandon, Man.: privately printed, 1943-?
Journal of No. 12 Service Flying Training School, RCAF.

Agreement Amending and Extending the British Commonwealth Air Training Plan Agreement of December 17, 1939, Relating to Training of Pilots and Aircraft Crews in Canada and their Subsequent Service, between the United Kingdom, Canada, Australia and New Zealand, dated at Ottawa, June 5, 1942. Ottawa: King's Printer, 1942. 28 pp.

The Air Force Guide, by "Group Captain". Toronto: Copp Clark, 1940. 180 pp.

Air Force Review. Vol. I-VI. Gardenvale, P.Q., Toronto: Anglo-American Pub. Co.,1940-45.
Title varies: Vol. IV-VI titled: Aviation Review.

The Aircraftsman. Vol. I-V? St. Thomas, Ont.: n.p., 1940-44?
Journal of the Technical Training School, RCAF, St. Thomas, Ont.

Allison, Les. *Canadians in the Royal Air Force.* Roland, Man.: privately printed, 1978. 216 pp.
220 pp. with separately printed epilogue.

Annis, Clare L. *Airpower 1952; Three Speeches.* n.p.: n.d. v.p.

Bank of Montreal. *Field of Honour; the Second World War, 1939-1945.* Montreal: n.p., 1950. 1 vol., unpaged.

Barrass, R., and T.J.H. Sloan. *The Story of 657 Air O.P. Squadron R.A.F., January 31st, 1943, to May 8th, 1945.* London: White-friars Press, n.d. 96 pp.

Beckles, Gordon, [*pseud.*] *see* Willson, Gordon Beckles.

Bernier, Robert. *Jacques Chevrier, chef d'escadrille, R.C.A.F.; tombé en service au large de Cap-Chat.* Montréal: Editions de l'A.C.J.C., 1943. 95 pp.

Beurling, George F., and Leslie Roberts. *Malta Spitfire; the Story of a Fighter Pilot.* Toronto: Oxford Univ. Press, 1943. 235 pp.

Birney, Earle, ed. *Record of Service in the Second World War; the University of British Columbia; a Supplement to the University of British Columbia War Memorial Manuscript Record.* Vancouver: privately printed, 1955. 46 pp.

Bishop, William A. *Winged Peace.* New York: Viking Press, 1944. 175 pp.

Bowering, Clifford H. *Service; the Story of the Canadian Legion, 1925-1960.* Ottawa: privately printed, 1960. 240 pp.

The British Commonwealth Air Training Plan. Ottawa: King's Printer, 1941. 10 pp.

The British Commonwealth Air Training Plan, 1939-1945; an Historical Sketch and Record of the Ceremony at R.C.A.F. Station Trenton. Ottawa: King's Printer, 1949. 58 pp.

Broadfoot, Barry. *Six War Years, 1939-1945; Memories of Canadians at Home and Abroad.* Toronto: Doubleday Canada. 1974. 417 pp.

Brock, Thomas Leith. *Fight the Good Fight; Looking in on the Recruit Class at the Royal Military College of Canada during a Week in February, 1931.* Montreal: privately printed, 1964. 30 pp.

The C.A.H.S. Journal. Vol. I- . Willowdale, Ont.: Canadian Aviation Historical Society, 1963- .

Calgary Wings. No. 1-? Calgary: privately printed, 1941-?
Journal of No. 37 Service Flying Training School, RAF.

Canada. Air Board. *Air Regulations 1920; with which are Printed the Air Board Act, the Convention Relating to International Air Navigation, and Certain Directions Given and Forms Approved for Use under the Regulations.* Ottawa: King's Printer, 1920. 139 pp.

_____. *Regulations for the Canadian Air Force and the Air Board Act, August 31, 1920.* Ottawa: King's Printer, 1920. 196 pp.

_____. *Report.* Ottawa: King's Printer, 1920-23. 4 vols.

Canada. Air Force. *The Canadian Air Force List.* Ottawa: King's Printer, 1921?-22?

_____. *Dress Regulations for the Royal Canadian Air Force, 1925.* Ottawa: King's Printer, 1926. 41 pp.

_____. *Exhibition of Paintings and Drawings.* Ottawa: King's Printer, 1944. 28 pp.

_____. *Final Report of the Chief of the Air Staff to the Members of the Supervisory Board, British Commonwealth Air Training Plan; a Summary of the British Commonwealth Air Training Plan from its Inception on December 17, 1939, to Termination on March 31, 1945.* n.p.: 1945. 63 pp.

_____. *Information Relating to Enlistment, Terms of Service, Pay, etc., of Airmen and Boys in the Royal Canadian Air Force.* Ottawa: King's Printer, 1930. 10 pp.

_____. *Regulations and Instructions for the Clothing of the Royal Canadian Air Force, 1927.* (C.A.P. 9.) Ottawa: King's Printer, n.d. 71 pp.

_____. *The Royal Canadian Air Force List.* Ottawa: n.p., 1942-66.
Issued in mimeographed form until 1942. Frequency varies.

_____. *Weekly Orders.* Ottawa: [King's Printer, 1920-25]. 1 vol., looseleaf.

Canada. Air Force. 409 Squadron. *1941-1945; the Nighthawks.* Hengelo, Neth.: n.p., n.d. 80 pp.

Canada. Air Force. 435 Squadron. *Chinthe.* Victoria, B.C.: privately printed, n.d. 166 pp.

Canada. Air Force. 436 Squadron. *Canucks Unlimited; the Record in Story and Picture of the History, Life and Experiences of the Men of 436 R.C.A.F. Squadron, India-Burma, 1944-1945.* Toronto: n.p., n.d. 93 pp.

[Canada. Air Force. 666 Squadron.] *Battle History 666.* Epe, Neth.: privately printed, 1945. 37 pp.

Canada. Air Force. 39 Reconnaissance Wing. *Flap; 39 Reconnaissance Wing.* J.H. Marsters, ed. Hamburg, Ger.: privately printed, 1945. 1 vol., unpaged.

Canada. Air Force. No. 8 Air Observer School. *From the First to the Last Flight; a Pictorial History of the Operations and Personnel of the Royal Canadian Air Force and Quebec Airways (Observers) Ltd., 1941-1945.* n.p.: n.d. 127 pp.

Canada. Air Force. No. 4 Initial Training School. *"All for One — One for All"; 1st Anniversary; No. 4 Initial Training School, Royal Canadian Air Force, Edmonton, Alberta.* Edmonton: privately printed, [1942]. 1 vol., unpaged.

_____. *Christmas and New Year's Greetings, 1942-43.* Edmonton: privately printed, n.d. 1 vol., unpaged.

[Canada. Air Force. No. 1 Technical Training School.] *St. Thomas, Ontario, Canada.* n.p.: n.d. 19 1., chiefly illus.

Canada. Air Force. No. 7 Air Observer School. *The Record; a Souvenir of No. 7 Air Observer School, R.C.A.F., Portage la Prairie, Manitoba, Operated by Portage Air Observer School Ltd., 1941-1945.* n.p.: n.d. 100 pp.

[Canada. Air Force. No. 24 Elementary Flying Training School.] *Sky; Memories of Abbotsford.* n.p.: [1944]. 23 pp.

[Canada. Air Force. No. 2 Bombing and Gunnery School.] *R.C.A.F. "Bomb Bursts".* Regina: Caxton Press, 1943. 1 vol., unpaged.

Canada. Air Force. Technical Training School. Y.M.C.A. Services. Supervisors, comp. *The Royal Canadian Air Force Technical Training School, St. Thomas, Ontario.* St. Thomas, Ont.: privately printed, n.d. 21 pp.

Canada. Air Force Headquarters. *Flying Regulations for the Royal Canadian Air Force.* (C.A.P. 100.) n.p.: 1940. 1 vol., looseleaf.

_____. *General and Routine Orders.* Ottawa: n.p., 1940-65. *Title varies: Routine Orders from 1947. Supplements also issued. Issued in mimeographed form from 1933.*

Canada. Air Force Headquarters. Air Historical Section. *Among the Few; a Sketch of the Part Played by Canadian Airmen in the Battle of Britain (July 10th — October 31st, 1940).* (A.F.P. 49.) n.p.: 1948. 36 pp.

_____. *RCAF Logbook; a Chronological Outline of the Origin, Growth and Achievement of the Royal Canadian Air Force.* Ottawa: King's Printer, 1949. 96 pp.

_____. *The R.C.A.F. Overseas.* Toronto: Oxford Univ. Press, 1944-49. 3 vols.

Canada. Air Force Overseas Headquarters. *Overseas Orders.* London: n.p., 1943-46.
Issued in mimeographed form from 1940.

_____. *Publication No. 1.* London: n.p., 1942. v.p.

[Canada. Armed Forces. 409 Squadron.] *Nighthawk! A History of 409 (Night Fighter) Squadron, 1941-1977.* Courtenay, B.C.: privately printed, n.d. 93 pp.

Canada. Armed Forces. 434 Squadron. *434 Squadron . . . a History.* n.p.: privately printed, [1977]. 155 pp.

Canada. Army. First Canadian Army Headquarters and Gt. Brit. Air Force. 35 Reconnaissance Wing. *Air Recce.* London: n.p., n.d. 66 pp.

Canada. Dept. of National Defence. *Canadian Prisoners of War and Missing Personnel in the Far East.* Ottawa: King's Printer, 1945. 59 l.

_____. *Defence Forces List, Canada (Naval, Military and Air Forces).* Ottawa: King's Printer, 1930-39.
Title varies somewhat. Superseded The Militia List. *Superseded by* The Canadian Navy List, The Canadian Army List *and* The Royal Canadian Air Force List.

_____. *Digest of Opinions and Rulings; Ottawa; March 31, 1944; Compiled from the Records of the Office of the Judge Advocate-General, at National Defence Headquarters.* n.p.: [1944]. 353 pp., looseleaf.

_____. *Financial Regulations and Instructions for the Royal Canadian Air Force on Active Service (Canada), effective September 1st, 1939.* Ottawa: King's Printer, 1940. 88 pp.

_____. *Financial Regulations for the Royal Canadian Air Force on Active Service, 1945.* (C.A.P. 2.) Ottawa: King's Printer, 1945. 154 pp.

_____. *Instructions for Engineer Services, Canada, 1936.* Ottawa: King's Printer, 1936. 152 pp.

Canada. Dept. of National Defence. *King's Regulations and Orders for the Royal Canadian Air Force, 1924.* Ottawa: King's Printer, 1924. 494 pp.

_____. *King's Regulations for the Royal Canadian Air Force, 1943.* (C.A.P. 4.) Ottawa: King's Printer, 1943. 404 pp.

_____. *Pay and Allowance Regulations for the Royal Canadian Air Force, Permanent and Auxiliary, 1924.* Ottawa: King's Printer, 1924. 1 vol., looseleaf.

*_____. *Report.* Ottawa: King's Printer, 1923-59.
Title varies. Annual most years.

*_____. *Report on Civil Aviation.* Ottawa: King's Printer, 1924-32. 9 vols.

Canada. Dept. of National War Services. *Annual Report.* Ottawa: King's Printer, 1945. 3 vols.

Canada. Dept. of Veterans Affairs. *30th Anniversary of the D-Day Landings in Normandy, 1944 — June 6 — 1974./30e anniversaire des débarquements en Normandie au jour J, 1944 — le 6 juin — 1974.* n.p./s.l.: s.i., 1974. 22 pp.
Bilingual text./Texte bilingue.

*Canada. Director of Public Information. *Canada at War.* No. 1-45. Ottawa: King's Printer, 1941-45.

*Canada. Ministère de la Défense nationale. *Rapport.* Ottawa: Imprimeur du Roi, 1923-59.
Divergence du titre. Annuel, la plupart des années.

*_____. *Rapport sur l'aviation civile.* Ottawa: Imprimeur du Roi, 1924-32. 9 tomes.

Canada. National Gallery. *Exhibition of Canadian War Art.* Ottawa: King's Printer, 1945. 22 pp.

Canada. National Research Council. *History of the Associate Committee on Aviation Medical Research, 1939-1945.* Edgar C. Black, ed. Ottawa: King's Printer, 1946. 212 pp.

*Canada. Parlement. Chambre des Communes. Comité spécial d'enquête sur les distinctions honorifiques et les décorations. *Procès-verbaux et témoignages.* No. 1-6. Ottawa: Imprimeur du Roi, 1942.

Canada. Parliament. House of Commons. Special Committee on Canteen Funds. *Minutes of Proceedings and Evidence.* No. 1-11. Ottawa: King's Printer, 1942.

*Canada. Parliament. House of Commons. Special Committee on Honours and Decorations. *Minutes of Proceedings and Evidence.* No. 1-6. Ottawa: King's Printer, 1942.

Canada. Royal Commission to Conduct an Inquiry into Certain Disorders Occurring May 7-8, 1945, in the City of Halifax. *Report on the Halifax Disorders, May 7th-8th, 1945.* Hon. Mr. Justice R.L. Kellock, Royal Commissioner. Ottawa: King's Printer, 1945. 61 pp.

*Canada. Service de l'Information. *Le Canada en guerre.* No. 1-45. Ottawa: Imprimeur du Roi, 1941-45.

Canadian Air Cadet. Vol. I-VII. Toronto: Air Cadet League of Canada, 1941-48.

Canadian Bank of Commerce. *War Service Records, 1939-1945; an Account of the War Service of Members of the Staff during the Second World War.* D.P. Wagner and C.G. Siddall, eds. Toronto: Rous & Mann, 1947. 331 pp.

Canadian Broadcasting Corporation. Publications Branch. *We have been There; Authoritative Reports by Qualified Observers who have Returned from the War Zones, as Presented Over the CBC National Network.* Toronto: Canadian Broadcasting Corporation, 1941-42. 2 vols.

Canadian Jewish Congress. *Canadian Jews in World War II.* Montreal: privately printed, 1947-48. 2 vols.

Canadian Legion War Services, Inc. *A Year of Service; a Summary of Activities on Behalf of His Majesty's Canadian Forces Rendered during Nineteen-Forty.* n.p.: n.d. 1 vol., unpaged.

[Canadian War Museum.] *La coopération canada-polonaise au cours des deux guerres mondiales./Polish-Canadian Co-operation in the Two World Wars.* Ottawa: n.p., 1973. 36 pp.
Texte bilingue./Bilingual text.

Carr, William Guy. *Checkmate in the North; the Axis Planned to Invade America.* Toronto: Macmillan, 1944. 304 pp.

Castonguay, Jacques. *Unsung Mission; History of the Chaplaincy Service (RC) of the R.C.A.F.* Montreal: Institut de Pastorale, 1968. 173 pp.

The Chinook. Vol. I-? Lethbridge, Alta.: n.p., 1942-?
Journal of No. 8 Bombing and Gunnery School, RCAF.

City of Winnipeg 402 Squadron, 1932-1974. n.p.: n.d. 1 vol., unpaged.

Collishaw, Raymond, and R.V. Dodds. *Air Command; a Fighter Pilot's Story.* London: W. Kimber, 1973. 256 pp.

Commonwealth War Graves Commission. *The War Dead of the Commonwealth; the Register of the Names of Those who Fell in the 1939-1945 War and are Buried; Cemeteries in Canada; Cemeteries in Ontario.* London: H.M. Stationery Office, 1961. 2 vols.

Commonwealth War Graves Commission. *The War Dead of the Commonwealth; the Register of the Names of Those who Fell in the 1939-1945 War and are Buried in Cemeteries in Canada; Cemeteries in British Columbia, Yukon Territory and Alberta.* Maidenhead, Eng.: [H.M. Stationery Office], 1972. 82 pp.

_____. *The War Dead of the Commonwealth; the Register of the Names of Those who Fell in the 1939-1945 War and are Buried in Cemeteries in Canada; Cemeteries in New Brunswick, Nova Scotia, Newfoundland and Prince Edward Island.* London: H.M. Stationery Office, 1962. 81 pp.

_____. *The War Dead of the Commonwealth; the Register of the Names of Those who Fell in the 1939-1945 War and are Buried in Cemeteries in Canada; Cemeteries in Quebec.* London: H.M. Stationery Office, 1962. 63 pp.

_____. *The War Dead of the Commonwealth; the Register of the Names of Those who Fell in the 1939-1945 War and are Buried in Cemeteries in Canada; Cemeteries in Saskatchewan and Manitoba.* London: [H.M. Stationery Office], 1963. 79 pp.

Contact! Vol. I-IV. Mossbank, Sask.: n.p., 1941-44.
Journal of No. 2 Bombing and Gunnery School, RCAF. Title varies. Vol. IV titled: Target.

Cosgrove, Edmund. *Canada's Fighting Pilots.* (Canadian Portraits.) Toronto: Clarke, Irwin, 1965. 190 pp.

_____. *The Evaders.* Toronto: Clarke, Irwin, 1970. 301 pp.

Coughlin, Tom. *The Dangerous Sky; Canadian Airmen in World War II.* Toronto: Ryerson Press, 1968. 214 pp.

Critchley, A. *Critch! The Memoirs of Brigadier-General A.C. Critchley.* London: Hutchinson, 1961. 256 pp.

The Dafoe Digest. Vol. I-? Saskatoon, Sask.: privately printed, 1942-?
Journal of No. 5 Bombing and Gunnery School, RCAF.

The Demon Squadron; 407 Squadron in War and Peace, May 1941 — June 1952, June 1952 — June 1975. n.p.: privately printed, [1975]. 46 pp.

Douglas, W.A.B., and Brereton Greenhous. *Out of the Shadows; Canada in the Second World War.* Toronto: Oxford Univ. Press, 1977. 288 pp.

The Drift Recorder. Winnipeg: n.p., ?-1945.
Journal of No. 5 Air Observer School, RCAF.

Ellis, Frank H. *Canada's Flying Heritage.* Toronto: Univ. of Toronto Press, 1954. 398 pp.

Ellis, Frank H. *Fifty Years of Adventure and Progress in Canadian Skies.* Toronto: Ryerson Press, 1959. 230 pp.

Ettenger, G.H. *History of the Associate Committee on Medical Research, Ottawa, 1938-1946.* Ottawa: n.p., n.d. 46 pp.

Fetherstonhaugh, R.C. *McGill University at War, 1914-1918; 1939-1945.* Montreal: McGill Univ., 1947. 437 pp.

Field, Peter J. *Canada's Wings.* London: Unwin, 1942. 126 pp.

The Fly Paper. Vol. I-? Jarvis, Ont.: privately printed, 1943-?
Journal of No. 1 Bombing and Gunnery School, RCAF.

The Flying Gopher; the Journal of the Royal Air Force, No. 41 Service Flying Training School, Weyburn, Saskatchewan, Canada. Vol. I-? Weyburn, Sask.: privately printed, 1942-?

Foothill Fliers. Vol. I-III? Calgary: privately printed. 1941-45?
Journal of No. 3 Service Flying Training School, RCAF.

416 Squadron see Hovey, H. Richard.

427 Lion Squadron, 1942-1970. Marceline, Mo.: Walsworth, n.d. 76 pp.

422 Sqn; This Arm shall do It, 1942-1970. Marceline, Mo.: Walsworth, n.d. 64 pp.

407 Squadron RCAF (Overseas). n.p.: 1945. 60 pp.

[General Motors of Canada, Limited.] *Achievement.* n.p.: [1943]. 74 pp.

Gibson, Colin. *"Air Power in Canada"; an Address by Col. the Hon. Colin Gibson, M.C., M.A., Minister of National Defence for Air, to the Empire Club of Toronto, February 28, 1946.* n.p.: n.d. 11 pp.

Gilman, William. *Our Hidden Front.* New York: Reynal & Hitchcock, 1944. 266 pp.

Giloteaux, Paulin. *Une "âme-hostie" canadienne; Jean-François Bittner, novice "père blanc" et aviateur-bombardier, 1919-1943.* Le Quesnoy, France: Oeuvres Charitable, 1952. 139 pp.

Godsell, Philip H. *The Romance of the Alaska Highway.* Toronto: Ryerson Press, 1944. 235 pp.

Gordon, John. *. . .Of Men and Planes.* Ottawa: Love Print., 1968. 3 vols.

_____. *Winged Sentries./Sentinelles de l'air.* Claude Rousseau, illus. n.p.: 1963. 104 pp.
Bilingual text./Texte bilingue.

[Gt. Brit. Air Force. No. 35 Elementary Flying Training School.] *A History of No. 35 E.F.T.S., R.A.F., Neepawa.* Neepawa, Man.: Neepawa Press, n.d. 1 vol., unpaged.

Gt. Brit. Imperial War Graves Commission. *The War Dead of the British Commonwealth and Empire; the Register of the Names of Airmen who Fell in the 1939-1945 War and have no known Grave; the Ottawa Memorial.* London: H.M. Stationery Office, 1959. 37 pp.

_____. *The War Dead of the British Commonwealth and Empire; the Register of the Names of Those who Fell in the 1939-1945 War and are Buried in Cemeteries and Churchyards in Surrey; Brookwood Military Cemetery, Woking.* London: [H.M. Stationery Office], 1958. 3 vols.

_____. *The War Dead of the British Commonwealth and Empire; the Register of the Names of Those who Fell in the 1939-1945 War and are Buried in Cemeteries in Italy; Ravenna War Cemetery.* London: [H.M. Stationery Office], 1956. 44 pp.

Gt. Brit. Ministry of Information. *Atlantic Bridge; the Official Account of R.A.F. Transport Command's Ocean Ferry.* London: H.M. Stationery Office, 1945. 75 pp.

Griffin, D.F. *First Steps to Tokyo; the Royal Canadian Air Force in the Aleutians.* Toronto: Dent, 1944. 50 pp.

Griffin, J.A. *Canadian Military Aircraft; Serials & Photographs, 1920-1968./Avions militaires canadiens; numéros de série et photographies, 1920-1968.* (Canadian War Museum Publication Number 69-2./Musée de guerre du Canada publication numéro 69-2.) Ottawa: Queen's Printer/Imprimeur de la Reine, 1969. 691 pp.
Bilingual text./Texte bilingue.

"Group Captain" *see The Air Force Guide.*

Gutta Percha and Rubber, Limited. *A Selection of Badge Designs of the Canadian Forces.* Toronto: n.p., n.d. 16 pp., chiefly illus.

Halliday, H.A. *Chronology of Canadian Military Aviation.* (National Museum of Man Mercury Series; Canadian War Museum Paper, no. 6.) Ottawa: [Queen's Printer], 1975. 168 pp.

_____. *The Tumbling Sky.* Stittsville, Ont.: Canada's Wings, 1978. 324 pp.

Hammond, H.R.L., and others, eds. [*401 Squadron*]. n.p.: privately printed, n.d. 1 vol., unpaged.

The Happy Warrior; a Book in Memory of the Life and Work of G/C the Rev. R.M. Frayne, C.D., D.D., Director of Religious Administration (P), the Royal Canadian Air Force. Toronto: United Church Pub. House, 1953. 103 pp.

Hearn, Owen. *Bing, R.C.A.F.; a Proud and Grateful Memory of Warrant Officer Albert Joseph Michael De Cruyenaere, R.C.A.F., Killed in Action in North Burma, March 1943.* n.p.: privately printed, n.d.

_____. *Verne, R.C.A.F.; a Companion Book to that of Bing, R.C.A.F.; Written in Proud and Grateful Memory of his Friend, Flying Officer Vernon Bartlett Graves Butler, R.C.A.F., Killed in Action in Manipur, Assam, March 1944.* n.p.: privately printed, n.d.

Hermann, J. Douglas. *Report to the Minister of Veterans Affairs of a Study on Canadians who were Prisoners of War in Europe during World War II./Rapport présenté au Ministre des Affaires des anciens combattants au sujet d'une enquête portant sur les Canadiens prisonniers de guerre en Europe au cours de la seconde guerre mondiale.* Ottawa: Queen's Printer/Imprimeur de la Reine, 1973. 56/60 pp.
Bilingual text./Texte bilingue.

Hill, B. Kirkbride, comp. *The Price of Freedom.* Toronto: Ryerson Press, 1942-44. 2 vols.

A History of No. 5 E.F.T.S. (R.C.A.F.); High River and Lethbridge, Alberta. D.C. Jones, comp. n.p.: 1945. 82 pp.

Hitchins, F.H. *Air Board, Canadian Air Force and Royal Canadian Air Force.* (National Museum of Man Mercury Series; Canadian War Museum Paper, no. 2.) Ottawa: Queen's Printer, 1972. 475 pp.

Hoare, John. *Tumult in the Clouds; a Story of the Fleet Air Arm.* London: Joseph, 1976. 208 pp.

Hodgins, J. Herbert, and others, comps. *Women at War.* Montreal: MacLean Pub., 1943. 190 pp.

Hopkins, Anthony. *Songs from the Front & Rear; Canadian Servicemen's Songs of the Second World War.* Edmonton: Hurtig Publishers, 1979. 192 pp.

[Hovey, H. Richard, and others.] *416 Squadron.* n.p.: 1974. 133 pp.

The Illustrated Review of Aviation in Canada; Celebrating the Golden Anniversary of Powered Flight in Canada. Montreal: privately printed, [1959]. 1 vol., unpaged.

In Transit; the Magazine of No. 31 R.A.F. Depot, Moncton, N.B. Vol. I-? Moncton, N.B.: n.p., 1942-?

Jackson, Fred, and others. *The Story of "418"; the City of Edmonton Intruder Squadron, R.C.A.F.* n.p.: n.d. 72 pp.

Johnson, J.E. *Wing Leader.* Toronto: Clarke, Irwin, 1956. 320 pp.

Jones, D.C., *see A History of No. 5 E.F.T.S. . . . .*

Journal of the Edmonton Military Institute. Vol. I-IV? Edmonton: Edmonton Military Institute, 1937-46?

*Kealy, J.D.F., and E.C. Russell. *A History of Canadian Naval Aviation, 1918-1962.* Ottawa: Queen's Printer, 1965. 164 pp.

*Kealy, J.D.F., et E.C. Russell. *Histoire de l'aéronavale canadienne, 1918-1962.* Ottawa: Imprimeur de la Reine, 1965. 185 pp.

Kellock, R.L., *see* Canada. Royal Commission to Conduct an Inquiry into Certain Disorders Occurring May 7-8, 1945, in the City of Halifax.

Kelsey Club, Winnipeg, Man. *Canadian Defence; What We have to Defend; Various Defence Policies.* Toronto: T. Nelson, 1937. 98 pp.

Kemp, Hugh. *28 True Adventure Stories; Canada's Aces.* Winnipeg: Contemporary Publishers, 1944. 50 pp.
  Also titled: *Adventure in the Skies; the Thrilling Achievements of Canada's Greatest Air Aces.* n.p.: n.d.

Kent, J.A. *One of the Few.* London: W. Kimber, 1971. 255 pp.

Kerr, W.K. *Bibliography of Canadian Reports in Aviation Medicine, 1939-1945.* n.p.: Defence Research Board, 1962. v.p.

King, W.L. Mackenzie. *Canada and the War; the Training of British Pilots and the Joint Air Training Plan; Mackenzie King Replies to Dr. Manion; a Radio Address by Right Honourable W.L. Mackenzie King, Ottawa, 8th March, 1940.* Ottawa: National Liberal Federation, n.d. 13 pp.

_____. *Plan d'entraînement des aviateurs du Commonwealth britannique; discours à la radio par le très honorable W.L. Mackenzie King, M.P., premier ministre du Canada, le dimanche, 17 décembre 1939.* Ottawa: Imprimeur du Roi, 1939. 15 pp.

Kostenuk, Samuel, and John Griffin. *RCAF Squadron Histories and Aircraft, 1924-1968.* (Canadian War Museum Historical Publication 14.) Toronto: S. Stevens, Hakkert, 1977. 255 pp.

Laing, Gertrude. *A Community Organized for War; the Story of the Greater Winnipeg Co-ordinating Board for War Services and Affiliated Organizations, 1939-1946.* Winnipeg: n.p., 1948. 103 pp.

Large, W.S. *The Diary of a Canadian Fighter Pilot.* K.B. Conn, ed. Toronto: R. Saunders, 1944. 64 pp.

London Air Observer; Published Monthly in the Interests of the Personnel of No. 4 Air Observer School, Leavens Bros. (Training) Limited. Vol. I-? London, Ont.: n.p., 1943-?

M.T.B. Vol. I-III? Rivers, Man.: privately printed, 1943-45?
Cover title: Message to Base. Journal of No. 1 Central Navigation School, RCAF.

McAlister, Alec. *Hi-Sky! The Ups and Downs of a Pinfeather Pilot.* Toronto: Ryerson Press, 1944. 124 pp.

Macdonald, Grant. *Our Canadian Armed Services,* sketches by Grant Macdonald. Montreal: Gazette, 1943. 1 vol., chiefly illus.

McGill Univ., Montreal, P.Q. *A Memorial Service for the McGill Men and Women who Gave Their Lives during the First and Second World Wars.* n.p.: [1946]. 1 vol., unpaged.

MacLaren, Roy. *Canadians in Russia, 1918-1919.* Toronto: Macmillan, 1976. 301 pp.

McLean, N.B. *Report of the Hudson Strait Expedition, 1927-28.* Ottawa: King's Printer, 1929. 221 pp.

MacMillan, D.A. *Only the Stars Know.* Toronto: Dent, 1944. 138 pp.

Main, J.R.K. *Voyageurs of the Air; a History of Civil Aviation in Canada.* Ottawa: Queen's Printer, 1967. 397 pp.

Manning the R.C.A.F.; Short History of the Directorate of Manning. n.p.: n.d. 25 pp.

Mazéas, Daniel. *Insignes armée canadienne, 1900-1914; Canadian Badges; supplément, 1920-1950.* Guincamp, France: privately printed, 1972. 116 pp.

*Melnyk, T.W. *Canadian Flying Operations in South East Asia, 1941-1945.* (Department of National Defence Directorate of History Occasional Paper, Number One.) Ottawa: Queen's Printer, 1976. 179 pp.

* _____. *Les opérations aériennes du Canada dans le sud-est Asiatique, 1941-1945.* Jacques Gouin, tr. (Ministère de la Défense nationale Service historique Document occasionnel, numéro 1.) Ottawa: Imprimeur de la Reine, 1976. 202 pp.

Memories of Linton; Home of the Goose and Thunderbird Squadrons. n.p.: n.d. 15 pp.

Merrick, Bob. *410 Squadron; a History.* n.p.: n.d. 114 pp.

Milberry, Larry. *Aviation in Canada.* Toronto: McGraw-Hill Ryerson, 1979. 272 pp.

Military Aviation. Vol. I-? Toronto: privately printed, 1940-?

Miville-Deschênes, Charles. *Souvenirs de guerre.* Québec, P.Q.: s.i., 1946. 128 pp.

The Mont Joli Target. Vol. I. Mont Joli, P.Q.: n.p., 1944-45.
Journal of No. 9 Bombing and Gunnery School, RCAF.

Morgan, Len. *The AT-6 Harvard.* (Famous Aircraft.) New York: Arco Pub. Co., 1965. 1 vol., unpaged.

Morneault, J.C. *424 Tiger Squadron, 1935-1977.* n.p.: [1978]. 31 pp.

Morris, Jerrold. *Canadian Artists and Airmen, 1940-45.* Toronto: The Morris Gallery, n.d. 207 pp.

The Moth Monthly. Vol. I-II. Caron, Sask.: privately printed, 1942-43.
Journal of No. 33 Elementary Flying Training School, RCAF. Vol. II, no. 3-12 titled: The Tailspin.

The Mount Hope Meteor. Vol. I-? Mount Hope, Ont.: privately printed, 1942-?
Journal of No. 33 Air Navigation School, RCAF.

Myles, Eugenie Louise. *Airborne from Edmonton.* Toronto: Ryerson Press, 1959. 280 pp.

National Aeronautical Collection. Ottawa: Queen's Printer, 1967. 36 pp.

National Aeronautical Collection./Collection aéronautique nationale. n.p.: n.d./s.l.: s.i., s.d. 36 pp.
Bilingual text./Texte bilingue.

Nicholson, G.W.L. *More Fighting Newfoundlanders; a History of Newfoundland's Fighting Forces in the Second World War.* [St. John's, Nfld.]: Govt. of Nfld., 1969. 621 pp.

Norway. Air Force. Training Centre, Ontario. *"Little Norway" in Pictures; R.N.A.F. in Canada.* n.p.: n.d. 1 vol., unpaged.

Nova Scotia. *Nova Scotia Helps the Fighting Man.* n.p.: [1942]. 32 pp.

No. 8 on Parade. Vol. I-? Winnipeg: n.p., 1942-?
Journal of No. 8 Repair Depot, RCAF.

Number Four Hundred & Four Squadron, Royal Canadian Air Force. n.p.: [1972]. 62 pp.

No. 9 Flyer. Vol. I. Centralia, Ont.: n.p., 1944-45?
Journal of No. 9 Service Flying Training School, RCAF.

No. 19 Service Flying Training School, Vulcan, Alberta, Royal Canadian Air Force, Annual, 1944. n.p.: privately printed, n.d. 51 pp.

Obodiac, Stanlee. *Pennfield Ridge.* Wembley, Eng.: privately printed, 1949. 100 pp.

[Ontario County Flying Training School, Limited.] *Souvenir Booklet, No. 20 Elementary Flying Training School, Limited, R.C.A.F., 1941-1944.* Oshawa, Ont.: privately printed, [1945].

Ottawa Air Training Conference, 1942. *Report of the Conference.* Ottawa: King's Printer, 1942. 25 pp.

Over Seas; the Magazine of the Royal Air Force, Greenwood, Nova Scotia, Canada. Vol. I-? n.p.: 1942-?

The Patrician. Vol. I-? Sydney, B.C.: privately printed, 1941-? *Magazine of the Royal Air Force, British Columbia.*

The Paulson Post. Vol. I-? Paulson, Man.: privately printed, 1942-? *Journal of No. 7 Bombing and Gunnery School, RCAF.*

Pearcy, Arthur. *The Dakota; a History of the Douglas Dakota in RAF and RCAF Service.* London: I. Allan, 1972. 320 pp.

Peden, Murray. *A Thousand shall Fall.* Stittsville, Ont.: Canada's Wings, 1979. 473 pp.

The Penhold Log. Vol. I-V. Penhold, Alta.: privately printed, 1941-44. *Journal of No. 36 Service Flying Training School, RCAF.*

Pilots, Observers and Air Gunners for the Royal Canadian Air Force. n.p.: n.d. [20 pp.]

Pioneer; Official Journal, No. 31 SFTS, Canada, Royal Air Force. Vol. I-II. Kingston, Ont.: privately printed, 1941-42.

*Le plan d'entraînement aérien du Commonwealth britannique. Ottawa: Imprimeur du Roi, 1941. 11 pp.

*Le plan d'entraînement aérien du Commonwealth britannique, 1939-1945; résumé historique et compte rendu de la cérémonie qui s'est déroulée à la station du CARC de Trenton. Ottawa: Imprimeur du Roi, 1950. 61 pp.

Prairie Flyer; the Magazine of No. 32 S.F.T.S. R.A.F. Vol. I-? Moose Jaw, Sask.: privately printed, 1941-?

Preston, Richard A. *Canada's RMC; a History of the Royal Military College.* Toronto: Univ. of Toronto Press, 1969. 415 pp.

Pukka Gen. Vol. I-IV. Debert, N.S.: privately printed, 1942-44. *Journal of No. 31 Operational Training Unit, RAF.*

RCA Victor Co. *Symbol of Air Supremacy.* n.p.: n.d. [12] pp.

The Rally Magazine. Vol. I-? Wrecclesham, Eng.: n.p., 1939?-? *A monthly magazine for Canadian Active Service Forces.*

Reader's Digest. *The Canadians at War, 1939/45.* Montreal: Reader's Digest, 1969. 2 vols.

_____. *The Tools of War, 1939/45, and a Chronology of Important Events.* Montreal: Reader's Digest, 1969. 96 pp.

The Record; a Souvenir of No. 7 Air Observer School, R.C.A.F. Portage la Prairie, Manitoba, Operated by Portage Air Observer School Ltd., 1941-1945. [Winnipeg: n.p., 1945.] 100 pp.

Recte Volare. Vol. I-? Port Albert, Ont.: n.p., 1942-?
Journal of No. 31 Air Navigation School, RAF.

The Regina Elementary Flying Training School Limited; a Company Incorporated under the Dominion Companies Act for the Sole Purpose of Operating No. 15 Elementary Flying Training School, a Unit of the British Commonwealth Air Training Plan, from November, 1940, to August, 1944. n.p.: n.d. 24 pp.

The Repair-O-Scope. Vol. I-? St. Johns, P.Q.: n.p., 1944-?
Journal of No. 9 Repair Depot, RCAF.

Rivac, Richard. *Tail Gunner Takes Over.* London: Jarrolds, n.d. 112 pp.

Roberts, Leslie. *Canada's War in the Air.* Montreal: A.M. Beatty, 1942. 157 pp.

_____. *There Shall be Wings; a History of the Royal Canadian Air Force.* Toronto: Clarke, Irwin, 1959. 250 pp.

Robertson, Heather, [comp.] *A Terrible Beauty; the Art of Canada at War.* Toronto: J. Lorimer, 1977. 239 pp.

Robertson, Peter. *Irréductible vérité/Relentless Verity/les photographes militaires canadiens depuis 1885/Canadian Military Photographers since 1885.* (Les Archives publiques du Canada/ Public Archives of Canada Series.) Québec, P.Q.: Les Presses de l'Université Laval, 1973. 233 pp.
Texte bilingue./Bilingual text.

Royal Military College of Canada, Kingston, Ont. *Regulations and Calendar of the Royal Military College of Canada, 1922.* Ottawa: King's Printer, 1923. 68 pp.

_____. *Standing Orders, Amended to January, 1924.* Ottawa: King's Printer, 1924. 120 pp.

_____. *Standing Orders, Amended to January, 1926.* Ottawa: King's Printer, 1926. 105 pp.

_____. *Standing Orders; the Royal Military College of Canada, 1938.* Ottawa: King's Printer, 1938. 67 pp.

The Royal Military College of Canada Review. Vol. I- . Kingston, Ont.: privately printed, 1920-   .

Sallans, G.H. *With Canada's Fighting Men.* Ottawa: King's Printer, 1941. 46 pp.

Sandwell, A.H. *Planes over Canada.* London: T. Nelson, 1938. 120 pp.

Savard, Adjutor. *Les ailes canadiennes françaises.* s.l.: s.i., 1944. 1 tome, non-paginé.

*_____. *The Defence of Our Land.* n.p.: 1943. 12 pp.

*_____. *La défense du territoire.* s.l.: s.i., 1943. 11 pp.

Segal, Jean Brown. *Wings of the Morning.* Toronto: Macmillan, 1945. 151 pp.

The Sentinel. No. 1-11? n.p.: 1944-45?
   Journal of No. 32 Radio Unit, RCAF, Port aux Basques, Nfld.

Shea, A.A., and E. Estoriak. *Canada and the Short-Wave War.* (Behind the Headlines, vol. III.) Toronto: Canadian Institute of International Affairs, 1942. 36 pp.

Smith, I. Norman. *The British Commonwealth Air Training Plan.* Toronto: Macmillan, 1941. 28 pp.

Sparks. Vol. I-? Guelph, Ont.: n.p., 1942-?
   Journal of No. 4 Wireless School, RCAF. Began publication as a newspaper.

*Stacey, C.P. *Armes, hommes et gouvernements; les politiques de guerre du Canada, 1939-1945.* Ottawa: Imprimeur de la Reine, 1970. 747 pp.

*_____. *Arms, Men and Governments; the War Policies of Canada, 1939-1945.* Ottawa: Queen's Printer, 1970. 681 pp.

Stalmann, Reinhart. *Die Ausbrecherkönige von Kanada.* [Hamburg, Ger.]: Sternbücher, 1958. 191 pp.

Stedman, Ernest W. *From Boxkite to Jet; Memoirs of Air Vice-Marshall Ernest W. Stedman.* [Toronto]: Univ. of Toronto Press, 1963. 1 vol., unpaged.
   Reprints of articles from Canadian Aviation. An enlarged edition was published as From Boxkite to Jet; the Memoirs of an Aeronautical Engineer (National Museum of Man Mercury Series; Canadian War Museum Paper no. 1.) Ottawa: Queen's Printer, 1972.

Summary of Memorandum of Agreement between the Governments of the United Kingdom, Canada, Australia and New Zealand Relating to Training of Pilots and Aircraft Crews in Canada and their Subsequent Service. n.p.: [1942]. 12 pp.

Sutherland, Alice Gibson. *Canada's Aviation Pioneers; 50 Years of McKee Trophy Winners.* Toronto: McGraw-Hill Ryerson, 1978. 304 pp.

Swan, Minto. *Props, Bars and Pulpits or Minto's Minutes.* Kingston, Ont.: privately printed, n.d. 143 pp.
   Cover title: Padre Minto Remembers.

Sweanor, George. *It's all Pensionable Time.* Vol. I. n.p.: n.d. v.p.

Swettenham, John. *D-Day./Jour-J.* Jacques Gouin, tr. Ottawa: National Museum of Man/Le Musée national de l'homme, [1970]. 27/30 pp.
Bilingual text./Texte bilingue.

The Swift; a Review of Current Events. No. 1-? Swift Current, Sask.: Sun Print. & Pub. Co., 1942-?
Journal of No. 39 Service Flying Training School, RAF.

Thompson, Roy J.C. *Wings of the Canadian Armed Forces, 1913-1972.* [Dartmouth], N.S.: n.p., 1973. 106 pp.

Thumbs Up. Vol. I-? Dartmouth, N.S.: privately printed, 1941-?
Published by airmen of RCAF Station Dartmouth. Vol. I, no. 1-4 were published by airmen of No. 4 Repair Depot, RCAF.

Tracer. Vol. I-? Winnipeg: privately printed, 1944-?
Journal of No. 3 Bombing and Gunnery School, RCAF.

Trinity College School Old Boys at War, 1899-1902, 1914-1918, 1939-1945. Port Hope, Ont.: privately printed, 1948. 245 pp.

25th Anniversary Reunion; Royal Canadian Air Force (Women's Division). Toronto: n.p., 1966. 1 vol., unpaged.

The University of Alberta in the War of 1939-45. Edmonton: n.p., 1948. 70 pp.

Vincent, Carl. *The Blackburn Shark.* (Canada's Wings, vol. 1.) Stittsville, Ont.: Canada's Wings, 1974. 98 pp.

Vincent, Carl, J.D. Oughton and E. Vincent. *Consolidated Liberator & Boeing Fortress.* (Canada's Wings, vol. 2.) Stittsville, Ont.: Canada's Wings, 1975. 246 pp.

[Virden Flying Training School, Limited.] *Virden Days; Memories of No. 19 E.F.T.S., R.C.A.F., 1941-1944.* Winnipeg: Saults and Pollard, [1945]. 94 pp.

Watt, Sholto. *I'll Take the High Road; a History of the Beginning of the Atlantic Air Ferry in Wartime.* Fredericton, N.B.: Brunswick Press, 1960. 169 pp.

Whitehead, William. *Dieppe, 1942; Echoes of Disaster.* Terence Macartney-Filgate, ed. (A Personal Library Publication.) Don Mills, Ont.: Nelson, 1979. 187 pp., chiefly illus.

Whitton, Charlotte. *Canadian Women in the War Effort.* Toronto: Macmillan, 1942. 56 pp.

[Willson, Gordon Beckles.] *Canada Comes To England,* by Gordon Beckles [*pseud.*] London: Hodder and Stoughton, 1941. 166 pp.

Wilson, J.A. *Development of Aviation in Canada, 1879-1948.* Ottawa: Dept. of Transport Air Services Branch, n.d. 105 pp.

Windy Wings. Vol. I-IV? Claresholm, Alta.: privately printed, 1941-44?
>Title varies. *Vol. I titled: <u>No. 15 S.F.T.S. Review</u>. Journal of No. 15 Service Flying Training School, RCAF.*

Wings. Vol. I-? Picton, Ont.: privately printed, 1941-?
>*Journal of RAF Station Picton and of No. 31 Bombing and Gunnery School, RAF.*

Wings. Vol. I-? Yorkton, Sask.: n.p., 1941-?
>*Journal of No. 11 Service Flying Training School, RCAF.*

Wings; Log of the R.C.A.F. Vol. I-? Ottawa: privately printed, 1943-?
>*Published monthly for Air Force personnel by the Air Force Headquarters Station Fund.*

*Wodehouse, R.F. *Aviation Paintings from the Art Collection of the Canadian War Museum.* Ottawa: [Queen's Printer], 1972. 84 pp.

_____. *A Check List of the War Collections of World War I, 1914-1918, and World War II, 1939-1945.* Ottawa: Queen's Printer, 1968. 239 pp.

*_____. *Tableaux de l'aviation militaire; provenant de la Collection d'art du Musée de guerre canadien.* Ottawa: [Imprimeur de la Reine], 1972. 84 pp.

Wynn, Edgar J. *Bombers Across.* New York: Dutton, 1944. 178 pp. *Atlantic Ferry Organization.*

Young Men's Christian Associations, Canada. *The 1st Year; a War Service Record of the Canadian Y.M.C.A. from the Outbreak of the War.* n.p.: [1940]. 23 pp.

Young Men's Christian Associations, Canada. National Council. War Services Executive. *With Arthur Jones through 5 Years of War; a Report of Canadian Y.M.C.A. War Services.* n.p.: n.d. 1 vol., unpaged.

Young, Scott. *Red Shield in Action; a Record of Canadian Salvation Army War Services in the Second Great War.* Toronto: F.F. Clarke, 1949. 149 pp.

Ziegler, Mary. *The Story of the Women's Division, Royal Canadian Air Force.* Hamilton, Ont.: privately printed, 1973. 173 pp.

1946-1967

Adelberg, Philip, ed. *414 Squadron (1941-1975); a Short History.* n.p.: 1975. 1 vol., unpaged.

Air Cadet Annual. Ottawa: Air Cadet League of Canada, 1949-69.

Air Force College Journal. Toronto: privately printed, 1956-64. 9 vols.
Title varies.

Annis, Clare L. *Airpower 1952; Three Speeches.* n.p.: n.d. v.p.

Aviation in Modern Defence; the Story of the Expanding Royal Canadian Air Force, n.p.: n.d. [12] pp.

*Barton, William H. *Science and the Armed Services.* (Current Affairs for the Canadian Forces, vol. II, no. 1.) Ottawa: King's Printer, 1952. 22 pp.

*_____. *La science et les Services armés.* (Actualités; revue destinée aux Forces canadiennes, vol. II, no. 1.) Ottawa: Imprimeur du Roi, 1952. 22 pp.

Bowering, Clifford H. *Service; the Story of the Canadian Legion, 1925-1960.* Ottawa: privately printed, 1960. 240 pp.

The C.A.H.S. Journal. Vol. I- . Willowdale, Ont.: Canadian Aviation Historical Society, 1963- .

Canada. Air Force. *Dress Orders for the Royal Canadian Air Force.* (C.A.P. 6.) Ottawa: Queen's Printer, 1958. v.p.

_____. *A Plan for Your Future.* Ottawa: King's Printer, 1948. 65 pp.

_____. *Regulations and Orders for the Royal Canadian Air Cadets.* (CAP 496.) n.p.: 1956. 1 vol., looseleaf.

_____. *The Royal Canadian Air Force List.* Ottawa: n.p., 1942-66.
Issued in mimeographed form until 1942. Frequency varies.

*Canada. Air Force. Air Defence Command Headquarters. *The Ground Observer Corps.* (Current Affairs for the Canadian Forces, vol. VIII, no. 6.) Ottawa: Queen's Printer, 1955. 31 pp.

Canada. Air Force. 1 Fighter Wing. *The First Year, 1951-52; 1 Fighter Wing, R.C.A.F.; North Luffenham, Rutland, England.* n.p.: 1953. 96 pp.

Canada. Air Force. Training Command. *Training in the Royal Canadian Air Force.* Scott Air Force Base, Ill.: n.p., n.d. 143 pp.

Canada. Air Force Headquarters. *Air Force Administrative Orders.* Ottawa: n.p., 1947?-65.
Issued as a non-chronological sequence in which orders were discarded when obsolete. Gradually superseded an older series of mimeographed administrative orders.

Canada. Air Force Headquarters. *General and Routine Orders.*
Ottawa: n.p., 1940-65.
Title varies: Routine Orders from 1947. Supplements also issued.
Issued in mimeographed form from 1933.

[Canada. Air Force Overseas Headquarters.] *Overseas Orders.*
London: n.p., 1943-66.
Issued in mimeographed form from 1940.

[Canada. Armed Forces. 409 Squadron.] *Nighthawk! A History of*
409 (Night Fighter) Squadron, 1941-1977. Courtenay, B.C.: privately printed, n.d. 93 pp.

Canada. Armed Forces. 434 Squadron. *434 Squadron . . . a History.*
n.p.: privately printed, [1977]. 155 pp.

*Canada. Aviation. Quartier général du Commandement de l'Air.
Le Corps des observateurs terrestres. (Actualités; revue destinée
aux Forces canadiennes, vol. VIII, no. 6.) Ottawa: Imprimeur de
la Reine, 1955. 31 pp.

Canada. Canadian Forces Headquarters. *Canadian Forces Administrative Orders.* Ottawa: n.p., 1965-71.
*Issued as a non-chronological sequence in which orders were dis-
carded when obsolete. Superseded by a bilingual format in 1972.*

Canada. Court Martial Appeal Board. *Court Martial Appeal Reports.*
Ottawa: Queen's Printer, 1957-73. 3 vols.

*Canada. Dept. of National Defence. *The Defence Research Board,
Canada.* n.p.: n.d. 1 vol., unpaged.

_____. *Defence Research Board; the First Twenty-five Years./
Conseil de recherches pour la défense; les 25 premières années.*
Ottawa: Queen's Printer/Imprimeur de la Reine, 1972. 46 pp.
Bilingual text./Texte bilingue.

_____. *The King's Regulations and Orders for the Royal Cana-
dian Air Force.* (C.A.P. 4.) Ottawa: King's Printer, 1951.
3 vols., looseleaf.

_____. *Manual of the Canadian Forces Medical Service in the
Field, 1959.* Ottawa: Queen's Printer, 1959. 324 pp., looseleaf.

*_____. *The Queen's Regulations and Orders for the Canadian
Forces.* Ottawa: Queen's Printer, 1965. 3 vols., looseleaf.

*_____. *The Queen's Regulations and Orders for the Royal
Canadian Air Force.* (CAP 4.) Ottawa: Queen's Printer, 1953.
3 vols., looseleaf.

_____. *The Queen's Regulations and Orders for the Royal Cana-
dian Air Force.* (CAP 4.) Ottawa: Queen's Printer, 1952. 3 vols.,
looseleaf.

*Canada. Dept. of National Defence. *Queen's Regulations for the Canadian Services Colleges.* Ottawa: Queen's Printer, 1958. 1 vol., unpaged.

*_____. *Report.* Ottawa: King's Printer, 1923-59.
Title varies. Annual most years.

*_____. *White Paper on Defence.* Ottawa: Queen's Printer, 1964. 30 pp.

Canada. Dept. of National Defence. Defence Research Board. *Annual Review./Revue annuelle.* n.p./s.l.: s.i., 1966- .
Bilingual text./Texte bilingue.

Canada. Dept. of Veterans Affairs. *Commemoration; Canadians in Korea, 1978./Souvenir; Canadiens en Corée, 1978.* n.p./s.l.: s.i., [1978. 14 pp.]
Bilingual text./Texte bilingue.

*Canada. Ministère de la Défense nationale. *Le conseil de recherches pour la défense, Canada.* s.l.: s.i., s.d. 1 tome, non-paginé.

*_____. *Livre blanc sur la défense.* Ottawa: Imprimeur de la Reine, 1964. 34 pp.

*_____. *Ordonnances et règlements royaux applicables au Corps d'aviation royal canadien.* (CAP 4.) Ottawa: Imprimeur de la Reine, 1953. 3 tomes, feuilles mobiles.

*_____. *Ordonnances et règlements royaux applicables aux Forces canadiennes.* Ottawa: Imprimeur de la Reine, 1965. 3 tomes, feuilles mobiles.

*_____. *Rapport.* Ottawa: Imprimeur du Roi, 1923-59.
Divergence du titre. Annuel, la plupart des années.

*_____. *Règlements royaux applicables aux Collèges des services armés du Canada.* Ottawa: Imprimeur de la Reine, 1958. 1 tome, non-paginé.

Canada. Parliament. House of Commons. Special Committee on Canteen Funds. *Minutes of Proceedings and Evidence.* No. 1-10. Ottawa: King's Printer, 1947.

Canadian Air Cadet. Vol. I-VII. Toronto: Air Cadet League of Canada, 1941-48.

Canadian Defence Quarterly./Revue canadienne de défense. Vol. I- . Toronto: Baxter Pub., 1971- .

Castonguay, Jacques. *Unsung Mission; History of the Chaplaincy Service (RC) of the R.C.A.F.* Montreal: Institut de Pastorale, 1968. 173 pp.

Childerhose, Chick. *Wild Blue.* Victoria, B.C.: Hoot Publications, 1978. 346 pp.

City of Winnipeg 402 Squadron, 1932-1974. n.p.: n.d. 1 vol., unpaged.

Collège militaire royal de Saint-Jean. *Ouverture officielle./Official Opening.* s.l.: s.i., s.d./n.p.: n.d. 27 pp.
Texte bilingue./Bilingual text.

Coup d'oeil sur le Collège militaire royal de Saint-Jean. Ottawa: Imprimeur de la Reine, 1959. 20 pp.

Le Défilé; la revue du Collège militaire royal de Saint-Jean. St-Jean, P.Q.: imprimé privé, 1952-   .
Divergence du titre.

The Demon Squadron; 407 Squadron in War and Peace, May 1941 — June 1952, June 1952 — June 1975. n.p.: privately printed, [1975]. 46 pp.

Ellis, Frank H. *Canada's Flying Heritage.* Toronto: Univ. of Toronto Press, 1954. 398 pp.

_____. *Fifty Years of Adventure and Progress in Canadian Skies.* Toronto: Ryerson Press, 1959. 230 pp.

The End of A Decade; a Pictorial Essay of 447 Surface to Air Missile Squadron from its Inception in 1962 until Closure in 1972. n.p.: n.d. 1 vol., unpaged.

Eternal Vigilance is the Price of Safety; an Active Auxiliary for Citizens of Ottawa. n.p.: n.d. 1 vol., unpaged.
No. 2416 Aircraft Control and Warning Squadron.

Flight Comment. Ottawa: King's Printer, 1949-   .
Title until 1953: Crash Comment. *Bilingual text from 1976, no. 3. Frequency varies.*

416 Squadron see Hovey, H. Richard.

427 Lion Squadron, 1942-1970. Marceline, Mo.: Walsworth, n.d. 76 pp.

422 Sqn; This Arm shall do It, 1942-1970. Marceline, Mo.: Walsworth, n.d. 64 pp.

4 Wing Baden-Soellingen, Sept 1953 — June 1970. J. David, ed. Marceline, Mo.: Walsworth, [1971]. 206 pp.

Fraser, Dan, ed. *CFS Sydney; 25 Jubilee Booklet, 1953-1978.* n.p.: [1978]. 40 pp.

Gibson, Colin. *"Air Power in Canada"; an Address by Col. the Hon. Colin Gibson, M.C., M.A., Minister of National Defence for Air, to the Empire Club of Toronto, February 28, 1946.* n.p.: n.d. 11 pp.

Goodspeed, D.J. *A History of the Defence Research Board of Canada.* Ottawa: Queen's Printer, 1958. 259 pp.

Gordon, John. . . .*Of Men and Planes.* Ottawa: Love Print., 1968. 3 vols.

_____. *Winged Sentries./Sentinelles de l'air.* Claude Rousseau, illus. n.p.: 1963. 104 pp.
Bilingual text./Texte bilingue.

Griffin, J.A. *Canadian Military Aircraft; Serials & Photographs, 1920-1968./Avions militaires canadiens; numéros de série et photographies, 1920-1968.* (Canadian War Museum Publication Number 69-2/Musée de guerre du Canada publication numéro 69-2.) Ottawa: Queen's Printer/Imprimeur de la Reine, 1969. 691 pp.
Bilingual text./Texte bilingue.

Halliday, H.A. *Chronology of Canadian Military Aviation.* (National Museum of Man Mercury Series: Canadian War Museum Paper, no. 6.) Ottawa: [Queen's Printer], 1975. 168 pp.

Hammond, H.R.L., and others, eds. [*401 Squadron*]. n.p.: privately printed, n.d. 1 vol., unpaged.

The Happy Warrior; a Book in Memory of the Life and Work of G/C the Rev. R.M. Frayne, C.D., D.D., Director of Religions Administration (P), the Royal Canadian Air Force. Toronto: United Church Pub. House, 1953. 103 pp.

Harvey, J.D. *426 Squadron Around the World Flight; North Star 17525 — Special Flight no. 160; Trip Diary 09 June — 07 July 1956.* n.p.: 1956. 22 pp.

Hinse, Jean-Robert, éd. *Station des Forces canadiennes/Canadian Forces Station/Senneterre, 1953-1978; album-anniversaire/ Anniversary Album.* s.l.: imprimé privé, [1978]./n.p.: privately printed, [1978]. 1 tome, non-paginé./1 vol., unpaged.
Texte bilingue./Bilingual text.

[Hovey, H. Richard, and others.] *416 Squadron.* n.p.: 1974. 133 pp.

Humby, P.A., ed. *CFS Sioux Lookout, 1953-1978.* Winnipeg: Inter-Collegiate Press, [1978]. 1 vol., unpaged.

The Illustrated Review of Aviation in Canada; Celebrating the Golden Anniversary of Powered Flight in Canada. Montreal: privately printed, [1959]. 1 vol., unpaged.

*Kealy, J.D.F., and E.C. Russell. *A History of Canadian Naval Aviation, 1918-1962.* Ottawa: Queen's Printer, 1965. 164 pp.

*Kealy, J.D.F., et E.C. Russell. *Histoire de l'aéronavale canadienne, 1918-1962.* Ottawa: Imprimeur de la Reine, 1965. 185 pp.

Kostenuk, Samuel, and John Griffin. *RCAF Squadron Histories and Aircraft, 1924-1968.* (Canadian War Museum Historical Publication 14.) Toronto: S. Stevens, Hakkert, 1977. 255 pp.

Langar Log. Vol. I-XI. Langar, Eng.: privately printed, 1952-63. *Journal of No. 30 Air Materiel Base, RCAF.*

The Link. Vol. I-V? Calgary: privately printed, 1955-59? *Journal of RCAF Station Lincoln Park.*

The Link. Vol. I-IV? Rivers, Man.: privately printed, 1948-51? *Journal of Canadian Joint Air Training Centre, Rivers, Man.*

The Log; Royal Roads Military College. Vol. V- . Victoria, B.C.: privately printed, 1942- .

McCaw, H.B., éd. *25 années de service; 1953-1978; 25 Years of Service.* n.p./s.l.: s.i., [1978]. v.p. *CFS/SFC Moisie. Bilingual text./Texte bilingue.*

*McCracken, George W. *Les aviateurs de l'OTAN au Canada.* (Actualités; revue destinée aux Forces canadiennes, vol. IV, no. 1.) Ottawa: Imprimeur de la Reine, 1953. 31 pp.

*_____. *NATO Air Training in Canada.* (Current Affairs for the Canadian Forces, vol. IV, no. 1.) Ottawa: Queen's Printer, 1953. 31 pp.

*_____. *Votre Aviation.* (Actualités; revue destinée aux Forces canadiennes, vol. V, no. 3.) Ottawa: Imprimeur de la Reine, 1953. 31 pp.

*_____. *Your Air Force.* (Current Affairs for the Canadian Forces, vol. V, no. 3.) Ottawa: Queen's Printer, 1953. 31 pp.

Main, J.R.K. *Voyageurs of the Air; a History of Civil Aviation in Canada.* Ottawa: Queen's Printer, 1967. 397 pp.

Marcoux, Jules, éd. *CMR, 1952-1977; album du 25e anniversaire./ 25th anniversary album.* St-Jean, P.Q.: s.i./n.p., 1977. 62 pp. *Texte bilingue./Bilingual text.*

Mazéas, Daniel. *Insignes armée canadienne, 1900-1914; Canadian Badges; supplément, 1920-1950.* Guincamp, France: privately printed, 1972. 116 pp.

The Medical and Dental Services of the Canadian Forces. (Current Affairs for the Canadian Forces, vol. VI, no. 1.) Ottawa: Queen's Printer, 1954. 31 pp.

Merrick, Bob. *410 Squadron; a History.* n.p.: n.d. 114 pp.

Milberry, Larry. *Aviation in Canada.* Toronto: McGraw-Hill Ryerson, 1979. 272 pp.

Mokler, R.J. *Aircraft Down; a Personal Account of Search, Survival and Rescue in the Canadian North.* New York: Exposition Press, 1968. 110 pp.

Morneault, J.C. *424 Tiger Squadron, 1935-1977.* n.p.: [1978]. 31 pp.

Myles, Eugenie Louise. *Airborne from Edmonton.* Toronto: Ryerson Press, 1959. 280 pp.

National Aeronautical Collection./Collection aéronautique nationale. n.p.: n.d./s.l.: s.i., s.d. 36 pp.
Bilingual text./Texte bilingue.

National Aeronautical Collection. Ottawa: Queen's Printer, 1967. 36 pp.

Number Four Hundred & Four Squadron, Royal Canadian Air Force. n.p.: [1972]. 62 pp.

Paré, Lorenzo. *Les canadiens français et l'organisation militaire.* (Oeuvre des tracts, 382.) Montréal: imprimé privé, [1951]. 16 pp.

Pearcy, Arthur. *The Dakota; a History of the Douglas Dakota in RAF and RCAF Service.* London: I. Allan, 1972. 320 pp.

Peden, Murray. *Fall of an Arrow.* Stittsville, Ont.: Canada's Wings, 1978. 182 pp.

Polumin, Nicholas. *Arctic Unfolding; Experiences and Observations during a Canadian Airborne Expedition in Northern Ungava, the Northwest Territories, and the Arctic Archipelago.* London: Hutchinson, 1949. 348 pp.

"Pourquoi je sers ma patrie". (Actualités; revue destinée aux Forces canadiennes, vol. X, no. 15.) Ottawa: Imprimeur de la Reine, 1956. 26 pp.

Preston, Richard A. *Canada's RMC; a History of the Royal Military College.* Toronto: Univ. of Toronto Press, 1969. 415 pp.

Roberts, Leslie. *There Shall be Wings; a History of the Royal Canadian Air Force.* Toronto: Clarke, Irwin, 1959. 250 pp.

Robertson, Peter. *Irréductible vérité/Relentless Verity/les photographes militaires canadiens depuis 1885/Canadian Military Photographers since 1885.* (Les Archives publiques du Canada/Public Archives of Canada Series.) Québec, P.Q.: Les Presses de l'Université Laval, 1973. 233 pp.
Texte bilingue./Bilingual text.

Roundel. Vol. I-XVII. Ottawa: Queen's Printer, 1948-65.
Journal of the RCAF.

Royal Military College of Canada, Kingston, Ont. *The Cadet Handbook.* Kingston: n.p., [1957?]. 59 pp., looseleaf.

The Royal Military College of Canada Review. Vol. I- . Kingston, Ont.: privately printed, 1920- .

Schwarzwaldflieger (Black Forest Flyer). Vol. I-X. Baden-Soellingen, Ger.: privately printed, 1954-63.
Journal of No. 4 (Fighter) Wing, RCAF.

*Les services medicaux et dentaires pour les Forces armées. (Actualités; revue destinée aux Forces canadiennes, vol. VI, no. 1.) Ottawa: Imprimeur de la Reine, 1954. 31 pp.

Snowy Owl; Journal of the Canadian Land Forces Command and Staff College. Kingston, Ont.: privately printed, 1952-73. 18 vols.
Title varies.

*Stacey, C.P., H.E.W. Strange and F.H. Hitchins. *Canada's Armed Forces Today.* (Current Affairs for the Canadian Forces, vol. II, no. 9.) Ottawa: Queen's Printer, 1952. 22 pp.

*Stacey, C.P., H.E.W. Strange et F.H. Hitchins. *Les Forces armées du Canada.* (Actualités; revue destinée aux Forces canadiennes, vol. II, no. 9.) Ottawa: Imprimeur de la Reine, 1952. 22 pp.

Sutherland, Alice Gibson. *Canada's Aviation Pioneers; 50 Years of McKee Trophy Winners.* Toronto: McGraw-Hill Ryerson, 1978. 304 pp.

Talepipe. Vol. I-?. North Luffenham, Eng., Marville, France: privately printed, 1952-?
Title varies: Vol. I, no. 1 & 2 titled: You Name It? Journal of No. 1 Fighter Wing, RCAF.

Thompson, Roy J.C. *Wings of the Canadian Armed Forces, 1913-1972.* [Dartmouth], N.S.: n.p., 1973. 106 pp.

25th Anniversary Reunion; Royal Canadian Air Force (Women's Division). Toronto: n.p., 1966. 1 vol., unpaged.

25th NORAD Region. Baton Rouge, La.: Army & Navy Pub. Co., n.d. 370 pp.

Vincent, Carl, J.D. Oughton and E. Vincent. *Consolidated Liberator & Boeing Fortress.* (Canada's Wings, vol. 2.) Stittsville, Ont.: Canada's Wings, 1975. 246 pp.

"Why I Serve", by the Serviceman. (Current Affairs for the Canadian Forces, vol. X, no. 15.) Ottawa: Queen's Printer, 1956. 26 pp.

Wilson, J.A. *Development of Aviation in Canada, 1879-1948.* Ottawa: Dept. of Transport Air Services Branch, n.d. 105 pp.

Ziegler, Mary. *The Story of the Women's Division, Royal Canadian Air Force.* Hamilton, Ont.: privately printed, 1973. 173 pp.